REFERENCE AND DESCRIPTION

REFERENCE

AND

DESCRIPTION

THE CASE AGAINST
TWO-DIMENSIONALISM

Scott Soames

PRINCETON UNIVERSITY PRESS

PRINCETON AND OXFORD

Published by
Princeton University Press,
41 William Street,
Princeton, New Jersey 08540

In the United Kingdom:
Princeton University Press,
3 Market Place,
Woodstock, Oxfordshire OX20 1SY

ISBN: 0-691-12100-1

Library of Congress Cataloging-in-Publication Data

Soames, Scott.
Reference and description: the case against two-dimensionalism /
Scott Soames.
p.   cm.
Includes bibliographical references and index.
ISBN 0-691-12100-1 (hardcover: alk. paper)
1. Description (Philosophy)   I. Title.

B105.D4S63 2005
121'.68—dc22

2004044533

British Library Cataloging-in-Publication Data is available

This book has been composed in Galliard.

www.pup.princeton.edu

Printed in the United States of America

1   3   5   7   9   10   8   6   4   2

FOR MARTHA

CONTENTS

A WORD ABOUT NOTATION ix

ACKNOWLEDGMENTS xi

INTRODUCTION 1

PART ONE
THE REVOLT AGAINST DESCRIPTIVISM 5

CHAPTER 1
The Traditional Descriptivist Picture 7

CHAPTER 2
Attack on the Traditional Picture
*Proper Names, Non-Descriptionality, and
Rigid Designation* 14

PART TWO
DESCRIPTIVIST RESISTANCE:
THE ORIGINS OF AMBITIOUS
TWO-DIMENSIONALISM 33

CHAPTER 3
Reasons for Resistance and
the Strategy for Descriptivist Revival 35

CHAPTER 4
Roots of Two-Dimensionalism in Kaplan and Kripke 43

CHAPTER 5
Stalnaker's Two-Dimensionalist Model of Discourse 84

CHAPTER 6
The Early Two-Dimensionalist Semantics of Davies
and Humberstone 106

PART THREE
AMBITIOUS TWO-DIMENSIONALISM   131

CHAPTER 7
Strong and Weak Two-Dimensionalism   133

CHAPTER 8
Jackson's Strong Two-Dimensionalist Program   149

CHAPTER 9
Chalmers's Two-Dimensionalist Defense of Zombies   194

CHAPTER 10
Critique of Ambitious Two-Dimensionalism   267

PART FOUR
THE WAY FORWARD   327

CHAPTER 11
Positive Nondescriptivism   329

INDEX   355

A WORD ABOUT NOTATION

In what follows, I will use either single quotation or italics when I want to refer to particular words, expressions, or sentences—e.g., 'good' or *good*. Sometimes both will be used in a single example—e.g., '*Knowledge is good*' *is a true sentence of English iff knowledge is good*. This italicized sentence refers to itself, a sentence the first constituent of which is the quote name of the English sentence that consists of the word 'knowledge' followed by the word 'is' followed by the word 'good'. In addition to using italics for quotation, sometimes I will use them for emphasis, though normally I will use boldface for that purpose. I trust that in each case it will be clear from the context how these special notations are being used.

In addition, when formulating generalizations about words, expressions, or sentences, I will often use the notation of boldface italics, which is to be understood as equivalent to the technical device known as "corner quotes." For example, when explaining how simple sentences of a language L are combined to form larger sentences, I may use an example like (1a), which has the meaning given in (1b).

1a. For any sentences A and B of the language L, ***A & B*** is a sentence of L.

b. For any sentences A and B of the language L, the expression which consists of A followed by '&' followed by B is a sentence of L.

Given (1), we know that if 'Knowledge is good' and 'Ignorance is bad' are sentences of L, then 'Knowledge is good & ignorance is bad' and 'Ignorance is bad & knowledge is good' are also sentences of L.

Roughly speaking, a generalization of the sort illustrated by (2a) has the meaning given by (2b).

2a. For any (some) expression E, ... ***E*** ... is so and so.

b. For any (some) expression E, the expression consisting of '...' followed by E, followed by '. . .' is so and so.

One slightly tricky example of this is given in (3).

3a. For any name n of L, ***'n' refers to n*** expresses a truth.

b. For any name n of L, the expression consisting of the left-hand quote mark, followed by n, followed by the right-hand quote mark, followed by 'refers to', followed by n, expresses a truth.

Particular instances of (3a) are given in (4).

4a. *'Brian Soames' refers to Brian Soames* expresses a truth.

b. *'Greg Soames' refers to Greg Soames* expresses a truth.

Finally, I frequently employ the expression *iff* as short for *if and only if*. Thus, (5a) is short for (5b).

5a. For all x, x is the referent of a description iff x, and only x, satisfies the description.

b. For all x, x is the referent of a description if and only if x, and only x, satisfies the description.

ACKNOWLEDGMENTS

The impetus for this book arose from two recent graduate seminars of mine at Princeton University. The first was a year-long seminar on *Naming and Necessity* and its aftermath jointly taught by David Lewis and me in the 1999–2000 academic year. At the first meeting, David announced that although the work of Kripke and other anti-descriptivists was often regarded as revolutionary, he himself was a counterrevolutionary. Accordingly, during the course of the year, he developed a version of two-dimensionalist descriptivism, and used it to accommodate and reinterpret central Kripkean doctrines and examples—while adhering to an essentially pre-Kripkean conception of meaning, belief, and modality. I was on the other side, having announced at the first meeting that the anti-descriptivist revolution begun in the 1970s by Kripke, Kaplan, Putnam, and others was a genuine advance that needed to be pushed even further. For me the seminar was extraordinarily productive. I benefited not only from David's inspired and often brilliant presentation of the opposing view, but also from the active participation of a number of accomplished graduate students and professors who regularly attended the meetings—including, among others, Cian Dorr, Mike Fara, Kit Fine, Delia Graff, Jonathan McKeown-Green, Benj Helle, Sean Kelly, Mark Johnston, Michael Nelson, and Jeff Speaks. The second major occasion on which I dealt with these issues was my seminar on two-dimensionalism in the spring of 2003. There I presented, in skeletal form, all the main themes developed more fully in this book. Again, I benefited from the comments of an exceptionally acute group of graduate students and professors from Princeton and Rutgers, including Eliza Block, Alexis Burgess, Sam Cumming, David Gordon, John Hawthorne, Jeff Kepple, Sarah-Jane Leslie, Stephen Leuenberger, David Manley, Mike McGlone, Jim Pryor, Dan Rothschild, Gillian Russell, Mark Schroeder, Adam Sennet, Brett Sherman, Ted Sider, and Jeff Speaks.

In addition to presenting material on two-dimensionalism at these seminars, I gave several lectures on the subject, first at the University of Calgary and the University of California, Los Angeles, in the fall of 2002, and then at Wayne State University, the University of Connecticut, the University of Massachusetts, and the University of Southern California, as well as at conferences in Birmingham, England, Barcelona, Spain, and Portland, Oregon, in 2003. Among the many who attended my lectures whose comments contributed to my thinking were Joseph Almog, John Baxter, J. C. Beall, Phil Bricker, Mark Johnston, David Kaplan, Ali Kazmi, Michael McKinsey, Barbara Partee, Larry Powers, Jonathan Schaffer, Michael Thau, and Stephen Yablo. Written versions of some of the material given as lectures will appear in the articles, "Kripke, the Necessary Aposteriori, and the Two-Dimensionalist Heresy," in Manuel Garcia-Carpintero and Josep Macià, eds., *The Two-Dimensional Framework* (Oxford: Oxford University Press) and "Reference and Description," in Frank Jackson and Michael Smith, eds., *The Oxford Handbook of Contemporary Analytic Philosophy* (Oxford: Oxford University Press). I am indebted to Ben Caplan, Ali Kazmi, and Jim Pryor for discussing those works with me, and helping me develop some of the issues.

The book manuscript itself was read and extensively commented upon by Alexis Burgess, Ben Caplan, Mark Kalderon, Mike McGlone, Ted Sider, and Jeff Speaks. Each one saved me from numerous mistakes, while also making many positive suggestions. The book would have been far worse without them, though all remaining errors are, of course, mine. I have, as usual, had the good fortune to work with an excellent and supportive editor—Ian Malcolm of the Princeton University Press. Last and most important, my greatest debt and deepest appreciation is owed to the person to whom this book is dedicated, my (future) wife and sine qua non, Martha.

REFERENCE AND DESCRIPTION

INTRODUCTION

A little over 30 years ago, a group of philosophers led by Saul Kripke, Hilary Putnam, David Kaplan, and Keith Donnellan ushered in a new era in philosophy by attacking a set of preconceptions about meaning that occupied center stage—not only in philosophizing about language, but also in the common practice of the discipline, and in the self-conception of many of its practitioners. Among the central presuppositions of the then reigning conception of language, and its role in philosophy, were the following:

(i)   The meaning of an expression is never identical with its referent. Rather, the meaning of a substantive, nonlogical term is a descriptive sense that provides necessary and sufficient conditions for determining its reference. For example, the meaning of a singular term is a descriptive condition satisfaction of which by an object is necessary and sufficient for the term to refer to the object, whereas the meaning of a predicate is a descriptive condition satisfaction of which by an object is necessary and sufficient for the predicate to be true of the object.

(ii) Understanding a term amounts to associating it with the correct descriptive sense. In the case of ordinary predicates in the common language, all speakers who understand them associate essentially the same sense with them. This is also true for some widely used ordinary proper names—such as *London*. However, for many proper names of less widely known individuals, the defining descriptive information, and hence the meaning, associated with the name can be expected to vary from speaker to speaker.

(iii) Since the meaning of a word, as used by a speaker, is completely determined by the descriptive sense that the speaker mentally associates with it, meaning is transparent. If two words mean the same thing, then anyone who understands both should easily be able to figure that out by consulting the sense that he or she associates with them.

(iv) Further, since the meaning of a word, as used by a speaker, is completely determined by the descriptive sense that he or she mentally associates with it, the meaning of a word in the speaker's language is entirely dependent on factors internal to the speaker. The same is true for the beliefs that the speaker uses the word to express. External factors—like the speaker's relation to the environment, and to the community of other speakers—are relevant only insofar as they causally influence the factors internal to the speaker that determine the contents of his or her beliefs.

(v) Apriori truth and necessary truth amount to essentially the same thing. If they exist at all, both are grounded in meaning. Such truths are knowable on the basis of understanding the words we use, and their necessity can be traced to our linguistic conventions.

(vi) Claims about objects having or lacking properties necessarily—independent of how they are described—make no sense. In some cases, a sentence *Necessarily t is F*, containing a singular term t designating o, might be true, but if so there will always be other sentences *Necessarily t* is F*, containing a different singular term t* designating o, which are false. (Here t and t* are coreferential terms that are associated with different descriptive conditions, which bear different conceptual relations to the property expressed by F.) Since sentences of both sorts exist, it would be arbitrary to take either one as indicating that the object designated has, or lacks, the relevant property necessarily. Such an idea is objectionably metaphysical, and devoid of clear sense.[1]

(vii) The job of philosophy is not to come up with new empirical truths. Its central task is that of conceptual clarification, which is grounded in the analysis of meaning.

These doctrines and their corollaries provided the framework for much of the philosophy done in the analytic tradition prior to the 1970s. Of course, not every analytic philosopher accepted all major tenets of the framework, and some, like W. V. Quine, rejected both the framework and the traditional notions of meaning, necessity, and apriority alto-

---

[1] Here and throughout, I use boldface italics to play the role of corner quotes.

gether. It is interesting to note, however, that even Quine—the framework's most severe critic—believed that **if** the traditional notions of meaning, necessity, and apriority make sense at all, then they must be related more or less as along the lines indicated above. What was, for the most part, absent at the time was a sense that all of these notions **do** make sense, and **are** important for philosophy, even though they are mischaracterized by the traditional framework.

This changed with Kripke, Putnam, Kaplan, Donnellan, and the line of research growing out of their work. Today, each of the doctrines (i–vii) has been vigorously challenged, and alternatives have been proposed to put in their place. Nevertheless, it would be wrong to say that a new, systematic consensus has been reached. Although everyone recognizes the need to take into account the observations and arguments of Kripke and his fellow anti-descriptivists, there are some who believe that the traditional descriptivist paradigm contained much that was correct, and that a new, more sophisticated version of descriptivism should be put in its place. Even those who reject the idea of a descriptivist revival and want to push the anti-descriptivist revolution further, have found the task of constructing a positive, non-descriptivist conception of meaning to be daunting. In short, all sorts of controversies remain, and the struggle to assess the legacy of the original anti-descriptivist challengers, and to forge a new understanding of meaning and its role in philosophy, is far from over.

This book is about what may be the most important aspect of that struggle. In the last 25 years a systematic strategy has grown up around a technical development, called *two-dimensional modal logic*, for reviving descriptivism, reconnecting meaning, apriority, and necessity, and vindicating philosophy as conceptual analysis along recognizably traditional lines. Although the logical and semantic techniques employed are new, a number of the motivating philosophical ideas are old. Since many of these ideas were not without plausibility, and since, in any case, old ideas die hard, it is not surprising that a vigorous attempt has been made to reinstate them. But there is more to the attempted revival than this. Anti-descriptivism has brought with it puzzles and problems of its own. On top of that, even the most important anti-descriptivist classics contain errors and missteps that have led others astray, and have sometimes seemed to point away from, rather than toward, their authors' most important insights.

The aim of this book is to sort through all of this—to assess the legacy of the original anti-descriptivist authors, to explain and evaluate the two-dimensionalist revival of descriptivism, and to provide the outlines of what I hope will prove to be a lasting, non-descriptivist perspective on meaning. In Part 1, I sketch the revolution against descriptivism led by Kripke and Kaplan, and I draw out some of its leading implications. In Part 2, I explain the reasons some philosophers have resisted this revolution, and I outline the strategy for descriptivist revival. This is followed by close examination and criticism of certain passages in Kaplan's "Demonstratives" and Kripke's *Naming and Necessity* that have been seized upon by philosophically motivated two-dimensionalists in an attempt to further their descriptivist agenda.[2] Part 2 closes with explication and criticism of the two most important early two-dimensionalist systems—the pragmatic model of Robert Stalnaker, and the semantic model of Martin Davies and Lloyd Humberstone. Part 3 is devoted to developing and evaluating two-dimensionalism in a systematic way. In the first chapter of Part 3, I define the two most philosophically important versions of this view. In the last chapter of Part 3, I give what I take to be decisive arguments against both, while arguing, in addition, that other, hybrid, versions of descriptive two-dimensionalism offer little hope of doing much better. In between those two chapters, I examine and criticize the systems of the leading philosophically motivated two-dimensionalists of our time, Frank Jackson and David Chalmers. Part 4, draws together the lessons learned along the way, provides positive non-descriptivist answers to several of the problems that motivated descriptive two-dimensionalism, assesses where the anti-descriptivist revolution stands today, and indicates further work that remains to be done.

---

[2] David Kaplan, "Demonstratives," in J. Almog, J. Perry, and H. Wettstein (eds.), *Themes from Kaplan* (New York and Oxford: Oxford University Press, 1989), and Saul Kripke, *Naming and Necessity* (Cambridge, MA: Harvard, 1980), originally published in Donald Davidson and Gilbert Harman (eds.), *Semantics of Natural Language* (Dordrecht: Reidel, 1972).

PART ONE

THE REVOLT AGAINST DESCRIPTIVISM

CHAPTER 1

THE TRADITIONAL DESCRIPTIVIST PICTURE

The modern discussion of reference begins with the reaction of Gottlob Frege and Bertrand Russell to an initially attractive but overly simple conception of meaning and reference. The conception is based on the observation that the most important feature of language is our ability to use it to represent the world. Different sentences represent the world as being different ways, and to sincerely accept, or assertively utter, a sentence is to believe, or assert, that the world is the way the sentence represents it to be. The reason sentences are representational in this way is that they are made up of words and phrases that stand for objects and the properties we take them to have—physical objects, people, ideas, institutions, shapes, sizes, colors, locations, relations, and the rest. What it is for language to be meaningful is for it to have this representational capacity. But if meaning is essentially representational, it would seem that the meaning of any word or phrase should be just what it represents, or stands for. In short, the meaning of an expression is the thing it refers to; and the meaning of a sentence is determined by the words that make it up.

Although attractive, and even undeniable in its broad outlines, this picture gives rise to puzzles in particular cases that led Frege and Russell to suggest significant modifications. In "On Sense and Reference," Frege considered an instance of the general problem posed by the observation that substitution of coreferential terms in a sentence sometimes changes meaning.[1] For example, in each of the following cases he would contend that the (a) sentence differs in meaning from the (b) sentence, even though they differ only in the substitution of terms that designate the same individual.

1a. The first Postmaster General of the United States was the author of *Poor Richard's Almanac*

  b. The first Postmaster General of the United States was the first Postmaster General of the United States.

[1] Gottlob Frege, "On Sense and Reference," in Peter Geach and Max Black (eds.), *Translations from the Philosophical Writings of Gottlob Frege* (Oxford: Basil Blackwell, 1970).

2a. Benjamin Franklin was the first Postmaster General of the United States.

  b. Benjamin Franklin was Benjamin Franklin.

3a. Ruth Marcus is Ruth Barcan.

  b. Ruth Marcus is Ruth Marcus.

In each case, this contention is supported by three facts: (i) a person can understand both sentences, and so know what they mean, without taking them to mean the same thing, or to have the same truth value; (ii) a person who assertively uttered the (a) sentence typically would be deemed to have said more, and conveyed more information, than someone who assertively uttered the (b) sentence; and (iii) the (a) and (b) sentences would standardly be used in belief ascriptions, *x believes that S*, to report different beliefs with potentially different truth values. If, on this basis, one agrees that the (a) sentences differ in meaning from the (b) sentences, then one must reject either T1, T2, or T3.

T1. The meaning of a genuinely referring expression is its referent.

T2. Both singular definite descriptions—i.e., expressions of the form *the so and so*—and ordinary proper names—e.g., *Benjamin Franklin*, *Ruth Barcan*, and *Ruth Marcus*—are genuinely referring expressions.

T3. The meaning of a sentence, of the sort illustrated by 1–3, is a function of its grammatical structure together with the meanings of its parts; in these sentences, substitution of expressions with the same meaning doesn't change meaning.

Whereas Frege rejected T1, Russell rejected T2. However, both agreed that the meaning of an ordinary proper name is not its bearer, and the meaning of a singular definite description is not the unique object that it denotes.

According to Frege, ordinary proper names and singular definite descriptions are terms that purport to refer to unique individuals. However, the meaning, or sense, of such an expression is never identical with its referent; instead, it is something that determines reference. For example, the meaning, or sense, of the description *the even prime number* is something like the property of being both an even number and prime (and being unique in this); its referent is whatever has this property—the number 2. Although different singular terms with the same sense must have the same referents, terms with the same referents may have different senses. This explains the difference in meaning between the (a) and (b) sentences in (1) and (2). The explanation is extended to the sentences in (3) by Frege's contention that, like descriptions, ordinary proper names have senses that determine, but are distinct from, their referents. This is, of course, consistent with there being certain contrasts between names and descriptions. One such contrast is that most ordinary names are grammatically simple, and so, unlike descriptions, their senses are not determined by the senses of their grammatically significant parts. Because of this, it is common for different speakers to use the same name to refer to the same object, even though they associate it with different properties, or senses. Although Frege doesn't dwell on this, the illustrations he provides support the contention that he regarded the sense of a proper name n, as used by a speaker s at a time t, to be the same as that of some description *the D* associated with n by s at t. Thus, he may be seen as adopting T4.[2]

T4. An ordinary proper name, n, as used by a speaker s at a time t, refers to (denotes) an object o iff o is the unique object that has the property expressed by *the D* (associated with n by s). When there is no such object, n remains meaningful while failing to refer to (denote) anything. In general, the meaning (for s at t) of a sentence ... *n* ... containing n is the same as the meaning (for s at t) of the corresponding sentence ... *the D* ... that arises by substituting the description for the name.

It follows from this that (3a) and (3b) differ in meaning for any speaker who associates the names *Ruth Marcus* and *Ruth Barcan* with descriptions that have different senses.

A second puzzle for the original conception of meaning and reference encompassing theses T1–T3 was Russell's problem of negative existentials, illustrated by (4).[3]

4a. Santa Claus does not exist.

b. The largest prime number does not exist.

---

[2] Although Frege seems to have regarded the sense of names to be descriptive, some latitude may be needed—including augmenting the descriptive vocabulary available to the agent—in specifying the descriptions themselves.

[3] Bertrand Russell, "On Denoting," *Mind* 14 (1905): 479–93.

It would seem, prima facie, that since these sentences are true, there must be no such individuals as Santa Claus or the largest prime number, and hence that the name *Santa Claus* and the definite description *the largest prime number* do not denote, or refer to, anything. T1 and T2 then lead to the result that the name and the description don't mean anything. But surely that can't be right, since if these expressions were meaningless, then either the sentences as a whole would be meaningless, or they would both have the same degenerate meaning, consisting of the meaning of their common predicate phrase, plus a gap corresponding to their meaningless subject expressions. Neither of these alternatives is correct.

The idea behind Russell's solution is illustrated by the proposal that the (b) sentences constitute analyses of the following (a) sentences.[4]

5a. Men are mortal.

  b. $\forall x$ (x is a man $\supset$ x is mortal)

> The propositional function that assigns to any object o the proposition expressed by *x is a man $\supset$ x is mortal* (relative to an assignment of o to 'x') is "always true"—i.e., always yields a true proposition.

6a. Honest men exist.

  b. $\exists x$ (x is a man & x is honest)

> The propositional function that assigns to any object o the proposition expressed by *x is a man & x is honest* (relative to an assignment of o to 'x') is "sometimes true"—i.e., sometimes yields a true proposition.

7a. Carnivorous cows don't exist.

  b. $\sim\exists x$ (x is a cow & x is carnivorous)

> It is not the case that the propositional function that assigns to any object o the proposition expressed by *x is a cow & x is carnivorous* (relative to an assignment of o to 'x') is "sometimes true"—i.e., it never yields a true proposition.

In each case, the simple subject-predicate grammatical form of the sentence differs from its more complex logical form, which is quantificational. For Russell, this means that it involves the attribution of a

---

[4] I ignore the suggestion of plurality in (6a).

higher order property to a lower level property. Here, one may think of propositional functions as playing the role of properties, and of "sometimes true" and "always true" as expressing the properties of being instantiated and universally instantiated, respectively. Hence, (5) tells us that the property of being mortal-if-human is instantiated by everything, (6) that the property of being an honest man is instantiated, and (7) that the property of being both carnivorous and a cow is not instantiated.

Russell's analysis of sentences containing singular definite descriptions (phrases of the form *the so and so*) is rather complicated.[5] For example, consider (8a), which he paraphrases as (8b), and analyzes as (8c).

8a. The largest prime number is even.

   b. There is a number n which has the property of being both (i) even and (ii) identical with absolutely any number m iff m is a prime number which is larger than all other prime numbers.

   c. $\exists x \, [\forall y \, (y$ is a prime number & y is larger than all other prime numbers $\leftrightarrow y = x)$ & x is even$]$

      The propositional function that assigns to any object o the proposition expressed by $\forall y$ *(y is a prime number & y is larger than all other prime numbers* $\leftrightarrow y = x)$ & *x is even* (relative to an assignment of o to 'x') is "sometimes true"—i.e., the property of being both even and a prime number larger than all others is instantiated.

Russell's analysis of (8a)—which may be seen as equivalent to *The largest prime number exists and is even*—contains his analysis of the "positive existential" (9a).

9a. The largest prime number exists.

   b. There is a number n which has the property of being identical with absolutely any number m iff m is a prime number which is larger than all other prime numbers.

   c. $\exists x \, \forall y \, [y$ is a prime number & y is larger than all other prime numbers $\leftrightarrow y = x]$

---

[5] For a more thorough explanation of Russell's analysis, see chapter 5 of Scott Soames, *Philosophical Analysis in the Twentieth Century*, vol. 1: *The Dawn of Analysis* (Princeton, NJ: Princeton University Press, 2003), hereafter referred to as *The Dawn of Analysis*.

The propositional function that assigns to any object o the proposition expressed by ∀y *[y is a prime number & y is larger than all other prime numbers ↔ y = x]* (relative to an assignment of o to 'x') is "sometimes true"—i.e., the property of being a prime number larger than all others is instantiated.

With this analysis of (9a) in place, the corresponding Russellian analysis, (4c), of the negative existential (4b) is obvious.

4c. ~∃x ∀y [y is a prime number & y is larger than all other prime numbers ↔ y = x]

It is not the case that the propositional function that assigns to any object o the proposition expressed by ∀y *[y is a prime number & y is larger than all other prime numbers ↔ y = x]* (relative to an assignment of o to 'x') is "sometimes true"— i.e., the property of being a prime number larger than all others is not instantiated.

For Russell, the virtue of this analysis is that (4b) is no longer seen as containing a constituent—*the largest prime number*—the job of which it is to refer to something (the thing which is supposed to be its meaning) which is then said not to exist. Hence there is nothing problematic, or paradoxical, in recognizing its truth.

Russell is able to give a similar analysis to (4a), since he holds that whenever one uses an ordinary proper name n, one always has some description in mind that one would be prepared to give in answer to the question **Who, or what, do you mean by n?** Precisely which description gives the content of the name may be expected to vary from speaker to speaker and time to time. However, whenever a name is used, there is always some description that may replace it, without changing meaning. Since Russell believes this to be true no matter what the grammatical form of the sentence, he is able to agree with Frege both in rejecting the conjunction of T1 and T2, and in accepting T4.[6] It is their common agreement on this thesis that philosophers have in mind when they speak of the traditional Frege-Russell view of ordinary proper names.

Two further points are worth noting. First, unlike Frege, Russell never rejected the idea that the meanings of some expressions are simply their referents; rather, he believed this to be true of a small category of *logically proper names*—including certain demonstratives and

⁶ Russell would use *denotes* rather than *refers* in T4.

pure indexicals—which have no other function than to refer. For example, he believed that when he said or thought to himself *I am a pacifist* or *This is red* the proposition he expressed consisted, in the first case, simply of the attribution of the property of being a pacifist to Russell himself, with no other descriptive information about him, and, in the second case, of the attribution of the property of being red to the object demonstrated, with no further attribution of descriptive properties to the object. Unfortunately, he combined his acceptance of this category of "names" with severe epistemological restrictions on the things capable of being named—essentially those about which Cartesian certainty is achievable, and mistakes are impossible.[7] Although this made for serious difficulties, including crippling problems explaining the use of such expressions in communication, Russell's embrace of the idea of a logically proper name was historically important in the later development of nondescriptive analyses of ordinary proper names and indexicals.

Second, the traditional Frege-Russell analysis of ordinary proper names was later modified by John Searle and others to incorporate the idea that the meaning of an ordinary name for a speaker, or a community, was not given by a single description, but by an open-ended family of descriptions.[8] On this view, the referent of the name is taken to be whatever object satisfies a sufficient number of a family of associated descriptions, and the meaning of a sentence *n is F* is, roughly, given by the claim *The thing of which most, or a sufficient number, of the claims: it is D1, it is D2, . . . are true is also F*. Two alleged virtues of this variant of the Frege-Russell view are (i) that it captures the Wittgensteinian idea that the meaning of a sentence containing a name is to some degree vague and indeterminate,[9] and (ii) that it accounts for the fact that even when D is one of the descriptions most strongly associated with n by speakers, the sentence *If n exists, then n is D* is not "true by definition"—sometimes, to our surprise, it can turn out to be false, and even when it is true, it often is not a necessary truth.

[7] Russell, "Knowledge by Acquaintance and Knowledge by Description," *Proceedings of the Aristotelian Society* 11 (1910–11). For discussion, see pp. 110–13 and 122–26 of Soames, *The Dawn of Analysis*.

[8] John Searle, *Mind* 67 (1958): 166–73.

[9] See section 79 of Ludwig Wittgenstein, *Philosophical Investigations* (New York: Macmillan Co., 1953); for discussion, see chapter 1 of Scott Soames, *Philosophical Analysis in the Twentieth Century*, vol. 2: *The Age of Meaning* (Princeton, NJ: Princeton University Press, 2003), hereafter referred to as *The Age of Meaning*.

CHAPTER 2

ATTACK ON THE TRADITIONAL PICTURE

PROPER NAMES, NON-DESCRIPTIONALITY, AND RIGID DESIGNATION

In 1970, Saul Kripke gave a series of arguments challenging traditional descriptive analyses of ordinary proper names, and suggesting an alternative picture.[1] He attacked both the view that the meanings of names are given by descriptions associated with them by speakers, and the view that their referents are determined (as a matter of linguistic rule) to be the objects that satisfy such descriptions. Assuming that meaning determines reference, Kripke takes the latter view, about reference, to follow from the former view about meaning, but not vice versa. Thus, all of his arguments against descriptive theories of the reference of proper names are also arguments against descriptive theories of their meanings, but some of his arguments against the latter do not apply to the former.

I begin with the more narrowly focused arguments, which are directed against two corollaries of the Frege-Russell thesis T4. Let n be a proper name, D be a description or family of descriptions associated with n by speakers, and ... D^* ... be a sentence that arises from ... n ... by replacing one or more occurrences of n with D^*. When D is a description, let $D^* = D$, and when D is a family of descriptions D_1 ... D_k, let D^* be the complex description *the thing of which most, or a sufficient number, of the claims: it is D_1, ..., it is D_k are true.* Kripke attacks the following corollaries of descriptivism about the meanings of names.

> T4(i)   Since the semantic content of (i.e., the proposition expressed by) ... n ... (as used in context C) is the semantic content of ... D^* ... (as used in C), ... n ... is true (as used in C) when evaluated at a possible world-state w iff ... D^* ... is true with respect to C and w. Since *If D^* ex-*

---

[1] Saul Kripke, *Naming and Necessity* (Cambridge, MA: Harvard, 1980), originally published in Donald Davidson and Gilbert Harman (eds.), *Semantics of Natural Language* (Dordrecht: Reidel, 1972).

ists, then D* is D* is a necessary truth, *If n exists, then n is D** is also necessary.

T4(ii) Since the semantic content of (i.e., the proposition expressed by) *... n ...* (as used in C) is the semantic content of *... D* ...* (as used in C), anyone who knows or believes the proposition expressed by *... n ...* (in C) knows or believes the proposition expressed by *... D* ...* (in C), and attitude ascriptions such as *Ralph knows/believes that n is F* and *Ralph knows/believes that D* is F* (as used in C) agree in truth value (with respect to any world-state w). Since the proposition expressed by *If n exists, then n is D** is the same as the proposition expressed by *If D* exists, then D* is D**, it is knowable apriori, and the claim *It is knowable apriori that if n exists, then n is D** is true.

Kripke's argument against T4(i) is known as *the modal argument.* Here is a particular version of it. Consider the name *Aristotle*, and the descriptions *the greatest student of Plato, the founder of formal logic,* and *the teacher of Alexander the Great.* Although Aristotle satisfies these descriptions,

1. *If Aristotle existed, then Aristotle was D*.*

is not a necessary truth, where D* is either any description in this family, or the complicated description *the individual of whom most, or a sufficient number, of the claims: . . . are true*, constructed from descriptions in the family. On the contrary, Aristotle could have existed without doing any of the things for which he is known; he could have moved to another city as a child, failed to go into philosophy, and never been heard from again. In such a possible scenario the antecedent of (1) is true, since Aristotle still exists, while the consequent is false, since he doesn't satisfy any of the relevant descriptions. But then, since (1) is false in this scenario, it is not a necessary truth, which means that the descriptions in the family do not give the meaning of *Aristotle*. According to Kripke, this is no accident; there is, he suggests, no family D_A of descriptions such that: (i) the referent of *Aristotle* is the unique individual who satisfies most, or a sufficient number, of the descriptions in D_A, (ii) ordinary speakers associate D_A with the name, believing its referent to be the unique individual who satisfies most, or a sufficient number, of the descriptions in D_A, and (iii) (1) expresses a necessary truth when D* is the complicated description constructed from D_A. If this is right, then both T4 and its corollary T4(i) are false, as is the view that names are synonymous with descriptions associated with them by speakers.

Why does this argument work? According to Kripke, there was a certain individual x—the person who actually was Aristotle—such that a sentence, ***Aristotle was F*** is true at an arbitrary world-state w iff at w, x had the property expressed by F. What does it mean to say that a sentence is true at w? It means that the proposition we actually use the sentence to express is a true description of what things would be like if the world were in state w. So, Kripke's view is that there was a unique individual x such that for any predicate F and world-state w, the proposition we actually use ***Aristotle was F*** to express would be true, if the world were in w, iff had the world been in state w, x would have had the property (actually) expressed by F. This is the basis of his doctrine that *Aristotle* is a **rigid designator**.[2]

DEFINITION OF RIGIDITY

A singular term t is a rigid designator of an object o iff t designates o in all worlds in which o exists, and t never designates anything else.

INTUITIVE TEST FOR RIGIDITY

A singular term t is a rigid designator iff *the individual who is t could not have existed without being t, and no one who is not the individual who is t could have been t* is true; otherwise t is nonrigid.

Using the notion of rigid designation, we can give the general form of Kripke's modal argument.

THE GENERAL VERSION OF THE MODAL ARGUMENT

(i)   Proper names are rigid designators.

(ii)   If a description D gives the meaning or content of a term t, then D is rigid iff t is.

[2] Here and throughout I use the notion of a singular term in a slightly extended sense to include variables, names, indexicals like *I* and *he*, and singular definite descriptions *the x: Fx*. Although this usage might lead one to think that I am treating *the* as a term-forming functor, rather than as a quantificational operator like *all* and *some*, that is not my intention. Even if *the x: Fx* is a generalized quantifier, I here extend the category of singular terms to include it. This terminological extension is made solely to simplify the discussion, and is not intended to have substantive import. For the same reason, sometimes when making claims about the extensions of singular terms in my sense, I will speak of their referents. This should be understood as including the denotations of singular definite descriptions.

(iii) So, the meanings or contents of proper names are not given by nonrigid descriptions.

Since the descriptions we have been considering are nonrigid, the meaning of *Aristotle* is not given by them. The same is true of other proper names. In *Naming and Necessity*, Kripke leaves the modal argument at that, concluding that there are no meaning-giving descriptions associated with names by speakers. In so doing, he appears, tacitly, to assume that the only candidates for being meaning-giving descriptions are nonrigid. Though understandable, this assumption is not beyond question, and will be revisited later.

We next consider Kripke's epistemological argument against T4, and its corollary T4(ii).

THE EPISTEMOLOGICAL ARGUMENT

(i)   If D gave the meaning (semantic content) of n, then T4(ii) would be true.

(ii) However, when D is a description or family of descriptions concerning well-known achievements or characteristics of the referent of an ordinary name n, it is not the case (a) that anyone who knows or believes the proposition expressed by *n is F* knows or believes the proposition expressed by *D* is F*, (b) that ascriptions such as *Ralph knows/believes that n is F* and *Ralph knows/believes that D* is F* invariably agree in truth value, (c) that the proposition expressed by *If n exists, then n is D** is knowable apriori, or (d) that *It is knowable apriori that if n exists, then n is D** is true.

(iii) So, descriptions concerning the well-known achievements or characteristics of the referents of ordinary names do not give their meanings (semantic contents).

(iv) Since these are the descriptions standardly associated with names by speakers, the meanings of names are not standardly given by the descriptions speakers associate with them.

Three features of this argument stand out. First, it shares the assumption, tacitly used to derive T4(ii) from the descriptivist account of meaning, that if n meant the same as D, then *Ralph believes, knows, or knows apriori that n is F* would have the same truth value as *Ralph believes, knows, or knows apriori that D* is F*. Although a case can be made that Kripke did tacitly assume this, the theoretical basis for the assumption goes beyond what is explicitly stated in his text. The important point is not so much the exact formulation of the needed doctrines, as the recognition that the argument needs some theoretical assumptions connecting the meanings of simple sentences with attitude ascriptions in which they figure, in order to draw the desired conclusion. Later, when the anti-descriptivist picture presented by Kripke is challenged, it will be important to be aware of these.

Second, the argument form is general, and not limited to claims about apriori knowledge, or even to claims about knowledge and belief as opposed to other propositional attitudes.[3] The point of the argument is to show that the proposition expressed by *n is F* is different from the proposition expressed by *D* is F*. This is done by showing that a person can bear a certain attitude relation to one of these propositions without bearing it to the other. Although the relation one bears to a proposition when one knows it apriori is useful for making this point, it is not the only such relation to which one might appeal.

Third, when used against certain views about the meanings of names, the epistemological argument has the task of distinguishing between necessarily equivalent propositions. In light of this, it should not be surprising that one has to appeal to intuitions, and theoretical assumptions, about propositions and propositional attitudes. There is something a little ironic here, though. Often it is assumed that whatever the difficulties faced by descriptive analyses of the meanings of names, at least they give plausible explanations of Frege's puzzle about substitution in attitude ascriptions, and a good account of the role of names in these sentences generally. Kripke's epistemological argument challenges this assumption.

I now turn to Kripke's reason for accepting the second premise of the epistemological argument. His text is replete with thought experiments supporting it, one of them being the Gödel/Schmidt example, concerning the origins of Gödel's famous incompleteness theorem.[4] In this example, Kripke imagines our belief that Gödel discovered the incompleteness theorem being proven false by historical scholarship that reveals that he stole it from Schmidt. Of course, Kripke is not saying that any such thing really happened, or even that we don't know that it didn't. The point is that we don't know this apriori. Rather, our

---

[3] The generalization is mine. Kripke contents himself with a specific version focusing on apriori knowledge. It should be acknowledged that when the argument is stated in its general form, the different clauses of (ii) tell differently against different forms of descriptivism.

[4] See *Naming and Necessity*, pp. 83–84.

knowledge that it was Gödel who proved the theorem (if anyone did) rests on, and is justified by, empirical evidence, and so is not apriori.[5] By contrast, we do know apriori that the discoverer of the incompleteness of arithmetic discovered the incompleteness of arithmetic (if anyone did). So, the epistemological argument shows that the proposition expressed by *Gödel discovered the incompleteness of arithmetic (if anyone did)* is not the same as the proposition expressed by *The discoverer of the incompleteness of arithmetic discovered the incompleteness of arithmetic (if anyone did)*.[6] Hence, the description does not give the meaning of the name for us—no matter how central attribution of the theorem to Gödel is to our beliefs about him. Kripke takes this point to extend to other descriptions speakers commonly associate with *Gödel*, and to proper names generally. He concludes that the meanings of the vast majority of proper names are not given by any descriptions that pick out the individual in terms of famous achievements, or important characteristics. Given this, one is hard-pressed to see how they could be given by any descriptions at all. Kripke therefore concludes that T4(ii) is false, and that the meanings of names are not synonymous with descriptions.

He is, however, careful to distinguish this conclusion from one that holds that the referents of proper names are not determined, as a matter of linguistic rule, to be whatever objects satisfy the descriptions associated with them by speakers. According to this weakened version of descriptivism, descriptions associated with a name semantically fix its referent at the actual world-state, without giving its meaning. Once its referent is determined, it is stipulated to retain that referent with respect to all other world-states; thus it is a rigid designator. Several corollaries are taken to follow. (i) The speaker has a description, or family of descriptions, D associated with n that the speaker takes to be uniquely satisfied by some object or other. (ii) It is semantically determined that o is the referent of n iff o uniquely satisfies D (or a sufficient number of the descriptions in D, if D is a family of descriptions). (iii) Since the speaker knows this on the basis of his or her semantic knowledge, the speaker knows on the basis of semantic knowledge alone that the sentence *If n exists, then n is D** expresses a truth. In sum, when D semantically fixes the reference of n, understanding n re-

---

[5] Ibid., p. 87.

[6] Note, in order to reach this conclusion it is not necessary to mention apriority at all. It is enough to observe that there is possible evidence that would make it rational for us to give up our belief in the proposition expressed by one of the two sentences but not the other.

quires knowing that its reference is fixed by D. This holds even though D does not give the meaning of n.

Kripke's arguments against this version of descriptivism are known as *the semantic arguments*, which are designed to constitute counterexamples to each of its corollaries. The Gödel/Schmidt scenario is taken to provide a counterexample to both (ii) and (iii). It is a counterexample to (iii) because we don't know, simply on the basis of our linguistic competence, that the sentence *If Gödel existed, then Gödel was D** is true, when D is a description or family of descriptions encompassing our most important knowledge of Gödel. It is a counterexample to (ii) because when one imagines a state of the world just like ours except that, unknown to speakers, Kripke's fantasy about Gödel's plagiarism is true, we take those speakers to be referring to Gödel, not Schmidt, when they use the name *Gödel*. Thus, the referent of *Gödel*, as used by those speakers, is not the individual that satisfies the descriptions they associate with it. If these arguments are correct, description theories of the referents of names are incorrect.

There is, however, a distinction to be made. Although Kripke suggests that the meanings of names are never the same as those of descriptions that speakers associate with them, he does allow that in some, relatively rare, cases the referent of a name may be semantically fixed by a description. However, the status of these names has become a matter of controversy. *Naming and Necessity* gives the appearance of endorsing three views about them that are difficult to jointly maintain: (i) that one is free to introduce a name n by stipulating that its reference is to be whatever object o satisfies some description D, even in cases in which one does not know of any o that it is has the property expressed by D, (ii) that in these cases what one means by *n is F* is that o has the property expressed by F,[7] and (iii) that in these cases (a) one knows apriori, simply on the basis of one's semantic knowledge, that the sentence *If n exists, then n is D* expresses a truth, (b) the proposition expressed by this sentence is one that can be known to be true apriori, on the basis of one's semantic knowledge, and (c) *It is knowable apriori, simply on the basis of one's semantic knowledge, that if n*

---

[7] Regarding (ii), Kripke says: "If, on the other hand, we merely use the description to **fix the referent** then that man will be the referent of 'Aristotle' in all possible worlds. The only use of the description will have been to pick out to which man we mean to refer. But then, when we say counterfactually 'suppose Aristotle had never gone into philosophy at all', we need not mean 'suppose a man who studied with Plato, and taught Alexander the Great, and wrote this and that, and so on, had never gone into philosophy at all', which might seem like a contradiction. We need only mean, 'suppose that **that man** had never gone into philosophy at all'" (p. 57).

exists, then n is D expresses a truth. Later, we will discuss the consequences of these views, the difficulties to which they give rise, and the proper lessons to draw from them.

There is another distinction to be noted regarding Kripke's response to the two kinds of descriptive theories that he criticizes. Although he argues that descriptive theories of the meaning of names and of their reference are both false, he offers a replacement for only the latter. According to Kripke, the vast majority of proper names have their reference semantically fixed not by a family of associated descriptions, but by a historical chain of reference transmission. Typically, the chain begins with an ostensive baptism in which an individual is stipulated to be the bearer of a name n. Later, when n is used in conversation, new speakers encounter it for the first time and form the intention to use it with the same reference as those from whom they picked it up. Different speakers may, of course, come to associate different descriptions with n, but usually this doesn't affect reference transmission. As a result, speakers further down the historical chain may use n to refer to its original referent o, whether or not they associate descriptions with n that uniquely denote o.

So Kripke does have an apparently plausible alternative to descriptivist theories of reference determination. What about meaning? On his account, it would seem that the only semantic function of a name is to refer, in which case one would expect ordinary proper names to be Russellian logically proper names (without Russell's epistemological restrictions on their bearers). However, Kripke does not draw this, or any other, definite conclusion about the meanings of names, or the propositions semantically expressed by sentences containing them. Along with nearly everyone else, he recognizes that one can understand different coreferential names without knowing that they are coreferential, and certainly without judging them to have the same meaning. However, this doesn't show that the names don't mean the same thing, unless one accepts the highly questionable principle that anyone who understands a pair of synonymous expressions must recognize them to be synonymous—something upon which Kripke never definitively pronounces.

In *Naming and Necessity*, he does argue that the proposition that Hesperus is Phosphorus is not knowable apriori, whereas the proposition that Hesperus is Hesperus is—and that one can know that Hesperus is Hesperus without knowing that Hesperus is Phosphorus.[8] These

---

[8] For explication and criticism of Kripke's argument, see chapter 15 of Soames, *The Age of Meaning*.

views together with natural assumptions about meaning, composition-ality, propositions, and propositional attitude ascriptions could be used to argue that the names *Hesperus* and *Phosphorus* differ in meaning, de-spite being coreferential. However, Kripke neither gives such an argu-ment, nor draws such a conclusion. Moreover, he has no account of what, over and above their referents, the meanings of these names might be. Finally, in "A Puzzle about Belief," he maintains that no definite conclusions should be drawn about the meanings of names from apparent failures of substitution of coreferential names in belief ascriptions.[9] On his view, these puzzles arise from principles of belief attribution that transcend any view about the meaning of names. Hence, he resists drawing any positive conclusion about their mean-ings, or about the propositions semantically expressed by sentences containing them.

Natural Kind Terms

The challenge to descriptive analyses of meaning and reference is not limited to proper names. In addition, both Saul Kripke and Hilary Putnam challenged descriptive analyses of natural kind terms like *gold, tiger, water, heat, light, color,* and *red*.[10] These philosophers, whose views were broadly similar, maintained that, like proper names, natural kind terms are not synonymous with descriptions associated with them by speakers; and, like names, they may acquire reference in two ways. One way involves direct presentation of samples, together with the stipulation that the term is to apply to all and only instances of the unique natural kind (of a certain sort) of which nearly all members of the sample are instances; the other involves the use of a description to pick out a kind by some, usually contingent, properties. Later, when the kind term is passed from speaker to speaker, the way in which the reference was initially established normally doesn't matter—just as with proper names. As a result, speakers further down the linguistic chain may use the term to apply to instances of the kind, whether or

[9] Saul Kripke, "A Puzzle about Belief," originally published in 1979, reprinted in Peter Ludlow (ed.), *Readings in the Philosophy of Language* (Cambridge, MA: MIT Press, 2003).
[10] Putnam, "Is Semantics Possible?," first published in 1970; "Explanation and Refer-ence," first published in 1973; and "The Meaning of 'Meaning,'" first published 1975; all reprinted in *Philosophical Papers*, vol. 2 (Cambridge: Cambridge University Press, 1975); Kripke, lecture 3 of *Naming and Necessity*.

not the descriptive properties they associate with the term really pick out its members. In addition, scientific investigation may lead to the discovery of properties that are necessary and/or sufficient for membership in the kind. These discoveries are formulated by theoretical identification sentences like those in (2), which are said to express truths that are necessary but knowable only aposteriori.

2a. Water is H_2O.

b. Lightning is electricity.

c. Light is a stream of photons.

d. Whales are mammals.

Examples like these are often thought to parallel corresponding sentences $\alpha = \beta$ in which α and β are rigid singular terms. It follows from the definition of rigidity that if α and β refer to the same individual, then they do so in every world-state in which that individual exists, and never refer to anything else. Thus, $\alpha = \beta$ *(if α exists)* is a necessary truth, if it is true at all. Nevertheless, Kripke regards many such truths, e.g., those in (3), to be knowable only aposteriori.

3a. Hesperus is Phosphorus (if Hesperus exists).

b. Cicero is Tully (if Cicero exists).

c. The man who actually won the U.S. Presidential election in 2000 was George W. Bush (if Bush exists).

However, there are two related difficulties with extending Kripke's theses about (3) to sentences like (2). First, many natural kind terms N are not singular terms, but general terms used to form simple predicates of the sort *is N, is an N*, or *are N's*. Since rigid designation is defined only for singular terms, it is not clear what role the notion of rigidity plays in explaining the putative fact that statements of theoretical identification involving natural kind predicates are necessary, if true. Second, many so-called statements of theoretical identification, including those in (2), are more naturally regarded as having the logical form $\forall x \ (Ax \supset Bx)$ rather than $A = B$.[11] Although, in my opinion, these difficulties do not undermine Kripke's attack on descriptivist accounts of natural kind terms, or his contention that many theoretical

---

[11] Note, although (2a) and (2b) and *Ice is H_2O* are true, *Electricity is lightning* and *H_2O is ice* are not.

identification statements involving natural kind terms are examples of the necessary aposteriori, they do raise questions about the proper way of extending his theses about names to this class of terms.[12]

Indexicals, Quantification, and Direct Reference

Starting with lectures given by David Kaplan in 1971, and continuing with published work of Kaplan and John Perry, a further challenge to descriptivism was mounted, focusing on the role of context in understanding indexicals like *I, now, today, here, actually, you, she,* and *that.*[13] Although the referents of these terms vary from one context of utterance to another, their meanings do not. For example, to know the meanings of *I, today,* and *she* is, roughly, to know the rules in (4).

4a. One who uses *I*—e.g., in a sentence *I am F*—refers to oneself, and says of oneself that one "is F."

   b. One who uses *today*—e.g., in a sentence *Today is F*—refers to the day the utterance takes place, and says of that day that it "is F."

   c. One who uses *she*—e.g., in a sentence *She is F*—refers to a contextually salient female, and says of her that she "is F."

These rules provide two kinds of information: they tell us how the referents of indexicals depend on aspects of contexts in which they are used, and they implicitly identify the semantic contents of these terms with their referents in contexts.

In order to understand this talk of content, one must grasp Kaplan's intuitive semantic framework. Sentences express propositions, which are their semantic contents; those containing indexicals express different propositions, and so have different contents, in different contexts. Nevertheless, the meaning of a sentence is constant; it is a function

---

[12] For further discussion, see chapters 9 through 11 of Scott Soames, *Beyond Rigidity* (New York: Oxford University Press, 2002). For critical discussion, see Nathan Salmon, "Naming, Necessity, and Beyond," *Mind* 112 (2003); Bernard Linsky, "General Terms as Rigid Designators," forthcoming in *Philosophical Studies*, and Scott Soames, "Reply to Critics," forthcoming in the same issue as Linsky.

[13] David Kaplan, "On the Logic of Demonstratives," *Journal of Philosophical Logic* 8 (1979) and "Demonstratives," in J. Almog, J. Perry, and H. Wettstein (eds.), *Themes From Kaplan* (New York and Oxford: Oxford University Press, 1989); John Perry, "The Problem of the Essential Indexical," *Nous* 13 (1979), and "Frege on Demonstratives," *Philosophical Review*, 86 (1977).

from contexts to contents. Kaplan's word for this is *character*. The picture is recapitulated for subsentential expressions. For example, the character of *I* is a function that maps an arbitrary context C onto the agent (often the speaker) of C, which is the semantic content of *I* relative to C.

There are two anti-descriptivist implications here. First, the referents of at least some indexicals are not determined by descriptions speakers associate with them. One example from Perry is Rip Van Winkle, who awakens on October 20, 1823 after sleeping for twenty years, and says, not realizing what happened, *Today is October 20, 1803*. In so doing, he speaks falsely because his use of *today* refers to the day of the context, no matter what description he may have in mind.[14] Another example involves Kaplan's identical twins, Castor and Pollux, raised in qualitatively identical environments to be molecule for molecule identical and so, presumably, to associate the same purely qualitative descriptions with the same terms.[15] Despite this, each refers to himself, and not the other, when he uses *I*. These examples show that the referents of indexicals are not always determined by purely qualitative descriptions that speakers associate with them. Although this leaves open the possibility that some indexicals may have their referents semantically fixed by descriptions containing other indexicals, it precludes the possibility that all indexical reference is determined in this way.

The second anti-descriptivist implication is that since the semantic content of an indexical in a context is its referent, its content is not that of any description. In order to make this point, one must move beyond the formal system developed in "On the Logic of Demonstratives," to the conception of structured contents that Kaplan characterizes in "Demonstratives" as the intuitive philosophical picture underlying his approach.[16] On this picture, the proposition expressed by S in C is a complex entity encoding the syntactic structure of S, the constituents of which are (or encode) the semantic contents in C of the words and phrases in S. For example, the proposition expressed in C

---

[14] Perry, "Frege on Demonstratives," p. 487.

[15] Kaplan, "Demonstratives," p. 531. By a *purely qualitative description*, I mean a description not containing indexicals, names, or any similar kinds of terms. Since the descriptivist view under attack holds that the reference of all such terms is descriptively fixed, it should countenance the elimination of any such terms from reference-fixing descriptions themselves.

[16] Pages 496–97. In the formal system, contents of expressions are functions from circumstances of evaluation (pairs of world-states and times) to extensions; thus contents of sentences are functions from circumstances to truth values. Though useful in formal work, Kaplan regards this conception of content as, at best, a very rough approximation of the more accurate and fine-grained conception of structured content.

by a sentence *i is F* is a complex in which the property expressed by F is predicated of the referent o of the indexical i; this is the same as the singular proposition expressed by *x is F*, relative to an assignment of o to the variable 'x'. By contrast, the proposition expressed by *The D is F* in C is a complex consisting of the property expressed by F plus a complex consisting of the content of *the* together with the structured complex which is the semantic content in C of the descriptive phrase *D*. On one natural analysis, this proposition predicates the higher order property of being instantiated by whatever uniquely instantiates the property expressed by D to the property expressed by F.

The claim that the semantic content of an indexical relative to a context is not the same as that of any description is supported by commonplace observations about propositional attitudes. Suppose, to adapt Russell's famous example, that on some occasion in which George IV spied Walter Scott, he gave voice to his newfound conviction, saying *He* [gesturing at Scott] *isn't the author of Waverley*. Had this occurred, each of the following ascriptions would have been true.

5a. The author of <u>Waverley</u>, namely Scott, is such that George IV said that he wasn't the author of <u>Waverley</u>.

 b. George IV said that you weren't the author of <u>Waverley</u>. (said addressing Scott)

 c. George IV said that I wasn't the author of <u>Waverley</u>. (said by Scott)

 d. George IV said that he [pointing at Scott] wasn't the author of <u>Waverley</u>. (said by a third party in another context)

On Kaplan's picture, these reports are true because the semantic content of the sentence George IV uttered (in his context), and so the proposition he asserted, is the same as the content of the complement clauses in the reports of what he said. Whatever descriptions speakers who utter (5b,c,d) may associate with the indexicals are irrelevant to the semantic contents of the reports. These indexicals, like the variable *he* in (5a), are used to report the attitude of an agent toward a particular person, abstracting away from the particular manner in which the agent thinks of, or characterizes, that person. All they contribute to the proposition George IV is reported as asserting is the individual Scott.

We are now ready to define the notion of a directly referential term, and contrast it with a generalized notion of rigid designation.[17]

DIRECT REFERENCE

A term t is directly referential iff for all contexts C, assignments A, and world-states w, the referent of t with respect to C, A, and w = the referent of t with respect to C and A = the content of t with respect to C and A.[18]

GENERALIZED RIGID DESIGNATION

A singular term t is a rigid designator iff for all contexts C, assignments A, world-states w, and objects o, if t refers to o with respect to C, A, and w, then t refers to o with respect to C, A, and w′, for all world-states w′ in which o exists, and t never refers to anything else with respect to C, A, and any world-state w*.

With this understanding, all directly referential singular terms are rigid designators, but not vice versa (e.g., *the square root of 25* is rigid but not directly referential). According to Kaplan, indexicals and variables are directly referential. Nathan Salmon and I extend this view to proper names.[19]

Before leaving Kaplan's framework, it is important to consider two indexical operators used to construct rigidified descriptions out of nonrigid descriptions. One, *dthat*, combines with a description **the D** to form a directly referential singular term **dthat [the D]** the content of which, relative to C and A, is the unique object o denoted by **the D** relative to C and A (if there is such an object). The other, *actually*, stands for the world-state C_W of the context in a manner analogous to the way in which *now* stands for the time C_T of the context, and *I* stands for the agent C_A of the context. *Actually* combines with a sentence S to form a complex sentence **Actually S** the content of which in C is a proposition that predicates of C_W the property of being a world-state in which the proposition expressed by S in C is true; hence **Actu-**

[17] Here, and in what follows, I treat what Kaplan calls *circumstances of evaluation* as world-states, rather than, as he does, pairs of times and world-states. Although there are real issues here, in order to keep the discussion as simple as possible, I will not pursue them.

[18] Intuitively, one can think of this as follows: (i) The content of t w.r.t. C and A is identified with its referent there. Since an object has already been determined, there is no further object determination to be done with respect to other world-states. So, for any world-state w, the referent of t with respect to C, A, and w is the referent of t with respect to C and A.

[19] Nathan Salmon, *Frege's Puzzle* (Cambridge, MA: MIT Press, 1986); Scott Soames, *Beyond Rigidity*.

ally S is true with respect to C and arbitrary world-state w iff S is true with respect to C and C_W, and whenever S is true in C_W, *Actually S* is a necessary truth.

The corresponding fact about descriptions is that whenever *the x: Fx* successfully denotes a unique individual o in the world-state of the context C, *the x: actually Fx* denotes o with respect to C and all possible world-states in which o exists, and never denotes anything else. Hence, *actually* is a rigidifier; however, the resulting rigidified descriptions are not directly referential. For example, if *the x: Fx* and *the x: Gx* are contingently codesignative descriptions of the same object o, then *the x: actually Fx* and *the x: actually Gx* will be non-directly referential, rigid designators of the same object, with different semantic contents, relative to a context and actual world state C_W of the context. The former may be paraphrased *the unique object which is F in C_W*, while the latter is paraphrased *the unique object which is G in C_W*. In Kaplan's intuitive semantic framework—in which the semantic content of a compound expression e is a structured entity constructed out of the semantic contents of the grammatical constituents of e—the semantic contents of *actually*-rigidified descriptions will be different whenever the semantic contents of the original, unrigidified descriptions are different. This is not so with descriptions rigidified using the *dthat* operator. Any pair of *dthat*-rigidified descriptions that refer to the same thing have the same semantic content. Hence, substitution of codesignative *dthat*-rigidified descriptions in a sentence (not containing quotation or quasi-quotational devices) always preserves the semantic content of the sentence, whereas substitution of codesignative *actually*-rigidified descriptions does not.[20]

Another difference between *dthat*-rigidified descriptions and *actually*-rigidified descriptions involves existence. A *dthat*-rigidified description, *dthat [the x:Fx]*, which designates an object o in the world-state of the context, designates o in all world-states, even those in which o does not exist. By contrast, an *actually*-rigidified description, *the x: actually Fx*, which designates o in the world-state of the con-

---

[20] This difference between *dthat*-rigidified descriptions and *actually*-rigidified descriptions (as well as between directly referential singular terms in general and other, merely rigid, terms) all but washes away in semantic systems in which the content of an expression in a context is identified with its intension (i.e., function from circumstances of evaluation to extensions) in the context. In such systems the content of a rigid designator in a context is a function from circumstances of evaluation that always returns the same object as extension (when it returns any extension at all). Though Kaplan uses such systems in his formal work, he does not believe that they capture the philosophical truth about content.

text, designates o in all world-states in which o exists. However, if different objects exist at different world-states, and the range of *the*, and other quantifiers, at a world-state is restricted to objects existing at that world-state (two very common assumptions), then *the x: actually Fx* will fail to designate anything at a world-state in which o does not exist.

For most discussions, this difference between *dthat*-rigidified descriptions and *actually*-rigidified descriptions doesn't matter much. However, there is one further peculiarity about *actually*-rigidified descriptions that is potentially more serious, and even calls into question the characterization of them as *rigid designators*. The peculiarity involves cases in which *the x: actually F* fails to designate an object at the world-state of a context C* because more than one object existing at that world-state has the property expressed by F.[21] Suppose further that there are exactly two such objects o_1, o_2, and that, of these two, only o_1 exists at possible world-state w_1, while only o_2 exists at w_2. Then, since *the x: actually Fx* designates an object o with respect to a context C and world-state w iff o is the unique object existing at w which, in the world-state C_W of the context, has the property expressed by F, *the x: actually Fx* will designate o_1 with respect to C* and w_1, while designating o_2 with respect to C* and w_2. Obviously, this description is not a rigid designator. Thus, not all descriptions to which *actually* has been added in this way qualify as rigid.

This does not materially affect our discussion thus far of what I have been calling *actually*-rigidified descriptions, since in introducing these descriptions, I said "whenever *the x: Fx* successfully denotes a unique individual o in the world-state of the context C, *the x: actually Fx* denotes o with respect to C and all possible world-states in which o exists, and never denotes anything else." This remains true. What is **not** true is that descriptions to which *actually* have been added in this way standardly satisfy the definition of generalized rigid designation just given. We can, however, bring such descriptions under the general rubric *rigid designation* by introducing the following contextualized notion.

CONTEXTUALIZED RIGID DESIGNATION
A singular term t is a rigid designator with respect to a context C and assignment A iff there is an object o such that (i) t refers to o with respect to C, A, and the world-state C_W of

---

[21] Thanks to Ali Kazmi for bringing this peculiarity to my attention.

C, and (ii) for all world-states w in which o exists, t refers to o with respect to C, A, and w, and (iii) t never refers to anything else with respect to C, A, and any world-state w*.

It is only this weakened, contextualized definition of rigid designation that is guaranteed to be satisfied by the description *the x: actually Fx* in contexts in which it successfully designates something. This is the sense in which I will refer to such descriptions as *rigid designators*.[22]

Philosophical Implications of Rigidity, Direct Reference, and Non-Descriptionality

Although it seems evident that the propositions expressed by (6) are knowable only aposteriori, it appears to be a consequence of the non-descriptive semantics of names, natural kind terms, and the actuality operator that each of these sentences expresses a necessary truth, if it is true at all.

6a. Saul Kripke ≠ David Kaplan

 b. Water is H_2O.

 c. Ice is H_2O.

 d. Actually it was the case that George Washington was the first President of the United States.

 e. If Thomas Jefferson existed, then the person who actually wrote the Declaration of Independence was Thomas Jefferson.

Since we know that (6a–e) are true, it follows that they are examples of the necessary aposteriori. Moreover, nondescriptional semantics of the

---

[22] A further point brought to my attention by Kazmi is that if we start with a sentence *The actual F is G* and (i) eliminate the description in favor of its Russellian expansion, while (ii) allowing ourselves to place the actuality operator between the quantifiers of that expansion, then we can give the sentence a highly intuitive reading—namely $\exists x$ *[actually* $\forall y$ *(Fy* $\leftrightarrow$ *x =y)* & *Gx]*—in which the uniqueness condition is correctly imposed on things that have the property expressed by F in the world-state of the context. This reading is not available if *the actual F* is treated in the usual manner as a singular term or restricted quantifier, *the x: actually Fx*, in which *the* is an operator with the usual semantics, ranging over objects existing at the world-state of evaluation. Perhaps we should allow *actual* to combine with *the* to form a complex quantifier *the-actual x*.

sort introduced by Kripke and Kaplan provide recipes for generating many more examples of the same type. One of the simplest such recipes involves examples containing the actuality operator. If S expresses an ordinary true, but contingent, proposition p that is knowable only aposteriori, then *Actually S* expresses a necessary truth that says of the actual world-state @ that it is a world-state with respect to which p is true. If, as seems evident, this proposition about @ is knowable apriori only if p is knowable apriori, then we have a recipe for cooking up instances of the necessary aposteriori, virtually at will. Another simple recipe involves directly referential singular terms. Let P be a predicate with the following two characteristics: (i) it expresses an essential property of anything that has it (i.e., a property that anything which has it couldn't exist without), and (ii) in order to know of a particular object that it has this property, one must possess empirical evidence to this effect. In addition, suppose (a) that o has the property expressed by P, and (b) that t is a directly referential term that designates o, and, hence, that the proposition expressed by *t is P* (relative to a context C) can be known only if one knows of o that it has the property which P expresses. It will then follow that (in C) *If t exists, then t is P* expresses a proposition that is both necessary and knowable only aposteriori. If nondescriptivists are right, then there are many examples of this type in which t is a name, an indexical, or a *dthat*-rigidified description. Similar recipes can be given for more complex sentences, as well as for sentences containing natural kind terms.[23]

The best examples of the contingent apriori are sentences like (7).

7. If some one person wrote the Declaration of Independence, then the person who actually wrote the Declaration of Independence wrote something.

It follows from the semantics of *actually*, plus the fact that Thomas Jefferson wrote the Declaration of Independence, that (7) is false at a world-state in which Thomas Jefferson wrote nothing, and someone else wrote the Declaration of Independence. Assuming that the world could have been in such a state, we conclude that (7) expresses a contingent truth. However, this truth can be known without doing any empirical investigation. Since anyone in the actual world-state can know it to be true simply by understanding (7), and reasoning about

---

[23] In the case of natural kind terms, the generation of instances of the necessary aposteriori raises a number of complicated and controversial questions. See chapters 9 through 11 of *Beyond Rigidity* for discussion.

it—without appeal to empirical evidence for justification—the proposition expressed would seem to be knowable apriori. Thus, it seems
that a proper understanding of nondescriptive semantics shows that—
contrary to what philosophers have thought for centuries—not all necessary truths are apriori, and not all apriori truths are necessary.

PART TWO

DESCRIPTIVIST RESISTANCE: THE ORIGINS OF AMBITIOUS TWO-DIMENSIONALISM

CHAPTER 3

REASONS FOR RESISTANCE AND THE
STRATEGY FOR DESCRIPTIVIST REVIVAL

Motivations

Despite the attack on descriptivism, some believe that the anti-descriptivists' conclusions are too extreme, and that properly modified descriptive analyses should be capable of withstanding their arguments. This view is fueled by three main factors. First is the conviction that anti-descriptivists have not adequately addressed Frege's puzzle about substitution of coreferential terms in attitude ascriptions and Russell's problem of negative existentials. There is still a widespread belief that these problems show that names cannot be directly referential. Although Kripke never asserted that they were, it is hard to see how, if his doctrines are correct, they could be anything else. According to him, the meaning of a name is never the same as that of any description, and the vast majority of names do not even have their referents semantically fixed by descriptions. If these names are so thoroughly nondescriptional, it is not clear how their meanings could be other than their referents. Consequently, one who takes that view to have been refuted by Frege and Russell will suspect that the power of Kripke's arguments must have been exaggerated, and will be motivated to find a way of modifying descriptivism that can withstand them.

The second factor motivating descriptivists is their conviction that critics like Kripke have focused on the wrong descriptions. To be sure, it will be admitted, for many speakers s and proper names or natural kind terms n, the descriptions most likely to be volunteered by s in answer to the question *To what, or to whom, do you refer when you use n?* neither give the meaning of n, nor semantically fix its reference. Often s will respond by citing what s takes to be the most well-known and important characteristics of the putative referent, about which s may be mistaken. However, the referents of these terms must be determined in some way, and surely, whatever way it is can be described. Thus, for each name or natural kind term n, there must be some description D that correctly picks out its referent(s)—perhaps one encapsulating Kripke's own causal-historical picture of reference transmission.

Is there any reason to believe that speakers associate D with n? Some descriptivists think so. In fact, the very success of Kripke and others in eliciting uncontroversial judgments about what names would refer to if used in various counterfactual situations has been taken to show that speakers must be implicitly guided by a descriptive theory that determines reference. For example, Frank Jackson argues that

> Our ability to answer questions about what various words refer to in various possible worlds, it should be emphasized, is common ground with critics of the description theory. The critics' writings are full of descriptions (*descriptions*) of possible worlds and claims about what refers, or fails to refer, to what in these possible worlds. Indeed, their impact has derived precisely from the intuitive plausibility of many of their claims about what refers, or fails to refer, to what in various possible worlds. But if speakers can say what refers to what when various possible worlds are described to them, description theorists can identify the property associated in their minds with, for example, the word 'water': it is the disjunction of the properties that guide the speakers in each particular possible world when they say which stuff, if any, in each world counts as water. This disjunction is in their minds in the sense that they can deliver the answer for each possible world when it is described in sufficient detail, but it is implicit in the sense that the pattern that brings the various disjuncts together as part of the, possibly highly complex, disjunction may be one they cannot state.[1]

This is a remarkable defense. If correct, it might seem to suggest that descriptive theories of reference are virtually guaranteed, apriori, to be irrefutable, since any refutation would require a clear, uncontroversial sketch of a possible scenario in which n referred to something o not satisfying the description putatively associated with n by ordinary speakers like us (or failed to refer to the thing that was denoted by this description)—whereas the very judgment that n does refer to o in this scenario (or does not refer to what the description denotes there) would be taken by Jackson to demonstrate the existence of a different,

---

[1] Frank Jackson, "Reference and Descriptions Revisited," *Philosophical Perspectives* 12 (1998): 212.

implicit description in our minds that successfully determines reference, whether or not we can articulate it.

The third factor motivating a descriptivist revival involves the inability of some to see how any single proposition could be either both necessary and aposteriori, or both contingent and apriori, as anti-descriptivists maintain. How, descriptivists ask, can evidence about the actual world-state be required to establish p, if p is true in every possible state in which the world could be (including states in which no such evidence exists)? Or again, if q is contingent, then there are states that the world could be in, such that were the world in them, q would be false. But how could one possibly know without appeal to evidence that the world is not in such a state? The former worry casts doubt on the necessary aposteriori, the latter on the contingent apriori.

In addition to endorsing these skeptical worries, some descriptivists— e.g., Frank Jackson, David Chalmers, and David Lewis—adhere to antecedent philosophical commitments that make the existence of propositions that are both necessary and knowable only aposteriori impossible. One of these commitments is to metaphysical possibility as the only kind of possibility. Although these theorists recognize different metaphysically possible ways that the world could be, they reject the idea that, in addition to these, there are also epistemically possible ways that the world might be—states which, though metaphysically impossible, cannot be known by us apriori not to obtain.[2] This restriction of epistemic possibility to metaphysical possibility renders the necessary aposteriori problematic from the start—since it precludes explaining this category of truth by citing metaphysically necessary propositions for which empirical evidence is needed to rule out metaphysically impossible, but epistemically possible, world-states in which they are false. When one adds to this Lewis's analysis of knowing p as having evidence that rules out all possible ways of p's being untrue, one has, in effect, defined propositions that are both necessary and knowable only aposteriori out of existence.[3] Since, when p is a necessary truth, there are no metaphysically possible ways of its being untrue, it follows that there are no possible ways of p's being untrue at all, and hence that knowledge of p never requires empirical evidence.

[2] David Chalmers, *The Conscious Mind* (New York and Oxford: Oxford University Press, 1996), pp. 136–8; Frank Jackson, *From Metaphysics to Ethics* (Oxford: Oxford University Press, 1998), pp. 67–74. The limitation of epistemic possibility to metaphysical possibility is tacitly assumed by Lewis in "Elusive Knowledge," originally published in 1996, reprinted in *Papers in Metaphysics and Epistemology* (Cambridge: Cambridge University Press, 1999).

[3] Lewis, "Elusive Knowledge," p. 422.

So, the necessary aposteriori is impossible. A different philosophical commitment that leads to the same conclusion identifies propositions with sets of metaphysically possible world-states (or functions from world-states to truth values). On this view, there is only one necessary proposition—which is known apriori.[4] But if that is right, then the anti-descriptivist semantics that leads to the conclusion that there are necessary aposteriori propositions must be mistaken.[5]

Strategy

The main strategy for constructing descriptive analyses of names and natural kind terms attempts (i) to find reference-fixing descriptions capable of withstanding Kripke's semantic arguments, (ii) to avoid the modal argument, either by rigidifying these descriptions, or by insisting that they take wide-scope over modal operators in the same sentence, and (iii) to use two-dimensional semantics to avoid the epistemological argument and explain away putative examples of the necessary aposteriori and the contingent apriori. The most popular strategy for finding reference-fixing descriptions is *causal descriptivism*, which involves extracting a description from Kripke's causal-historical account of reference transmission. Details aside, the general idea is clear enough, as is illustrated by the following passage from David Lewis.

> Did not Kripke and his allies refute the description theory of reference, at least for names of people and places? Then why should we expect descriptivism to work any better for names of colors and color experiences? . . . I disagree. What was well and truly refuted was a version of descriptivism in which the descriptive senses were supposed to be a matter of famous deeds and other distinctive peculiarities. A better version survives the attack: *causal descriptivism*. The descriptive sense associated with a name might for instance be *the place I have heard of under the name "Ta-*

[4] See Robert Stalnaker, "Assertion," originally published in 1978, reprinted in *Context and Content* (Oxford: Oxford University Press, 1999), and *Inquiry* (Cambridge, MA: MIT Press, 1984); Lewis, "Elusive Knowledge," pp. 422–23; Frank Jackson, *From Metaphysics to Ethics*, pp. 71–74 and 75–78.

[5] Attacks on nondescriptivist accounts of the semantic contents of names have also been based on puzzles about the contingent apriori. For example, see Michael Dummett, *Frege* (London: Duckworth, 1973), p. 121, and Gareth Evans, "Reference and Contingency," *Monist* 62 (1979): 161–89 reprinted in *Collected Papers* (Oxford: Clarendon Press, 1985).

romeo", or maybe *the causal source of this token: Taromeo,* and for an account of the relation being invoked here, just consult the writings of causal theorists of reference.[6]

The second part of the descriptivists' strategy is the attempt to avoid Kripke's modal argument. The simplest way of doing this, once one has what one takes to be a reference-fixing description, is to rigidify it using *actually* or *dthat.* An alternative method is to analyze names as meaning the same as nonrigid descriptions that are required to take wide-scope over modal operators (and modal predicates) in the same sentence, while taking narrow-scope when embedded under verbs of propositional attitude.[7] Although the details can be complicated, the guiding idea is simple. Descriptivists want to explain apparent instances of substitution failure involving coreferential proper names in attitude ascriptions by appealing to descriptive semantic contents of names occurring in the complement clauses; however, they also want to guarantee substitution success when one coreferential name is substituted for another in modal constructions. The different strategies of dealing with Kripke's modal argument are designed to do that.

The final weapon in the descriptivists' strategic arsenal is (ambitious) two-dimensionalism, which is illustrated by the following line of thought about a simple example of the contingent apriori.

1. If there is a unique F, then the x: actually Fx = the x: Fx.

Here, we let *the x: Fx* be a nonrigid description which designates some individual o in the actual world-state, but which designates other individuals with respect to other world-states. The semantics of *actually* guarantees that (1) is a contingent truth that is false with respect to world-states in which *the x: Fx* designates something other than o. However, although the proposition expressed by (1) is contingent, the knowledge reported by (2) is, at bottom, nothing over and above the knowledge reported by (3).

---

[6] David Lewis, fn. 22 of "Naming the Colors," originally published in 1997, reprinted in *Papers in Metaphysics and Epistemology;* see also "Putnam's Paradox," originally published in 1984, and reprinted in *Papers in Metaphysics and Epistemology;* Fred Kroon, "Causal Descriptivism," *Australasian Journal of Philosophy* 65 (1987); John Searle, chapter 9 of *Intentionality* (Cambridge: Cambridge University Press, 1983), and David Chalmers, "On Sense and Intension," in J. Tomberlin (ed.), *Philosophical Perspectives* 16; *Language and Mind* (Oxford: Blackwell, 2002), pp. 135–82.

[7] Jackson advocates the rigidifying strategy in "Reference and Description Revisited," pp. 213–14; Michael Dummett advocated the wide-scope strategy in *Frege: Philosophy of Language* (New York: Harper & Row, 1973).

2. x knows that if there is a unique F, then the x: actually Fx = the x: Fx.

3. x knows that if there is a unique F, then the x: Fx = the x: Fx.

Hence, if the latter is apriori, so is the former. But the latter is apriori, since it is nothing more than knowledge of the trivial, necessary truth expressed by (4).

4. If there is a unique F, then the x: Fx = the x: Fx.

It follows that the knowledge reported by (2) must also be apriori, despite the fact that the proposition expressed by its complement clause, (1), is contingent. How can this be?

The two-dimensionalist answer is based on the observation that sentences (1) and (4) are equivalent in one respect and nonequivalent in another. They are nonequivalent in that they express different propositions. They are equivalent in that the conditions under which they express truths are identical—and known to be so by anyone who understands them. Any context of utterance in which one of them could be used to express a truth is a context in which the other would also express a truth. What contexts are these? Since (4) expresses the same proposition in all contexts, they are precisely the contexts in which the proposition that (4) always expresses is true. Putting this all together, we see that sentence (1) is, in fact, semantically associated with two propositions—the one it expresses in our own present context (which, two-dimsensionalists call *the secondary proposition*), and the one—expressed by (4)—that states the conditions under which (1) expresses a truth (which is accorded the honorific *the primary proposition*). Since this "primary proposition" is obviously both necessary and apriori, anyone who understands (1) thereby has all the information needed to know that it expresses a truth.

How does this provide the two-dimensionalist with an explanation of the apriori status of (1)? Two main possibilities suggest themselves (between which informal discussions of two-dimensionalism do not always carefully distinguish). The first may be seen as arising from a systematic semantic theory called *strong two-dimensionalism*, which we will investigate in Part 3. It holds that although the proposition expressed by (1) is a contingent truth, the knowledge reported by (2) is **not** knowledge of this truth, but knowledge of the conditions under which (1) expresses a truth—i.e., knowledge of the proposition expressed by (4). On this view, there is no puzzle explaining how the proposition expressed by (1) can be both contingent and knowable apriori, because it isn't. Instead, the sentence is associated with two propositions: its "secondary proposition," which is relevant to its status as being necessary or contingent, and its "primary proposition," which is relevant to its status as being knowable apriori or only aposteriori. In general, sentences like (1)—which express different propositions in different contexts—are seen as semantically associated with two propositions relative to any context C: the proposition the sentence expresses in C (its secondary proposition relative to C) and the proposition that states the conditions that must be satisfied by the world in any context in which the sentence expresses a truth (its primary proposition). It is the primary proposition associated with a sentence S that provides the argument to the operators *it is knowable apriori that, it is knowable only aposteriori that,* and *Jones knows (apriori* or *aposteriori) that,* when S is combined with them to form a knowledge ascription. By contrast, it is its secondary proposition—the one S expresses in C—that provides the argument to modal operators like *it is a necessary truth that, it could have been the case that,* and *if it had been the case that* ____, *then it would have been the case that* ____. This semantic framework provides the basis for the strong two-dimensionalist's hypothesis that the explanation given of the contingent apriority of (1) can be extended to cover every case of the contingent apriori. A corresponding explanation is postulated for the necessary aposteriori.

A slightly different two-dimensionalist explanation of all these examples arises from a different semantic theory called *weak two-dimensionalism,* which will also be examined in Part 3. On this view, sentences that express different propositions in different contexts are semantically associated with primary and secondary propositions in any context C—just as with strong two-dimensionalism. However, according to weak two-dimensionalism, the argument provided by such a sentence S to the operators *it is knowable apriori that, it is knowable only aposteriori that,* and *Jones knows (apriori* or *aposteriori) that* is **not** its primary proposition, but its secondary proposition in C. On this view, the knowledge reported by (2) **is** knowledge of the contingent proposition expressed by (1). However, this knowledge is apriori because this proposition—the secondary proposition associated with (1) in C—can be known simply by virtue of knowing (1)'s primary proposition, which is the apriori truth expressed by (4). As before, what makes the knowledge reported by (2) apriori is that the primary proposition associated with (1) is apriori. However, whereas the strong two-dimensionalist claims that knowledge of the primary proposition is reported **instead** of knowledge of the secondary proposition, the weak two-dimensionalist claims that knowledge of the primary proposition **counts** as knowledge of the secondary proposition. The weak two-dimensionalist hypothesizes that a similar explanation can be given for all cases of the contingent apriori. A corresponding explanation is offered for the necessary aposteriori.

Both of these two-dimensionalist responses aim to take the sting out of the contingent apriori and the necessary aposteriori for the descriptivist. The strong two-dimensionalist response does so by treating sentences that fall into these categories as giving rise to an **illusion** to be dispelled by laying bare a previously unnoticed equivocation between the two different propositions associated with each such sentence. The weak two-dimensionalist response is more charitable—alleging no equivocation, but attempting to explain the existence of certain propositions that are both contingent and knowable apriori, and others that are both necessary and knowable only aposteriori, by citing the intimate epistemological relations these propositions bear to other, less puzzling propositions. In Part 3, we will examine both responses in detail, and subject them to critical scrutiny. For now, it is enough to notice two important ways in which these responses are connected to descriptivism. First, they promise a way of accommodating compelling examples of the contingent apriori and the necessary aposteriori without embracing the nondescriptive semantic theses that led Kripke and others to give these examples in the first place. Second, the two-dimensionalist explanations offered for examples involving names or natural kind terms are predicated on analyzing them as rigidified descriptions—hence the attractiveness of the explanations for descriptivists.

CHAPTER 4

ROOTS OF TWO-DIMENSIONALISM IN KAPLAN AND KRIPKE

Overview

In chapter 3, I indicated how certain forms of two-dimensionalism—those I called *strong* and *weak* two-dimensionalism—have become associated with an ambitious attempt to revive descriptivism in a way that renders it immune from Kripke's attacks, and provides deflationary accounts of the contingent apriori and the necessary aposteriori. In this chapter, I will trace some of the sources of this ambitious use of two-dimensionalist ideas to certain parts of the classic anti-descriptivist texts of Kaplan and Kripke. There is, of course, an irony in this, since neither Kaplan nor Kripke would endorse any version of two-dimensionalism that led to a resurgence of descriptivism. Nevertheless, I will show how certain parts of their discussions have encouraged descriptive two-dimensionalists. In all such cases, I will argue that the passages by Kaplan and Kripke contain errors, slips, or misleading suggestions that are all too easily interpreted as pointing away from the guiding insights and lasting lessons of their brilliant works. However, the argument to this effect is only begun in this chapter. The full argument requires the development and criticism of ambitious two-dimensionalism given in Part 3.

Benign Two-Dimensionalism

Before isolating sources of what I take to be two-dimensionalist error in Kaplan and Kripke, I need to distinguish ambitious two-dimensionalism (of either the strong or weak variety) from what might be called *benign two-dimensionalism*. Roughly put, benign two-dimensionalism is the view that there are two dimensions of meaning—character and content. As indicated in the discussion of Kaplan in chapter 2, character is a function from contexts of utterance (which include designated possible world-states) to contents expressed in those contexts. Content either is, or determines, a function from circumstances of evaluation (again including possible world-states) to extensions. Characters, which are occasionally referred to as *two-dimensional intensions*,[1] are, as Kaplan taught us, crucial to the semantics of context-sensitive expressions and the sentences that contain them. It is Kaplan who gave us benign two-dimensionalism, the *locus classicus* of which is his "Demonstratives." In Kaplan's benign sense, "we are all two-dimensionalists now."

In recent years, however, *two-dimensionalism* has come to stand for something more pointed and ambitious—a cluster of views that build on Kaplan's benign two-dimensionalism, while going beyond it in philosophically significant ways. The defining characteristic of *ambitious two-dimensionalism*, as I will call it, is the attempt to use a Kaplan-like distinction between content and character to revive descriptivism, and to explain, or explain away, all instances of the necessary aposteriori and the contingent apriori. The revival of descriptivism is linked to the conviction that all names and natural kind terms can be treated as rigidified descriptions. Examples of the necessary aposteriori and the contingent apriori involving these expressions are thus assimilated to examples containing such descriptions—like (1) *If there is a unique F, then the x: actually Fx = the x: Fx* in chapter 3. Instances of the necessary aposteriori and the contingent apriori are then "explained" in the manner indicated there by appealing to the pairs of "primary" and "secondary" propositions associated with each such instance. The details of these explanations, and the reasons ambitious two-dimensionalists are intent on offering them, will be carefully scrutinized in later chapters. This chapter will focus on passages in Kaplan and Kripke that can be read (or, in some cases, misread) as encouraging this ambitious philosophical program.

Sources of Ambitious Two-Dimensionalism in Kaplan's "Demonstratives"

I begin with Remark 10 of section XIX, "Remarks on the Formal System," which is concerned with the relationship between necessity, apriority, and logical truth (validity) in Kaplan's formal logic of demonstratives. In Kaplan's system, contexts include a designated

---

[1] See Robert Stalnaker, *Context and Content*, p. 10 of the introduction.

world-state C_w, a designated time C_T, a designated place C_P, and a designated agent C_A. A sentence S in LD (the logic of demonstratives) is a logical truth iff for every model structure M, S expresses a truth in every context C of M—i.e., S expresses a proposition in C which is true at the world-state C_w and time C_T of C. Roughly speaking, logical truths are sentences that are semantically guaranteed to express truths by the logical vocabulary—the interpretation of which remains invariant from one model to the next—of the logic of demonstratives.

Remark 10 focuses on uses of the *dthat*-operator to express necessary aposteriori and contingent apriori truths. It must be remembered that Kaplan's remark is about his formal system, in which the content of an expression relative to a context is identified with its intension—which, in turn, is a function from world-state/time pairs to the extensions of the expression at those pairs. In this system, rigid designators are identified with expressions the contents of which in a context are constant functions—i.e., functions that assign the same extension to every world-state/time pair. These expressions are said to have a "Stable Content." By contrast, an expression is said to have a "Stable Character" iff (for each model) it has the same content in every context, and thus its character is a constant function which assigns to each context, as argument, the same content, as value. For Kaplan, nonindexicals—names, natural kind terms, and many ordinary predicates—have Stable Characters, whereas indexicals do not. As indicated in chapter 2, he regards the identification of contents with intensions as an artifact of the formal system which, though useful, is, at best, a rough, and sometimes misleading, approximation of the real truth.[2] As he sees it, the real truth about contents of expressions is that they are structured complexes the constituents of which are the semantic contents of the grammatically significant units that make them up.

Here is Remark 10.

Rigid designators (in the sense of Kripke) are terms with a Stable Content. Since Kripke does not discuss demonstratives, his examples all have, in addition, a Stable Character (by Remark 8). Kripke claims that for proper names α, β it may happen that $\alpha = \beta$, though not apriori, is nevertheless necessary. This, in spite of the fact that the names α, β may be introduced by means of descrip-

---

[2] The identification of contents with intensions is misleading because, among other things, it obliterates the distinction between rigid designators that are directly referential and those that are not, and because it recognizes only one necessary proposition.

tions α', β' for which $\alpha' = \beta'$ is not necessary. An analogous situation holds in LD [the logic of demonstratives]. Let α', β' be definite descriptions (without free variables) such that $\alpha' = \beta'$ is not apriori, and consider the (rigid) terms *dthat[α']* and *dthat[β']* which are formed from them. We know that

$\vDash (\text{dthat}[\alpha'] = \text{dthat}[\beta'] \leftrightarrow \alpha' = \beta')$

Thus, if $\alpha' = \beta'$ is not apriori, neither is *dthat[α'] = dthat[β']*. But since:

$\vDash (\text{dthat}[\alpha'] = \text{dthat}[\beta'] \rightarrow \Box\text{dthat}[\alpha'] = \text{dthat}[\beta'])$

it may happen that *dthat[α'] = dthat[β']* is necessary. The converse situation can be illustrated in LD. Since $(\alpha = \text{dthat}[\alpha])$ is valid (see Remark 3), it is surely capable of being known apriori. But if α lacks a Stable Content (in some context C), $\Box (\alpha = \text{dthat}[\alpha])$ will be false.[3]

In this passage, Kaplan makes two significant assumptions about the relationship between the epistemological notion of apriori truth and the notions of logical equivalence and logical truth (or validity). In discussing the first example, *dthat [α'] = dthat [β']*, which is supposed to be an instance of the necessary aposteriori, he tacitly assumes A1.

A1. Any sentence logically equivalent to an apriori truth is apriori.

In discussing the second example, $\alpha = $ *dthat [α]*, which is supposed to be an instance of the contingent apriori, he tacitly assumes A2.

A2. If S is valid (logically true), then it is apriori.

I will argue that these assumptions are false—as well as being in obvious tension with other things Kaplan says.

Kaplan's remarks in this passage are not isolated ones. For example, at the end of section XVII, "Epistemological Remarks," he talks about the relationship between logical truth, apriority, and necessity. He begins on page 538 by telling us that logical truth "is a form of apriority." Next follows a discussion of the two examples summarized in Remark 10. He then continues:

How can something be both logically true, and thus *certain*, and *contingent* at the same time? In the case of indexicals the answer is easy to see.

---

[3] Page 550. The symbol '$\vDash$' means that the sentence that follows it is a logical truth in the logic of demonstratives; '$\Box$' is the necessity operator. I have added boldface italics where corner quotes are needed.

*E. Corollary 3 The bearers of logical truth and of contingency are
different entities. It is the character (or, the sentence, if you prefer)
that is logically true, producing a true content in every context. But
it is the content (the proposition, if you will) that is contingent or
necessary.*[4]

We are told that the bearers of logical truth are characters. Since we
are also told that logical truth is a species of the apriori, it would be
natural to think that, according to Kaplan, the things known apriori or
aposteriori are characters. What we have here is nothing less than one
of the wellsprings of ambitious two-dimensionalism. How is it that
one sentence can be logically true, and hence an example of the apriori, while also being contingent? Because the sentence is associated
with two different semantic values—one, its character, which is logically true and knowable apriori, the other, the proposition it expresses
in a context, which is contingent.

This is very close to the strong two-dimensionalist claim that such
sentences are associated with a primary proposition (which is true at a
world-state w iff the character of the sentence assigns w—considered
as a context—a proposition true at w) and a secondary proposition
that is expressed in the context. Kaplan's examples of sentences that
are contingent, yet logically true, express contingent (secondary)
propositions. However, since their characters express truths in every
context, the primary propositions associated with them by strong two-
dimensionalists are seen as necessary. Given the strong two-dimensionalist's claim that no necessary propositions are knowable only
aposteriori, he concludes that the primary proposition must be knowable apriori, if it is knowable at all—a qualification that comes to nothing in classic strong two-dimensionalist systems, which identify propositions with functions from world-states to truth values, and thereby
recognize only a single necessary proposition.

Of course, Kaplan himself doesn't say all this. Still, the passage from
section XVII points in a strong two-dimensionalist direction. By my
lights, there are three things in the passage that are wrong or misleading. First, the contention that characters are the bearers of logical
truth is false; at any rate, it is false if characters are also what Kaplan repeatedly insists that they are—namely, the meanings of sentences. Second, the suggestion that the bearers of logical truth are also the bearers of apriority is incorrect. Third, the claim that logical truth is a

---

[4] Page 539. The italics are Kaplan's, for emphasis.

species of the apriori is questionable; there is reason to believe that some sentences that are logically true do not express propositions that are knowable apriori.

What are the bearers of logical truth in Kaplan's system? It is not clearly right to say that they are characters—in the sense of rules grasped by competent speakers that map contexts into propositions expressed by sentences. For Kaplan, logical truth is truth in all contexts of **every model structure**—where a model structure is a sextuple <C,W,U,P,T,I> in which C is a non-empty set of contexts (each containing a designated world-state, time, place, and agent), W is a non-empty set of world-states, U is a nonempty set of individuals, P is a nonempty set of positions, T is a nonempty set of integers (playing the role of moments of time), and I is an interpretation function that assigns intensions to the primitive nonlogical vocabulary of Kaplan's language.[5] The inclusion of the interpretation function—which is indispensable in model theoretic semantics—ensures that the interpretations, and hence, meanings of the nonlogical vocabulary will vary from model to model. This is significant, because the nonlogical vocabulary includes all primitives of the language—all names, predicates, and function signs—other than the standard logical symbols, the modal and tense operators, and the special indexical terms and operators introduced by Kaplan in his formal system.

This means that when a and b are names, $a = b$ is never a logical truth, since the two names can be assigned different referents in different model structures. Within a model structure the characters of names are constant, but from model to model they vary. Surely, if we are going to identify the meaning of a sentence with its character, we must identify it with its character **in a certain model structure**. So to give a theory of meaning for the language of Kaplan's system, one would have to specify an intended model. By contrast, character can be thought of as the bearer of logical truth only when character is **not** relativized to a model. For any sentence S, S is a logical truth iff the character of the sentence schema that results from replacing all nonlogical symbols in S with schematic letters returns a truth in any context for any assignment to the schematic letters in any arbitrary model structure. Call the characters of these schematic sentences *schematic*, or *unrelativized*, characters. These, rather than full-blown characters—i.e., meanings of sentences—can be regarded as the bearers of logical truth.

[5] Page 543–44.

I don't think that Kaplan would disagree. As I read "Demonstratives," sometimes when he speaks of characters it is in the context of providing a semantics, or theory of meaning, for his language of demonstratives. On these occasions, he has in mind full-blown meanings—characters in the intended model, if you will. At other times, when thinking about the formal logic of demonstratives, he has in mind characters unrelativized to models—what I have called *schematic*, or *unrelativized*, characters. There is no real conflict here, just the need to be alert. Still, getting clear about this has an advantage. Once one sees the point, one is less likely to slip into thinking that the bearers of logical truth—schematic characters—are also the things that are known apriori. This, in turn, makes it less likely that one will view logical truth as a species of the apriori.

This brings me to my second point about Kaplan's two-dimensionalist passage—the implicit suggestion that the bearers of logical truth are the same as the bearers of apriority. Though the suggestion is clearly there, it is hard to take this to be Kaplan's final, considered view—since it is in tension with other things he says. For example, at the beginning of section XVII he asks whether it is content or character that is the object of thought.

> Is character, then the object of thought? If you and I both say to ourselves,
>
> (B) "I am getting bored"
>
> have we thought the same thing? We could not have, because what you thought was true while what I thought was false.
>
> What we must do is disentangle two epistemological notions: *the objects of thought* (what Frege called "Thoughts") and the *cognitive significance of an object of thought*. As has been noted above, a character may be likened to a manner of presentation of a content. This suggests that we identify objects of thought with contents and the cognitive significance of such objects with characters. . . .
>
> According to this view, the thoughts associated with ***dthat[α]* = *dthat[β]*** and ***dthat[α]* = *dthat[α]*** are the same, but the thought (not the denotation, mind you, but the *thought*) is *presented* differently.[6]

---

[6] Page 530.

Here Kaplan says that contents, not characters, are the objects of thought; they are what we think and believe. In addition, he notes that when the expressions α and β are coreferential, *dthat [α] = dthat [β]* expresses the same thought as *dthat [α] = dthat [α]*. But since thoughts are for Kaplan the things thought, believed, and known, it follows that anyone who knows the thought expressed by one of these sentences knows the thought expressed by the other. So it can't be that one of these thoughts is knowable apriori while the other is not. Presumably, that which is known—namely the proposition expressed by both sentences—is capable of being known apriori.

A similar point emerges in section XX, "Adding Says." There, Kaplan starts off remarking:

> I have already mentioned, in connection with Dr. Lauben, that when x says 'I have been wounded' and y wishes to report in indirect discourse exactly what x said, y has a problem. It will not do for y to say 'x said that I have been wounded'. According to our earlier remarks, it should be correct for y to report x's *content* using a character appropriate to the context of the report. . . . I will try to show that such constructions are the inevitable result of the attempt to make (third person) *indirect discourse* reports of the first person *direct discourse* sayings when those sayings involve indexicals.
>
> The situation regarding the usual epistemic verbs—'believes', 'hopes', 'knows', 'desires', 'fears', etc.—is, I believe, essentially similar to that of 'says'. Each has, or might have, a *direct discourse* sense in which the character which stands for the cognitive significance of the thought is given (he thinks, 'My God! It is *my* pants that are on fire.') as well as an *indirect discourse* sense in which only the content need be given (he thinks that it is *his* pants that are on fire).[7]

On the next page, Kaplan gives an analysis of the standard, indirect-discourse sense of propositional attitude verbs. According to the analysis, the things known are contents of sentences, or propositions, and an ascription *Mary knows that S* reports that Mary bears a certain relation to the content of (proposition expressed by) S in the reporting context—to the "secondary intension or proposition," as ambitious two-dimensionalists would put it. According to Kaplan, this two-place knowledge relation between an agent a and a true proposition p holds

[7] Page 553.

in virtue of a three-place relation holding between a, a character M, and p, when M expresses p in a's context, and a justifiably accepts M (and believes it to express a truth). However, the attitude ascription *Mary knows that S* does not identify this character. Rather, it simply reports that there is some character or other with the features needed in order for Mary to know the content of (or proposition expressed by) S (its "secondary proposition") in the reporting context. This proposition (content) is the thing that is reported to be known. But if this is true of the ascription *Mary knows that S*, then surely it is also true of the ascriptions *Mary knows apriori that S, It is possible for someone to know apriori that S, It is knowable apriori that S,* and *It is knowable only aposteriori that S*. In short, the things that are apriori or aposteriori—the bearers of apriority and aposteriority—are, like the bearers of necessity and possibility, propositions (contents of sentences). They are the so-called secondary intensions of the clauses that occur in both attitude and modal ascriptions.[8]

So far we have two conclusions. (i) The bearers of apriority are **not** the bearers of logical truth; rather, the bearers of apriority are propositions (in particular, secondary propositions expressed by the complement sentences in attitude ascriptions), while the bearers of logical truth are schematic characters. (ii) Kaplan's example *dthat [α] = dthat [β]* in Remark 10 is a case in which a sentence which is not a logical truth expresses a proposition that is both necessary and (presumably) knowable apriori.[9] Hence, it is **not** a genuine example of the necessary aposteriori (contrary to Remark 10). My third and final point is that some logical truths in Kaplan's system express propositions that are not knowable apriori, and so logical truth isn't a species of the apriori.

The relevant examples are those like *α = dthat [α]*, which, in my opinion, Kaplan mischaracterizes. In Remark 10, he tells us that they are examples of the contingent apriori (when α is not rigid).[10] The rea-

---

[8] In drawing this conclusion, we need to be clear about what it involves, and what it does not. In general, when we ask *What are the bearers of X?*—e.g., of truth, necessity, or apriority—we are asking *What sorts of things is X correctly predicated of?*—e.g., *What things are true, necessary, or (knowable) apriori?* What we have shown is that since, for Kaplan, the things that are known apriori are contents rather than characters, for him, contents and not characters should be seen as the bearers of apriority. To say this is not to deny that characters may play a key role in explaining apriori knowledge, or that accepting a certain sort of character may be either necessary, sufficient, or both for knowing apriori the proposition it expresses. On the contrary, it is claims of this sort at which Kaplan's implicit suggestion that characters are the bearers of apriority should be seen as pointing.

[9] If you deem it to be required, add an existence clause *if dthat [α] exists.*

[10] Kaplan defines away worries about cases in which α doesn't denote.

son I take this to be incorrect is that it requires something that seems to be impossible—namely that one can know apriori of the individual who is the referent of, for example, *the youngest Chinese spy,* that this individual is the youngest Chinese spy (if anyone is) just by knowing that the youngest Chinese spy is the youngest Chinese spy (if anyone is) and understanding how *dthat* works.[11] Against this, I would maintain that knowing that sentence (1)

1. Dthat [the youngest Chinese spy] is the youngest Chinese spy (if anyone is).

expresses a truth is one thing, while knowing of a particular person that he or she is the youngest Chinese spy (if anyone is) is quite another.

But this is precisely what must be known, and known apriori, if (2a) is to be true.[12]

2a. Jones knows apriori that dthat [the youngest Chinese spy] is the youngest Chinese spy (if anyone is).

On Kaplan's account (2a) is true only if Jones knows p apriori, where p is the proposition expressed by (1). This proposition is none other than the proposition expressed by *x is the youngest Chinese spy (if anyone is)* relative to an assignment of the individual who really is the youngest Chinese spy to 'x'. Thus, (2a) is true only if (2b) is true.

2b. There is an individual x who is the youngest Chinese spy, and Jones knows apriori that this individual x is the youngest Chinese spy (if anyone is).

Let us suppose, for the sake of argument, that there are Chinese spies, that one among them is the youngest, and that I know these two things. Then I can be sure that (1) expresses a truth. Still, there is no individual whom I know to be the youngest Chinese spy, and, no matter what my powers of apriori reasoning, I cannot—without doing empirical investigation—come to know of the individual who is in fact the

---

[11] This example is an adaptation (with a different lesson) of Quine's famous example about Bernard J. Ortcutt in "Quantifiers and Propositional Attitudes," *Journal of Philosophy* 53 (1956): 183–94.

[12] For the connection between believing of an object o that it is F and believing the singular proposition that predicates being F of o, see David Kaplan, "Opacity," in Lewis E. Hahn and Paul A. Schilpp (eds.), *The Philosophy of W. V. Quine* (La Salle, IL: Open Court, 1986), and my "Donnellan's Referential/Attributive Distinction," *Philosophical Studies* 73 (1994): 149–68, at pp. 150–51.

youngest Chinese spy that he or she is the youngest Chinese spy (if anyone is). Hence, (1) is not an example of the apriori, and (2a) is false.

In "Demonstratives," Kaplan takes the opposite view.

> There is nothing inaccessible to the mind about the semantics of direct reference, even when the reference is to that which we know only by description. What allows us to take various propositional attitudes towards singular propositions is not the form of our acquaintance with the objects but is rather our ability to manipulate the conceptual apparatus of direct reference.[13]

In effect, what Kaplan is saying here is that knowing how *dthat* works, plus understanding the other words in (1), is sufficient not only for knowing that (1) expresses a truth, but also for knowing the proposition it expresses, and hence for knowing of the individual who is, in fact, the youngest Chinese spy that he or she is the youngest Chinese spy (if anyone is). As I have indicated, I do not find this claim credible. Although I will say more about this shortly, I won't go into it further now.[14] Suffice it to say that if I am right, then we should not accept Kaplan's claim that $\alpha = dthat\ [\alpha]$ is an instance of the contingent apriori, when α is not rigid.

We should also understand that later, when we come across ambitious two-dimensionalists making claims about the contingent apriori and the necessary aposteriori similar to those in Kaplan's Remark 10, they are doing so, at least in part, on the basis of natural inferences drawn from selected parts of his text. Strong two-dimensionalists can point to his (unfortunate) remarks in section XVII, on pages 538–39, that logical truth is a species of the apriori and that the reason certain sentences can be logically true, and hence instances of the apriori, while still being contingent, is that the bearers of logical truth and apriority, on the one hand, are different from the bearers of necessity, on the other. Weak two-dimensionalists can point (i) to his identification, on page 530, of thoughts with contents rather than characters, (ii) to his analysis, in section XX, of the semantics of indirect discourse and other propositional attitude ascriptions *x v's that S* as reporting two-place relations between agents and propositions expressed by S that are mediated by three-place relations between agents, propositions, and characters, and (iii) to his, I believe unduly permissive, idea

---

[13] Page 536.
[14] See chapter 16 of *The Age of Meaning* for further relevant discussion.

that one can know the singular proposition expressed by ... *dthat [α]* ... simply by knowing how *dthat* works, and understanding and accepting ... *α* ... (without any antecedent *de re* knowledge of the object denoted by α that it is so denoted).

Of course, Kaplan himself was neither a strong two-dimensionalist—as is shown by the passages friendly to weak two-dimensionalism—nor a weak two-dimensionalist—as is shown by the fact that he takes names and natural kind terms to be nonindexical expressions with Stable Characters, and so implicitly rejects any ambitious two-dimensionalist attempt to assimilate all examples of the contingent apriori and the necessary aposteriori to those involving rigidified descriptions (like the ones discussed in chapter 3). Nevertheless, Kaplan's various two-dimensionalist suggestions have taken on lives of their own in the hands of others. It is all too easy for ambitious two-dimensionalists of different stripes to look back at Kaplan's text and find passages that seem to support their particular two-dimensionalist theses. More generally, they can all find encouragement for two ideas dear to their hearts: (i) that linguistic devices for turning descriptions into directly referential singular terms are readily available, easily mastered, applicable to any arbitrary description, and (ii) that understanding, accepting, and knowing of a sentence S that contains such a rigidified description that it expresses a truth is sufficient for one to satisfy *x* *knows that S*.

Sources of Ambitious Two-Dimensionalism in Kripke's *Naming and Necessity*

As I see it, ambitious two-dimensionalism is, at bottom, an attempt to accommodate many of Kripke's most persuasive arguments and examples, while avoiding the deepest and most important philosophical consequences of his work. Particularly important are his nondescriptive treatments of names and natural kind terms, his implicit recognition of the nonreducibility of epistemic possibility to metaphysical possibility, and his robust conception of the necessary aposteriori, based on substantive, metaphysical doctrines. Since so much of ambitious two-dimensionalism is devoted to revising, and diminishing, these central Kripkean legacies, it is unfortunate that the very text that so worries his critics should contain flaws so useful to them.

These flaws can be found in four threads of *Naming and Necessity*.

The first is Kripke's view that important examples of the contingent apriori may be explained by the fact that the referents of names and natural kinds are, in some cases, fixed by description. The second involves the blurring of a crucial distinction between semantic and presemantic senses of "reference fixing," and a resulting exaggeration of the extent of descriptive reference fixing for natural kind terms, and of instances of the apriori involving them. The third thread concerns the effects of this unclarity about reference fixing on a proper understanding of the role of historical chains of reference transmission in the semantics of names and natural kind terms. The final thread involves the proper response to puzzling questions about how empirical evidence can be required for knowledge of a necessary proposition p, even though—since p is true in all possible world-states—the evidence does not rule out any possible way in which p could be false. In what follows, I will deal with these one by one.

Reference-Fixing Descriptions and the Contingent Apriori

This point is essentially a replay of the last point made about Kaplan. As just discussed, according to Kaplan one can know apriori the contingent proposition expressed by

1. Dthat [the youngest Chinese spy] is the youngest Chinese spy (if anyone is).

simply by understanding how *dthat* works, and knowing the trivial, necessary, and apriori truth that the youngest Chinese spy is the youngest Chinese spy (if anyone is). The same is true for Kripke, except that instead of rigidifying the description with *dthat*, one uses it to introduce a rigid name, *Lee*, which is then used to construct the alleged example, (3), of the contingent apriori.

3. Lee is the youngest Chinese spy (if anyone is).

In fact, as the initial sentences of Remark 10 indicate, Kaplan saw his point about indexicals as reiterating points that Kripke had already made about names.

Thus, essentially the same criticism applies to Kripke as applied to Kaplan. In Kripke's case we may put the point by contrasting two different scenarios in which one might attempt to use a description to introduce and fix the referent of a name. In the first scenario, one does not know, or believe, of any object that it is denoted by the description introducing the name—e.g., one doesn't know, or believe, of any individual i that i is the youngest Chinese spy. Clearly, the mere performance of a linguistic ceremony of using the description to introduce a name can't change this. If, despite this, one's introduction of the name *Lee* for i is successful, then (3) will come to express a proposition about i that one doesn't know to be true, and can't come to know except by gaining *de re* knowledge of i through further empirical investigation. Regarding this scenario, one must say either (i) that the name hasn't successfully been introduced after all, (ii) that the speaker doesn't understand the name he has introduced, or (iii) that understanding and justifiably accepting a true sentence containing the name is not sufficient for knowing the proposition p which it expresses to be true. Either way, apriori knowledge of a contingent truth has not been achieved.

In the second scenario, one already knows, on the basis of current perception or previous empirical investigation, that a certain object o is the denotation of a description D. Thus, prior to using D to introduce n, one knows, on the basis of empirical evidence, the proposition expressed by *x is D*, relative to an assignment of o to 'x'. If one then uses D to introduce and fix the referent of n, one can come to express the proposition one already knows empirically with the sentence *n is D*, but this doesn't change the fact that one's knowledge is aposteriori. For example, suppose that I see one and only one man standing in front of me, and think to myself, *He is standing in front of me*. My knowledge, of the man in question, that he is standing in front of me is based on, and justified by, my perceptual experience. Hence it is aposteriori. This fact would not change if I were to introduce the name *Saul* with the stipulation that it is to refer to the man standing in front of me. If I were to do that, the sentence *Saul is standing in front of me* would **not** express a proposition that I knew apriori. It would simply express a proposition that I already knew aposteriori, and that can be known only in that way.

A similar point holds regarding my knowledge of the weaker proposition I might express by saying, or thinking, *He is the man standing in front of me, if anyone is*, in a situation in which I see the man, believe him to be standing in front of me, but don't feel absolutely sure that anyone is standing in front of me because I harbor some (unfounded) doubts about perceptual illusions. Still, my knowledge, of this man m, that if anyone is standing in front of me, then **he**, m, is standing in front of me is aposteriori, not apriori. In addition to being based exclusively on the perceptual experience that presents the man to me, and allows me to entertain the proposition known to be true, my knowledge is also **justified** by this experience. I am justified in believing what I do about m because of my perceptual experience of m. As Jim Pryor has usefully reminded us, the fact that a certain perceptual experience may play a crucial role in allowing one to entertain a certain proposition does not negate the fact that it may also play a crucial role in justifying one's knowledge of that proposition.[15] Hence, the knowledge I express by saying *If anyone is standing in front of me, then he* [demonstrating m] *is standing in front of me* is aposteriori, as is the knowledge I express by saying *If anyone is standing in front of me, then Saul is standing in front of me* (if I have introduced the name *Saul* to stand for that man).

There is a further wrinkle here worth noting. Suppose—to go beyond anything Kripke says in *Naming and Necessity*—(i) that in order for one to understand a name n the referent of which is semantically fixed by D, one must know, of the denotation o of D, that it "is D," and (ii) that one who understands and justifiably accepts a true sentence S which expresses a proposition p thereby counts as knowing p.[16] If these conditions are correct, then anyone who understands *n is D, if anything is D*, where D semantically fixes the referent of n, will thereby have all the information needed to know, not only that the sentence expresses a truth, but also the truth that the sentence expresses. As we have seen, however, this is **not** sufficient for that knowledge to qualify as apriori.

The upshot of all this is that, contrary to Kripke and Kaplan, there are no cases of contingent apriori knowledge arising from the use either of *dthat*-rigidified descriptions or names the referents of which are fixed by descriptions. However, this does not mean that there is no such thing as the contingent apriori. Examples containing the actuality operator, like (1) in chapter 3, remain untouched. Indeed, for most **failed** Kripke- or Kaplan-style examples of the contingent apriori involving descriptive reference-fixing or *dthat*-rigidified descriptions, there are corresponding **successful** examples that can be constructed using the actuality operator. As I will later indicate, the effect of this result on ambitious two-dimensionalism is by no means negligible.[17]

---

[15] Jim Pryor, *Thinking about Water*, in preparation.

[16] Here and throughout, I adopt the simplifying fiction that knowledge can be taken to be justified, true belief. In so doing, I assume that what I say here can be adapted to whatever the solution to the Gettier problem turns out to be.

[17] The main points in this section are discussed in greater detail in chapter 16 of *The Age of Meaning*.

Natural Kind Terms, Reference Fixing, and the Apriori

As pointed out in chapter 2, Kripke's account of natural kind terms like *gold, water, tiger*, and *green* is similar to his treatment of names. Like names, these terms are not synonymous with descriptions associated with them by speakers. Moreover, the way in which they are introduced, and have their reference fixed, is similar to the way in which names are introduced and acquire reference. What Kripke says about the general term *cat* is the model for a great many natural kind terms:

> The original concept of cat is: *that kind of thing*, where the kind can be identified by paradigmatic instances. It is not something picked out by any qualitative dictionary definition.[18]

Although this may be a little cryptic, the point is clear. Just as ordinary proper names are normally introduced by stipulating that they are to apply to certain objects with which one is already acquainted, so general terms are often introduced with the intention that they are to designate certain kinds with which we are already acquainted through their paradigmatic instances. For example, we may imagine the term *gold* introduced by the following stipulation:

> The general term *gold* is to designate the unique substance of which all, or nearly all, of these things [demonstrating some particular pieces of metal] are instances (and of which none, or nearly none, of those things [demonstrating contrasting particulars] are instances).

In understanding this stipulation, we may take it for granted that substances are understood to be physically constitutive kinds—i.e., kinds instances of which share the same basic physical constitution. Hence, the effect of the stipulation is to introduce a predicate *is gold* that applies (with respect to any world-state) to all and only those items that share the basic physical constitution that nearly all the paradigmatic *gold* samples mentioned in the stipulation actually have (and that none, or nearly none, of the paradigmatic *non-gold* samples do).

This stipulation is, of course, idealized. The term *gold* could have been introduced in this way, and it behaves pretty much as it would if it had been so introduced. However, it need not have been introduced by any formal stipulation. It is enough if at some point speakers started calling certain things *gold*, with the intention that the predicate *is gold*

[18] Kripe, *Naming and Necessity*, p. 122.

was to apply not only to the particular objects they encountered, but also to all and only instances of the relevant kind to which those objects actually belonged. An analogous point holds for proper names. Although formal baptisms are common, there are also cases in which a proper name is introduced more informally, as when people start calling a certain body of water *Green Lake* and the habit catches on. In each of these cases, both the formal and the informal, we may speak of a name or natural kind term as being introduced ostensively.

How are examples of the ostensive definitions of natural kind terms related to instances of the apriori? In lecture 3, Kripke says the following:

> [T]he present view asserts, in the case of species terms as in that of proper names, that one should bear in mind the contrast between the *a priori* but perhaps contingent properties carried with a term, given by the way its reference was fixed, and the analytic (and hence necessary) properties a term may carry, given by its meaning. For species, as for proper names, the way the reference of a term is fixed should not be regarded as a synonym for the term. . . . If we imagine a hypothetical (admittedly somewhat artificial) baptism of the substance [gold], we must imagine it picked out as by some such 'definition' as, 'Gold is the substance instantiated by the items over there, or at any rate, by almost all of them'. Several features of this baptism are worthy of note. First, the identity in the 'definition' does not express a (completely) necessary truth: though each of these items is, indeed, essentially (necessarily) gold, gold might have existed even if the items did not. The definition does, however, express an *a priori* truth, in the same sense as (and with the same qualifications applied as) '1 meter = length of S': it *fixes a reference.*[19]

The suggestion here seems to be that if one introduces the term *gold* with the stipulation that *is gold* is to apply to all and only instances of the (unique) substance of which these things [demonstrating certain particulars] are instances, then the claim that these things are gold (if there is any unique substance of which they are instances) is apriori. This, I believe, is a mistake—though a revealing one.

Here, it is important to resist the temptation of an all-too-common line of argument. The tempting line goes something like this:

[19] Ibid., p. 135.

(i)   To introduce a name or natural kind term n by stipulating that it is to stand for that which satisfies a certain condition, is to use a description D expressing that condition to semantically fix the reference of n.

(ii) When D semantically fixes the reference of n, competent speakers who understand n associate D with it, and know that the semantic rules governing n guarantee that it refers to whatever, if anything, satisfies D.

(iii) Because of this, competent speakers know apriori that which is expressed by *n is D (if there is a unique thing that is D)* when n is a proper name, and *For all x, x is an n iff x is an instance of the kind D (if there is such a thing as the kind D)* when n is a general term.

Here, (ii) may serve as a definition of what it is for a description to semantically fix the reference of a term. The idea it expresses is, essentially, the one behind Kripke's weak, fix-the-referent version of the descriptivism described in chapter 2, and defined by the first five theses listed at the beginning of lecture 2 of *Naming and Necessity*. Terms that have their reference fixed in this way are seen as analogous to descriptions rigidified using *dthat*. Although the semantic content of *dthat D* is simply the denotation, if any, of D, in order to understand the rigidified description, one must know that its referent is, by definition, whatever satisfies D. The same is true of names and natural kind terms that have their reference fixed by descriptions in the sense of (ii).

Given this conception of what it is for a description to semantically fix the referent of a term, one can isolate two mistakes in the reasoning from (i) to (iii). (i) is in error because it is possible to use a description as a tool to introduce a term without the description semantically fixing its referent, and hence becoming part of what a competent speaker must master in order to understand it. For example, when looking at our firstborn son and naming him *Greg Soames*, his mother and I did not intend the name to have the force of any *dthat*-rigidified description incorporating the content we used in singling him out. Although our stipulation relied on descriptive information to initially endow the name with meaning, that information was not incorporated into either the content of the name, or the conditions required to understand it. (iii) is in error because—whether or not a description used to introduce a term also semantically fixes its reference—the description associated with the term does **not** give rise to apriori knowledge. As was shown by the example in the previous section, in stipulating that *Saul* was to be the name of the person standing in front of me at a certain time and place (if anyone was), I did not thereby come to know **apriori**, of that man, that he was standing in front of me, if anyone was. On the contrary, it was because I was looking at him, and knew him to be standing in front of me, if anyone was, that I was able to name him with my stipulation. This knowledge was, of course, aposteriori.

Applying these lessons to natural kind terms leads one to two significant conclusions. First, although stipulations introducing natural kind terms—like the one I have imagined for *gold*—make use of descriptions of kinds in terms of their instances, typically the descriptions do **not** semantically fix the reference of these terms. The descriptions usually don't enter into their meanings, and competence with the terms, and the predicates containing them, normally doesn't require speakers to understand anything about the instances used to introduce them. Second, even those introducing a term like *gold* with the stipulation imagined don't know apriori of the particular objects mentioned in the introduction that they are gold (if anything is)—any more than Greg's mother and I knew apriori that Greg Soames was our son (if anyone was). We did know, in virtue of knowing our own stipulation, that he was named *Greg Soames* (if he indeed was our son). However, even that metalinguistic knowledge was not apriori, since our justification rested on our knowledge of the empirical facts that endowed the name with its semantic content.

By the same token, one who introduces the general term *gold* with the stipulation imagined thereby knows the metalinguistic truth that nearly all of the objects mentioned in the stipulation are ones to which the predicate *is gold* applies (if nearly all of them share the same physical constitution). However, such a person does **not** know apriori that nearly all those sample objects are gold, since that would require knowing that they are instances of the same substance (physically constitutive kind), and that can be known only aposteriori. Is anything weaker known apriori? Does such a person know apriori that **if** nearly all of those sample objects are of the same (unique) physically constitutive kind, then they are gold? To ask this is to ask whether such a person knows apriori, of the kind gold, that nearly all those sample objects are instances of it, if nearly all of them are instances of any (unique) physically constitutive kind at all.

In answering this question one must distinguish two related claims.

4a. The *gold*-stipulator knows apriori that if there is a (unique) physically constitutive k of which nearly all *gold* samples are instances, then nearly all those samples are instances of k.

   b. If there is a (unique) physically constitutive kind k of which nearly all *gold* samples are instances, then the *gold*-stipulator knows apriori that nearly all those samples are instances of k, if they are instances of any (unique) physically constitutive kind.

Although (4a) is trivially true, it has nothing to do with reference determination. Although (4b) is relevant to the semantics of reference fixing, it is not true. However, seeing this takes a little work.

There are two main cases to consider. In the first case, the stipulator already knows aposteriori that nearly all the samples are instances of the same (unique) physically constitutive kind, even though he or she is not able to describe the kind in any very informative way except by reference to the samples themselves. It is, I think, reasonable to regard this as a case in which the agent is acquainted with the kind by virtue of being acquainted with some of its instances, and knowing of them that they are instances of a single physically constitutive kind. In this case, the agent's knowledge of the kind gold is aposteriori, and remains aposteriori when he or she introduces the predicate *is gold* to apply to instances of it. But what about the knowledge mentioned in (4b)—knowledge of the kind gold that nearly all of the stipulator's paradigmatic samples are instances of it, **if they are instances of any unique physically constitutive kind at all?** Isn't that something that the *gold*-stipulator knows apriori? No, it isn't. Think again about the man I see standing in front of me. My knowledge, of this man m, that if one and only one man is standing in front of me, then **he**, m, is standing in front of me is aposteriori, not apriori. It is justified by my perceptual experience of m. Something similar is true of the *gold*-stipulator who thinks: *If nearly all those samples are instances of a single physically constitutive kind, then nearly all of them are instances of it* [demonstrating the kind, gold], or *If nearly all those samples are instances of a single physically constitutive kind, then nearly all of them are gold* [if the agent has introduced the term *gold*]. What justifies this knowledge is the agent's acquaintance with, and empirically justified beliefs about, a certain natural kind—gold. Hence, his or her knowledge is aposteriori, and for this *gold*-stipulator (4b) is false.

The second case to be considered is one in which we imagine the *gold*-stipulator as **not** knowing in advance that the items in the sample are of the same physically constitutive kind—even though in fact they are. The stipulation will be a little strange, if the stipulator doesn't at least **believe** that they are of the same kind, and take himself or herself to have some evidence for this. However, if this evidence falls short of knowledge, then stipulatively introducing the term won't put the agent in a better epistemic position than before—any more than introducing the name *Saul* when I am not sure anyone is standing in front of me would improve my epistemic situation in that case. The *gold*-stipulator will, presumably, assent to the sentence *If nearly all these items in the sample are of the same physically constitutive kind, then they are all gold*, and to the extent that he or she is justified in believing that the sample does uniquely determine such a kind, he or she will be justified in believing the proposition expressed by the sentence. The agent may even know this weaker proposition to be true. But if so, this knowledge is justified by the fact that the items the agent is perceptually acquainted with, and has beliefs about, **are** instances of one particular kind—gold—as opposed to any other. Hence, this knowledge is aposteriori, and (4b) is false.

In order to successfully introduce a name or natural kind term like *gold*, one must have some acquaintance with the object to be named or the natural kind to be designated. Often, this will involve being perceptually acquainted with, and believing certain things of, the object or the kind—though there are cases in which the relevant form of acquaintance is more remote.[20] In the case of many natural kinds, the normal way of being acquainted with, and believing things of, them is by being acquainted with, and believing things about, some of their instances. In order to successfully introduce a general term designating one of these kinds k (for which one has no other name), to use it to express propositions of which k is a constituent, and to know these propositions to be true, typically one must be acquainted with some particulars that are instances of k, and one must have reason to believe that they are instances of a unique kind of the type that k is. In virtue of this, when one knows, of the particulars, that they are instances of k, if they are instances of any one relevant kind at all, this knowledge is aposteriori.

Having said this, I need to add three clarifying qualifications. First, I have **not** said that in order to have beliefs about natural kinds—e.g., the color green, the substances gold or water, or the species tiger—one

---

[20] For example, naming a deer whose regular effects on your garden you have noticed, or a boat you have drawn up plans for and are about to build.

must believe of some particular instances of these kinds that they are, e.g., green, gold, water, or tigers (if they are instances of any one relevant kind). Someone introducing these terms with stipulations of the sort imagined typically must have such beliefs, but once the terms have been successfully introduced, they can be picked up by other competent speakers of the language, provided these speakers intend to use the terms with the semantic contents they have already acquired. These speakers need have no beliefs about particular instances of the kinds.

Second, some account must be given of what happens when a speaker introduces a term with a stipulation like the following one for *tiger*, without realizing that the supposedly paradigmatic items in the *tiger* sample are **not** animals at all.

> The general term *tiger* is to designate the species of animal of which all, or nearly all, of these things [demonstrating some salient individuals] are instances (and of which none, or nearly none, of those things [demonstrating other individuals] are instances). Hence, the predicate *is a tiger* will apply (with respect to any world-state) to all and only those animals that are members of the species of which nearly all the paradigmatic *tiger* samples are actually members (and of which none, or nearly none, of the paradigmatic *non-tiger* samples are actually members).

Borrowing from Putnam, we may imagine a world-state in which speakers stipulate that the predicate *is a tiger* is to apply to all members of the same species of animal as the tawny, striped, catlike individuals they have seen in various zoos, as well as in the wild—even though, unknown to them, these so-called tiger specimens are not animals at all, but cleverly disguised robots controlled by space aliens.[21] Putnam's intuition, which I share, is that in this fantastic scenario—in which speakers are under a monumental misimpression—the predicate *is a tiger* nevertheless turns out to be meaningful, and to truly apply to paradigmatic members of the *tiger* sample. However, its meaning (semantic content) in the imagined world-state is **not** the animal species which is its meaning for us, in the world as it actually is. The imagined world-state is **not** one in which tigers fail to be animals; there are no tigers in that scenario (in our sense of *tiger*), even though there are things that speakers in the scenario correctly call *tigers*. Nor is the scenario one in which speakers wrongly **believe** that tigers are animals; speakers in the

[21] Hilary Putnam, "It Ain't Necessarily So," *Journal of Philosophy* 59 (1962): 658–71.

scenario have **no** beliefs about tigers, or the kind tiger, in our sense—even though they have beliefs which they express using the word *tiger.* Given all this, we can only conclude that there must be a process by which a word introduced with the intention that it is to designate a natural kind of a certain sort may acquire a quite different meaning.

I suspect that what is going on is something like this: one who introduces the predicate *is a tiger* with the stipulation I have suggested intends (i) that it apply to nearly all specimens in the paradigmatic *tiger* sample, (ii) that it apply to other things iff they bear a certain important relation of similarity to specimens in the sample, and (iii) that this similarity relation be the relation of being-an-instance-of-the-same-animal-species-as. In our fantastic Putnam-style scenario, these intentions cannot all be fulfilled, and the predicate acquires a different meaning by default—one which conforms to the first two intentions, but not the third. Depending on the beliefs and intentions of speaker-hearers, plus further empirical facts about the world-state, a new similarity relation comes to be the salient one—with the result that the predicate *is a tiger* acquires a meaning that is as close as is reasonably possible, given the situation, to the one intended by speakers.

The third point of clarification to be added to the picture involves the question of whether it is part of the meaning of the predicate *is a tiger* (in the sense of its semantically determined reference-fixing conditions) that it applies only to animals. Nothing we have said so far settles this question. Since, in the Putnam-style scenario, the predicate means something other than what it actually means to us, the fact that it applies to non-animals in that scenario does not, by itself, resolve the question of whether its actual meaning involves reference to animals. By the same token, the scenario doesn't rule out the possibility that the proposition actually expressed by *Tigers are animals* (understood as $\forall x\ (x\ is\ a\ tiger \supset x\ is\ an\ animal)$) may be knowable apriori. It isn't, of course, but not because the presuppositions of the stipulation used to introduce the term might be false. The reason it is not knowable apriori that tigers are animals is that, like other *de re* knowledge, *de re* knowledge of the kind tiger that instances of it are animals requires empirical justification.[22] Nevertheless, it is conceivable that it **is** part of

---

[22] To know that tigers are animals is to know the proposition expressed by $\forall x(x\ is\ a\ tiger \supset x\ is\ an\ animal)$, one of the constituents of which is the kind tiger, contributed by the term *tiger.* If an agent A knows this proposition, then the kind tiger is such that A knows that for all x, if x is an instance of it, then x is an animal. For A to have this knowledge is for A to know of the kind tiger that instances of it are animals. Knowing that this is true of the kind requires empirical evidence.

the meaning of *is a tiger* that anything it applies to is an animal. A predicate P can be semantically restricted to apply only to individuals with the property expressed by F, even though the proposition expressed by *P's are F's*—i.e., $\forall x(Px \supset Fx)$—is not knowable apriori.

Consider the following analogy with names. Suppose I introduce the name *Φ-Saul* with the stipulation that it is to be synonymous with the rigidified description *dthat [the x: x is a philosopher and x = Saul Kripke]*. In order to understand the name, one must know that it refers to an individual iff that individual is both Saul Kripke and a philosopher. In this sense, it is part of the meaning of the name that it refers to the philosopher Saul Kripke, if it refers to anything at all. However, the proposition semantically expressed by (5a)

5a. If *Φ-Saul* has a referent, then Φ-Saul is a philosopher

is just the singular proposition that says of Saul Kripke that if a certain name has a referent, then he is a philosopher. Since this proposition can be known only aposteriori, it is **not** knowable apriori that if *Φ-Saul* has a referent, then Φ-Saul is a philosopher. This is true, even though the knowledge needed to understand (5a) is, arguably, sufficient for knowledge of the proposition (5a) expresses. This illustrates the larger point that in order for a proposition p to be knowable apriori, it is not enough that there be some sentence S which both expresses p and is such that understanding S provides one with all the justification one needs to know p. Such sentences and propositions do have an interesting epistemological status. The sentences might well be termed *analytic*, and the propositions they express are knowable without any empirical justification beyond that required to understand certain sentences that express them. Nevertheless, these propositions are not knowable apriori.[23]

The point can be made even more graphic by adding a further semantic assumption—namely that understanding *Φ-Saul* requires knowing of its referent, Saul Kripke, that he satisfies the associated description, and hence is a philosopher. The idea behind this assumption is that if n is a genuine name which refers to some object o (which is its semantic content), then understanding n requires knowing that which is expressed by *'n' refers to n*, which in turn amounts to knowing, of o, that n refers to it. If this is correct, and *Φ-Saul* is a genuine name, then (5b) will qualify as analytic in the sense that understanding it provides

---

[23] For further discussion, see chapter 16 of *The Age of Meaning*.

one with all the justification one needs to know the proposition it expresses.

5b.   Φ-Saul is a philosopher.

Nevertheless, the singular proposition about Saul Kripke to the effect that he is a philosopher, which is semantically expressed by (5b), is clearly not knowable apriori.

Applying these lessons to the predicate *is a tiger*, we get the results (i) and (ii):

(i)   **If** understanding *tiger* requires knowing that it designates a kind of animal (if it designates anything at all), then, even though the proposition that tigers are animals (if *tiger* designates anything at all) is **not** knowable apriori, it **is** knowable solely by virtue of the knowledge required to understand the (analytic) sentence—*Tigers are animals (if 'tiger' designates anything at all)*—that expresses it.

(ii)   **If**, in addition to requiring one to know that *tiger* designates a kind of animal (if it designates anything at all), understanding *tiger* requires one to know of the kind it actually designates that it is so designated, and hence that its instances (if any) are animals, then, even though the proposition that tigers are animals is **not** knowable apriori, it **is** knowable solely by virtue of the knowledge required to understand the (analytic) sentence—*Tigers are animals*—that expresses it.

Let us focus on the assumption that understanding *tiger* requires knowing that it designates a kind of animal (if it designates anything at all), and hence that the predicate *is a tiger* applies only to instances of an animal kind. On this assumption, the proposition mentioned in (i) has the status indicated there. What is there to be said for this assumption? On the one hand, we are, I think, inclined to suppose that someone who doesn't realize that *is a tiger* applies only to animals (if *tiger* designates anything at all) doesn't understand *tiger*. On the other hand, we can easily imagine a skeptic who routinely applies *tiger* to the things that the rest of us do, while wrongly believing they aren't animals, because he mistakenly believes that the fantastic Putnam-style scenario was the report of a genuine scientific discovery. Does he understand the word, or not? It is not easy to tell. One way of describing the case would be to say that although he knows how natural kind terms work, including how they can sometimes be assigned meanings different from those originally intended, he doesn't correctly understand what *tiger* actually means, because he fails to associate it with the right reference-fixing conditions. That seems a bit forced. Moreover, there is a problem in describing the skeptic's beliefs in the scenario in which he is wrong (and in which he never sees tigers but simply picks up the word from others). How, in that scenario, does his acceptance of *Tigers are not really animals*—which, by hypotheses, he doesn't understand—justify **our** clearly correct characterization of him as believing that tigers are not really animals?[24] It is not clear. Perhaps the right thing to say is that although it is a commonly known fact that *tiger* picks out a species of animal, knowing this fact is not **required** in order to understand the term, after all.

Fortunately, for our purposes, we need not resolve this issue here, since the chief lessons derived from my critique of Kripke's account of reference fixing for natural kind terms are independent of it. They are (i) that even though descriptions are often used to introduce natural kind terms, and to endow them with semantic properties, this does **not** show that those descriptions semantically fix the reference of the terms, or become parts of the meanings of, or the conditions for understanding, the terms; (ii) that despite the impression one gets from certain passages in lecture 3 of *Naming and Necessity*, most natural kind terms do **not** have their reference semantically fixed by descriptions; and (iii) that neither the descriptions used to introduce natural kind terms, nor the relatively sparse descriptive information which could, perhaps, be seen as playing a genuinely semantic role in determining reference, give rise to significant examples of apriori knowledge. As I will argue in later chapters, these lessons apply with even greater force to the two-dimensional revisionists of Kripke than they do to Kripke himself.[25]

Semantics, Reference Fixing, and Historical Chains

As noted in chapter 2, Kripke distinguishes two versions of the description theory of names, both of which he rejects. According to the strong version, the descriptions associated with names by speakers give

---

[24] Thanks to Jeff Speaks for raising this question.

[25] The material in this section draws heavily on my unpublished paper "Knowledge of Manifest Natural Kinds," which was given as a talk at the Third Barcelona Workshop on Issues in the Theory of Reference on June 5, 2003 in Barcelona, Spain.

their meanings, in the sense of providing synonyms. According to the weak version, these descriptions are said to *fix the referent* of the name, even though they don't provide synonyms. The idea behind the weak version of the theory is something like this: Even though proper names don't have meanings in the usual sense, something must be responsible for establishing and maintaining the link between a name and what it refers to; e.g., something must determine what one's utterance of 'Aristotle' refers to. Perhaps descriptions semantically associated with names do this after all; perhaps each proper name is associated with descriptions that provide the criteria for determining what it refers to—descriptions that are aspects of its meaning mastered by competent speakers, even though they do not provide synonyms for the name. Once these descriptions have fixed what the name designates with respect to the actual world-state, the connection between the name and the referent becomes rigid, and the name refers to the same thing in all world-states in which it refers to anything at all.

In understanding this theory, it is crucial to recognize that the descriptive reference-fixing conditions postulated by it are **semantically** associated with names in the sense of being requirements for understanding the names that must be mastered by competent speakers. It is because the theory is understood in this way that the interesting, though contentious, claim it makes can be distinguished from the trivial and uninteresting claim that it is possible to describe the process by which names get their referents. For any word whatsoever—'and', 'necessarily', 'if', 'obviously', etc.—there is some description that correctly describes the process by which the word acquired its meaning, or referent. However, that does not mean that all words have their meanings, or referents, semantically fixed by descriptions, in the sense of the weak version of the description theory.

Although Kripke doesn't spend much time explicating this point, it is clear from the way he argues against the weak version of the theory that he presupposes it. In testing the theory, he isolates corollaries (i–iv).

If a description D semantically fixes the referent of a name n for a speaker, then

(i)   the speaker believes that D applies to a unique individual;

(ii) if D does apply to a unique individual o, then o is the referent of n;

(iii) if D does not apply to a unique individual, then n has no referent.

(iv) the speaker knows (or is capable of knowing) *a priori* that the sentence *If n exists, then n is D* expresses a truth.

He then proceeds to give counterexamples to these corollaries. His point is to demonstrate that for the vast majority of proper names there is no linguistic rule, mastered by competent speakers, which specifies their referents as being whatever satisfies the descriptions speakers associate with them.

Corollary (iv) is especially useful in illustrating this point. Why is it part of the theory? If the linguistic rule by which the referent of a name is fixed is that the name is to refer to whoever or whatever is designated by a certain description D, then, presumably, one who understands the name, and hence knows this rule, needs no further information to conclude that the sentence *If n exists (existed), then n is (was) D* must be true.[26] Since one knows (or is capable of knowing) this just by knowing the rules of the language, without doing any extra empirical investigation, Kripke characterizes it as apriori. Though he can be criticized for using the term *apriori* in this way, it is clear that, according to the weak version of the description theory, the examples do end up having a special epistemological status.

Kripke's arguments in lecture 2 are designed to show that this theory is false. Except for some relatively rare special cases—like *Jack the Ripper* and *Neptune* (for a period before the planet was observed)—the vast majority of ordinary proper names do not, according to Kripke, have their referents semantically fixed by description. So how is their reference determined? In answer to this question, he offers his historical chain conception of reference transmission. Although much of this discussion is correct and unexceptionable, the way in which he sometimes poses the question can, I think, be misleading. As we have seen, when he discusses the fix-the-referent version of the description theory, he is clearly discussing a proposal about the semantics of names. Because of this, his way of framing the general discussion—

---

[26] If D fails to designate anything, then n fails as well, and the sentence may be taken to be trivially true by falsity of antecedent. If D does designate something, then n designates the same thing, and the consequent is true. Either way, the truth of the conditional is guaranteed. If one is worried that a sentence containing a name that fails to refer may not express a proposition, and so may fail to be true, then one may change (iv) to read *the speaker knows (or is capable of knowing) apriori that if 'n exists' expresses a truth, then 'n is D' also expresses a truth.* Since this issue does not affect the outcome of the discussion, I will leave it to one side.

What fixes reference?—may seem to suggest that the two answers he gives to this question—*Descriptions in certain unusual cases* and *Historical chains of reference transmission for the great mass of proper names*—are on a par. Since the claim about descriptions is understood to be semantic, and hence about the linguistic rules that speakers must master in learning various names, this encourages the unwary reader to think of the claim about historical chains in the same way.

I believe this to be a mistake. There is nothing special here about the semantics of names. Standardly, when one uses any word in the language of one's community, one does so with the intention that it should carry whatever meaning and reference it has already acquired. This is a fact about the **use** of all expressions, not about the **semantics** of any of them. To the extent that there are additional questions about names (or natural kind terms), they are questions of a different sort. If one asks *How were these terms originally introduced into the language, and in virtue of what did they come to refer to what they do?*, then Kripke's comments about initial baptisms and ostensive introductions of terms are relevant. If one asks *How do speakers normally acquire and become competent users of these terms?* or *In virtue of what do these terms retain their reference in the language?*, then his comments about chains of reference transmission are apropos. However, there is no genuinely semantic question about the linguistic rules mastered by competent speakers of the language to which Kripke's historical chains of reference transmission provide, or are intended to provide, an answer.[27]

The failure to grasp this point is, as I will argue later, one of the principle sources of descriptivists' last-gasp attempt to interpret Kripke's historical-chain theory of reference transmission as providing the descriptions needed for a correct descriptive theory of the semantics of names. In this case, I believe, the error is essentially theirs, with Kripke's fault being, primarily, the relatively innocuous one of not making the semantic/nonsemantic distinction more clearly and explicitly.[28]

A Puzzle about the Necessary Aposteriori

In the middle of lecture 3, after summing up his treatment of natural kind terms and illustrating their role in generating examples of the

---

[27] This way of looking at Kripke's discussion of reference fixing via baptism and historical chains of reference transmission is explained and forcefully defended by Jonathan McKeown-Green in his unpublished Princeton doctoral dissertation, *The Primacy of Public Language*, 2002.

[28] The material in this section draws substantially on chapter 14 of *The Age of Meaning*.

necessary aposteriori, Kripke takes up a challenge to his view. Up to this point, when discussing necessary aposteriori truths, he has emphasized that although they are necessary, and hence true with respect to every possible world-state, nevertheless, for all we knew prior to empirically discovering their truth, they, in his words, "could have turned out otherwise." Realizing that this may sound puzzling, he gives voice to the following objection.

> Theoretical identities, according to the conception I advocate, are generally identities involving two rigid designators, and therefore are examples of the necessary *a posteriori*. Now in spite of the arguments I gave before for the distinction between necessary and *a priori* truth, the notion of *a posteriori* necessary truth may still be somewhat puzzling. Someone may well be inclined to argue as follows: 'You have admitted that heat might have turned out not to have been molecular motion, and that gold might have turned out not to have been the element with the atomic number 79. For that matter, you also have acknowledged that . . . this table might have turned out to be made from ice from water from the Thames. I gather that Hesperus might have turned out not to be Phosphorus. What then can you mean when you say that such eventualities are impossible? If Hesperus might have *turned out* not to be Phosphorus, then Hesperus might not have *been* Phosphorus. And similarly for the other cases: if the world could have *turned out* otherwise, it could have *been* otherwise.[29]

The problem here starts out being about theoretical identity sentences involving natural kind terms, but quickly expands to cover all instances of the necessary aposteriori. Let p be such an instance. Since p is aposteriori, its falsity must be conceivable, and we need empirical evidence to rule that out. Without such evidence, **it could turn out that** p is false. But, the objector maintains, if p is necessary, there are no possibilities in which p is false. So, if p really is necessary, we don't require empirical evidence to know p after all; and if p really is aposteriori, then p isn't necessary. The necessary aposteriori is an illusion.

Kripke begins his reply to this objection with the following passage.

> The objector is correct when he argues that if I hold that this table could not have been made of ice, then I must also hold that it could not have turned out to be made of ice; *it could have*

[29] *Naming and Necessity*, pp. 140–41.

turned out that P entails that P could have been the case. What, then, does the intuition that the table might have turned out to have been made of ice or of anything else, that it might even have turned out not to be made of molecules, amount to? I think that it means simply that there might have been *a table* looking and feeling just like this one and placed in this very position in the room, which was in fact made of ice. In other words, I (or some conscious being) could have been *qualitatively in the same epistemic situation* that in fact obtains, I could have the same sensory experience that I in fact have, about *a table* which was made of ice.[30]

Imagine the following scenario: a table has been brought in, and I have examined it and determined it to be made out of wood, not ice. I point to the table and say *I know that this table is not made out of ice.* I know this because I have empirically ruled out what otherwise would have been an epistemologically relevant possibility. Prior to my checking, **it could have turned out**, for all I knew, that the table was made of ice. The intuition that things could have turned out that way is, Kripke suggests, nothing more than the judgment that it is genuinely possible for me, or some other agent, to be in a situation qualitatively identical to this one, and be pointing at a table that **is** made out of ice.[31]

He generalizes this point in the next paragraph.

The general answer to the objector can be stated, then, as follows: Any necessary truth, whether *a priori* or *a posteriori*, could not have turned out otherwise. In the case of some necessary *a posteriori* truths, however, we can say that under appropriate qualitatively identical evidential situations, **an appropriate corresponding qualitative statement** might have been false. The loose and inaccurate statement that gold might have turned out to be a compound should be replaced (roughly) by the statement that it is logically possible that there should have been a compound with

[30] Ibid., pp. 141–42.

[31] The suggestion is, as we shall see, problematic. However, even at this stage there is something surprising about the application of this idea to the intuition that the table might have turned out not to be made of molecules. Is Kripke suggesting that it is genuinely metaphysically possible for **some table** not be made out of molecules? If so, then it doesn't seem at all obvious that the suggestion is correct, even though it is obvious that the table could have turned out not to be made of molecules, in the sense in which how things could have turned out is relevant to questions about what is apriori and what is aposteriori.

all the properties originally known to hold of gold. The inaccurate statement that Hesperus might have turned out not to be Phosphorus should be replaced by the true contingency mentioned earlier in these lectures: two distinct bodies might have occupied, in the morning and the evening, respectively, the very positions actually occupied by Hesperus-Phosphorus-Venus.[32]

This paragraph and the one preceding it mark the beginning of what in my opinion is the most misleading passage in *Naming and Necessity*, and the one most encouraging to ambitious two-dimensionalists.

Two main issues are addressed: the necessity of certain propositions, and the fact that they can be known only aposteriori. Regarding the former, Kripke makes three points:

(i)   There is a natural and correct way of understanding the locution *It could have turned out that ~S* in which it entails *It is not necessary that S*.

(ii) When understood in this way, his previous remarks—that when S is both necessary and aposteriori, empirical evidence is needed because *It could have turned out that ~S* was true—were strictly speaking inaccurate.

(iii) In these cases, the necessary proposition expressed by S is easily confused with certain descriptive propositions that are both contingent and knowable only aposteriori. These are the propositions that could genuinely have turned out not to be true.

Kripke maintains that when the objector protests that his examples can't be necessary, given that they are aposteriori, the objector is **confusing** the propositions expressed by the examples with other, related propositions that really are contingent. The objector confuses the singular proposition that **this** table in front of me is made out of ice, with the related general proposition that the, or a, table in front of me is made out of ice. He also confuses the necessary truth expressed by (6a) with the contingent truths expressed by (6b–c).

6a. Hesperus is Phosphorus.

b. 'Hesperus' and 'Phosphorus' are coreferential.

c. 'Hesperus is Phosphorus' expresses a truth in our language.

---

[32] *Naming and Necessity*, pp. 142–43, my emphasis.

Since the two names are associated with a pair of descriptions that can't be satisfied unless the heavenly body that appears in the evening sky is the heavenly body that appears in the morning sky, the objector also ends up confusing the necessary truth expressed by (6a) with the contingent truth expressed by (6d).

6d. The heavenly body that appears in the evening sky (at time t and place p) is the heavenly body that appears in the morning sky (at t* and p*).

This response of Kripke's is unobjectionable, as far as it goes. However, it doesn't go far enough. Although it deals with objectors who grant that his examples are aposteriori, but doubt they are necessary, it doesn't deal with objectors who grant that the examples are necessary, but doubt that they are aposteriori. More importantly, the reply fails to deal with the general form of the objection, which purports to demonstrate, without relying on any particular example, that no proposition can be both necessary and knowable only aposteriori. To the extent that his remarks do suggest a reply to these worries, it is puzzling and inadequate. In the passage, Kripke seems to suggest that his earlier argument that the claim that Hesperus is Phosphorus is knowable only aposteriori provides the pattern of explanation for all other examples of the necessary aposteriori. This is unfortunate.

Kripke's argument that it is not knowable apriori that Hesperus is Phosphorus, given in the last four pages of lecture 2, is based on the observation that evidence available to us simply by virtue of understanding the names *Hesperus* and *Phosphorus* is insufficient to show that they are coreferential. Since agents in epistemological situations qualitatively identical with ours might use the names exactly as we do, yet be referring to different things, the qualitative evidence we have by virtue of understanding the names is insufficient to justify the claim that they are coreferential. Thus, the metalinguistic claims (6b) and (6c), as well as the non-metalinguistic claim (6d), are not knowable apriori. This is, of course, correct. However, it is not the conclusion Kripke is interested in. The conclusion he explicitly draws is that it is not knowable apriori that Hesperus is Phosphorus.[33] Unfortunately, this non-metalinguistic conclusion does **not** follow from his stated

---

[33] See pp. 103–4 of *Naming and Necessity*. Although in the passage on pp. 142–43 quoted above Kripke mentions the non-metalinguistic (6d) without mentioning the metalinguistic (6b) and (6c), he implicitly refers the reader to the passage on pages 103–4, where he mentions both types of examples, emphasizing the metalinguistic.

premises. The proposition that Hesperus is Phosphorus is, as he insists, true in all possible world-states. So it is true in all world-states in which agents are in epistemic situations qualitatively identical to ours. Hence, the principle that only propositions true in all such states are knowable apriori does not rule out that this proposition may be knowable apriori.

Perhaps, however, the gap in Kripke's argument can be filled. Throughout the passage, he exploits a familiar connection between speakers' understanding and acceptance of sentences and our ability to use those sentences to report what they believe. In his example, before we learned of the astronomical discovery, we understood but did not accept (6a); hence it is natural to conclude that we didn't believe that Hesperus was Phosphorus. Moreover, we would not have been **justified** in accepting (6a) based on the evidence we had at that time. Because of this, it is natural to think that we wouldn't have then been justified in **believing** that Hesperus is Phosphorus. If so, then the proposition that Hesperus is Phosphorus must require empirical justification, in which case it must **not** be knowable apriori—exactly as Kripke says.

With this in mind, we may reconstruct Kripke's implicit reasoning as follows.

(i)   One who understands *Hesperus is Phosphorus* accepts it and believes it to be true iff one believes that Hesperus is Phosphorus.

(ii) Similarly, one who understands *Hesperus is Phosphorus* would be justified in accepting it and believing it to be true iff one would be justified in believing that Hesperus is Phosphorus.

(iii) In order to be justified in accepting *Hesperus is Phosphorus* and believing it to be true, it is not sufficient for one simply to understand it; in addition one needs empirical evidence that the two names refer to the same thing.

(iv) Therefore, understanding *Hesperus is Phosphorus* is not sufficient for one to be justified in believing that Hesperus is Phosphorus; in addition, one must have empirical evidence that the two names refer to the same thing.

(v)   Therefore the statement that Hesperus is Phosphorus is not knowable apriori.

This, I take it, is the reasoning Kripke uses to support his conclusion that the necessary truth that Hesperus is Phosphorus is knowable only aposteriori, and it is the reasoning that he seeks to generalize to other cases of the necessary aposteriori. The key elements in the reasoning are the principles of Strong Disquotation and Strong Disquotation and Justification, which, without fussing over details, may be formulated roughly as follows:

STRONG DISQUOTATION

If x understands S, uses it to express p, and knows that S expresses p, then x believes p iff x accepts S (and believes it to be true).

STRONG DISQUOTATION AND JUSTIFICATION

If x understands S, uses it to express p, and knows that S expresses p, then x would be justified in believing p on the basis of evidence e iff x would be justified in accepting S (and believing it to be true) on the basis of e.

How are these principles used? If I understand the sentence (6a), *Hesperus is Phosphorus*, while associating the two names with the descriptions *the heavenly body seen in the evening sky (at t and p)*, and *the heavenly body seen in the morning sky (at t* and p*)*, then I will justifiably accept (6a) **only if** I justifiably believe that the heavenly body seen in the evening sky (at t and p) is the heavenly body seen in the morning sky (at t* and p*). Since my justification for this descriptive belief is empirical, my justification for accepting sentence (6a) is also empirical. Strong Disquotation and Justification will then tell us that my belief in the proposition I use the sentence to express—presumably the proposition that Hesperus is Phosphorus—is empirically justified. Hence, my knowledge of this proposition is aposteriori. **If** one assumes that this result carries over to other agents, times, and sentences expressing the same proposition, then one will arrive at Kripke's conclusion that this proposition can be known **only** aposteriori.

Next consider the table that has been brought into the room. In pointing at it and saying *This table is not made out of ice*, I express a necessary truth—since **this very table** could not have been made out of ice. Nevertheless, in this context I would not accept, and would not be justified in accepting, the sentence *This table* (pointing) *is not made out of ice* unless I **also** believed, and was **justified** in believing, the descriptive proposition that the, or a, table directly in front of me is not made out of ice. This descriptive proposition q is, of course, contingent rather than necessary, and hence not to be confused with the proposition expressed by the indexical sentence I uttered. Since I am justified in believing q only on the basis of empirical evidence, and since this evidence is **included** in the evidence on which I base my utterance, my evidence for accepting the sentence uttered must also be empirical. From strong disquotation and justification, it follows that although it is a necessary truth that this table is not made out of ice, my knowledge of this truth is based on empirical evidence, and so is aposteriori. Generalizing to other agents, times, and ways of expressing the same proposition, one might well conclude that this proposition is both necessary and knowable **only** aposteriori.

These examples illustrate Kripke's strategy for answering the objection to the necessary aposteriori. Confronted with someone who grants that S expresses a necessary proposition p, but objects that since p is necessary, knowledge of it cannot require empirical justification, Kripke suggests that empirical evidence is required in order to know a **different** but qualitatively similar proposition q that is related to p in a certain way. When he says *It could have turned out that ~S*, and follows this with *So knowing that S requires empirical justification*, what he takes to stand in need of justification is **not** the necessary proposition p actually expressed by S, but a related proposition q that **is** false in certain possible world-states involving agents in epistemic situations qualitatively identical to ours. This contingent proposition is one the agent must know in order to be counted as satisfying *x knows that S*.

That is the view suggested by Kripke's final, problematic response to the objector. Recall the objector's argument. If p is knowable only aposteriori, then empirical evidence is needed to rule out certain possible circumstances in which p is false. But, if p is necessary, there are no such circumstances to rule out. Thus, no proposition can be both necessary and knowable only aposteriori. To this, two main replies could be made; one could reject either of the two implicit premises, P1 and P2, presupposed by the objector.

P1. When an instance S of the necessary aposteriori expresses a necessary proposition p, and empirical evidence is required in order for one to satisfy *x knows that S*, the function of this evidence is to rule out (epistemic) possibilities in which p is false.

P2. All epistemic possibilities are genuine, metaphysical possibilities—roughly, every way that, for all we know apriori, the world might be is a way that the world genuinely could be.

One might have thought that Kripke was committed to rejecting P2 anyway, in which case nothing more would need to be said to rebut the objector's argument.[34] What we have seen, however, is that these few pages of Kripke's text can be read as suggesting something quite different—namely, the rejection of P1, and its replacement by P3 and P4.

P3. When empirical evidence is required for the truth of *A knows that S*, its function is always to rule out possibilities. However, sometimes the possibilities to be ruled out are **not** those in which the proposition expressed by S is false; instead they are possibilities in which a certain related proposition is false.

P4. Examples of the necessary aposteriori are those in which even though S expresses a necessary truth p, the truth of *A knows that S* always requires knowing some contingent, aposteriori proposition q that is related to p in a certain way.

Since it is P3 that is most objectionable, I will concentrate on it. Along with P4, it is also an important cornerstone of ambitious two-dimensionalism. In later chapters, I will deal with its incarnation there. Here, I will finish up by indicating the flaws in Kripke's route to it, and explaining how his apparent endorsement of it had the effect of obscuring his genuine insight into the necessary aposteriori, which is incorporated in a natural strategy that rebuts the objector's argument by rejecting P2 rather than P1.

As we have seen, Kripke's route to P3 was based on the principles of Strong Disquotation and Strong Disquotation and Justification. The problem with these principles is that they require an unrealistic degree of transparency of meaning. Sentences S_1 and S_2 may mean the same thing, and express the same proposition p, even though a competent speaker who understands both sentences, associates them with p, and knows of each that it expresses p, does not realize that they express the same proposition. Such an agent may accept S_1, and believe it to be true, while refusing to accept S_2, or to believe it to be true—even though the agent satisfies both *x believes that 'S_1' expresses the proposition that S_1* and *x believes that 'S_2' expresses the proposition that S_2*, and thereby believes that S_1 expresses p while also believing that S_2 expresses p. This is the situation that Kripke's well-known character

---

[34] Kripke's discussion of Goldbach's conjecture, p. 35ff of *Naming and Necessity*, indicates that he doesn't rule out epistemic possibilities that are not metaphysical possibilities. Below, I will indicate why he should be understood as embracing them.

Pierre finds himself in with the sentences *Londres est jolie* and *London is pretty*.[35] Although both mean that London is pretty, and although Pierre understands both, he does not realize that they say the same thing, and so he accepts one while rejecting the other. Since applying Strong Disquotation gives us the contradictory result that Pierre both believes and does not believe one and the same thing, the strong disquotational principles cannot be accepted.[36]

However, the source of their plausibility should be understood. Here is my own, contentious, diagnosis of the matter. As I argued in chapter 3 of *Beyond Rigidity*, it is common for an utterance of a sentence to result in the assertion not only of the proposition it **semantically** expresses, but also of other propositions, the contents of which depend on background assumptions in the context. For example, the sentence

7a. Peter Hempel lived on Lake Lane

might be used in one context to assert the proposition that my former neighbor, Peter Hempel, lived on Lake Lane, while in another it might be used to assert that the famous philosopher, Peter Hempel, lived on Lake Lane. The meaning of the sentence is what is common to what is asserted in **all** normal contexts in which it is used by speakers who understand it. This turns out to be nothing more than the singular, Russellian proposition that is also semantically expressed by (7b).

7b. Carl Hempel lived on Lake Lane.

Since (7a,b) **mean** the same thing, even though speakers who understand them may not realize that they do, anyone who understands both while accepting only one is a threat to principles of strong dis-

---

[35] "A Puzzle about Belief."

[36] This is just one of many similar examples in the literature. Another is Nathan Salmon's character Sasha, who learns the words *catsup* and *ketchup* from independent ostensive definitions, in which bottles so labeled are given to him to season his foods at different times. As a result, Sasha comes to learn what catsup is and what ketchup is. However, since the occasion never presents itself, no one ever tells him that the two words are synonymous, which of course they are. As a result, he does not accept the sentence *Catsup is ketchup*—because he suspects that there may be some, to him indiscernible, difference between them. Nevertheless he understands both words. As Salmon emphasizes, nearly all of us learn one of the words ostensively. The order in which they are learned doesn't matter, and if either term may be learned ostensively, then someone like Sasha could learn both in that way. But then there will be sentences S_1 and S_2 which differ only in the substitution of one word for the other, which Sasha understands while being disposed to accept only one—just as with Kripke's Pierre. Nathan Salmon, "A Millian Heir Rejects the Wages of *Sinn*," in C. A. Anderson and J. Owens (eds.), *Propositional Attitudes: The Role of Content in Logic, Language, and Mind* (Stanford, CA: CSLI, 1990). See also Stephen Rieber, "Understanding Synonyms without Knowing That They Are Synonymous," *Analysis* 52 (1992): 224–28.

quotation. If, in those principles, the proposition p the speaker uses S to express is identified with the proposition **semantically** expressed by S, then the existence of such a speaker falsifies the principles. However, if the principles allow p to be a modestly enriched proposition that the speaker would assert were he to assertively utter S in the context, no counterexample may result.

Thus, small differences in formulation can affect whether or not the principles are compatible with certain problematic examples.[37] When stated in terms of the semantic contents of sentences, strong disquotational principles are straightforwardly false. When stated in terms of descriptively enriched propositions that speakers would use sentences to assert in particular contexts, the principles are less easily falsified. Unfortunately, these principles are often either left implicit or stated imprecisely, with the resulting danger of equivocation. If Kripke's implicit use of strong disquotation in *Naming and Necessity* is taken as involving a modestly **enriched** proposition that speakers might naturally use the sentence *Hesperus is Phosphorus* to assert—say the proposition that the bright object, Hesperus, seen in the evening sky is the bright object, Phosphorus, seen in the morning sky—then his conclusion that **this proposition** is knowable only aposteriori is correct, and the needed version of strong disquotation is **not** subject to immediate falsification. However, this way of taking the argument is of no help to the larger project of vindicating the necessary aposteriori—since the **enriched** propositions speakers associate with (1a) are **not** necessary truths. On the other hand, if we focus on the necessary proposition that the sentence **semantically** expresses, then the strong disquotational principles needed for Kripke's argument cannot be accepted. Either way, when equivocation is avoided, Kripke's use of examples like (6a) to explain the necessary aposteriori fails, and his apparent embrace of P3 is undermined.[38]

In my opinion, this is all to the good, since there is a much better

---

[37] Thanks to Mike McGlone for helping me appreciate this point.

[38] The best one might do, I think, would be to imagine an assertive utterance of *If Hesperus exists and Phosphorus exists, then Hesperus is Phosphorus* in which the speaker asserted the enriched proposition expressed by *If the bright object, Hesperus, seen in the evening sky exists and the bright object, Phosphorus, seen in the morning sky exists, then the bright object, Hesperus, seen in the evening sky is the bright object, Phosphorus, seen in the morning sky.* This proposition is, arguably, both an example of the necessary aposteriori and something which might be predicted to be aposteriori by appropriately formulated strong disquotational principles appealing to enriched propositions asserted by speakers. Nevertheless, there appears to be little prospect of finding any formulation of strong disquotational principles that both avoids all falsifying counterexamples and explains the aposteriority of all Kripke-style examples of the necessary aposteriori. Thanks to Ben Caplan for a useful discussion of this point.

way of responding to the objector's argument against the necessary aposteriori. As indicated in chapter 2, Kripke's views about this class of truths are connected to his views about essential properties. He argues that we know **apriori** that various properties and relations are essential to anything that has them. This means that certain propositions which predicate these properties and relations of objects are such that we know apriori that **if** they are true, **then** they are necessarily true. Still, finding out whether they are true requires empirical investigation. According to this way of looking at things, in order to find out whether certain things are true with respect to **all** possible states of the world, and other things are true with respect to **no** possible states of the world, we sometimes must **first** find out what is true with respect to the **actual** state of the world. Sometimes in order to find out what could or could not be, we first must find out what is. This will seem problematic only if one has restricted the ways things could coherently be **conceived** to be (consistent with what can be known apriori) to ways things **really** could be—i.e., only if one has restricted epistemic possibility to metaphysical possibility. Although the passages in lecture 3 of *Naming and Necessity* that we have been discussing may seem to show Kripke backsliding on this point, they don't, in my opinion, negate the central lesson of his work—that one must sharply distinguish these two kinds of possibility. Thus, the proper response to the Kripkean objector is to reject the skeptic's premise P2.[39]

For Kripke, as I understand him, what is epistemically possible is not always metaphysically possible. Here it is helpful to remember that, for him, possible states of the world are not alternate concrete universes. Instead, they may be taken to be maximally complete ways the real concrete universe could have been. They are, in effect, maximally

---

[39] Kripke's fn. 72, toward the end of the main passage under discussion, shows that even there he was aware of the importance of the distinction between epistemic and metaphysical possibility. He says, referring to some of the remarks we have been discussing: "Some of the statements I myself make above may be loose and inaccurate in this sense. If I say, 'Gold *might* turn out not to be an element,' I speak correctly; 'might' here is *epistemic* and expresses the fact that the evidence does not justify *a priori* (Cartesian) certainty that gold is an element. I am also strictly correct when I say that the elementhood of gold was discovered *a posteriori*. If I say, 'Gold *might have* turned out not to be an element,' I seem to mean this metaphysically and my statement is subject to the correction noted in the text." Here, it is important to remember that the footnotes were added to the lectures by Kripke after they were given and a written transcript had been produced. I believe that when writing the footnote he noticed that his discussion had neglected the distinction between epistemic and metaphysical necessity, and he wished—without changing the text—to call attention to his commitment to it.

complete properties that the universe could have instantiated. Thinking of them in this way suggests an obvious generalization. Just as there
are properties that ordinary objects could possibly have had and other
properties they couldn't possibly have had, so there are certain maximally complete properties that the universe could have had—possible
states of the world—and other maximally complete properties that the
universe could not have had—impossible states of the world. Just as
some of the properties that objects couldn't have had are properties
that one can coherently conceive them as having, and that one cannot
know apriori that they don't have, so some maximally complete properties that the universe could not have had (some metaphysically impossible states of the world) are properties that one can coherently
conceive it as having, and that one cannot know apriori that it doesn't
have. Given this, one can explain the informativeness of certain necessary truths as resulting (in part) from the fact that learning them allows one to rule out certain impossible, but nevertheless coherently
conceivable, states of the world. Moreover, one can explain the function played by empirical evidence in providing the justification needed
for knowledge of necessary aposteriori propositions. Empirical evidence is required to rule out certain impossible world-states which
cannot be known apriori not to be instantiated, with respect to which
these propositions are false.[40] Thus, by expanding the range of epistemically possible states of the world to include some that are metaphysically impossible, one can accommodate Kripkean examples of the
necessary aposteriori. This, not the ambitious two-dimensionalist principle P3, is the true lesson that emerges from Kripke's discussion of
this important category of truths.[41]

[40] I here assume that names (unlike definite descriptions such as *the stuff out of which this
table, if it exists, is constituted*) rigidly designate the same thing with respect to all world-
states, metaphysically possible or not.

[41] Thanks to Ali Kazmi and Ben Caplan for useful comments and discussion. The material
in this section is taken, with some changes, from my "Saul Kripke, the Necessary Aposteriori,
and the Two-Dimensionalist Heresy," in Manuel Garcia-Carpintero and Josep Macià (eds.),
The Two-Dimensional Framework (Oxford: Oxford University Press, forthcoming).

CHAPTER 5

STALNAKER'S TWO-DIMENSIONALIST
MODEL OF DISCOURSE

At the end of the last chapter, I emphasized Kripke's essentialist route to the necessary aposteriori. According to him, we know apriori that certain properties—being made out of molecules, being a table not made out of ice, not being Saul Kripke, etc.—are essential properties of anything that has them, even though our knowledge of which objects have them can only be aposteriori. Given this, plus rigid designation, Kripke was able to construct many examples of the necessary aposteriori. However, although his examples were persuasive, and his explanation commonsensical, his conclusion collided with certain influential doctrines favored by a number of leading philosophers.

Chief among these doctrines were (i) the restriction of epistemic possibility to metaphysical possibility, (ii) the identification of propositions with sets of (metaphysically) possible world-states (or functions from such states to truth values), and (iii) the characterization of the goal of rational inquiry as that of locating the actual world-state within the space of (metaphysically) possible world-states compatible with what one already knows, or has established. As indicated in chapter 4, (i) leads to a puzzle about how empirical evidence could possibly be required for knowledge of any necessary truth. In chapter 3, I noted that if (ii) is correct, there can't be propositions that are both necessary and knowable only aposteriori, since there is only one necessary proposition (which is apriori). The necessary aposteriori is also problematic for (iii). According to the model of which it is a part, acquiring new information always involves learning truths that distinguish the way the world actually is from certain ways that it isn't, but could have been. Acquiring information is equated with narrowing down the range of (metaphysically) possible world-states compatible with what one knows. But if this is so, then necessary truths—which are true in all possible world-states—will be uninformative, and will never advance the goal of rational inquiry or discourse.

For these reasons, philosophers committed to (i), (ii), or (iii) were faced with a dilemma. They could either accept Kripke's examples at face value while abandoning, or modifying, their previous commitments, or they could retain those commitments while attempting to explain away Kripke's examples. One of those who found himself in this position was Robert Stalnaker. Although strongly committed to (i), (ii), and (iii), he also recognized the power of Kripke's examples. His 1978 article "Assertion" was an important, and historically influential, attempt to find a way of accommodating Kripke's discussion, while draining it of any content incompatible with (i–iii).[1]

The Two-Dimensionalist Model of Assertion

The idea for accommodating Kripke's examples was simple. Stalnaker accepted Kripke's contention that examples like (1a–e)

1a. This table [demonstrating a particular table] is made out of molecules.

 b. This table [demonstrating a table that is made of wood] is not made out of ice.

 c. Lassie was a dog.

 d. Hesperus is Phosphorus.

 e. David Kaplan is not Saul Kripke.

express necessary truths that predicate essential properties (or relations) of objects (or pairs of objects). Stalnaker also accepted the obvious fact that a speaker who assertively utters one of these sentences often asserts something informative that is knowable only aposteriori. However, he maintained that in every such case the proposition asserted is contingent, and hence not identical with the necessary proposition semantically expressed by the sentence uttered. He believed that he could show this by appealing to a plausible and independently motivated model of discourse.

According to the model, conversations take place against a set of background assumptions shared by the conversational participants which rule out certain possible world-states as not obtaining, or

---

[1] "Assertion" was originally published in Peter Cole (ed.), *Syntax and Semantics 9: Pragmatics* (New York: Academic Press, 1978), pp. 315–32. It is reprinted in Robert Stalnaker, *Context and Content* (New York and Oxford: Oxford University Press, 1999). Citations will be to this volume.

"being actual." As the conversation proceeds, and assertions are made and accepted, new propositions are admitted into the set of shared background assumptions, and the set of possible world-states that remain compatible with what has been assumed or established shrinks. The set of possible world-states that are compatible with everything that has been assumed or established up to a given point in the conversation is called the *context set* at that point in the conversation. The aim of further discourse is to further narrow down this set of possibilities, within which the actual state of the world is assumed to be located. When one asserts p, the function of one's assertion is to shrink the context set by eliminating from it all world-states in which p is not true.

Stalnaker postulates three rules governing assertion, as understood in this model.[2]

R1. A proposition asserted should always be true in some but not all of the possible world-states in the context set.

R2. Any assertive utterance should express a proposition relative to each possible world-state in the context set, and that proposition should have a truth value in each possible world-state in the context set.

R3. The same proposition should be expressed relative to each possible world-state in the context set.

The rationale for the first rule is that a proposition true in all world-states of the context set would be uninformative, and would fail to perform the essential function of assertion, which is to narrow down the range of world-states that conversational participants take to be candidates for being the way the world actually is. By the same token, a proposition false in all world-states in the context set would contradict what has already been conversationally established—since it would eliminate the entire context set, it would also fail to narrow down the range in which the actual world-state is to be located. Of course, this rule, like the others, allows for some flexibility in how it applies. If someone **seems** to say something that violates it, one may sometimes conclude that no violation has really taken place because the context set isn't quite what one originally thought, or because the speaker didn't really assert, or mean, what he at first seemed to assert or mean.

[2] *Context and Content*, p. 86.

This is not to say that violations never occur, but it is to say that common knowledge of the rule can sometimes be exploited for conversational purposes—as when a speaker deliberately says something the literal interpretation of which would violate the rule, knowing full well that he will be reinterpreted in a certain obvious way so as to be seen as conforming with it.[3]

Stalnaker's rationale for the second rule is that if an utterance violates it, then for some world-state w in the context set, the assertive utterance won't determine whether it should remain in the set, or be eliminated. If the sentence uttered does not express a proposition at w, or if it does express a proposition, but one for which no truth value—true or untrue—is defined at w, then the verdict on whether w stays or goes will, Stalnaker thinks, be undetermined. This is to be avoided.[4]

In explaining the rational for R3, Stalnaker employs his notion of *the propositional concept associated with an assertion*. A propositional concept is very much like one of David Kaplan's characters. For Stalnaker, it is a function from world-states, considered as possible contexts of utterance, to propositions—where propositions are taken to be nothing more than assignments of truth values to world-states considered as circumstances of evaluation. The propositional concept associated with an utterance of a sentence S at a certain moment m in a conversation is a function that maps each world-state w in the context set at m onto a proposition—which is simply an assignment of truth values to **all** the world-states in the context set. This assignment of truth values is identified with the proposition that would be expressed by S at m, if the context of utterance were to turn out to be w.

Propositional concepts associated with utterances are often given pictorial representations, as is indicated by Stalnaker's example D.

D	i	j	k
i	T	T	T
j	F	F	T
k	F	T	T

D represents the propositional concept associated with the use of a sentence S at a moment m in which the context set consists of the

---

[3] See ibid., p. 89.
[4] Ibid., pp. 89–90.

world-states i, j, and k. What D tells us is (i) that if i is the state the world is really in at m, then the proposition (semantically) expressed by the speaker's utterance of S is the proposition that assigns truth to every world-state of the context set; (ii) that if j is the state the world is in at m, then the proposition (semantically) expressed by the speaker's utterance of S is the proposition that assigns truth to k and falsity to i and j; and (iii) that if k is the state the world is in at m, the proposition (semantically) expressed by the speaker's utterance of S is the proposition that assigns falsity to i and truth to the other two world-states.[5]

Stalnaker uses the propositional concept D to give the following rationale for R3.

> To see why the principle must hold, look at the matrix for the propositional concept D. Suppose the context set consists of i, j, and k, and that the speaker's utterance determines D. What would he be asking his audience to do? Something like this: If we are in the world i, leave the context set the same; if we are in the world j, throw out worlds i and j, and if we are in world k, throw out just world i. **But of course the audience does not know which of those worlds we are in, and if it did the assertion would be pointless**. So the statement, made in that context, expresses an intention that is essentially ambiguous. Notice that the problem is not that the speaker's utterance has failed to determine a unique proposition. Assuming that one of the worlds i, j, or k, is in fact the actual world, then that world will fix the proposition unambiguously. **The problem is that since it is unknown which proposition it is that is expressed, the expression of it cannot do the job that it is supposed to do**.[6]

The idea is that if R3 is violated, the conversational participants won't know which proposition is (semantically) expressed by the sentence uttered. But if the proposition asserted is always the one (semantically) expressed by the sentence uttered (in the context), then the conversational participants won't know what is asserted, and so will be at a loss

---

[5] It is not entirely clear from Stalnaker's discussion what status the propositions "expressed by" S at the world-states of the context set have. It is clear that they are not always the propositions asserted, if those world-states turn out to obtain. In many cases, they may be the propositions semantically expressed by S in that eventuality—hence the parenthetical "semantically" above. However, Stalnaker also indicates that propositional concepts are not always semantic characters—thus throwing this identification into doubt. We need not resolve this issue now, but will return to it later.

[6] Pages 90–91, my emphasis.

as to how to update the context set and proceed with the conversation. Hence one should avoid violations of R3.

With R1–R3 in place, Stalnaker is ready to use them to explain assertive utterances of Kripkean examples of the necessary aposteriori. He continues from the end of the previous passage as follows:

> As with the other principles, one may respond to apparent violations [of R3] in different ways. One could take an apparent violation as evidence that the speaker's context set was smaller than it was thought to be, and eliminate possible worlds relative to which the utterance receives a divergent interpretation. Or, one could reinterpret the utterance so that it expresses the same proposition in each possible world. Consider an example: hearing a woman talking in the next room, I tell you, *That is either Zsa Zsa Gabor or Elizabeth Anscombe.* Assuming that both demonstrative pronouns and proper names are rigid designators—terms that refer to the same individual in all possible worlds—this sentence comes out expressing either a necessary truth or a necessary falsehood, depending on whether it is one of the two mentioned women or someone else who is in the next room. Let i be the world in which it is Miss Gabor, j the world in which it is Professor Anscombe, and k a world in which it is someone else, say Tricia Nixon Cox. Now if we try to bring the initial context set into conformity with the third principle [R3] by shrinking it, say by throwing out world k, we will bring it into conflict with the first principle [R1] by making the assertion trivial. But if we look at what is actually going on in the example, if we ask what possible states of affairs the speaker would be trying to exclude from the context set if he made that statement, we can work backward to the proposition expressed. A moment's reflection shows that what the speaker is saying is that the actual world is either i or j, and not k. What he means to communicate is that the diagonal proposition of the matrix E exhibited below, the proposition expressed by †E, is true.[7]

E	i	j	k
i	T	T	T
j	T	T	T
k	F	F	F

†E	i	j	k
i	T	T	F
j	T	T	F
k	T	T	F

[7] Page 91.

It may be helpful to summarize Stalnaker's reasoning here. The propositional concept associated with the sentence uttered is E. Looking at E tells us two things: (i) we don't know which proposition is (semantically) expressed by the sentence S the speaker uttered in his actual context, because which proposition is expressed depends on which context actually obtains, and we don't know which context does obtain; (ii) none of the possible propositions expressed would serve any useful purpose in the conversation. To assert a necessary truth is to assert something trivially uninformative which is of no use in narrowing down the location of the actual world-state within the context set; and asserting a necessary falsehood is even worse. Thus, E violates R3, and any attempt to avoid the violation—by excluding either k alone, or both i and j, from the context set—will violate R1. So, if we are to avoid violation entirely, and to regard the speaker's utterance as informative, we must take it as asserting some proposition other than the proposition it (semantically) expresses at i, j, or k. What proposition should we choose? Well, whatever context in fact turns out to obtain, the speaker will surely be committed to his utterance of S expressing a truth in the context. So that is what we should take his utterance as asserting. The proposition asserted is **the** proposition that is true (false) at a world-state w (of the context set) just in case the proposition (semantically) expressed by S in w is true (false) at w—it is the assignment of truth values that arises from E by looking along the diagonal to find the truth value that appears in row w of column w, for each w. This is what Stalnaker calls the *diagonal proposition*. Since, in this example, the diagonal proposition is neither true in all world-states of the context set nor false in all these states, it can do the job that asserted propositions are supposed to do—shrink that set. Hence, he maintains, this is the proposition that is really asserted by the speaker's utterance—no matter which member of the context set turns out, in fact, to obtain. This is what †E represents, where '†' (pronounced "dagger") is an operator that maps a propositional concept C1 onto the propositional concept C2 that arises from C1 by taking each of the rows of C2 to be the diagonal proposition determined by C1.

This example is the prototype for Stalnaker's treatment of the necessary aposteriori, which—extrapolating and generalizing from his explicit remarks—we may take as suggesting the following thesis.

> T1. Although no necessary propositions are knowable only
> aposteriori, a sentence S, as used in a particular conver-

sation C, is an example of the necessary aposteriori iff the proposition (semantically) expressed by S relative to the world-state that really obtains in the speaker's context is necessary, but the diagonal proposition asserted, which arises from applying the '†' operator to the propositional concept associated with the use of S in C is contingent, and hence knowable only aposteriori.

Given T1, plus Stalnaker's discussion of the example—*That is either Zsa Zsa Gabor or Elizabeth Anscombe*—motivating it, one might get the impression that he thought that all genuine examples of the necessary aposteriori were indexical, in the sense of semantically expressing different propositions in different contexts of utterance. This might well seem problematic, since many instances of the necessary aposteriori arise from the use of names and natural kind terms, which neither Kripke nor Kaplan view as indexicals. Of course, others might see things differently. If one thought (i) that every name and natural kind term had its reference semantically fixed by description and (ii) that when the reference of t is semantically fixed by a description **the x: Dx**, the analysis of t is either **the x: actually Dx** or **dthat [the x: Dx]**, then all names and natural kind terms could be taken to be indexicals, and standard Kripkean instances of the necessary aposteriori could be assimilated to Stalnaker's explicitly indexical example. However, neither Kripke, Kaplan, nor Stalnaker accept (i) and (ii).

In spite of this, Stalnaker believed that the same sort of explanation given for his indexical example could be given for non-indexical examples of the necessary aposteriori—like, allegedly, *Hesperus is Phosphorus*—as is indicated by the way in which he continues the previously quoted passage.

I suggest that a common way of bringing utterances into conformity with the third principle [R3] is to interpret them to express the diagonal proposition, or to perform on them the operation represented by the two-dimensional operator DAGGER. There are lots of examples. Consider: *Hesperus is identical with Phosphorus, it is now three o'clock, an ophthalmologist is an eye doctor.* In each case, to construct a context which conforms to the first principle [R1], a context in which the proposition expressed is neither trivial nor assumed false, one must include possible worlds in which the sentence, interpreted in the standard way, expresses different propositions. But in any plausible context in which one of these sentences might reasonably be used, it is clear that the diagonal proposition is the one that the speaker means to communicate. The two-dimensional operator DAGGER may represent a common operation used to interpret, or reinterpret, assertions and other speech acts so as to bring them into conformity with the third principle [R3] constraining acts of assertion.[8]

This is puzzling. If, as Stalnaker presumably thinks, (2a,b) don't contain indexicals, then their meanings—i.e., their Kaplan-style characters—will, on his view, be constant functions, and each will express the same (necessary) proposition in every context of utterance.

2a. Hesperus is identical with Phosphorus.

  b. An ophthalmologist is an eye doctor.

But if that is so, then it would seem that the propositional concepts associated with their use will be unaffected by the application of the dagger operation, and Stalnaker's explanation of their use won't get off the ground.

Perhaps Stalnaker intends to include some contexts in the context set in which the words—*Hesperus, Phosphorus,* and *ophthalmologist*—stand for something other than what they actually do. Presumably, the justification for this would be the idea that (2a) or (2b) would be used only if it were **not** taken for granted that all conversational participants knew what these words meant—with the result that world-states in which the words mean something different from what they actually mean would be among the genuine possibilities left open by the conversation prior to the assertive utterances. But then, the thought continues, different propositions would be expressed when the sentences were "interpreted in the standard way," at these world-states, considered as contexts.

Although something like this is, I suspect, what Stalnaker had in mind, there are two potential worries to be addressed. First, if the meaning of a sentence S is represented by its Kaplan-style character S_C, then information about what the expressions of S mean and refer to with respect to the world-state of an arbitrary counterfactual context C are **irrelevant** to what proposition S semantically expresses relative to C. The proposition expressed is the proposition one gets by applying S_C to C. But since S_C is determined by what S **actually** means, what S would mean if C were to obtain has no effect on this result, and is completely beside the point. For example, the proposi-

---

tion semantically expressed by *I live in Princeton* relative to any possible context C is the proposition that attributes the property of living in a certain town (the one in central New Jersey called 'Princeton' in the actual world-state) to the agent of the context—irrespective of whether the agent of the context speaks English or any other language, and irrespective of what meanings and referents, if any, speakers in the counterfactual world of that context attach to the terms 'I' and 'Princeton'. This means that no matter what information about meaning is, or is not, included in members of the context set for utterances of (2a) and (2b), the meanings of those sentences—their Kaplan-style characters—will ignore this information, and always return the same propositions. Since this would block Stalnaker's explanations, he must maintain that, the propositional concept PC_{Sm} corresponding to a use of a sentence S at a given moment m in a conversation is **not** the actual meaning of S (thought of as a function from contexts to propositions) restricted to the world-states in the context set at m—despite the fact that understanding S as giving rise to PC_{Sm} involves "interpreting S in the standard way." Presumably this propositional concept is some function from contexts to propositions which differs in certain ways from the actual character of S, but not others. Clearly, this aspect of the view needs further elaboration.

The second worry is more serious. No matter what elaboration might be offered, it is **not** true that (2a) would be used only in a conversation in which it is not presupposed that conversational participants know what *Hesperus* and *Phosphorus* mean and refer to, in the sense most relevant to Stalnaker's model. Certainly, each of the conversational participants may know perfectly well that 'Hesperus' refers to this object [pointing in the evening to Venus] and that 'Phosphorus' refers to that object [pointing in the morning to Venus]. They may even have done the pointing themselves. Clearly, these speakers know of the referent of each name that it is the referent of that name. Hence the (contingent) propositions expressed by *'Hesperus' refers to x* and *'Phosphorus' refers to x*, relative to an assignment of Venus to 'x', should be among those that have already been assumed or established in the conversation. But then, metaphysically possible world-states in which the names mean and refer to different things will already have been eliminated from the context set as incompatible with what has been assumed or established. Nevertheless, (2a) could be used in these circumstances perfectly intelligibly. Since Stalnaker's explanation cannot successfully be applied to this case, his account of the necessary aposteriori, and his attempt to accommodate Kripkean examples of it, remains incomplete at best.

In a moment, we will see that the problem with his account of the necessary aposteriori is considerably worse than this. Before that, however, a word should be said about his view of the contingent apriori. This category of truth doesn't pose as direct a threat to his identification of propositions with sets of (metaphysically) possible world-states (or functions from such states to truth values) as does the necessary aposteriori, and he doesn't say nearly as much about it. Nevertheless, he seems to endorse a version of the orthodox ambitious two-dimensionalist position.

> Let me mention one complex operator, square-dagger, which says that the diagonal proposition is necessary. This can be understood as the A PRIORI TRUTH operator, observing the distinction emphasized in the work of Saul Kripke between apriori and necessary truth. An apriori truth is a statement that, while perhaps not expressing a necessary proposition, expresses a truth in every context. This will be the case if and only if the diagonal proposition is necessary, which is what the complex operator says. I will illustrate this with a version of one of Kripke's own examples. Suppose that in worlds i, j, and k, a certain object, a metal bar, is one, two, and three meters long, respectively, at a certain time t. Now suppose an appropriate authority fixes the reference of the expression *one meter* by making the following statement in each of the worlds i, j, and k: *This bar is one meter long.* Matrix †C represents the propositional concept for the claim that this statement is apriori true.

C	i	j	k
i	T	F	F
j	F	T	F
k	F	F	T

$\dagger C$	i	j	k
i	T	T	T
j	T	T	T
k	T	T	T

> The proposition expressed by the authority is one that might have been false, although he couldn't have expressed a false proposition in that utterance.[9]

---

[9] Pages 83–84. Note an apparent equivocation in Stalnaker's use of the term *statement* in this passage. He speaks of statements expressing propositions, which suggests that he thinks of them as sentences. However, he also talks about some statements being apriori truths, which suggests that he thinks of them as propositions—i.e., of things that are known, and so capable of being known apriori. This looseness, though understandable, is both a source of trouble and something that is characteristic of many two-dimensionalist discussions.

These comments, which essentially exhaust Stalnaker's treatment of the subject, point to something like T2.

T2. A sentence S, as used on a given occasion in a context C, is an instance of the contingent apriori iff the proposition semantically expressed by S in C is contingent, but the diagonal proposition associated with the use of S in C is necessary (since S would express a truth no matter what the context).

Taken together, this thesis plus Stalnaker's discussion suggests the strong two-dimensionalist position that when we say *It is knowable apriori that S* we are reporting on the epistemic status of the diagonal proposition associated with S, whereas when we say *It is not a necessary truth that S* we are reporting on the modal status of a different proposition—the one semantically expressed by S. In later chapters we will see that this view is unsustainable. For now it is enough to notice two worries about the right-to-left direction of T2. First, we are normally inclined to think that there may be necessary truths that are not knowable at all, and so are not apriori. An approach that identifies "the A PRIORI TRUTH operator" with one that "says that the diagonal proposition is necessary" simply defines away this possibility without doing anything to address the worry itself. Of course, anyone who, like Stalnaker, is committed to the idea that propositions are nothing more than sets of possible world-states won't take this worry seriously, since on his account there is only one necessary proposition. However, that is little comfort to the rest of us, who are impressed with the many, well-known difficulties with that view.[10]

The second worry regarding Stalnaker's thesis T2 involves Kaplan-style examples like $\alpha = dthat\ [\alpha]\ (if\ \alpha\ exists)$. Here, the diagonal proposition clearly is both necessary and knowable apriori, while the proposition expressed is contingent. However, as we saw in chapter 4, it is not at all obvious that this is a genuine instance of the contingent apriori. In order for it to be so, *It is knowable apriori that $\alpha = dthat\ [\alpha]$* must be true, which in turn requires *There is an x such that it is knowable*

---

[10] For more on these difficulties, see my "Direct Reference, Propositional Attitudes, and Semantic Content," *Philosophical Topics* 15 (1987): 47–87, reprinted in Peter Ludlow (ed.), *Readings in the Philosophy of Language*. Stalnaker attempts to deal with the difficulties in his Inquiry (Cambridge, MA: MIT Press, 1984). Strong responses to Stalnaker may be found in Mark Richard, *Propositional Attitudes* (Cambridge: Cambridge University Press, 1990), pp. 12–16; Hartry Field, "Stalnaker on Intentionality: On Robert Stalnaker's 'Inquiry'" in *Pacific Philosophical Quarterly* 67 (1986): 98–112; and Jeff Speaks, *Three Views of Language and the Mind* (unpublished Ph.D. dissertation, Princeton University, 2003).

apriori that $\alpha = x$ to be true. However, for many choices of α, it is hard to see how one could know apriori of some object that it "is α."

For all these reasons, Stalnaker's attempt to use his pragmatic model of assertion and conversational dynamics to accommodate the necessary aposteriori and the contingent apriori—while remaining committed to the restriction of epistemic possibility to metaphysical possibility, and the identification of propositions with functions from possible world-states to truth values—is, at best, questionable. In the next section, we will see that this is an understatement. The model of discourse and inquiry he proposed is unworkable, and is vitiated by the limitation of world-states to those that are metaphysically possible. Given his commitments, Stalnaker cannot successfully explain the necessary aposteriori.

Failure of the Model

This point is brought out by the following example in which you are sitting across from me in my office, you point to a paperweight in plain view on my desk, and ask *What is that paperweight made out of?*, and I respond *It is made of wood*. Although you don't know, prior to my utterance, what the paperweight is made of, we both assume that, whatever it is made of, it is an essential property of that paperweight that it be made of that stuff. Since, in fact, the paperweight is made out of wood, my remark is an example of the necessary aposteriori. How would Stalnaker represent the conversation? Well, prior to the utterance he would have different possible world-states in the context set that were compatible with everything we had assumed or established in the conversation up to that point. Presumably, he would maintain that these would include a context i in which the thing which, in i, is the one and only one paperweight on the desk is made of wood, a context j in which the paperweight on the desk in j is made of something else, e.g., plastic, and context k in which a paperweight in front of us in k is made out of something else again—perhaps, metal. Thus, Stalnaker would associate the following *propositional concept* with my utterance.

PW	*i*	*j*	*k*
i	T	T	T
j	F	F	F
k	F	F	F

His rules for assertion would then yield two conclusions: (i) that on hearing my utterance you had no way of knowing which proposition was (semantically) expressed by my sentence, because which proposition was expressed depended on which context—i, j, or k—actually obtained, and you didn't know, in advance of accepting my remark, which context did obtain, and (ii) that none of the propositions that might have been (semantically) expressed would have served any useful purpose. To have asserted a necessary truth would have been to have asserted something trivially uninformative, and of no use in narrowing down where the actual world-state was located within the context set; and to have asserted a necessary falsehood would have been a nonstarter. So, if you regarded my utterance as informative, you must have taken it as asserting some proposition other than any of the candidates for being the one it (semantically) expressed.

Which proposition might that have been? Since you knew that whatever the world-state of the context turned out to be, I would be committed to my remark expressing a truth, you must have taken me to have asserted the diagonal proposition—which is true (false) at one of the world-states of the context set iff the proposition (semantically) expressed by my sentence relative to that world-state is true (false) when evaluated at that world-state. Since this proposition is neither true at all world-states in the context set, nor false at them all, asserting it does the job that assertions are intended to do—namely, shrink the context set. Implicitly recognizing all of this, we both rightly understood the diagonal proposition to be the proposition I asserted.

That is the explanation provided by Stalnaker's model. There are two things wrong with it. First, in point of actual fact, it is wrong to suppose that you had any relevant doubt about what proposition was (semantically) expressed by my utterance of *It is made of wood* in response to your question *What* [pointing at the paperweight] *is that made of*? The proposition I expressed is one that predicates being made of wood of that very paperweight—the one we both were looking at, and saw clearly sitting on the edge of my desk. You knew that it was the object you had asked about, and about which I had given an answer. Since you also knew what wood was, you knew precisely which property was predicated of which object by my remark. How, then, could there have been any real doubt in your mind about what proposition my sentence expressed?

The natural description of this case is one which recognizes that there is a proposition p such that you and I both knew that my utterance expressed p, even though you didn't know, in advance of accepting my remark, whether or not p was true, and hence didn't know whether or not p was a necessary truth. However, given Stalnaker's identification of propositions with sets of possible world-states, he can't say this—since the fact that p is necessary would require him to say (i) that you knew p all along, and (ii) that you knew that my utterance expressed a trivial truth, simply by virtue of understanding what it said. Since this is absurd, he is forced to the patently counterintuitive conclusion that upon hearing my utterance, you didn't know what proposition it expressed.

The second thing wrong with Stalnaker's explanation is that the world-states j and k in the context set must either be (a) ones that are **not** really metaphysically possible (contrary to one of his central philosophical commitments), or (b) ones that are **not** compatible with all the shared assumptions of the conversational participants prior to my utterance (contrary to the dictates of his model). What are the world-states i, j, and k in the context set? They are total possibilities regarding how the world might be in which one and only one paperweight is sitting on my desk, seen by both of us, and the subject of our discourse. The paperweight satisfying these conditions in i is made out of wood, whereas the paperweights satisfying them in j and k are made out of plastic in one case and metal in the other. What paperweights do satisfy these conditions in j and k? If j and k are really metaphysically possible, as Stalnaker insists, then the paperweights in j and k **can't be** the paperweight that is really on my desk. Since that paperweight is made out of wood in every genuinely possible world-state in which it exists, it is not made out of plastic in j or metal in k. It follows that j and k must be world-states in which **some other paperweight** is between us on the desk, seen by us, and the subject of our conversation.

But how can that be? Surely, one thing that was part of the shared conversational background prior to my remark was the knowledge that this very paperweight [imagine me demonstrating it again now] was between us on the desk, seen by us both, and the subject of our conversation. To deny this would be tantamount to denying that we ever know directly, of anything we perceive or talk about, that it has one property or another. Even if we put the question of knowledge aside, surely we both believed these things about this very paperweight, which is all the model requires. But if we did have this *de re* knowledge, or these *de re* beliefs, of this particular paperweight, then Stalnaker's requirement that the world-states in the context set be compatible with **everything** assumed and established in the conversation must have eliminated all metaphysically possible world-states in which any other paperweight, not made out of wood, is the one and only paperweight under discussion—in which case there is no room for the diagonalization required by his explanation. This is the fundamental problem. Unless some persuasive defense can be found for excluding obvious, shared *de re* belief and knowledge from the conversational model, Stalnaker's explanation can't get off the ground. Since he doesn't offer any such defense, and I can see none myself, his account must be rejected.[11] (We will return to this in a moment.)

Now notice what happens if we drop one of Stalnaker's antecedent philosophical commitments, and think of the context set as including world-states that are metaphysically impossible but epistemically possible—i.e., as properties that the world couldn't really have had, but which we cannot know apriori that it doesn't have. When we allow such world-states, the propositional concept associated with the utterance turns out to be different from the one we originally took it to be. On this way of looking at things, i, j, and k are different epistemic possibilities involving the very same object o—where o is the paperweight that we actually see on my desk, are talking about, and know that we are talking about. In world-state i, o is made of wood; in j, o is made of plastic; and in k, o is made of metal. When we think of things in this way we get the following matrix.

---

[11] Stalnaker himself indicates that *de re* knowledge and belief routinely contribute to the common conversational background—compatibility with which determines the context set. For example, on page 86 he says,

> A conversation is a process taking place in an ever-changing context. Think of a state of a context at any given moment as defined by the presuppositions of the participants as represented by their context sets. In the normal, nondefective case, the context sets will all be the same, so for this case we can talk of the context set of the conversation. Now how does an assertion change the context? There are two ways, the second of which, I will suggest, should be an essential component of the analysis of assertion. I will mention the first just to set it apart from the second: The fact that a speaker is speaking, saying the words he is saying in the way he is saying them, is a fact that is usually accessible to everyone present. Such observed facts can be expected to change the presumed common background knowledge of the speaker and his audience in the same way that any obviously observable change in the physical surroundings will change the presumed common knowledge. If a goat walked into the room, it would normally be presupposed, from that point, that there was a goat in the room. And the fact that this was presupposed might be exploited in the conversation, as when someone asks, *How did that thing get in here?*, assuming that others will know what he is talking about. **In the same way, when I speak, I presuppose that others know I am speaking. . . . This fact, too, can be exploited in the conversation, as when Daniels says *I am bald*, taking it for granted that his audience can figure out who is being said to be bald.** [my emphasis]

PW*	i	j	k
i	T	F	F
j	T	F	F
k	T	F	F

Since the same proposition is expressed with respect to each epistemologically possible context, and since it is neither trivially true nor trivially false, no diagonalization is needed.

This is an improvement. It also encourages a certain thought. Perhaps Stalnaker's model of inquiry can be divorced from philosophically contentious motivations that partially inspired it. The idea is to give up the identification of epistemic possibility with metaphysical possibility, to give up the goal of explaining away the necessary aposteriori, and to give up the analysis of propositions as sets of metaphysically possible worlds. We retain the idea that utterances are associated with propositional concepts or matrices, plus the general model of discourse that makes use of these matrices. In particular, we retain the idea that the point of a discourse is to locate the actual state of the world among all the possible world-states—now thought of as including both epistemic and metaphysical possibilities. As before, an assertion is supposed to narrow the set of possibilities compatible with everything that has previously been assumed or established in the conversation. So on the new picture, Stalnaker's conversational rules, R1–R3, remain intact.

I will illustrate this revised model with another example. I say *He is John Hawthorne* in a conversation in which it is common knowledge, prior to my remark, that this person—the one I am talking about—is either John Hawthorne or Ted Sider. We suppose that the utterance takes place in a context in which everyone knows a few facts about John and Ted already, but not everyone knows what they look like. Perhaps everyone has talked to each of them on the phone, or read their work, or corresponded with them, or some combination of the three, even though many would not recognize them by sight. Let us stipulate that everyone already knows of John that his name is 'John', that he is a Rutgers professor, and that he is not Ted—similarly for everyone's antecedent knowledge of Ted. Moreover, this shared knowledge is known to be shared, and so the propositions known are part of the conversational background presupposed at this point in the conversation. It is in this situation that I utter the sentence *He is John*

Hawthorne, demonstrating John, who is sitting at the end of the table. The sentence uttered contains a name which, like the demonstrative *he*, is a rigid designator with respect to all possible world-states— including those that are epistemically, but not metaphysically, possible. To say this is to say that when describing these world-states using a sentence containing one of these terms, we are always talking about the same individual.

What are the epistemic possibilities prior to my utterance? Let us consider just two—j and t. I **begin** by describing them as follows: in j there is a unique person sitting there at the end of the table and it is John, and in t there is a unique person sitting there and it is Ted. This gives us the following matrix.

JT	*j*	*t*
j	T	T
t	F	F

Stalnaker's principles then dictate that we perform the diagonalization operation, with the result that the diagonal proposition is asserted—a proposition which is true just in case John is sitting there, and false otherwise. That is a good result in the sense that it, or something quite like it, would, I think, normally be regarded as having been asserted by such an utterance. If you were to report my remark by saying *Scott said that John Hawthorne was sitting there*, I think most people would judge what you said to be true.

Nevertheless, the way we reached this result is problematic. World-states j and t are supposed to be epistemic possibilities compatible with **everything** taken for granted in the conversation prior to my remark. But, as in the earlier example, I left out of my specifications of j and t certain things known by all conversational participants. I ignored the fact that it was known (prior to my remark) that he [imagine me point-ing again at John] was sitting there and also the fact that it was known (prior to my utterance) that since there weren't two people sitting there, and since John and Ted are different people, if John was sitting there, then Ted wasn't. When these things are added to the model, t becomes incompatible with what is known or assumed by conversa-tional participants, and so is excluded from the context set.

Why? First, since it is commonly known (prior to my utterance) that he [pointing at John] is sitting there, it follows that he, John, is an x, such that it is commonly known that x is sitting there. This is just to say that the singular proposition p which says of John that he is sitting there is known to be true by the conversational participants, and so must be true with respect to t, if t is to be compatible with everything commonly known or assumed. Second, since it is commonly known (prior to my remark) that if John is sitting there, Ted isn't, it again follows that John is an x such that it is commonly known that if x is sitting there, then Ted isn't. But it has already been stipulated that the proposition q that Ted is sitting there is true in t. Hence, t can be compatible with everything which is known or assumed in the conversation (prior) to my utterance only if a certain trio of propositions are compatible—where the trio consists of p, q, and the conditional proposition the antecedent of which is p and the consequent of which is the negation of q. Since these propositions are **incompatible**, t must be excluded from the context set—in which case our revised Stalnaker-style explanation of what I have asserted fails for the same reason that his original explanation failed for my assertion about the paperweight.

How then is it that my utterance of *He is John Hawthorne* was informative? Since I discuss this sort of issue in considerable detail in chapters 3 and 4 of *Beyond Rigidity*, I will say only a brief positive word about it here. We know that prior to the utterance my audience already believed of John that he was John. So the new belief acquired by virtue accepting my utterance wasn't that one. What might it have been? One such belief was surely that he, the person sitting there, was John Hawthorne. Everyone in the audience could see—without any appeal to propositional concepts or diagonalization—that I was attributing the property of being John Hawthorne to the guy sitting there, at whom I was pointing. So naturally I was committed to that being true. Notice something else: if someone in the audience were to describe what I said to a third party who hadn't been present, he might say *At first several of us didn't know who was sitting at the end of the table, but then Scott said that John Hawthorne was the man sitting there.* In ordinary life such a report would be taken to be completely accurate. If it is accurate, then not only did I convey this informative proposition, I actually said (i.e., asserted) it. This is evidence either that what I asserted went a little beyond the strict semantic content of the sentence I uttered in the context, or else that the sentence I uttered had a rather rich semantic content relative to that context. My own view, presented in *Beyond Rigidity*, is that the former is correct.

So in the end I agree with Stalnaker that in cases like this the speaker does assert a proposition which is not the proposition semantically expressed by the sentence he utters. But the mechanism by which this happens is a rather ordinary one, and typically it does not involve any forced two-dimensionalist diagonalization.

As for Stalnaker's model of discourse, what our discussion of this example has shown is that it cannot be saved simply by liberalizing it so as to allow for epistemically possible world-states over and above those that are metaphysically possible. The fundamental assumption leading to the failure of the model is the presumption that conversational participants can do two things: (i) identify, at the time of each utterance, precisely which possible world-states are compatible with everything previously assumed or established in the conversation, and (ii) determine which of these possible states are compatible with propositions expressed by the sentence we utter under different assumptions about which possible context actually obtains. In reality, we can't always do these things—no matter whether the possible world-states in question are metaphysical or epistemic. We can't do them because the relationship between sentences and the propositions they express is **nontransparent** in a certain way. There are pairs of sentences S1 and S2—or more accurately sentences plus contexts of utterance—such that

(a) S1 expresses a proposition p1, S2 expresses p2, and a speaker understands both sentences, while knowing that accepting S1 is sufficient for believing p1 and accepting S2 is sufficient for believing p2, and

(b) p1 bears some intimate logical relation to p2—e.g., p1 is the negation of p2, or p1 is identical with p2, or p1 is a conditional and p2 is its antecedent—

even though

(c) the speaker has no way of knowing that the logical relation mentioned in (b) holds between the proposition he believes in virtue of accepting S1 and the proposition he believes in virtue of accepting S2.

Because of this, there are cases in which a speaker believes p1, and yet is in no position to recognize that in believing p2 he is believes something inconsistent with this, which—in terms of the model—rules out all epistemologically possible world-states. In other cases, in which p1 and p2 are consistent, but some different logical relation holds between them, the fact that the speaker believes both p1 and p2 may result in ruling out some but not all possible world-states, without the speaker's recognizing precisely which. Because of this nontransparency in the relationship between sentences, the propositions we believe in virtue of accepting them, and the world-states in which these propositions are true, our beliefs cannot always interact with one another in the way presupposed by the model. Hence, the model fails.[12]

It is important to realize how modest are the assumptions that lead to this result. In order to derive it, one may, but need not, endorse the contentious, but I believe correct, doctrine that the semantic contents of names and indexicals (relative to contexts) are their referents, or the similarly contentious but correct doctrine that the semantic contents of natural kind terms are the kinds they designate. One reason these semantic assumptions are not needed is that we can generate the relevant problems for the model using pairs of synonymous expressions of other sorts—for example *catsup/ketchup* and *dwelling/abode*—where in each case a speaker can understand both expressions without realizing that they are synonymous.[13] Another reason that contentious semantic assumptions are not necessary is that what generates problems for Stalnaker's model are not so much **semantic** facts about the sentences involved, as **cognitive** facts about speakers who use them. When an agent looks directly at the paperweight on my desk, and sincerely utters *That* [pointing at the paperweight] *is the paperweight I am talking about*, he is correctly described as believing, of the paperweight, that he is talking about it—where the proposition believed is that expressed by *x is the paperweight I am talking about*, relative to an assignment of the object itself to 'x'. It is believing this proposition that creates trouble for the model, whether or not we identify it with the semantic content of the sentence uttered. Similar points hold for examples in which the sentence uttered contains a proper name or natural kind term, understood by speakers and hearers. In all these cases, the propositions that prove problematic for the model are clearly among those that conversational participants come to believe and assume at later stages of the conversation. Since these assumptions determine the context set for later utterances, the only hope for saving

---

[12] This is, in my view, one of the chief lessons of Saul Kripke, "A Puzzle about Belief," in A. Margalit (ed.), *Meaning and Use* (Dordrecht: Reidel, 1979).

[13] See Nathan Salmon, "A Millian Heir Rejects the Wages of Sinn," and Stephen Rieber, "Understanding Synonyms without Knowing That They Are Synonymous."

the model is to exclude all beliefs of this sort from playing this role. However, this is unacceptable. First, there is no independent motivation for such an exclusion, and second, if I am right, so much would have to be excluded that the model would be eviscerated. For these reasons, I conclude that there is no reasonable prospect for saving it.

Remember, this conclusion comes on top of the failure of Stalnaker's initial model to account for the example involving my paperweight, and after our improvement of it by expanding the model to allow for metaphysically impossible, but epistemically possible, world-states (which cannot be known apriori not to obtain). In light of this double failure, it seems clear that Stalnaker's two-dimensionalist model of discourse cannot successfully explain Kripkean examples of the necessary aposteriori. Since giving such an explanation is an important part of the two-dimensionalist program to revive descriptivism, we must look elsewhere for different ways of implementing that program.

CHAPTER 6

THE EARLY TWO-DIMENSIONALIST
SEMANTICS OF DAVIES AND HUMBERSTONE

The hallmark of ambitious two-dimensionalism, as it has come to be known in recent years, is the attempt to use the two dimensions of semantic assessment in modern, post-Kaplanean semantic theories—contexts of utterance (in which sentences express propositions) vs. circumstances of evaluation (in which the propositions are evaluated)—and the two dimensions of semantic value—character vs. content—to give analyses of names and natural kind terms as rigidified descriptions, with the aim of reproducing Kripke's characterization of examples of the necessary aposteriori and the contingent apriori, while draining those categories of any content incompatible with certain philosophical commitments of yesteryear—including the restriction of the epistemically possible to the metaphysically possible. Although in the previous chapter we saw some of this in Stalnaker, we didn't see it all. On the one hand, he made heavy use of the distinction between context and circumstance of evaluation, his propositional concepts were closely related to Kaplan's characters, his deflationary treatments of the necessary aposteriori and the contingent apriori were designed to explain them away in accord with certain antecedent philosophical commitments, and his strategy for doing this was to associate utterances of sentences that are instances of these categories with two different objects of evaluation, one of which was meant to explain their characterization as necessary or contingent, and the other of which was meant to explain their characterization as apriori or aposteriori. On the other hand, the system he proposed was **not** a semantic theory (specifying the meanings of sentences, and semantic information they encode relative to contexts), but a pragmatic theory of the propositions asserted by utterances of sentences in conversations. Thus, Stalnaker did not claim that names and natural kind terms should be analyzed semantically as rigidified descriptions.

Martin Davies and Lloyd Humberstone take a different tack in their classic paper, "Two Notions of Necessity," which provides a formal, two-dimensional semantic theory in the service of the philosophical

program of deflating the contingent apriori and the necessary aposteriori.[1] Their paper was highly influential in the later development of
ambitious two-dimensionalism, and its chief contribution was to explicitly link this deflationary philosophical program with a specific and
reasonably well-understood semantic framework.

The Two-Dimensional Semantic System

In the paper, Davies and Humberstone articulate a formal semantics
for a simple language—a modal version of the propositional calculus
with a normal necessity operator, an actuality operator, and a new operator that takes one outside the usual modal model in a certain way.
Such models are triples—consisting of a set W of world-states (called
"worlds"), a designated actual world-state @, and a valuation function
that assigns intensions (functions from world-states to extensions) to
the nonlogical vocabulary. The basic operators are 'necessarily', 'A',
and 'F'.

> *Necessarily S* is true in a model M w.r.t. w iff S is true in M w.r.t.
> all world-states in W.
> *AS* is true in M w.r.t. w iff S is true in M w.r.t. @.
> *FS* is true in M w.r.t. w iff for all models M' that differ from M at
> most regarding which world-state @' is designated as "actual," S
> is true in M' w.r.t. w.

The operator 'A' is commonly called *the actuality operator*, while 'F' is
called *the fixedly operator*. A further operator, *FA*, often called *the
fixedly actual operator*, is definable in terms of these two.

> *FAS* is true in M w.r.t. w iff for all models M' that differ from M
> at most regarding which world-state @' is designated as "actual,"
> S is true in M' w.r.t. @'.

This is the most interesting operator in their system. They give their
interpretation of it, in words that echo through decades of later two-
dimensionalist writing, by remarking: "*FAα* says: whichever world
[-state] had been actual, α would have been true at that world[-state]
considered as actual."[2] Unfortunately, this formulation is not very edi-

[1] Martin Davies and Lloyd Humberstone, "Two Notions of Necessity," *Philosophical
Studies* 38 (1980): 1–30.
[2] Ibid., p. 3.

fying, since it is not altogether clear, nor was it ever satisfactorily explained, what it means to "consider a possible world[-state] as actual."

There is, I think, a serious problem with this terminology, which we might as well get out of the way. We know that the adverb *actually* is standardly treated as a rigidifier. If we treat the adjective *actual* as merely a grammatical variant of *actually*—on analogy with the way in which *me* is a grammatical variant of *I*—then just as there is and could be only one me, even though everyone can correctly **call** himself or herself *me*, so there is only one possible world-state that either is, or could be, the actual world-state, even though for any world-state, had it obtained, agents could have corrected **called** it "actual." (Think of *the actual world-state* as short for *the world-state that actually obtains.*) Of course, using the word in this way, we can't make sense of Davies and Humberstone's statement that the sentence *FAS* says that whichever world-state had been actual—i.e., whichever world-state had been this very world-state (the one that actually obtains)—S would have been true at that world-state, considered as actual—i.e., considered as this very world-state. That makes no coherent sense, and is **not** what they intend.

Here is a different way of understanding what they might mean. Think of possible world-states as maximal properties that the world—i.e., the universe—could have instantiated. The actual world-state is the one that is instantiated. The other world-states are not instantiated, but could have been. (*Could* is taken as primitive and world-state talk is correlated with some, but not necessarily all, *could* talk.) So perhaps *considering a world-state as actual* can be understood as *considering a world-state as being instantiated.* If this is right, then when Davies and Humberstone tell us

> *FAS says: whichever world[-state] had been actual, S would have been true at that world[-state] considered as actual*

they are telling us something that starts out as follows:

> *FAS* says: whichever maximal property of the world had been instantiated (i.e., whichever way the world had been), S would have been true. . . .

But now we are left with the task of completing the paraphrase by translating the phrase *at that world[-state] considered as actual.* It is not clear how to do that. If we simply treat the phrase as adding nothing, and leave it out of our translation, we won't get Davies and Humberstone's interpretation of *FAS* right—because what we have so far wrongly assimilates it to *Necessarily S*. We get the same result if we simply complete the paraphrase in a way that parallels our translation of the first part of their remark—translating *S would have been true at that world considered as actual* as *S would have been true had that property been instantiated*, or as *S would have been true had the world been that way*. Completing the translation from two-dimensionalese into something comprehensible in these ways doesn't change the meaning of what we already had, since, on these translations, the final phrase is redundant—with the result that *FAS* is, again, wrongly assimilated to *Necessarily S*. So we still haven't gotten an acceptable paraphrase of Davies and Humberstone's informal explanation of their most important formal operator.

Fortunately, there is a better way of interpreting what it means to *consider a world[-state] as actual* that makes good sense of their system, and the uses to which they wish to put it. On this interpretation, to consider a world-state as actual is to consider its role as a possible context of utterance, in the sense of a perspective from which sentences are taken to express propositions. On this interpretation, for a sentence to be true at a world-state "considered as actual" is for the sentence to express a proposition with respect to that world-state which is true when evaluated at that world-state. **Roughly put, then, what *FAS* "says" is that S (understood as carrying the meaning it actually has) would express a truth in any context of utterance, no matter what the world-state of the context.** This, I believe, is the correct way of understanding what Davies and Humberstone have in mind. To understand them in this way is to understand their actuality operator as being the same as Kaplan's, and as being similar to his temporal indexical *Now*. Given this, their "fixedly operator" is, as we shall see, an operator on the analogs of Kaplan-style characters.[3]

If I am right about this, then we can use David Kaplan's distinction

---

[3] Despite the fact that this is the correct interpretation of the Davies-Humberstone system, it is **not** the way that they understand themselves. In the last paragraph of section 2 of their paper they cite a discussion by Evans of certain real asymmetries between time and modality in his article "Does Tense Logic Rest on a Mistake?" They indicate that, on the basis of these asymmetries, they, following him, do **not** count the actual world-state in their system as a context, and hence they do **not** count their actuality operator as an indexical. I take this to be a serious mistake on their part. Moreover, without this way of understanding their semantics, they have no clear interpretation to offer. In my opinion, Davies and Humberstone are led astray by an important error in Evan's paper. For a brief discussion of that error see pp. 150–53 of my review of Evans's *Collected Papers* in *Journal of Philosophy*, 86 (1989): 141–56.

between character and content to explain what is going on in the Davies-Humberstone formal system. Given a model, we consider the family of all models that differ from it at most in what world-state is designated as *actual*. This family of models corresponds to what Kaplan would call a single *model structure*. For each sentence S we define a function f_{CS} that assigns to each model M in the family the set of possible world-states in M at which S is true. This function corresponds to Kaplan's notion of the character of S (relative to a single model structure). The set of world-states assigned by the function to a model is the content of S at that model; so character is a function from models to contents. Since models differ from one another **only** in which world-state is designated as *actual*, and since to designate a world-state as *actual* is to treat it as a context of utterance, one can think of the character of the sentence as a function from different world-states, functioning as possible contexts of utterance, to the contents (i.e. propositions) expressed by the sentence relative to those contexts.

Given that the only indexical operator in the Davies and Humberstone formal language is the actuality operator, we know that the contents of sentences without it will not vary from model to model, and their characters will be constant functions. These sentences express the same propositions in all contexts/models (in the specified family of models). By contrast, many sentences containing the actuality operator will express different propositions with respect to different contexts/models. For example, let M be a model with designated actual world-state @, and let S be a sentence that is true at @ with respect to M, but which is false at some other world-states of M. Then *AS* will be true at every world-state with respect to M, and the character of *AS* will assign to each model M* the set of all world-states in M* (the necessary proposition) if S expresses a truth at the designated actual world-state @* of M*, and it will assign the empty set of world-states (the inconsistent proposition) to M* if S is false at @* in M*. By the same token, *FAS* will be true at an arbitrary model and world-state iff S is true at the designated actual world-state in every model. If we think of *FA* as itself being a single operator, then it is an operator on the characters of sentences; it assigns truth to the character of its argument S iff that character expresses a truth in every context—i.e., in the designated actual world-state of every model. Thus, we can think of *FAS* as "saying" that a certain character—the one which is the meaning of S—expresses a truth in every context. This claim will always be either necessarily true or necessarily false.

Applying the System to the Contingent Apriori

What is philosophically interesting about the Davies and Humberstone system is their use of the difference between *FA* and *necessarily* to capture Gareth Evans's distinction between what he called (somewhat tendentiously) *deep necessity* and *superficial necessity*. His idea was that sentences are associated with two different semantic values—one which is the argument to modal operators and predicates, and the other which is the argument to epistemic operators and predicates, as well as that which is asserted by utterances of sentences. **Superficial** necessity is what is reported by modal sentences like *It is a necessary truth that S*, whereas **deep** necessity is reported not by modal sentences at all, but by sentences that characterize something as knowable apriori. Evans used these ideas in "Reference and Contingency" in arguing for an early version of the strong two-dimensionalist thesis that no single thing is really both contingent and knowable apriori.[4] For him, what are **called** instances of the contingent apriori are **sentences** that are superficially contingent, yet deeply necessary—i.e., sentences one of the semantic values of which—the superficial one—is properly deemed contingent, while its other semantic value—the deep one—is properly deemed necessary apriori. Evans's distinctions are translated into the Davies and Humberstone system as follows.[5]

A true sentence S is superficially contingent iff *Necessarily S is false.*

A true sentence S is deeply contingent iff *FA S* is false.

S is superficially necessary iff *Necessarily S* is true.

S is deeply necessary iff *FA S* is true.

Davies and Humberstone support Evans's contentions (i) that all examples of the contingent apriori are sentences that are superficially

[4] Gareth Evans, "Reference and Contingency," reprinted in his *Collected Papers*. For criticism, see my review of this volume, cited in the previous footnote.
[5] These definitions are those of Davies and Humberstone; see "Two Notions of Necessity," p. 9.

contingent, but deeply necessary, and (ii) that this provides an explanation of their status as contingent, yet knowable apriori. However, it is less than fully clear from their discussion what, precisely, the explanation mentioned in (ii) is supposed to be. How is it, exactly, that *It is a necessary truth that S* may be false when *It is knowable apriori that S* is true? Since Davies and Humberstone do not provide a formal treatment of any epistemic operators, we need to supplement their account with explicit semantics for *it is knowable apriori that__* in order to answer this question. After doing this, we will look carefully at selected passages of their text to see if this is a reasonable interpretation of what they really had in mind.

We have already seen that *FA* is an operator on Kaplan-style characters, that *FAS* is true iff the character of S expresses a truth at every context, and that the proposition expressed by *FAS* can be taken to say that for every context C, the character of S assigns to C a proposition true at C. The obvious two-dimensionalist hypothesis to be investigated is that S is apriori iff *FAS* is true. Let us suppose, for the moment, that this hypothesis is correct. How, then, should we think about the epistemic operator, *it is knowable apriori that___*? Although Davies and Humberstone don't say, a natural way to extend their explicit remarks would be to characterize it as also operating on the character of its complement sentence—even as being synonymous with *FA*. It may be objected that this can't be so, since we understand the epistemic operator on the basis of understanding the two-place predicates *__knows apriori__* and *___ knows___*. Surely, the second arguments of these predicates must be propositions, rather than characters, since the things that are known are true, and propositions are bearers of truth. However, there is less to this objection than meets the eye. Although characters are not themselves straightforwardly true or false, relative to world-states, they do expresses propositions that are true or false, relative to contexts, which in the Davies-Humberstone system are simply world-states. So, a character could be characterized as true at a world-state iff the proposition it expresses at that world-state is true at that world-state.

Alternatively, for each character, we can associate it with the proposition that it expresses a truth. This proposition will be true at a world-state iff the character is true at the world-state in the sense just indicated. (In the Davies-Humberstone formal system, this proposition will be the set of those world-states w that are members of the set of world-states that the character assigns to w.) Suppose, now, that we take this proposition to be both the object of the attitude verb *know*, and the object on which *it is knowable apriori that* operates. On this account, S will be an example of the apriori iff this proposition is knowable apriori—in effect, iff the character of S is such that it is knowable apriori that it expresses a truth. When will that be so? Well, when *FAS* is true, the character of S expresses a truth in every possible context, and the proposition p which says of this character that it expresses a truth will be a necessary truth. Suppose, further, it is assumed that this (somehow) guarantees that p is knowable apriori—perhaps because one identifies propositions with sets of world-states, in which case the unique necessary proposition must be knowable apriori. Then, of course, S will be an example of the apriori.

We can now give a tidy two-dimensionalist explanation of the contingent apriori. For any sentence S, the *primary intension* of S is the proposition that its character expresses a truth—i.e., the set of contexts/world-states C to which the character of S assigns a proposition that is true at C. The proposition expressed by S in C is the *secondary intension* of S in C. Although the primary and secondary intensions of some sentences will be the same, in many cases in which S contains the actuality operator, they will be different. *It is a necessary truth that S* is true in C iff the secondary intension of S in C is true at all possible world-states; *It is knowable apriori that S* is true in C iff the primary intension of S is knowable apriori. Davies and Humberstone suggest that in every genuine case of the contingent apriori, the two intensions/propositions are different. For example, sentence (1a)—which is simply a repetition of sentence (1) of chapter 3—is a case of the contingent apriori, since its secondary intension is contingent, while its primary intension—which is also the secondary intension of (1b)—is both necessary and apriori.

1a. If there is a unique F, then the x: actually Fx = the x: Fx.

  b. If there is a unique F, then the x: Fx = the x: Fx.

There is no puzzle about how any one proposition can be both contingent and apriori, since none is.

Interpreting Davies and Humberstone

The explanation just given of the contingent apriori status of (1a) is identical with the **strong** two-dimensionalist explanation of it given in chapter 3. Although this is a natural way of extending Davies and Humberstone's use of their semantic system to support Evans's philosophical approach to the contingent apriori, it is not the only possible extension. A good deal of what they say could be preserved by a weak two-dimensionalist interpretation as well—in which *knows (apriori)* operates on the secondary intensions of, or propositions expressed by, its sentential complements, but the explanation of how those intensions/propositions are known appeals to an agent's justifiably accepting the relevant primary intensions/propositions (as spelled out in chapter 3). Thus, it is important to look more closely at the text to see which, if either, of these interpretations makes the most sense of their remarks. As we shall see, the resulting picture is less than fully definitive, indicating that Davies and Humberstone should not be seen as advocating any single, unified treatment of the contingent apriori and the necessary aposteriori, but as exploring a range of what they took to be promising two-dimensionalist ideas.

One factor indicating their sympathy with strong two-dimensionalism has already been mentioned. Davies and Humberstone see themselves as supporting Gareth Evans's approach to the contingent apriori, which was strong two-dimensionalist in the sense of taking what is contingent in these cases to be one semantic value associated with a sentence while taking what is apriori to be a different semantic value. Since Davies and Humberstone give an elegant account of what these two semantic values are, while claiming to vindicate Evans's approach to the contingent apriori, it is natural to read them as suggesting strong (rather than weak) two-dimensionalism.

The second factor suggesting strong two-dimensionalism is that their formal system doesn't make available any semantic values to serve as contents of sentences that are more fine-grained than sets of possible world-states. If they really intend to identify what sentences are used to assert, and what one knows apriori or aposteriori, with sets of world-states—as opposed to using the formal system as a convenient fiction in the way that Kaplan does—then, since there is only one necessary truth, which is obviously knowable apriori, (i) there is, in general, no need for any further explanation of why, in different cases, the fact that the primary intension of a sentence is necessary should be thought sufficient to explain why it is knowable apriori, and (ii) there simply can't be any necessary truth that is knowable only aposteriori—as would be required under weak two-dimensionalism. Since, as we shall see in a moment, Davies and Humberstone do accept the necessary aposteriori, this would mean that they could invoke only a strong two-dimensionalist explanation of it.

At this point, however, it is important to qualify these remarks. Although Davies and Humberstone lean strongly toward the view that every instance of the apriori is a sentence the primary intension of which is necessary, they remain cautiously agnostic about whether every sentence with such a primary intension is a genuine instance of the apriori. For example, unlike virtually all later ambitious two-dimensionalists, they assume that ordinary proper names (unlike special "descriptive names") are **not** to be analyzed as rigidified descriptions. Because of this, they take true identity sentences involving such names to be "deeply" as well as "superficially" necessary (and hence to have primary intensions which are necessary truths). Nevertheless, they are agnostic about whether or not such sentences should be classified as apriori.[6] They couldn't be agnostic about this if they were definitely advocating either a view of propositions as sets of possible world-states, or the strong two-dimensionalist thesis that there are no propositions that are both necessary and knowable only aposteriori.[7] In fact, it is hard to see how they could be agnostic about such identities while definitely advocating the weak two-dimensionalist thesis that the explanation of every example S of the necessary aposteriori involves the fact that knowing the secondary intension of S requires justifiably accepting some "deeply contingent character" that expresses it (typically the character of S itself).[8] In light of this, Davies and Humberstone cannot be seen as advocating any systematically descriptive thesis about names, or any unified treatment of all examples of the contingent apriori and the necessary aposteriori. Rather, their own relatively cautious exploration of the possibility of using two-dimensionalist semantic ideas to explain **some** instances of the contingent apriori and the necessary aposteriori provided the basis for the later development of more systematic versions of ambitious two-dimensionalism.

---

[6] Ibid., p. 10.

[7] Assuming, of course, that S is correctly classified as apriori iff *It is knowable apriori that S* is true, where *it is knowable apriori that* operates on either the primary or the secondary intension (or both) of S.

[8] Call a character "deeply contingent" iff the proposition it assigns to some (but not every) context is false at that context—in effect, iff any sentence with that character would be "deeply contingent" and so have a contingent primary intension.

Discussion of a Famous Case

Next we turn to their explicit discussion of Evans's most famous example of the contingent apriori.

S. If anyone uniquely invented the zip [zipper], Julius invented the zip.

In Evans's example, *Julius* is taken to be a "descriptive name" introduced by the stipulation that it is to rigidly designate the inventor of the zip (in a situation in which one does not know, of any particular person p, that it was p who invented the zip). According to Evans, S is contingent, since *Julius* rigidly designates someone who, though he invented the zip, could have existed even if someone else had done so instead. Nevertheless, Evans takes S to be knowable apriori, since knowing it involves nothing more than knowing S'.

S'. If anyone uniquely invented the zip, the inventor of the zip invented the zip.

Here is how Davies and Humberstone frame the issue.

The sentence (S) is true, but the □-modalization of (S) is false. So (S) is a (superficially) contingent truth. On the other hand, to understand (S) is merely to understand that it states that if anyone uniquely invented the zip, then whoever invented the zip did. So the statement expressed by (S) is knowable *a priori*. One way of putting the puzzle, then, is this. An outright assertion using (S) intuitively has the same content as an assertion using (S'). Yet (S) and (S') embed differently in □-contexts: (□S) is false while (□S') is true.[9]

The view here seems to be (a) that sentences S and S' are such that utterances of them assert the same apriori truth, (b) that for each sentence, understanding it amounts to understanding that it "states" this proposition, but (c) that one of the sentences is properly regarded as contingent and the other as necessary, since the modal ascription *Necessarily S* is false whereas the ascription *Necessarily S'* is true—in which case, the modal operator cannot be operating on the apriori truth associated with both sentences. How can this be? The answer (for Evans) is supposed to be that, in general, sentences bear **two** se-

[9] Davies and Humberstone, "Two Notions of Necessity," p. 8.

mantic values—one relevant to occurrences of the sentence in modal ascriptions, and the other which gives the assertive content of the sentence, and is relevant to occurrences of the sentence under propositional attitude verbs, like *is knowable apriori*. Supposedly, S and S' agree on that latter value while disagreeing on the former value. Hence, Evans's treatment of this example, as seen by Davies and Humberstone, is strong two-dimensionalist.

Davies and Humberstone continue their discussion of S and S' as follows:

> Evans' solution to this puzzle is best seen if one employs possible worlds terminology with a fixed actual world w* (the *actual* actual world) playing the role of the actual world throughout. Associated with (S) is the property:
>
> λw (if anyone uniquely invented the zip in w then whoever invented the zip in w* invented the zip in w).
>
> The actual world w* has this property, but some other worlds lack it. Associated with (S') is the following property, which no world lacks:
>
> λw (if anyone uniquely invented the zip in w then whoever invented the zip in w invented the zip in w).
>
> This is why (S) and (S') embed differently in □-contexts. **On the other hand, an outright assertion of either (S) or (S') in the actual world has the force of an assertion that w* has the associated property, and λ-conversion reveals that these two assertive contents are precisely the same. . . .** Evans' solution to the puzzle strikes us as both elegant and convincing.[10]

The "elegant and convincing" view expressed here seems to involve the claim that assertive utterances of S and S' have the same content, and so make the same assertion, where the proposition asserted is taken to be about the actual world-state w*. Presumably, this proposition—which constitutes the common assertive content of the two sentences—is the semantic value on which the sentences agree (their primary intension), whereas the semantic values on which they differ are their secondary intensions.

What should we think about this view? As I see it, there is something importantly right about it, but also something seriously wrong.

---

[10] Ibid., pp. 8–9 (my emphasis).

Moreover, what is right and important for explaining the contingent apriori has nothing essential to do with ambitious two-dimensionalism. In spelling this out, I will follow Davies and Humberstone in treating *Julius* as synonymous with *the actual inventor of the zip*, and S as synonymous with S_A.[11] Hence, everything said about S may be understood as applying to S_A (as well).

> S_A. If anyone uniquely invented the zip, the actual inventor of the zip invented the zip.

The problems with the view sketched by Davies and Humberstone lie in the claims that the "assertive contents" of S and S′ are the same, that this assertive content is what must be understood in order to understand the sentences, and hence, that this content is one of their semantic values. Why should we accept these claims? A natural way to reconstruct the implicit argument that the assertive contents of these sentences are the same is as follows.

(i) An assertive utterance of S in w* results in the assertion of the proposition expressed by (a) *λw (if anyone uniquely invented the zip in w, then whoever invented the zip in w* invented the zip in w) w**.

(ii) An assertive utterance of S′ in w* results in the assertion of the proposition expressed by (b) *λw (if anyone uniquely invented the zip in w, then whoever invented the zip in w invented the zip in w) w**.

(iii) Since (a) and (b) are related by λ-conversion, the contents asserted are the same (even though the properties involved are different).

(iv) Hence the "assertive contents" of S and S′ "are precisely the same."

This argument is fraught with difficulties. One worry is that although (a) and (b) are indeed related by λ-conversion, and so are necessarily equivalent, it does **not** follow from this that they have the same content, and so express the very same proposition—unless it is assumed that contents/propositions are sets of possible world-states. Although Davies and Humberstone might here be implicitly relying on this as-

---

[11] I do this for the sake of argument only. My own view, explained in chapter 16 of *The Age of Meaning*, is that genuine names cannot be introduced in the manner indicated by Evans.

sumption, as noted earlier they do not, in the end, definitively endorse it. Moreover, if one doesn't identify propositions with sets of world-states, then one is forced to articulate a different conception of propositions and to show that, on this conception, the propositions expressed by (a) and (b) do count as identical. Although I will not pause over this, the problem should not be assumed to be trivial, since there is considerable intuitive support for the hypothesis that at least **some** sentences related by λ-conversion express **different** propositions.[12]

The second problem with the argument is that there is little reason to suppose that assertive utterances of S and S′ invariably result in the assertion of the propositions expressed by (a) and (b). These propositions are special in that they attribute properties to the actual world-state w*—in the case of S′, the property attributed to w* is, in effect, the property of being a world-state with respect to which it is true that if anyone uniquely invented the zip, then the inventor of the zip invented the zip, whereas in the case of S (or S_A) it is the property of being a world-state with respect to which it is true that if anyone uniquely invented the zip, the inventor of the zip in w* invented the zip. Why is it assumed that **these** propositions are asserted? Not all propositions predicate properties of world-states, and surely, those that are not about world-states can be asserted too. As far as I can tell, the view that assertive utterances of S (or S_A) and S′ result in the assertion of the world-state–specific propositions (a) and (b) can be defended only if it can be defended that an assertive utterance of any sentence P in a world-state w results in the assertion that w has the property φ expressed by $\lambda w(Pw)$—an assertion tantamount to the assertion that w is a world-state with respect to which the proposition p expressed by P is true. But this is highly dubious, since it has the seemingly absurd consequence that whenever one asserts **any** true proposition p in world-state w, one also asserts the **necessary truth** that w is a world-state with respect to which p is true, as well as the consequence that whenever anyone asserts anything false one also asserts a **necessary falsehood**.[13] Surely, one is inclined to object, **sometimes** our as-

[12] See p. 144 of my review of Evans's *Collected Papers*, also my "Pronouns and Propositional Attitudes," *Proceedings of the Aristotelian Society*, vol. 90, part 3, 1989/90, 191–212; and my "Attitudes and Anaphora, *Philosophical Perspectives* 8: *Logic and Language* (1994): 251–72.

[13] Not only is this result counterintuitive, it is one that anyone who both (i) identifies propositions with sets of possible world-states and (ii) recognizes that asserting that expressed by *P & Q* involves asserting that expressed by Q cannot accept—since together (i) and (ii) entail that anyone who has asserted a necessary falsehood has asserted every proposition. Surely, however, no one would claim that anyone who has asserted an ordinary falsehood has asserted every proposition.

sertions are merely contingent—and if they are sometimes contingent, then presumably normal assertive utterances of S (or S_A) are sometimes merely contingent, even though normal assertive utterances of S′ always involve the assertion of a necessary truth. If this is right, then the claims made by (i) and (ii) about the propositions asserted by utterances of S (or S_A) and S′ cannot be accepted.[14] For these reasons, the "elegant and convincing" two-dimensionalist solution to Evans's puzzle embraced by Davies and Humberstone seems quite dubious.

Nevertheless, as I mentioned a moment ago, Evans was on to something right and important for explaining examples of the contingent apriori like S_A. However, the important principles one needs are those that validate certain inferences, rather than principles about assertive content. These principles are illustrated in the following derivation, which we will illustrate by going through it step by step.[15]

2. (i) P iff P

   (ii) So, $\lambda w[(P \text{ iff } P) w] @$

   (iii) So, $\lambda w[P(w) \text{ iff } P(w)] @$

   (iv) So, $\lambda w[P(w) \text{ iff } P(@)] @$

   (v) So, $\lambda w[(P \text{ iff } P@) w] @$

   (vi) So, P iff P@

   (vii) So, P iff actually P

The argument begins with the obvious apriori truth stated in (i). The aim is to show is that anyone who knows this truth is in a position

[14] Even if those claims were accepted, it would still be a long step to the conclusion, (iv), that S (S_A) and S′ have the same "assertive content"—where this is taken to mean that there is some one proposition which is both asserted by utterances of these sentences, and one of their fundamental semantic values. The mechanism responsible for the assertion of world-state-specific propositions of the sort illustrated by (a) and (b) must surely be substantially pragmatic—opening up the likelihood that in some cases it may yield equivalent assertive outcomes from nonequivalent semantic inputs.

[15] I use '@' to designate that actual state of the world, and I use 'w' as a variable over world-states. When S is any sentence, I use *S@* to express the claim that attributes the property of being true with respect to the actual world-state to the proposition that S expresses, and I use the formula *S(w)* to express the claim that that proposition is true with respect to the world-state which is the value of 'w'. Where ... v ... is any formula containing one or more free occurrences of the variable v, $\lambda v[... v ...]$ is a predicate expressing a property that is true of an object o iff ... v ... is true of o relative to an assignment of o to 'v'. The explanation of argument (2) given here replaces the flawed explanation given in chapter 16 of *The Age of Meaning*.

to derive the conclusion (vii) from it by steps that one can determine, apriori, to be truth-preserving. Then since (vii) is an apriori consequence of (i), which is knowable apriori, (vii) is also knowable apriori, despite the fact that it is contingent (when 'P' is replaced by a contingent truth). If this is right—and if, as I will show, the argument doesn't depend on any version of two-dimensionalism beyond Kaplan's benign two-dimensionalism (which recognizes *actually* as an indexical operator that directly refers to the world-state of the context)—then the contingent apriori status of **P iff actually P** can be explained without positing one proposition semantically associated with it that is relevant to its modal status, and another that is relevant to its epistemic status and "assertive content." The same sort of non-two-dimensional explanation can be given of why Evans's examples S and S_A are knowable apriori, despite the fact that they are contingent.

The step from (i) to (ii) is based on the principle that for any proposition p, if in world-state w, an agent a knows p, then a (who is, by hypothesis, acquainted with w) needs no further evidence to be able to conclude, or come to know, of w, that it has the property of being a world-state with respect to which p is true. So, when @ is the state that the world is actually in, our apriori knowledge of the proposition expressed by (i) is sufficient to enable us to come to know of @ that it has the property of being a world-state with respect to which that proposition is true. This is the (apriori) knowledge expressed by (ii). But if we know, of @, that it has the property of making a biconditional proposition true, then we need no further evidence to be able to conclude, or come to know, of @, that it has the property of making one side of the biconditional true iff it makes the other side true. This is the (apriori) knowledge expressed by (iii). Next comes the move to (iv), which is the key step in the argument. Consider an analogy. Suppose that m has the property that any man has just in case he loves Anna iff he loves Betty—i.e., $\lambda x[Lxa$ iff $Lxb]$ m. It is an apriori consequence of this that m also has the property that any man has just in case he loves Anna iff m loves Betty—i.e., $\lambda x[Lxa$ iff $Lmb]$ m. Similarly, (iii) tells us that @ has the property that any world-state has just in case a certain proposition p (expressed in the derivation by 'P') is true with respect to that world-state iff p is true with respect to that world-state—i.e., $\lambda w[P(w)$ iff $P(w)]$ @. It is an apriori consequence of this that @ also has the property that any world-state has just in case p is true with respect to that world-state iff p is true with respect to @— i.e., $\lambda w[P(w)$ iff $P(@)]$ @. Thus, the knowledge expressed by (iv) is apriori. The move to step (v) is just the mirror image of the move to step (iii), and can be known apriori to be truth-preserving for the same reason. The next step, to (vi), is also sound, but it is a little tricky.

One might think that one could appeal to the principle that, for any proposition p and world-state w, if in w an agent a can know of w that p is true with respect to it on the basis of evidence e (or on the basis of no empirical evidence at all), then a can know p on the basis of e (or on the basis of no empirical evidence at all). But this is, arguably, not so, as is indicated by the following case.[16] Suppose one describes a possible world-state w to oneself in some detail, and concludes, correctly, just by contemplating w, that it is a possible world-state with respect to which a certain proposition q is true. It would seem that this might well count as knowledge, of w, that p is true with respect to it. Let us suppose that it does. Suppose further that w is, in fact, the actual world-state—the world-state in which one is doing the relevant describing and thinking—but that one doesn't realize that the world-state one has been describing and thinking about is the state that the world is actually in. In such a case, one might know (apriori), of the actual world-state @, that q is true with respect to it, without believing q, and without having any justification for believing q. If this is right, then one can't use the principle just stated to get from (v) to (vi).

Nevertheless, the move can be made. In the scenario relevant to the derivation, the agent starts at (i) with apriori knowledge of a certain proposition, and moves at (ii) to knowledge, of the actual world-state, that it is one with respect to which the proposition in question is true—where this is knowledge that he can express using the demonstrative *this world-state*, with the understanding that it refers to the state the world really is in (which he directly experiences). Throughout the entire derivation, where we use '@' the agent can use *this world-state* with that understanding. If he does this, then all the argumentative moves, including the move from (v) to (vi), will be transparent. In particular, his knowledge at (v) will be knowledge, of @, that it is a state which is both the one that the world really is in and one with respect to which a certain proposition p is true. From this he can conclude, without further evidence, that p is true. Since his knowledge at (v) is apriori, his knowledge of p at step (vi) is too. Given that (vii) expresses the same proposition as (vi), we have shown that (vii) is apriori, despite being contingent. Since nowhere have we had to appeal to

---

[16] This case is taken from fn. 20, p. 421 of *The Age of Meaning*.

principles of ambitious two-dimensionalism, we have done what we set out to do.

Remarks on the Necessary Aposteriori

Finally, I turn to what Davies and Humberstone have to say about the necessary aposteriori. They begin by focusing on examples involving so-called *descriptive names*. On their analysis, descriptive names, such as Evans's *Julius*, are synonymous with descriptions rigidified using the actuality operator.[17] *Julius* itself is synonymous with *the actual inventor of the zip,* or (more properly) *the x: actually x invented the zip.* By contrast, we let *Tom* be an ordinary nondescriptive name which refers to the same person as *Julius* does. Then (3a) is taken to be synonymous with (3b).

3a. Tom is Julius.

b. Tom is the actual inventor of the zip.

Since *Tom, Julius,* and *the actual inventor of the zip* are rigid designators, the proposition expressed by these sentences (their secondary intension) is necessary, and **It is a necessary truth that S** is true, when S is (3a) or (3b).[18] Nevertheless, **It is knowable apriori that S** is not true in these cases, since in order for that to be so we would have to be able to know apriori that Tom is the inventor of the zip, which is impossible. Hence, Davies and Humberstone take (3a) and (3b) to be examples of the necessary aposteriori, and their explanation of them is broadly compatible with either strong or weak two-dimensionalism.

However, the range of examples of the necessary aposteriori that can be explained in this way is quite limited. Here, it is instructive to quote a passage from their discussion. Note in particular the contrast drawn between "descriptive names" and ordinary "proper names."

> Consider again the descriptive name 'Julius' of the man who actually invented the zip, and the proper name 'Tom' of that same man. Then it is an *a posteriori* truth that Julius is Tom and yet 'Julius is Tom' is necessarily true since '□(Julius is Tom)' is (modulo problems of contingent existence) true. So **descriptive names** give rise to necessary *a*

[17] Davies and Humberstone, "Two Notions of Necessity," p. 11.

[18] For simplicity, I here put aside consideration of world-states at which Tom doesn't exist.

posteriori truths. But clearly there is more to be said. Certainly, 'Julius is Tom' is superficially necessary, and certainly that necessity is guaranteed by the fact that 'Julius is Tom' is an identity statement using names. But, equally clearly, 'Julius is Tom' is **deeply contingent**, and that contingency rests on the fact that while both names are in a sense rigid designators . . . **'Tom' does, while 'Julius' does not, retain its reference under changes in which world is considered as the actual world.**

These distinctions enable us to make sense of what might otherwise look like a disagreement over the modal status of 'Julius is Tom'. For one party might say, 'Julius, the man who actually invented the zip, could not have failed to be Tom even if he had failed to invent the zip', while the other urged that in an imagined counterfactual situation in which Tom did not invent the zip, the speakers of *our* language would speak truly were they to say: Julius is not Tom. **Apparent disagreement would be multiplied if some speakers came to know that Tom invented the zip and allowed this knowledge so to infect their use of 'Julius' that it too became a *proper* rather than a *descriptive* name of Tom.** For although these speakers would agree with the rest as to the truth-values of all sentences free of 'F' [the Davies and Humberstone "Fixedly" operator on characters], **they would judge that *in no sense* is 'Julius is Tom' contingent; in the imagined counterfactual situation, 'Julius' would have a different meaning from that which it has in *their* language.**[19]

There are two important points to notice here. First, the examples of the necessary aposteriori that Davies and Humberstone recognize and purport to explain all essentially involve either the actuality operator itself, or names which are taken to be synonymous with *actually*-rigidified descriptions. It is this descriptive analysis that allows them to view the primary and secondary intensions of these examples as being (modally) different propositions, thereby allowing a two-dimensionalist explanation to get off the ground. Second, Davies and Humberstone do **not** assimilate ordinary proper names to "descriptive names" like *Julius*. Instead, ordinary names are treated as vehicles for expressing *de re* knowledge of individuals one is acquainted with.[20] Moreover, they hypothesize that even if n starts out as a "descriptive name" des-

[19] Pages 17–18, my emphasis.
[20] See pp. 7–8.

ignating o, when speakers become acquainted with o, and come to know that o is the referent of n, this is likely to convert n into an ordinary nondescriptive name.[21]

This treatment of ordinary proper names as nondescriptive is profoundly **anti–two-dimensional** in the ambitious, programmatic sense that has grown up in the decades after their paper was published. In their system, sentences containing ordinary names, but no "descriptive names" or occurrences of the actuality operator, do **not** express different propositions with respect to different contexts. Hence, their primary intensions are indistinguishable from their secondary intensions, and no two-dimensionalist explanations of the necessary aposteriori involving such sentences can be given. Since most of Kripke's classical examples were of precisely this sort, the loophole left open by Davies and Humberstone for later ambitious two-dimensionalists to close was very large.

This raises an obvious question about natural kind terms. Are they to be treated on analogy with descriptive names or ordinary proper names? Here, Davies and Humberstone take a hesitant, somewhat ambivalent, step in the direction of what has become the ambitious two-dimensionalist program. They suggest that natural kind terms be understood on the model of "descriptive names," and analyzed as descriptions rigidified using the actuality operator. On this view, (4a) is synonymous with something along the lines of (4b).

4a. Water is H_2O.

  b. The actual chemical kind instances of which fall from clouds, flow in rivers, are drinkable, odorless, etc. is H_2O.

Sentence (4b) is true because the chemical kind in question has the molecular structure H_2O. It is taken to be necessary because the two terms are both rigid designators of the kind. But (4b) is supposed to be knowable only aposteriori, since in order for one to satisfy

5. x knows that the actual chemical kind instances of which fall from clouds, flow in rivers, are drinkable, odorless, etc. is H_2O.

it is supposed that one must know the primary intension of (4b) to be true, which is nothing other than the contingent, aposteriori proposition that is the secondary intension of (4c).

[21] See p. 20.

4c. The chemical kind instances of which fall from clouds, flow in rivers, are drinkable, odorless, etc. is H_2O.

Since (4a) is taken to be synonymous with (4b), all of this is supposed to carry over to (4a) itself. The suggestion is that all examples of the necessary aposteriori involving natural kind terms can be given similar two-dimensionalist explanations.

> [W]e suggest that at least some light may be cast on the semantics of natural kind words by seeing them as analogous to descriptive names, rather than proper names, of chemical, physical, or biological kinds. Thus, suppose that 'water' is a descriptive name with its reference fixed by the description 'the chemical kind to which that liquid belongs which falls from clouds, flows in rivers, is drinkable, colourless, odourless, . . .' so that with w_1 as the actual world [context of utterance] the reference of 'water' with respect to w_2 [circumstance of evaluation] is that chemical kind of stuff which *in w_1* falls from clouds. . . . **To understand 'water' it would not be necessary to know *which* chemical kind actually has those properties and so it would be an *a posteriori* discovery that water is H_2O;** what is more, this would have to be recognized as *a posteriori* even by those who hold that all true identities using proper names express *a priori* truths. The true identity statement 'Water is H_2O' would be deeply but not superficially contingent, **but for those among the chemically informed for whom 'water' had become another proper name of H_2O, 'Water is H_2O' would be contingent in no sense.**
>
> On the suggested view, one would hold 'that "water" was *world-relative* [indexical] but *constant* in meaning', and that in one sense, for worlds w_1 and w_2, 'water is H_2O in w_1 and water is XYZ in w_2', namely the sense which answers to the fact that 'Water is H_2O' is true$_{w1,w1}$ [i.e., the sentence expresses in w_1 a proposition true in w_1] and yet 'Water is XYZ' is true$_{w2,w2}$. Yet one would also hold that in a sense 'water is H_2O in all worlds (the stuff called 'water' in w_2 isn't water)', namely that sense which answers to the fact that for w^* as the actual world, 'Water is H_2O' is true$_{w^*,w}$ for all worlds w [the proposition expressed by the sentence in w^* is true at all worlds], and 'Water is XYZ' is false$_{w^*,w}$ for all worlds w.[22]

[22] Pages 18–19, my emphasis.

This is just the analysis of 'water' as an indexical, rigidified description, used as the basis of a descriptive, two-dimensionalist explanation of the necessary apriori status of (4a). I have, of course, already explained in chapter 4 why I don't think that natural kind terms like 'water' are descriptive in this way, and I have indicated what I take to be the proper explanation of their status as examples of the necessary aposteriori.[23] Here, I simply draw attention to three peculiarities in the passage that are worth noting. The first is the suggestion that many speakers who use the term 'water' may not know what kind it stands for, and may remain ignorant of this as long as they are ignorant about the molecular structure of water. The second is the suggestion that it is because these speakers don't know what kind 'water' stands for that their knowledge that water is H_2O is aposteriori. The third is the suggestion that for those who know what 'water' stands for, (4a) may be apriori. Davies and Humberstone do not, I think, definitively commit themselves to the truth of these suggestions, but they do seem to flirt with these ideas. This is significant, since—as we shall see in chapter 8—these suggestions were picked up by later two-dimensionalists, who enthusiastically embraced them.

These suggestions are, in my opinion, misguided. All of us knew which kind 'water' stood for—in the sense of knowing, of the kind water, that 'water' stood for it—long before we knew chemistry. One no more has to know the essential, molecular properties of water in order to know what 'water' stands for than one has to know my genetic code in order to know that 'Scott Soames' stands for me. Of course, if one (wrongly in my view) identifies propositions with sets of possible world-states, then one will take the proposition expressed by (4a)—its secondary intension—to be **the** trivial, apriori necessary truth, and one will be inclined to explain why the chemically ignorant don't accept (4a) by saying that they don't know which proposition it expresses—despite understanding its meaning—because they don't know what the disguised, rigidified description 'water' refers to. Similarly, on this account, the natural way to explain why

6. x doesn't know that water is H_2O.

is satisfied by many of the chemically ignorant is to adopt the **strong** two-dimensionalist view that what it reports not to be known is the **pri-**

---

mary, rather than the secondary, intension of its complement clause, (4a). In chapter 10, I will explain in detail why this view cannot be correct. For now, I simply note that the natural way in which this view arises from the passage just cited constitutes another respect in which Davies and Humberstone laid the groundwork for the later development of stronger, more systematic versions of ambitious two-dimensionalism.[24]

Davies and Humberstone finish up their discussion of (7a) with some honest and well-founded doubts.

> A final objection is more serious. Imagine that every speaker of the language containing 'Julius' had a visual confrontation with Tom and was told 'This man is Julius'. Then one expects that 'Julius' would become a proper name of Tom. This is not, of course, to say that for the identity statement 'This man is Julius' or even for 'This man is called "Julius"' to be *true*, 'Julius' must be a proper name, but only that, given the knowledge which each speaker would now have (knowledge *by acquaintance* of Julius) it would be natural for the semantic function of 'Julius' to change. **But now consider the fact that practically every speaker of our language has had a visual confrontation with (a sample of) the chemical kind H_2O and been told, 'This stuff (this chemical kind) is water (is called "water")'. Is it not unlikely that 'water' remains, in our language, a merely descriptive name of H_2O?** A reply to this objection will depend upon claiming that physical ostension of a sample of H_2O accompanied by the words 'This stuff' ('the chemical kind here exemplified') is similar not to physical ostension of a man accompanied by the words 'this man', but rather to physical ostension of a screen ac-

---

[24] Another (unfortunate) aspect of their discussion of (4a) that was picked up by later two-dimensionalists was their way of responding to the natural objection that their account of the descriptive content of 'water' was far too detailed and complex. Surely, speakers can understand the word without knowing all that. In response to this, Davies and Humberstone say, "we might modify the reference-fixing description by introducing a new word 'waterish' which is to be a (*quasi-*) *functional* word, rather than a real natural kind word: one can imagine speakers being trained with this word in the presence of stuff which fell from clouds, and so on, and then being introduced to the descriptive name 'water' via the reference-fixing description 'the chemical kind to which waterish stuff belongs' (pp. 19–20). This, it seems to me, is an artful but ineffective dodge. Either the alternative sketched is not really descriptive reference fixing at all, but simply an instance of the kind of nondescriptive, Kripkean ostensive explanation discussed in chapter 4—*Water is the substance (physical kind) of which those* [demonstrating some instances of water] *are samples*—or else it is genuinely descriptive, like the original Davies and Humberstone proposal, only made vague so as to avoid obvious counterexamples.

companied by 'the man behind this screen', or even physical os-
tension of a zip accompanied by 'the inventor of this device'.
**Since we do not know whether such a claim can be defended,
we are not confident that the suggested view is correct.**[25]

Thus, even where natural kind terms are involved, Davies and Humberstone were merely exploring, rather than definitely advocating, an
analysis in terms of rigidified descriptions. What they showed was that
if a certain descriptivist approach was taken, then certain avenues of
two-dimensionalist explanation of the necessary aposteriori and the
contingent apriori could be placed on the table.

The Legacy of "Two Notions of Necessity"

"Two Notions of Necessity" provided the semantic foundations for
later, more systematic developments of ambitious two-dimensionalism. Davies and Humberstone provided the sketch of an elegant semantic model incorporating Evans's suggestion that some sentences—
including paradigmatic examples of the contingent apriori—were
associated with two semantic values, one of which was responsible for
their contingency and the other of which was responsible for their
apriority. They extended this suggestion to important examples of the
necessary aposteriori, and made clear the role of analyses of names and
natural kind terms as rigidified descriptions in this explanatory strategy. However, they did not pursue the strategy to its logical conclusion, because they retained well-founded doubts about descriptive
analyses of many proper names and natural kind terms. Somehow
these doubts got lost in the decades to come, as later ambitious two-
dimensionalists swept them aside in search of a systematically descriptivist semantic theory, and a unified, all-encompassing two-dimensionalist account of the necessary aposteriori and the contingent apriori.
When these theorists did this, the Davies-Humberstone semantic
framework was ready and waiting for them. In the next chapter, we
will use this framework to explicitly formulate two precise and systematic versions of ambitious two-dimensionalism. In the following chapters, these semantic theories will serve as interpretive templates in
examining the most influential and philosophically far-reaching contemporary examples of ambitious two-dimensionalism.

[25] Page 20, my emphasis.

PART THREE

AMBITIOUS TWO-DIMENSIONALISM

CHAPTER 7

STRONG AND WEAK TWO-DIMENSIONALISM

Having explored the roots of ambitious two-dimensionalism, we now turn to the task of gathering together leading two-dimensionalist ideas, extending them, and blending them into a systematic program for reviving descriptivism, and explaining, or explaining away, the contingent apriori and the necessary aposteriori. As I indicated in chapter 3, there are two natural ways of doing this—one which I dubbed *strong two-dimensionalism* and the other, *weak two-dimensionalism*. Since strong two-dimensionalism is, I believe, the purest form of the view, we will begin with it.

Strong Two-Dimensionalism

The central tenet of strong two-dimensionalism introduces and defines the distinction between primary and secondary intension.

T1. Each sentence is semantically associated with a pair of semantic values—its primary intension, and its secondary intension. Its primary intension is a proposition which is true with respect to all and only those contexts C to which the Kaplan-style character of S assigns a proposition that is true at C. When contexts are identified with world-states, and propositions are taken to be sets of such states, the primary intension (proposition) associated with S is the set of world-states w which are such that the character of S assigns to w (considered as a context of utterance) a set of world-states (i.e., a proposition) that contains (i.e., is true at) w. The secondary intension of (or proposition expressed by) S at a context C is the proposition assigned by the character of S to C.

The key notion here is that of the primary intension of a sentence S. Although, in principle, one could identify it with the character of S, the standard practice has been to take it to be a proposition defined in terms of the character, as indicated above. Propositions themselves can be, and frequently are, treated as sets of world-states. However, although there are substantial reasons internal to strong two-dimensionalism for understanding propositions in this way, strong two-dimensionalism *per se* does not require this. What is required is a certain relationship between primary and secondary intension. For some sentences—not containing indexicals—the primary intension of S and the secondary intension of S (at C) are (for all intents and purposes) identical. However, when S contains indexicals, and the character of S is a nonconstant function, then for (at least) some contexts C, the secondary intension of S at C will differ from the primary intension of S. For such sentences, the primary intension of S is constant and invariant, whereas the secondary intension varies from context to context. Since this primary intension is supposed to be a proposition, it must make some claim. A natural way of thinking of this claim is to take it to be one which asserts, of the character of S, that it expresses a truth. Here, it is crucial not to confuse this claim with one that asserts, of the character of S, that it expresses a truth with respect to **some specified context**. In order for the primary intension to remain invariant from context to context, the claim it makes must **not** be relativized to context.

How is this possible? Since characters are functions that require contexts as arguments to express anything (as values for those arguments), one might wonder how it could make sense to claim simply that the character of S expresses a truth, without specifying any context whatsoever. The key to answering this question lies in the strong two-dimensionalist's identification of contexts with possible world-states. Given this identification, we take the property of expressing a truth to be a property that the character of S has at all and only those contexts/world-states w to which it assigns a proposition that is true with respect to w. This will work so long as being a world-state is all there is to being a context, or, to put it another way, so long as being a context at which sentences express propositions, and being a circumstance of evaluation at which propositions are assessed for truth or falsity, are just two roles played by the very same things—possible states of the world.

But is this really so? Are contexts nothing more than world-states? They are, or at least they may be taken to be, when the only indexicals to be considered are *dthat* and *actually*. However, the situation becomes more complicated when ordinary indexicals like *I* and *now* are added. Surely, some contextual parameters are needed to determine the different propositions expressed at different contexts by sentences containing these new indexicals. If, as seems plausible, these new contextual parameters involve new designated semantic values (to interpret the new indexicals) over and above the designated actual world-state, then the identification of contexts with world-states will fall by the wayside, and our characterization of the primary intension of a sentence will have to be revised.

As later chapters will make clear, this will indeed be necessary. However, since this involves some difficulties and complications, it is best for now to limit ourselves to simple cases in which these difficulties do not arise. For this reason, I will temporarily restrict the scope of discussion to examples in which the only indexicals are *actually* and *dthat*; and in this chapter I will formulate the theses of strong two-dimensionalism as if these were the only indexicals to be considered. Only after the strong two-dimensionalist treatment of this restricted range of cases has been presented and critically evaluated will we turn to the problems and complications that other indexicals pose for the theory.

The next tenets to be added to the formulation of two-dimensionalism are T2–T4.

> T2. Understanding S consists in knowing its character and primary intension. Although this knowledge, plus complete knowledge of a context C, would always give one knowledge of the secondary intension of—i.e., the proposition expressed by—S in C, sometimes one does not have such knowledge. Since we never know all there is to know about the context/world-state C, sometimes we don't know precisely which proposition is expressed by S in C. However, this does not prevent us from using S correctly in C.

> T3a. Examples of the necessary aposteriori are sentences the secondary intensions of which are necessary, and the characters of which assign false propositions to some contexts. Since the character of such a sentence sometimes assigns propositions to contexts that are false in those contexts, the primary intension of such a sentence is contingent.

> T3b. Examples of the contingent apriori are sentences the secondary intensions of which are contingent, and the charac-

ters of which assign true propositions to every context. Since the character of such a sentence always assigns propositions to contexts that are true in those contexts, the primary intension of such a sentence is necessary.

T4a. All proper names and natural kind terms have their reference semantically fixed by descriptions not containing any (uneliminable) proper names or natural kind terms.

T4b. These names and natural kind terms are synonymous with context-sensitive, rigidified descriptions (using *dthat* or *actually*).

As will later become clear, these theses of strong two-dimensionalism differ only minimally from their weak two-dimensionalist counterparts. For various reasons—connected both with the impossibility, within weak two-dimensionalism, of identifying propositions with sets of possible world-states, and with the way in which weak two-dimensionalism ultimately extends to cases involving indexicals other than *dthat* and *actually*—it turns out to be more natural to identify the primary intension of S in such systems with its character than it is to identify it with any proposition defined in terms of that character. Other than this difference, strong and weak two-dimensionalism are essentially equivalent regarding T2–T4. Regarding the analyzability thesis T4, it is important to avoid a potential misunderstanding. In advancing this thesis, the ambitious two-dimensionalist is **not** committed to the claim that the object language L contains sufficient nonindexical vocabulary to construct the relevant descriptions. Rather, the claim is that the reference of names and kind terms is fixed by their association with purely descriptive properties, not containing any objects as constituents (except perhaps for certain contextual parameters like agent and time), and that the terms are synonymous with rigidified versions of descriptions expressing these properties that could, in principle, be constructed using all the vocabulary of L, together with the addition of new purely descriptive vocabulary, if necessary.

The crucial difference between the two versions of ambitious two-dimensionalism concerns the explanations they give of T3a and T3b, involving the necessary aposteriori and the contingent apriori. As indicated in chapter 3, strong two-dimensionalism tends to be driven by three philosophical commitments: (i) the conviction that metaphysical possibility is the only genuine kind of possibility, (ii) the view that the function of evidence required for aposteriori knowledge of a proposition p is that of ruling out possibilities in which p is false, and (iii) the view that propositions are sets of possible world-states. Given (i), plus either (ii) or (iii), one has no choice but to hold that no necessary proposition is ever knowable only aposteriori. It follows, according to strong two-dimensionalism, that if a sentence S is an instance of the necessary aposteriori, it is **not** because the proposition that S expresses, its so-called secondary intension, is both necessary and knowable only aposteriori. Rather, it is because the secondary intension of S is necessary, whereas its primary intension is contingent. On this view, *It is a necessary truth that S* and *It is knowable only aposteriori that S* are jointly true, but the proposition said to be necessary is not the one reported to be knowable only aposteriori. In general, when one says *Jones knows, or knows apriori, that S*, what one reports is that Jones knows p (or knows p apriori), where p is the primary, rather than the secondary, intension of S. Similarly, when one says *It is knowable apriori that S* or *It is knowable only aposteriori that S*, the proposition one reports on is the primary intension of S, not its secondary intension.

This idea is reflected in T5 and T6.

T5a. *It is a necessary truth that S* is true with respect to a context C and world-state w iff the secondary intension of S in C is true with respect to all (metaphysically possible) world-states w* that are possible relative to w.

T5b. *It is knowable apriori that S* is true with respect to C and w iff the primary intension of S in C is knowable apriori in w; *x knows/believes that S* is true of an individual i with respect to C and w iff in w, i knows/believes the primary intension of S with respect to C. Similar clauses hold for other modal and epistemic operators.

T6a. S is an example of the necessary aposteriori iff the secondary intension of S (with respect to C) is a necessary truth, but the primary intension of S is contingent and, though knowable, not knowable apriori. To say that the primary intension of S is contingent is, in effect, to say that there are contexts C* to which the character of S assigns a proposition that is false in C*. Thus, examples of the necessary aposteriori express necessary truths in our actual context, while expressing falsehoods in other contexts. Primary intensions of these sentences are not knowable apriori because we require empirical information to determine that our context is not one to which the character assigns a falsehood.

T6b. S is an example of a contingent apriori truth iff the secondary intension of S (with respect to C) is true, but not necessarily true, while the primary intension of S is necessary and knowable apriori. To say that the primary intension of S is necessary is, in effect, to say that for every context C*, the proposition assigned to C* by the character of S is true at C*. Thus, sentences that are examples of the contingent apriori express propositions which, while true in our actual context/world-state, are false when evaluated at some world-states, even though these sentences express truths in every context/world-state. Primary intensions of these sentences are knowable apriori because no empirical information is needed to determine that our context is one to which the character assigns a truth.

These theses carry with them certain additional implications which, although they go a little beyond what is asserted by T1–T6, are more or less inevitable corollaries of them. One of these corollaries is T7a.

T7a. There is no proposition that is both necessary and knowable only aposteriori; nor is there any proposition that is contingent yet knowable apriori.

The thought here is that if there were such propositions, then there would be no reason why it shouldn't be possible to express them using nonindexical sentences—where the primary and secondary intensions of any such sentence would have to be both necessary or both contingent. Since this is ruled out by T6, the strong two-dimensionalist should be seen as committed to T7a. The next implication, which follows naturally on this one, is T7b.

T7b. The necessary aposteriori and the contingent apriori are, in effect, linguistic illusions, born of a failure to notice the different roles played by primary and secondary intensions in modal and epistemic sentences. (This is so even if they are deep illusions, which could be expected to arise in any language used by creatures like us.)

In what follows, I will take T7a and T7b to be included in the characterization of strong two-dimensionalism.

One final thesis suggests itself, even though it is not strictly entailed by what we already have.

T8. A proposition is necessary iff it is knowable apriori.

Prior to T8 we already have both its right-to-left direction and the claim that any necessary truth that is knowable at all is knowable apriori. Thus, what T8 adds to T1–T7 is the claim that all necessary truths are knowable. In systems that identify propositions with sets of possible world-states, this claim is, of course, trivial, and in effect already presupposed. In fact, the acceptance by a strong two-dimensionalist of T8 would seem to go hand in hand with a possible-world-state analysis of propositions. Since it is difficult to imagine another conception of propositions that would justify the claim that all necessary truths are knowable, it is easy to understand why a strong two-dimensionalist who adopted T8 would find this analysis of propositions congenial.

It is worth mentioning why such a theorist might want to do this. Consider again the standard strong two-dimensionalist explanation of the contingent apriori. This explanation hinges on two alleged facts: the contingency of the secondary intension of the sentence, and the necessity of its primary intension—i.e., of the "diagonal proposition" determined by the Stalnaker-style propositional function (character) associated with it. But how does the necessity of this proposition guarantee that it is knowable apriori, unless it is somehow guaranteed that every necessary truth is knowable? And how is this guaranteed unless it is assumed that propositions are just sets of possible world-states (or functions from such states to truth values)? To the extent that strong two-dimensionalists want simply to take it for granted that necessity of primary intension is enough for apriori truth, they have reason to embrace the possible-world-state analysis of propositions, and with it, T8.

In what follows, I will use the term *strong two-dimensionalism* to refer to systems incorporating T1–T7, whether or not they also incorporate T8. In those cases where I wish to be more specific, I will characterize strong two-dimensionalist systems that do include T8 as examples of *very strong two-dimensionalism*. I will presuppose that all and only those systems of strong two-dimensionalism that identify propositions with sets of possible world-states (or functions from such states to truth values) are very strong two-dimensionalist systems.

Weak Two-Dimensionalism

The fundamental difference between strong and weak two-dimensionalism, which tends to drive all other differences, is that whereas the
strong two-dimensionalist seeks to explain away the necessary aposteriori and the contingent apriori—in the manner of T7—the weak two-
dimensionalist accepts the existence of propositions that are both necessary and knowable only aposteriori, as well as those that are both
contingent and knowable apriori, while attempting to give deflationary, two-dimensionalist explanations of how there can be such propositions. In taking this explanatory perspective, the weak two-dimensionalist rejects T7, T8, and the possible-world-state analysis of
propositions, while sharply modifying the semantic analysis of epistemic sentences given in T5b, and the explanations of the necessary
aposteriori and the contingent apriori given in T6. As noted earlier,
the weak two-dimensionalist counterparts of T1–T5a are at most
minor variations on those earlier theses.

WT1. Each sentence is semantically associated with a pair of semantic values—primary intension, and secondary intension. The primary intension of S is its Kaplan-style character. The secondary intension of (or proposition expressed
by) S at a context C is the proposition assigned by its primary intension to C.

WT2. Understanding S consists in knowing its primary intension—i.e., its meaning, or character. Although this
knowledge, plus complete knowledge of the context C,
would always give one knowledge of the proposition expressed by S in C, sometimes one does not have such
knowledge. Since we never know all there is to know
about the designated world-state of C, sometimes we
don't know precisely which proposition is expressed by S
in C. However, this does not stop us from using S correctly in C.

WT3a. Examples of the necessary aposteriori are sentences the
secondary intensions of which are necessary, and the primary intensions of which assign false propositions to
some contexts.

WT3b. Examples of the contingent apriori are sentences the secondary intensions of which are contingent, and the primary intensions of which assign true propositions to every context.

WT4a. All proper names and natural kind terms have their reference semantically fixed by descriptions not containing any (uneliminable) proper names or natural kind terms.

WT4b. These names and natural kind terms are synonymous with descriptions rigidified using *actually* or *dthat*.

WT5a. ***It is a necessary truth that*** *S* is true w.r.t. a context C and world-state w iff the secondary intension of S in C is true w.r.t. all (metaphysically possible) world-states w* that are possible relative to w.

In understanding WT3a and WT3b, it is important to realize that these are to be taken as universally quantified conditionals, rather than universally quantified biconditionals. For example, WT3a tells us that for every sentence S, if S is an example of the necessary aposteriori, then the secondary intension of S is necessary and the primary intension of S assigns false propositions to some contexts. It does **not** assert the converse of this claim. Thus, when α and β are contingently codesignative descriptions, it is possible for a weak two-dimensionalist to classify *dthat[α] = dthat[β]* as an example of the necessary **apriori** on the grounds that the proposition it actually expresses (its secondary intension) is the same as that expressed by *dthat[α] = dthat[α]*. If this is correct, then *dthat[α] = dthat[β]* is **not** an example of the necessary aposteriori, even though its secondary intension is necessary, while its primary intension assigns false propositions to contexts in which α and β designate different objects.

Next we come to the semantic analysis of attitude ascriptions, which provides the theoretical basis for the weak two-dimensionalist explanation of the necessary aposteriori and the contingent apriori. The central thesis used in this explanation is WT5b. WT5c specifies an additional reading of some attitude ascriptions posited by some theorists to handle a limited range of special so-called *de se* cases.

WT5b. Standardly, an attitude ascription *x v's that S*, when taken in a context C, is true of an individual a with respect to a

possible world-state w iff there is some meaning (character) M such that (i) in w, a bears a certain relation R to M
(which relation depends on which verb v is involved), and
(ii) M assigns the **secondary intension** of S relative to C
to a related context with a as agent and w as world-state.
So propositions are objects of the attitudes, and attitude
verbs are two-place predicates of agents and their objects.
However, this two-place relation holds between an agent
a and a proposition p in virtue of a three-place relation
holding between a, a character, and p. To believe p is to
accept a character M that expresses p (and to believe that
M expresses a truth). To know a true proposition p is to
justifiably accept a character M that expresses p (and to
know that M expresses a truth).

WT5c. In addition, some attitude ascriptions *x v's that S* have a
secondary reading in which they are true of an individual
a with respect to a context C and world-state w iff in w, a
bears a certain relation R to the character M of S (or, in
certain cases, to the character of a specified transformation of S). For example, when v = 'believe', R is the attitude of accepting M (and believing it to express a truth);
when v = 'know', R is the attitude of justifiably accepting
M (and knowing it to express a truth).

Let us pause for a moment over WT5c, the rationale for which is illustrated by John Perry's amusing example of an amnesiac, Rudolf
Lingens, trapped in a library.[1] Rudolf is suffering from amnesia and
doesn't know where he is, when it is, or who he is. But he knows many
other things. He comes across a book in the library which details
everything about him in the third person, under the name 'Lingens'.
The book includes all significant facts about him, right down to his
being lost in a library and his reading a book about someone named
Lingens. The book may even have photos of Lingens which he no
longer recognizes, since he has forgotten how he looks, and has had
no access to a mirror. Now it seems possible that Lingens might know
all the facts indicated in the book without, as we would ordinarily put
it, "knowing who he is." When he finally has some flash of memory
and discovers who he is, or at least comes to think he knows who he is,

---

[1] "Frege on Demonstratives," p. 492.

he says *I am Rudolf Lingens! This book is about me!* Nevertheless, he need not thereby come to believe any proposition he had not believed before. For the propositions expressed by the sentences he now comes to accept are, arguably, also expressed by other sentences he has accepted for some time—e.g., by *He* [pointing at his photo in the book] *is Rudolf Lingens!, This book is about him!* [pointing again], and perhaps even by *Rudolf Lingens is Rudolf Lingens,* and *This book is about Rudolf Lingens!* So, it would seem, the propositions expressed by *I am Rudolf Lingens!* and *This book is about me!* in Lingens's present context are propositions he already believed prior to his discovery.

Notice also that it doesn't help to go metalinguistic. When Lingens makes the discovery, he says to himself *The sentence 'I am Rudolf Lingens' expresses a truth in my context.* But again, there is reason to think that is something he already believed, since he believed that the sentence expressed a truth in Lingens's (or in his [pointing at the picture in the book]) context. Thus, it would seem that he already believed, prior to his discovery, that the characters of these sentences expressed truths in his context. What has changed is that he now **accepts** a character that he did not previously accept. What the example seems to show is that acceptance of a character cannot always be assimilated to believing some proposition about it.

The important point for our purposes is that the ambiguity in belief and other attitude ascriptions posited by (some) weak two-dimensionalists cannot, in general, be viewed as an ambiguity about which of two different propositions associated with the complement clause the agent may bear one and the same attitude toward; instead, it must be seen as an ambiguity involving two different attitudes toward two different sorts of things. Though there is a serious question about whether this is a genuine **semantic** ambiguity in propositional attitude verbs (as opposed to a pragmatic fact about what information certain unambiguous propositional attitude ascriptions can sometimes be used to assert or convey), there is certainly something here to be captured. Scenarios like Perry's would ordinarily be described as cases in which one is ignorant about who one is, where one is, what time it is, and so on, even though, as we have seen, this ignorance, arguably, cannot be attributed to the failure to believe any proposition. Moreover, if we imagine Lingens reporting, after he has regained his memory, *I just now came to believe that I am Rudolf Lingens,* we would, I think, ordinarily be inclined to take him as having said something true. In the weak two-dimensionalist framework we are considering, this is because *believe* can sometimes mean *accept*, and a *that* clause in a belief ascription can sometimes denote a character. Similar remarks apply to the attitude ascription *Rudolf just now came to believe that he is Rudolf Lingens*. The only difference is that in this case the character Rudolf is reported as coming to accept is the one associated with a certain transform—*I am Rudolf Lingens*—of the complement sentence, rather than the one associated with the complement sentence itself.[2]

Though I have my doubts about this semantic analysis, I will not here attempt to evaluate it—much of which can, I think, be separated from distinctively two-dimensionalist theories. It should be noted, however, that examples covered by WT5c don't have anything special to do with the necessary aposteriori and the contingent apriori—standard instances of which are given weak two-dimensionalist explanations based on WT5b. These explanations are summarized in WT6.

WT6a. For all propositions p, p is both necessary and knowable only aposteriori iff (i) p is necessary; (ii) p is knowable **in virtue of** one's justifiably accepting some meaning M (and knowing that it expresses a truth), where M is such that (a) it assigns p to one's context, (b) it assigns a false proposition to some other context, and (c) one's justification for accepting M (and believing it to express a truth) requires one to possess empirical evidence; and (iii) p is knowable **only** in this way.

WT6b. For all propositions p, p is both contingently true and knowable apriori iff in addition to being contingently true, p is knowable **in virtue of** one's justifiably accepting some meaning M (and knowing that it expresses a truth), where M is such that (a) it assigns p to one's context, (b) it assigns a true proposition to every context, and (c) one's justification for accepting M (and believing it to express a truth) does not require one to possess empirical evidence.

The aim of these doctrines is to give deflationary explanations of the necessary aposteriori and the contingent apriori by analyzing our knowledge of these propositions in terms of the conditions in which

---

[2] This is how the weak two-dimensionalist handles David Lewis's examples in "Attitudes *De Dicto* and *De Se*" (originally published in 1979, reprinted in *Philosophical Papers*, New York: Oxford University Press, 1983).

we are justified in accepting characters that assign these propositions to the contexts in which we find ourselves. In a moment, I will give examples of such explanations.

Before doing that, however, I wish to raise certain general questions regarding these explanations which, I hope, will shed further light on weak two-dimensionalism. The explanations of the necessary aposteriori and the contingent apriori summarized in T6 seem to presuppose that there is some connection between a character expressing a falsehood in some, or no, contexts, and one's needing, or not needing, empirical evidence in order to justifiably accept it. What exactly does this connection amount to? Since weak two-dimensionalists reject the possible-world-state analysis of propositions, there is nothing that guarantees that all necessary truths are knowable, let along knowable without empirical justification. Thus, the mere fact that a character M expresses a truth with respect to every context/world-state (and hence that the proposition that M expresses a truth is necessary) is not, in and of itself, sufficient to show that one can ever be justified in accepting M (or believing that it expresses a truth). In many particular cases it may be clear that one is justified, and even that this justification does not depend on having empirical evidence. But there is nothing that I can see in weak two-dimensionalism which guarantees that this will always be so.

Another, closely related, question is why there can't be any necessary proposition p expressed by a sentence S satisfying the following conditions: (a) the character M of S expresses a truth in every context, (b) one can know p by virtue of understanding S, accepting it (i.e., M) (and knowing it to express a truth), (c) accepting M (and knowing it to express a truth) requires empirical evidence, and (d) there is no other apriori route to p. Thesis WT6 tells us that there are no examples like this, but it doesn't tell us why not. The reason, in my opinion, why cases like this are **not** countenanced by weak two-dimensionalists involves two views that are parts of the standard motivation for both strong and weak two-dimensionalism. They are (i) the restriction of epistemic possibility to metaphysical possibility, and (ii) the claim that the role of empirical evidence in justifying one's acceptance of a character M lies in excluding possibilities incompatible with that evidence in which M expresses a falsehood. For the strong two-dimensionalist theorist, (ii) is the companion to (iii), which the theorist also accepts: (iii) the role of empirical evidence in justifying one's knowledge of a proposition p lies in excluding possibilities incompatible with that evidence in which p is false. This principle—which, together with (i), rules out the existence of any propositions that are both necessary and knowable apriori—is rejected by the weak two-dimensionalist. However, its companion (ii) (argued against at the end of chapter 4) remains.

Examples of Strong and Weak
Two-Dimensionalist Explanations

The different explanations of the contingent apriori and the necessary aposteriori given by strong and weak two-dimensionalists can be illustrated by considering two rather transparent examples. The first is the instance of the contingent apriori discussed informally in chapter 3.

1. If there is a unique F, then the x: actually Fx = the x: Fx.

Here, we let **the x: Fx** be a nonrigid description which designates some individual o in the actual world-state, but which designates other individuals with respect to other world-states. The semantics of *actually* guarantees that the secondary intension of (1) is a contingent truth that is false with respect to world-states in which **the x: Fx** designates something other than o. However, although that proposition is contingent, the primary intension of (1) is a necessary truth. In very strong two-dimensionalist systems, this fact guarantees that it is knowable apriori, and hence that sentence (1) is an instance of the contingent apriori. However, even in strong two-dimensionalist systems that don't include T8, the primary intension of (1) is so obviously equivalent to the apriori proposition which is the secondary intension of (2) that the primary intension of (1) must also be knowable apriori.

2. If there is a unique F, then the x: Fx = the x: Fx

The weak two-dimensionalist explanation is similar, except that it characterizes the **secondary** intension of (1) as being knowable apriori in virtue of the fact that empirical evidence is not needed in order to be justified in accepting the character of (1), and knowing that it expresses a truth (i.e., in knowing what the strong two-dimensionalist describes as its *primary intension*). The reason empirical evidence isn't needed is that the character of (1) is trivially equivalent to the character of (2), which clearly requires no empirical evidence in order for one to justifiably accept it, or know it to express a truth. The strong and

the weak two-dimensionalist agree in identifying this as the basis of the
apriority of sentence (1). They differ in that the weak two-dimensionalist takes this to be sufficient to establish that the proposition expressed by (1)—its secondary intension—itself counts as knowable
apriori, whereas the strong two-dimensionalist insists that the secondary intension of (1) is not knowable apriori.

Next consider (3), which is an example of the necessary aposteriori
when **the x: Fx** and **the x: Gx** are contingently codesignative descriptions.

3. If there is a unique object that is actually F and a unique object
    that is actually G, then the x: actually Fx = the y: actually Gy.

Since the rigidified descriptions are codesignative, the secondary intension of (3) is a necessary truth. By contrast, its primary intension—
which, according to the strong two-dimensionalist, is either trivially
equivalent to, or identical with, the secondary intension of (4)—is
both contingent and knowable only aposteriori.

4. If there is a unique object that is F and a unique object that is
    G, then the x: Fx = the x: Gx.

For the strong two-dimensionalist, this is just what it means for (3) to
be an instance of the necessary aposteriori.

For the weak two-dimensionalist, the explanation of the aposteriority of (3) is a little more involved. According to weak two-dimensionalism, the secondary intension of (3) counts as knowable only aposteriori because (a) it is knowable in virtue of one's justifiably accepting
the character of (3) and knowing that it expresses a truth (which
amounts to knowing what the strong two-dimensionalist calls its *primary intension*), (b) this character assigns false propositions to counterfactual contexts in which **the x: Fx** and **the x: Gx** denote different
things, (c) one's justification for accepting this character in the actual
context, and believing it to express a truth, requires one to possess empirical evidence that the two descriptions are codesignative, and (d)
the secondary intension of (3) isn't knowable in any fundamentally
different way.

As before, the strong and the weak two-dimensionalist are in at least
partial agreement about what they identify as the source of the epistemic status of (3). They agree that the sentence is to be classified as
aposteriori in part because the claim that its character expresses a truth
(what the strong two-dimensionalist calls its *primary intension*) is con-

tingent, and knowable only on the basis of empirical evidence (which is, of course, also required to justifiably accept the character). However, whereas this is all there is to the explanation for the strong two-dimensionalist, the weak two-dimensionalist insists on two further points—(i) that it is sufficient in order to know the secondary intension of (3) either that one justifiably accepts the character of (3) and knows that it expresses a truth, or that one justifiably accepts some other character that assigns to one's context the proposition which is the secondary intension of (3), and knows of that character that it expresses a truth; and (ii) that any such character shares with (3) the properties of assigning false propositions to some contexts, and of requiring empirical evidence in order for one to justifiably accept it, and know it to express a truth. In the case of (3) itself, (i) and (ii) may not seem to come to much, since it is not easy to imagine characters fundamentally different from (3) assigning relevant contexts the proposition that (3) actually expresses, and hence providing fundamentally different routes for coming to know that proposition. However, in chapter 10 I will revisit these points, and present examples in which characters with very different modal and epistemic properties do provide alternative ways of expressing the very same proposition, and different apparent routes for coming to know it. These examples will play a role in assessing both weak two-dimensionalism itself, and how it differs from strong two-dimensionalism. For now, I simply note that, in the case of examples like (3), the chief difference between these two forms of ambitious two-dimensionalism concerns the classification of the secondary intension of (3). Whereas both strong and weak two-dimensionalism count the **sentence** as an example of the necessary aposteriori, only weak two-dimensionalism classifies the proposition expressed by the sentence—its secondary intension—in that way.

CHAPTER 8

JACKSON'S STRONG
TWO-DIMENSIONALIST PROGRAM

In this chapter and the next, I will use the strong and weak two-dimensionalist frameworks formulated in chapter 7 to shed light on the work of two leading proponents of ambitious two-dimensionalism—Frank Jackson and David Chalmers. My discussion will focus on, though not be limited to, their most systematic, well-known, and widely influential works. In this chapter, I will concentrate primarily on Jackson's 1995 John Locke lectures, published in 1998 (in revised and expanded form) as *From Metaphysics to Ethics*. In the next, I will discuss Chalmers's *The Conscious Mind*, published in 1996.[1] Although my discussion will be critical as well as expository, I will not attempt any final evaluation of strong or weak two-dimensionalism until chapter 10.

In the first three chapters of *From Metaphysics to Ethics*, Jackson presents his view of a central issue connecting metaphysics, supervenience, and conceptual analysis. The issue is the status of physicalism, thought of as a doctrine about the relationship between explicitly physical facts and truths, on the one hand, and facts and truths of other sorts—especially semantic and psychological facts and truths—on the other. Physicalism is committed to the view that all genuine facts or truths of any sort are **necessary** consequences of the explicitly physical facts and truths—or, as Jackson sometimes puts it, that $\Phi \supset \Psi$ is a necessary truth, where Φ is an enormously complex, explicitly physicalistic sentence that gives a complete account of all explicitly physical facts in the world, and Ψ is a true sentence expressing any other fact (e.g., any semantic or psychological fact). The question at issue is whether physicalism is also committed to the view that all genuine facts and truths are **apriori** consequences of the explicitly physical facts and truths—or, in Jackson's words, whether $\Phi \supset \Psi$ is always an apriori truth. He claims both that physicalism is committed to this, and that it is true. Thus, he concludes that all genuine facts and truths

---

[1] Frank Jackson, *From Metaphysics to Ethics* (Oxford: Clarendon Press, 1998); David Chalmers, *The Conscious Mind* (New York and Oxford: Oxford University Press, 1996).

of any kind are apriori consequences of the explicitly physical facts and truths.

There is, however, an obvious problem that must be faced. Since *Naming and Necessity*, it has been recognized that some necessary truths are knowable only aposteriori, and, by implication, that some necessary consequences of a given statement are **not** apriori consequences of that statement. How, then, does Jackson know that his statements $\Phi \supset \Psi$ aren't necessary without being apriori, or that the semantic or psychological Ψ isn't a necessary consequence of the all-encompassing physical statement Φ, without being an apriori consequence of Φ? He addresses this problem in chapter 3, in the section entitled "Conceptual Necessity and Physical Necessity."

Jackson's Restriction of Epistemic Possibility to Metaphysical Possibility

Jackson begins by describing an approach—similar to the one I outlined at the end of chapter 4—which he rejects. He says:

> There are two quite different ways of looking at the distinction between necessary aposteriori sentences like 'Water = H_2O', and necessary apriori ones like '$H_2O = H_2O$' and 'Water = water'. You might say that the latter are analytically or conceptually or logically (in some wide sense not tied to provability in a formal system) necessary, whereas the former are metaphysically necessary, meaning by the terminology that we are dealing with two senses of 'necessary' in somewhat the way that we are when we contrast logical necessity with nomic necessity. On this approach, the reason the necessity of water's being H_2O is not available a priori is that though what is conceptually possible and impossible is available in principle to reason alone given sufficient grasp of the relevant concepts and logical acumen, what is metaphysically possible and impossible is not so available. Knowledge of the metaphysically necessary and possible is, in general, a posteriori. Similarly, it is often suggested that essential properties show that we need to make a distinction in kinds of necessity between metaphysical and conceptual necessity.[2]

About this view, he says:

[2] *From Metaphysics to Ethics*, p. 69.

I think, as against this view, that it is a mistake to hold that the necessity possessed by 'Water = H$_2$O' is different from that possessed by 'Water = water', or, indeed, '2 + 2 = 4'. . . . I have two reasons for holding that there is only one sense of necessity and possibility in play here. The first is Occamist. We should not multiply senses of necessity beyond necessity. The phenomena of the necessary a posteriori, and of essential properties, can be explained in terms of one unitary notion of a set of possible worlds. The phenomena do not call for a multiplication of senses of possibility and necessity, and in particular for a distinction among the possible worlds between the metaphysically possible ones and the conceptually possible ones.[3]

The important thing here is Jackson's attitude toward the relationship between epistemic and metaphysical possibility. His mention of **senses**—i.e., meanings—of the words 'necessary' and 'possible' (in everyday language? as technical terms?)—is beside the point. After all, there surely **is** such a thing as the sense of the phrase *maximally complete property which could not have been instantiated, but which cannot be known apriori not to be instantiated*, whether or not any properties satisfy this condition (and play a role in explaining the necessary aposteriori).

The substantive issue concerning the necessary aposteriori is whether, if w is a way that the world genuinely could **not** have been, we can know apriori that w does not obtain, or whether, on the contrary, this is something that may turn out to be knowable only aposteriori. What Jackson, in effect, asserts is that every such way that the world could not be is a way that can be known apriori not to obtain (assuming this to be knowable at all). Although he doesn't here give much by way of a reason to believe this thesis, the fact that he advances it shows something important about how he approaches the problem. If w could not have obtained, then the proposition that w does not obtain is necessary. Jackson's position is that no necessary truth of this sort can be knowable only aposteriori. But if none of **these** (maximally contentful) propositions is both necessary and knowable only aposteriori, then it is hard to see how any propositions whatever could be both necessary and knowable only aposteriori. It would seem that if p is both necessary and knowable only aposteriori, then there will be ways $w_{\sim p}$ that the world could not be, with respect to which p is untrue,

---

[3] Ibid., pp. 69–70.

which are such that it is knowable only aposteriori that they do not obtain. Since this contradicts Jackson's view, it appears that he approaches the problem of explaining the necessary aposteriori with a prior commitment to the view that **no proposition** is both necessary and knowable only aposteriori. This fits perfectly with strong two-dimensionalism. Thus, we should not be surprised that, in setting up the problem, he begins by insisting that it is about how **sentences** can properly be characterized as both necessary and aposteriori.

Jackson's Statement of the Problem Posed by the Necessary Aposteriori

Here is how Jackson states the problem:

> The phenomenon of the necessary a posteriori calls for more discussion. We need, it seems to me, to have before us from the beginning two central facts. First, it is **sentences**, or if you like statements or stories or accounts in the sense of assertoric sentences in some possible language, that are necessary aposteriori. Secondly, the puzzle . . . is how a sentence can be necessarily true and understood by someone, and yet the fact of its necessity be obscure to that person.[4]

According to Jackson it is puzzling how a person can understand a sentence that expresses a necessary truth, and yet not know that it is necessary. But what is the puzzle? There are lots of sentences of mathematics that express necessary truths that people seem to understand, without knowing that they are necessary, or even that they are true. Why, one wants to know, should this be puzzling?

For Jackson, the puzzle arises from a certain view—which he takes to be a platitude—about what it means to understand a sentence.

> Consider what happens when I utter the sentence, 'There is a land-mine two metres away.' I tell you something about how things are, and to do that is precisely to tell you which of the various possibilities concerning how things are is actual. My success in conveying this urgent bit of information depends on two things: your understanding the sentence, and your taking the sentence to be true. **We have here a folk theory that ties together**

[4] Page 71, my emphasis.

understanding, truth, and information about possibilities; and the obvious way to articulate this folk theory is to identify, or at least essentially connect, understanding a sentence with knowing the conditions under which it is true; that is knowing the possible worlds in which it is true and the possible worlds in which it is false; that is, knowing the proposition it expresses on *one* use of the term 'proposition'. This kind of theory in its philosophically sophisticated articulations is best known through the work of David Lewis and Robert Stalnaker. But it would, I think, be wrong to regard the folk theory as being as controversial as these articulations. The folk theory is, it seems to me, a commonplace.[5]

The reference here to Lewis and Stalnaker is to the view that propositions—thought of as semantic contents of sentences, objects of propositional attitudes, and the primary bearers of truth and falsity—are sets of possible world-states (or functions from such states to truth values). On this view, there is only one necessary proposition, which everyone knows apriori to be both true and necessary. If, as is often assumed, to understand a sentence S that expresses p is to know that S expresses p, and hence to know that S is (necessarily) true iff p is (necessarily) true, then anyone who understands a sentence S* that expresses the necessary proposition q should thereby know that S* is (necessarily) true. Necessarily true sentences for which this is not so will then seem puzzling—as do examples of the necessary aposteriori—to theorists who assume that the Lewis-Stalnaker view is correct.

This, however, is just one of the many ways in which the Lewis-Stalnaker view is breathtakingly at odds with what we ordinarily think.[6] What is surprising is that Jackson regards this highly revisionary view as merely the articulation of an underlying platitude that connects understanding a sentence with knowing the conditions under which it is true. The platitude, apparently, is that the former either is, or essentially involves, the latter. It is not clear what Jackson takes to be potentially controversial about the Lewis-Stalnaker "articulations"—perhaps it is their use of the word 'proposition', which he seems to regard as subject to varying interpretations, or perhaps it is the identification of conditions in which a sentence is true with "possible worlds" (I would

---

[5] Ibid., my emphasis.

[6] For further discussion of the difficulties with this view, see the works cited in fn. 10 of chapter 5.

say "world-states") in which it is true. But whatever it is, I believe there is a glaring problem with what Jackson says about this.

Let us take a stab at what really is platitudinous about the commonplace that understanding a sentence involves knowing the conditions in which it is true. Principles (1) and (2)—which may themselves be regarded as obvious, and in some sense widely (if only implicitly) accepted—are good candidates for articulating this view.

1. Anyone who understands the sentence 'There are no numbers x, y, z, and n, where n is greater than 2, which are such that $x^n + y^n = z^n$' knows (or could come to know solely on the basis of reflection) that it is true iff there are no numbers x, y, z, and n, where n is greater than 2, which are such that $x^n + y^n = z^n$.

2. Anyone who understands the sentence 'There are no numbers x ,y, z, and n, where n is greater than 2, which are such that $x^n + y^n = z^n$' knows (or could come to know solely on the basis of reflection) that for all possible ways w that the world might be, this sentence is true, when taken as a description of how things would be if w obtained, iff it would be the case, if w obtained, that there are no numbers x, y, z, and n, where n is greater than 2, which are such that $x^n + y^n = z^n$.

Next we extend these principles to cover all normal, putatively fact-stating sentences. For any such sentence S, we may grant that counterparts of (1) and (2) involving S are obvious and widely accepted—elements of a "folk theory," if you must. However, there is nothing in these principles that generates a puzzle about the necessary aposteriori, or that would lead one to expect that anyone who understands a necessary truth should know (or be able to come to know in the absence of further empirical evidence) that it is necessary, or even true.

Perhaps, then, Jackson thinks of the connection between understanding a sentence and knowing its truth conditions in some other way. Looking back at the passage, we see that he equates knowing the conditions under which a sentence is true with "knowing the possible worlds in which it is true and the possible worlds in which it is false." What exactly does that mean? Let's try something easier. What is it to know the major American cities which have Republican mayors and the major American cities which do not have Republican mayors? A natural answer is that it is to know, for every major American city c which has a Republican mayor, that c has a Republican mayor, and also to know, for every major American city c which does not have a Republican mayor, that c doesn't have a Republican mayor. By parity of reasoning, a natural way of understanding what it is to know the possible world-states in which S is true, and those in which S is false, is to identify it with knowing that S is true in w, for every possible world-state w in which S is true, and knowing that S is false in w, for every possible world-state in which S is false. On this understanding, the platitudes (1) and (2) are replaced by (3).

3. Any speaker s who understands the sentence 'There are no numbers x, y, z, and n, where n is greater than 2, which are such that $x^n + y^n = z^n$' is such that for all possible ways w that the world might be, if that sentence is true when taken as a description of how things would be if w obtained, then s knows (or could come to know solely on the basis of reflection) that the sentence is true with respect to w, and for all possible ways w that the world might be, if that sentence is false when taken as a description of how things would be if w obtained, then s knows (or could come to know solely on the basis of reflection) that the sentence is false with respect to w.

Here we have a principle that might well be thought to generate a puzzle. Since the arithmetical sentence is true with respect to all possible world-sates, the principle tells us that anyone who understands it should know (or be capable of coming to know solely on the basis of reflection) of every one of those states—including the state the world actually is in—that the sentence is true with respect to that state.[7] Granted, this is not quite the same as knowing (or being capable of coming to know solely on the basis of reflection) that the sentence is true with respect to all world-states, and, hence, is necessary. Still, it is close enough to make one wonder how a speaker who understands the

---

[7] There is a hidden difficulty here which I will simply note, without pausing over. The knowledge that is postulated is *de re* knowledge of each world-state w that S is true with respect to w. However, the only account of *de re* knowledge of an entity e standardly recognized by ambitious two-dimensionalists is that which arises from justifiably accepting indexical sentences expressing singular propositions concerning e. Obviously, this account cannot be given for the *de re* knowledge presupposed here, since the alleged knowledge is supposed to underlie and explain all linguistic understanding. But if the ambitious two-dimensionalist has to assume a primitive source of *de re* knowledge, what is there to assure us that one can't have primitive *de re* empirical knowledge of an ordinary object o that it has a certain essential property P? The question is pressing because if one can have such knowledge, then there will be instances of the necessary aposteriori that do not fit the ambitious two-dimensionalist model. Thanks to Mark Kalderon for raising this issue.

sentence, and hence is in a position to know all this, might neverthe-less fail to know—and even be incapable of knowing—that it is neces-sary. One might also be puzzled about how such a speaker could fail to know that the sentence is **true**, and have no idea how to go about finding out whether or not it is—which, of course, is the position in which many competent speakers find themselves. Given that their un-derstanding of the sentence is supposed to guarantee that they know (or are capable of coming to know on the basis of reflection alone) that it is true in the actual world-state (i.e., in the world as it actually is), one may feel hard pressed to explain how they could be as ignorant about it as many of us in fact are. If principles corresponding to (3) were accepted for all normal, potentially fact-stating sentences, then similar puzzles would be generated for many other necessary truths—including all instances of the necessary aposteriori (which cannot be known to be either true or necessary by anyone who understands them, without appeal to further empirical evidence).

Perhaps, then, Jackson's claim is that what makes the necessary aposteriori puzzling are the problems it poses for the obvious and widely accepted "folk theory" that encompasses all instances of the following universal generalization.

4. Any speaker x who understands a normal, potentially fact-stat-ing sentence S is such that for all possible ways w that the world might be, if S is true when taken as a description of how things would be if w obtained, then x knows (or could come to know solely on the basis of reflection) that S is true with re-spect to w, and for all possible ways w that the world might be, if S is false when taken as a description of how things would be if w obtained, then x knows (or could come to know solely on the basis of reflection) that S is false with respect to w.

But now the problem is apparent; (4) is **not** part of any obvious or widely accepted "folk theory." Moreover, it is not at all clear that it can serve Jackson's purposes. For example, one of its consequences is that whenever any sentence is true in the world as it actually is, then some-one who understands it will know (or be capable of coming to know solely on the basis of reflection) that it is true with respect to the actual world-state @. However, it had better not follow from this that the speaker will know (or be capable of coming to know without appeal to empirical evidence) that the sentence is true *simpliciter*—and, hence, that it is an accurate description of how things really stand. But, if knowing that a sentence is true with respect to @ does **not** provide the basis for knowing that the sentence is true *simpliciter*, then it remains mysterious, how, if at all, the condition stated by (4) for understanding a sentence can be seen as shedding any light on the role played by understanding and accepting sentences as true in guiding our actions, and providing us with information about the world. (Recall Jackson's discussion of the utility of the information one gains from understanding and accepting *There is a land-mine two metres away*.)

Perhaps the idea is that understanding a sentence provides the speaker with the ability to determine whether it is true with respect to a world-state w, **when w is described, or presented, to the speaker in an appropriate and complete way**, and that this ability is important in guiding action and providing information about the world. If this is the idea, then although it may not be obviously false, it is far too unclear to inspire confidence. How, for example, are the world-states to be described, and what explanation can be given one's ability to understand the description? Obviously, we cannot use to describe w the very sentences the truth of which, in w, the speaker is supposed to determine—while also taking it for granted that the speaker can understand the description. But how then are we to proceed? I doubt that there is any realistic way to do so.[8] Nevertheless, we might pretend, for the sake of argument, (i) that a proposition p, specifying the content of w, could be expressed by some enormously long conjunctive sentence Φw and (ii) that the speaker could, in principle, entertain p as a hypothesis, independently of his mastery of any of the sentences of L, where L is the speaker's language—the one mastery of which we are trying to explain. Supposing all this, we let q be one of the conjuncts of p, and S be a sentence of L that expresses q which the speaker un-

---

[8] For many speakers s and propositions p, the only way available to s by which to entertain p is via understanding a sentence of s's language that expresses p. But if we are explaining s's competence in L using the present interpretation of (4), then these sentences won't be available to present possible world-states to s. If one insists that s's competence could be explained by attributing to s the ability to make the needed judgments about truth in different world-states—in a counterfactual situation in which s is taught a new language in which to describe the states—then (i) (as indicated below) the resulting view rests on the unsupported premise that when a sentence in the new world-state language expresses the same proposition as a sentence in the object language, and s understands both, s will be able to recognize the fact that they do, and (ii) one will have lost the generality of what was supposed to be a puzzle about all necessary truths, in any case—since, prior to learning the new world-state language, s will have no way of judging certain necessary truths to be true with respect to different world-states, because s will have no independent means describing the world-states, or entertaining hypotheses about them.

derstands. Does the speaker's linguistic competence guarantee that he must be in a position to judge that S is true with respect to w (when w is presented to him via p)? Does the linguistic competence of a speaker who understands the English sentences 'London is pretty', 'Catsup is a condiment', and 'Carl Hempel was a philosopher', while knowing that London is pretty, that ketchup is a condiment, and that Peter Hempel was a philosopher, guarantee that he knows that the English sentences are true? I don't think so. But whether or not one agrees with me about this, no one who has studied the recent literature on the subject can take it for granted without argument that the answer to the question is *yes*.[9] Interpreted in this way, (4) is no platitude. Nor is it something for which Jackson gives any argument; and this is the best we have been able to do.

In sum, nothing Jackson says provides any reason whatsoever to believe that there is any obvious, widely accepted, or even defensible view about the connection between understanding a sentence and knowing its truth conditions which generates a puzzle about how sentences that express necessary truths can be understood and yet not known, simply on that basis, to be necessary, or true. By contrast, this is, as we have seen, a puzzle for anyone who accepts, as Jackson does, the Lewis-Stalnaker view of propositions. In light of this, the best way to understand Jackson is to see him as accepting this highly contentious theory without argument, and wrongly taking it to be essentially platitudinous. Given this starting point, he sees the problem of the necessary aposteriori as that of explaining how a speaker x can understand a sentence S that expresses the trivial, apriori, and necessary proposition p—which x already knows to be true—without knowing that S is true, and without being able to come to know that S is true in the absence of further empirical information. It is not surprising that from this starting point he arrives at a solution that is an instance of what I have called *very strong two-dimensionalism*.

The Logic of Jackson's Proposed Solution

With this as his starting point, the logic of his proposed solution to the "puzzle" about the necessary aposteriori is transparent. In recon-

---

[9] For example, see the sources cited in fn. 13 of chapter 5 above, plus Saul Kripke, "A Puzzle about Belief," in A Margalit (ed.), *Meaning and Use* (Dordrecht: Reidel, 1979), and chapter 3 of *Beyond Rigidity*.

structing his position, I begin with an argument that all sentences that are instances of the necessary aposteriori must be indexical.

(i)   If p is a (the) necessary proposition, then it either already is, or can be, known apriori to be both true and necessary.

(ii) If understanding a nonindexical sentence S that expresses a proposition p involves knowing that S expresses p, then understanding S will be sufficient to know that S is both true and necessary without appeal to additional empirical information, provided that p already is, or can be, known apriori to be both true and necessary.

(iii) Understanding a nonindexical sentence S that expresses p does involve knowing that S expresses p.

(iv) If S is an instance of the necessary aposteriori, then understanding S is not sufficient, without additional empirical information, to know that it is true or necessary.

(v)   So all sentences that are instances of the necessary aposteriori must be indexical.

(i) represents the Lewis-Stalnaker baggage that Jackson brings to the problem. (ii) is based on the compelling idea that the truth (and modal) value of a sentence is inherited from the truth (and modal) value of the proposition the sentence expresses. So if one knows the truth (and modal) value of p, and one knows that S expresses p, then one should know the truth (and modal) value of S. Although this principle is certainly not beyond question, it is, I think, one that Jackson takes for granted.[10] (iii) states a plausible and widely accepted condition on understanding a sentence. If S is nonindexical, then it expresses the same proposition p in every context of utterance. Hence, it is natural to suppose that in order to understand S—and hence to be able to use it competently to assert and express one's belief in p—one must know that S expresses p. (iv) is simply an observation about the sentences that are now widely recognized to be instances of the necessary aposteriori.

This brings us to the conclusion, (v), and the semantics of indexicality given by Kaplan. Along with indexicality comes the strong two-dimensionalist's distinction between primary and secondary intension,

---

[10] I do not accept the principle myself—for Kripkean Pierre-type reasons that we may here put aside.

and the possibility that sometimes the latter may be necessary, but not known by a competent speaker to be the proposition that the sentence actually expresses, while the former—which is grasped by the speaker and which states the conditions under which the sentence expresses a truth—may be knowable only aposteriori. A good example of this is provided by (5), when the two unrigidified descriptions on which *dthat* operates are contingently codesignative.

5. Dthat [the x: Fx] = dthat [the x: Gx]

If the speaker s doesn't know of the object o that is designated by these descriptions that it is so designated, then s won't know that the secondary intension of (5) is the necessary proposition that predicates the identity relation of o and itself. Nevertheless, s may understand **the x: Fx** and **the x: Gx** perfectly well, and be fully apprised of how *dthat* works. Thus, s may know that it is a necessary and sufficient condition for (5) to express a truth that the proposition expressed by (6) be true.

6. The x: Fx = the x: Gx

In the words of the strong two-dimensionalist, s may know what the primary intension of (5) is. However, since this proposition is knowable only aposteriori, s may lack the empirical information needed to know that it is true. Thus, (5) is a sentence that expresses a necessary truth, even though knowledge that (5) expresses a truth (i.e., knowledge of the truth of its primary intension) requires empirical evidence over and above that which is needed to understand it. Strong two-dimensionalists—Jackson included—will therefore characterize it as an example of the necessary aposteriori. In this they differ from weak two-dimensionalists, who would characterize (5) as apriori, on the grounds that what is known apriori—namely the secondary intension of (5)— can be known in ways other than by understanding and accepting (5); moreover, some of these ways—e.g., those that involve accepting and understanding *dthat [the x: Fx] = dthat [the x: Fx]*—(arguably) do not rely on empirical evidence to justify one's knowledge.[11]

Of course, (5) is a rather atypical example of the necessary aposteriori, containing as it does Kaplan's invented *dthat* operator. By contrast, the overwhelming majority of Kripke's examples crucially involve proper names or natural kind terms. In order to fit these into the pattern of his proposed solution, Jackson must analyze names and natural

[11] For simplicity I here ignore questions about the existence of Fs. If one is worried about this, one can add the clause *if there is a unique F* to the relevant sentences.

kind terms as both indexical and rigid. In short, he must treat them as rigidified descriptions that don't contain any names or natural kind terms that aren't themselves, in principle, eliminable by further analysis. In the end, all names and natural kind terms—*water, tiger, gold, red, light, heat, hot, sound, loud,* etc.—must be noncircularly eliminable, so that each such term is ultimately analyzable as a rigidified description that contains **no** names or natural kind terms.[12] Jackson advances this extraordinarily ambitious and far-reaching analytic program on the narrowest of grounds. His commitment to it does not arise from the successful culmination of careful and detailed investigations of particular names and natural kind terms, but simply from the theoretical baggage he brings to the problem. Turning the later Wittgenstein on his head, one might sum up the approach on offer with the aphorism *Don't look and see what words mean; let me tell you what they have to mean!*

This approach leads Jackson to conclude that Kripke's example (7) of the necessary aposteriori must be on a par with (5).

7. Water is H_2O.

Just as the secondary intension of (5)—the proposition it expresses—is the trivial, necessary truth that predicates identity of an object and itself, so, Jackson thinks, the secondary intension of (7)—the proposition it expresses—is the trivial, necessary truth that predicates identity of the chemical kind H_2O and itself. The reason for this is that, according to Jackson, 'water' is analyzed as a rigidified description that denotes the kind H_2O.[13] Also as in the case of (5), understanding (7) does not require knowing the proposition it expresses, but rather knowing the conditions under which it expresses a truth. These are

[12] The descriptions D to be rigidified (using *actually* or *dthat*) may themselves contain indexicals of various sorts, and the other, nonindexical, vocabulary in D need not be restricted to expressions of English.

[13] In a system that did not incorporate the Lewis-Stalnaker view of propositions, one would get this analysis of the secondary intension of (7) if one analyzed *water* as a *dthat*-rigidified description designating the chemical kind H_2O, but not if one analyzed it as an *actually*-rigidified description. On the latter analysis, the secondary intension of (7) would be the proposition that the stuff satisfying a certain description in **this** world-state is H_2O—a proposition which, though necessary, is not the mere predication of the identity relation of the kind and itself. However, since both propositions are necessary, this difference between the two analyses is obliterated in a system like Jackson's that adopts the Lewis-Stalnaker view of propositions. Jackson seems not to mind this, and speaks repeatedly of one's not knowing the proposition expressed by a sentence containing *water* unless one is able to identify its referent as the chemical kind H_2O.

just the conditions under which the proposition expressed by (8)—which is also the primary intension of (7)—is true, where *the watery stuff of our acquaintance* is Jackson's stand-in for the description that **must** semantically fix the referent of 'water' (though he is noncommittal about what its content really is).

8. The watery stuff of our acquaintance = the chemical compound molecules of which contain two hydrogen atoms and one oxygen atom.

Since this (contingent) proposition is knowable only aposteriori, and since it must, according to Jackson, be known by anyone who understands (7) in order for that person to know that (7) expresses a truth, Jackson characterizes (7) as an example of the necessary aposteriori. This is his general model for all Kripkean examples of the necessary aposteriori.[14]

Finally, there is the question of what propositions are asserted by utterances of such sentences, what beliefs they are used to express, and what propositional attitudes they are used to attribute to others when they occur as complement clauses in attitude ascriptions. For the strong two-dimensionalist, the answer is straightforward. In all of these cases the propositions asserted, believed, or ascribed to others are the **primary intensions** of the relevant sentences. In the case of (7), it is the proposition expressed by (8). This also appears to be Jackson's view. Clearly, when someone assertively utters (7), that person does not assert that H_2O is H_2O—which is what Jackson takes its secondary intension (proposition expressed) to be. Rather, Jackson takes the person to assert the proposition expressed by (8). Similarly, when we say *x knows/believes that water is H_2O but y doesn't know/believe that*, we are not asserting that x knows or believes that H_2O is H_2O but y doesn't know or believe that. Rather, Jackson thinks, we are asserting that x knows or believes that "the watery stuff of our acquain-

---

[14] Throughout his discussion, Jackson routinely treats sentences like (7) as if they were simple identities in which a pair of terms flank '='—thereby overlooking the parallel between *Water is H_2O* and *Ice is H_2O*. Although both are naturally understood as true, they are not both simple identities, since it is not the case that water is ice. The most natural way to understand these, and many other Kripkean examples of the necessary aposteriori involving natural kind terms, is as universally quantified conditionals (or in some cases biconditionals) in which the natural kind terms function as predicates (or are used to construct predicates such as *is water*). See chapters 9–11 of *Beyond Rigidity* for discussion and implications. In discussing Jackson (and Chalmers) I ignore these issues, and restrict attention to uses of natural kind expressions in which they function non-predicatively.

tance" is H$_2$O but y doesn't know or believe that. The same must be true regarding what we assert when we say *It is not knowable apriori that water is H$_2$O*. In order for this to come out true, as it must, the proposition said not to be knowable apriori cannot be the proposition which, on Jackson's view, is the secondary intension of its complement clause. Presumably, it must be the proposition which is its primary intension. If so, then Jackson is a classic example of a (very) strong two-dimensionalist.

In His Own Words

I now turn to a brief examination of Jackson's text in order to further document that the position just outlined is the one he advocates. He gives his solution to the "puzzle" posed by the necessary aposteriori in a passage that starts on page 72 with the first of the following two quotes, and ends on page 74 with the second.

> I think—unoriginally—that the way out of our puzzle is to allow that we understand some sentences without knowing the conditions under which they are true, in *one* sense of the conditions under which they are true, though, as we will note later, we must know the conditions under which they are true in *another* sense of the conditions under which they are true.[15]

> The explanation of the necessary a posteriori is now straightforward. Our question is: How can you understand a necessarily true sentence and yet need a posteriori information to tell you that it is necessary? The answer is because understanding does not require knowing the proposition expressed, and yet it is the nature of the proposition expressed that determines that the sentence is necessary. And the important point for us is that this story about the necessary a posteriori does not require acknowledging two sorts of necessity. The story was all in terms of one set of possible worlds.[16]

Immediately after the first of these remarks Jackson announces that his account "is a sketch of the approach naturally suggested by the two-dimensional modal logic treatment of the necessary a posteriori, as in,

[15] Page 72.
[16] Page 74.

. . . [Stalnaker, Davies and Humberstone, and Kaplan—as well as Tichy, Vlach, and David Lewis]," and he adds, "What immediately follows in the text can be put in Stalnaker's terminology by saying that understanding requires knowing the propositional concept associated with a sentence, though not necessarily the proposition expressed, and in Kaplan's by saying that understanding requires knowing character but not necessarily content."[17] Evidently Jackson's position is that all sentences that are examples of the necessary aposteriori are indexical. Since the character of a nonindexical sentence is a constant function from arbitrary contexts to the one proposition p it always expresses, there is no significant difference between knowing its character and knowing that it expresses p. According to Jackson, however, there is always a difference between these two things when the sentence in question is an instance of the necessary aposteriori. Although the propositions these sentences express are necessary, he maintains that understanding them does **not** require knowing, or having all the information needed to know, that those propositions are expressed. What is required is knowing their characters, which encode the conditions under which the sentences express truths. Since these sentences are instances of the necessary aposteriori, knowledge that these conditions obtain always requires aposteriori knowledge over and above what is needed to understand the sentences themselves.

Problems with Jackson's Thesis That Natural Kind Terms Are Indexicals

The remainder of the passage is taken up with two examples meant to illustrate this approach. One involves the overtly indexical sentence, *He has a beard*, while the other involves the Kripkean example of the necessary aposteriori, *Water is H_2O*. The two are supposed to be parallel, illustrating Jackson's commitment to analyzing 'water'—and by extension every natural kind term and proper name—as a rigidified, and therefore indexical, description. In fact, the examples are more telling than Jackson realizes. As we will see, the two sentences differ sharply from one another in ways that undermine the story he wishes to tell.

Jackson's comments about the overtly indexical sentence are as follows:

[17] Page 72, fn. 26.

Here is an illustrative example, familiar from discussions of two-dimensional modal logic, of understanding a sentence without knowing its truth-conditions in one sense. Suppose I hear someone say 'He has a beard'. I will understand what is being said without necessarily knowing the conditions under which what is said is true, because I may not know who is being spoken of. That is, I may not know which proposition is being expressed. If I am the person being spoken of, the proposition being expressed is that Jackson has a beard; if Jones is the person being spoken of, the proposition being expressed is that Jones has a beard; and so on. Hence, if I don't know whether it is Jackson, Jones, or someone else altogether, I don't know which proposition is being expressed in the sense of not knowing the conditions under which what is said is true. But obviously I do understand the sentence. I understand the sentence because I know how to move from the appropriate contextual information, the information which in this case determines who is being spoken of, to the proposition expressed.[18]

The point here is unexceptionable. To understand the demonstrative *he* is to know the constraints it places on individuals that may be its referent in different contexts of utterance, and to know that when, in some context C, it is used in a sentence *He is so and so*, the proposition expressed in C is one that says, of the referent r of *he* in C, that r is so and so. Obviously, one can know the meaning of *he* in this sense, and of a sentence S containing it, without knowing, in some particular context of utterance, to whom *he* is used to refer, in which case one will not know the proposition expressed in the context by S. This much is clear and uncontroversial.

The use to which Jackson puts this observation is not. Think of how the necessary aposteriori would appear if the quintessential example of it were *He is him*, said in a context C in which *he* and *him* were accompanied by different demonstrations referring to the same man. Although the proposition expressed would be a trivial necessary truth p, the sentence itself could be understood by someone who, not knowing to whom the terms referred in C, didn't know that p was expressed. Moreover, acquiring this knowledge would be an empirical, aposteriori matter. If this were what it was for a sentence to be an instance of the necessary aposteriori, and if all of Kripke's examples could properly be given an analysis modeled on this one, then the phe-

---

[18] Pages 72–73.

nomenon of the necessary aposteriori would be a linguistic triviality, with no real significance for our understanding of necessity, possibility, apriority, or other philosophically important notions. The philosopher yearning for the modal and epistemic certainties of pre-Kripkean days could scrupulously attach the label *necessary aposteriori* to all of Kripke's examples, while leaving his or her preconceptions about modality, apriori knowledge, and conceptual analysis blissfully undisturbed. That is Jackson's program.

Clear indication of this is given in the paragraph starting on page 73 that immediately follows the one about *he* just quoted. In this passage, Jackson uses the natural kind term *water* to illustrate his broader commitment to treating all proper names and natural kind terms as indexicals on analogy with *he*.

> A similar point can be made about 'water' sentences. The propositions expressed by, in the sense of the truth-conditions of, our 'water' sentences depend on how things are in the actual world—in particular, on whether the watery stuff of our acquaintance is H_2O. **This means that those who do not know this fact do not know the proposition expressed by, for example, 'Water covers most of the [E]arth'.** . . . Nevertheless, they understand 'water' sentences. It follows that understanding 'Water covers most of the Earth' does not require knowing the conditions under which it is true, that is, the proposition it expresses. Rather it requires knowing how the proposition expressed depends on context of utterance—in this case, how it depends on which stuff in the world of utterance is the watery stuff of our acquaintance.[19]

On this analysis, both the contingent truth *Water covers the Earth* and the necessary truth *Water is H_2O* can be understood without knowing the propositions they express. In both cases, the proposition expressed is (allegedly) about the chemical kind H_2O in the strong sense that one who does not know that *water* designates the chemical compound molecules which consist of two hydrogen atoms and one oxygen atom does not know what propositions are expressed by these sentences— just as one who does not know the man referred to in an utterance of *He has a beard* doesn't know what proposition is expressed. In the case of *Water is H_2O*, Jackson evidently takes the proposition expressed to be the trivial, necessary identity that predicates identity of H_2O and it-

---

[19] Pages 73–74, my emphasis.

self. The sentence is necessary because the proposition it expresses is necessary. However, the sentence is also aposteriori, because in addition to understanding it, one needs further information—which can be known only aposteriori—to come to know that it expresses a truth. Jackson's idea is that all instances of the necessary aposteriori are like this.

There are several problems with this idea. One is the sheer implausibility of the claim that if I don't know that *water* designates the chemical kind H_2O, then I don't know what proposition is expressed by *I drank a glass of water at lunch today* or *The water in the bathtub is cold* (in the sense that I don't know of any propositions that they are expressed by these sentences). Consider a parallel case. If, looking out my window, I say *That is a fine red one* and you can't see, and don't know, what I am referring to, then, although you may know that I said of something that it is red, there is an obvious sense in which you don't know what proposition my remark expressed (in the sense of knowing of any p that my remark expressed p), and hence don't know what I said. You are not similarly in the dark if I say *The water in the bathtub is cold* even if you don't know the chemical composition of water. The problem is worse when one sees that what Jackson says about *water* is supposed to extend to all names and natural kind terms—including *air, tiger, man, woman, gold, color, red, light, heat, hot, cold, sound, loud,* and on, and on, and on. Since all of these figure in sentences that are examples of the necessary aposteriori, his solution to the "puzzle" about the necessary aposteriori dictates that ordinary speakers ignorant of the relevant constitutive facts about these individuals or kinds must not know what propositions are expressed by sentences containing any of them.

This conclusion and the implicit methodology used to reach it are highly counterintuitive. If I were to say to you *This paperweight is not made out of metal*, pointing at the wooden paperweight in plain view on my desk, which we are both looking at, my remark would be a good example of the necessary aposteriori. Suppose, however, that you hadn't examined the paperweight carefully and didn't know what material it was made of. Then you would understand my sentence, yet be in no a position to know that it was true, without examining it further. Applying Jackson's treatment of *water* to this case, he would have to say that, just as you wouldn't know what proposition I expressed if you didn't know to whom *he* referred when I said *He has a beard,* so you didn't understand the proposition I expressed when I said *This paperweight is not made of metal* because you were ignorant of certain properties of the referent of my utterance of *this paperweight*. But the fact that we don't know **all** of the essential properties of the thing referred to doesn't mean that we don't know that it is referred to, or that we don't know what proposition is expressed by an utterance of a sentence involving such reference. The reasoning that applied perfectly to Jackson's example involving *He has a beard* has no application in these cases.

The same point holds for sentences containing names. Surely there are some necessary aposteriori truths in which my name, *Scott Soames,* as well as the names of my two sons, *Greg Soames* and *Brian Soames*, figure essentially—e.g., the necessary aposteriori truths that we are all composed in part of H_2O molecules, as well as other, more abstruse, truths of which I may be ignorant. If my understanding of these sentences does not by itself guarantee that I know that they express truths, and if I am unable to come to know that they do in the absence of further empirical evidence, then, by Jackson's lights, this very fact shows that, in the absence of this evidence, I must not know the propositions expressed by these sentences—or by any other sentences containing the names. But surely I do. I do know who is designated by the names *Scott Soames, Greg Soames,* and *Brian Soames,* and I do know, of the propositions that are expressed by sentences containing them, that they are so expressed. Imagine what it would be like to deny this—i.e., to maintain that for every name and natural kind term that figures in instances of the necessary aposteriori of which competent speakers may be ignorant, these speakers don't know the propositions expressed by sentences containing those terms. With ignorance so vast, one wonders what privileged class of sentences—analogous to the mysterious "elementary propositions" of the *Tractatus*—do express propositions that speakers recognize as expressed, according to Jackson's aprioristic approach to what language **must** be like.

There is another crippling problem, connected to all this, with his assimilation of natural kind terms like *water* to indexicals like *he*. To see this, let S be some instance of the necessary aposteriori, like *Water is H_2O, Heat is mean molecular kinetic energy,* or *Gold is the element with atomic number 79*. About these cases, Jackson wants to say:

A. that understanding S is **not** sufficient for us to know what proposition S expresses—it is **not** sufficient, in the absence of additional empirical facts that can be known only aposteriori, for us to know, of the proposition p that S does express, that S expresses p;

B. that we **do** know p (apriori)—either simply because p is necessary, or (at least in these cases) because p is a trivial, necessary identity that predicates identity of a kind and itself;

C. that this fact does **not** make the ascription *x knows that S* or the ascription *x knows apriori that S* true of us—e.g., this is not sufficient to make it the case that one knows that water is H_2O, let alone that one knows apriori that water is H_2O; and

D. that what would make the ascription *x knows that S* true of us is our learning that S expresses a truth in our context—which, when S = *Water is H_2O*, Jackson would describe as learning that "the watery stuff of our acquaintance" is H_2O—though, of course, even this wouldn't make the ascription *x knows apriori that S* true of us.

Yet the very analogy, or supposed analogy, between *water* and the demonstrative *he* used to support this treatment of the necessary aposteriori can be shown to undermine the story that Jackson tells—as is illustrated by the fact that if we substitute his example *He has a beard* for S in (C) and (D), these points fail.

Regarding (C), let the context of utterance be one in which (i) the speaker utters *He has a beard,* referring demonstratively to Saul Kripke, (ii) Jackson overhears the remark but cannot see to whom the speaker is referring, but (iii) Jackson knows independently, of Saul Kripke, that he has a beard. Contrary to (C), the ascription *Jackson knows that he has a beard*, said in the same context by the same speaker referring demonstratively to Saul Kripke, would, intuitively, be **true**, not false— even though Jackson may have no confidence in the speaker, no idea to whom the speaker is demonstratively referring, and no belief that the speaker's utterance of *He has a beard* expresses a truth. By parity of reasoning, if (α) *water* really were an indexical like *he*, and (β) the proposition expressed by *Water is H_2O* really were already known apriori to be true by a speaker (as indicated in (B)), then the ascriptions *x knows that water is H_2O* and *x knows apriori that water is H_2O* would also be true of the speaker (whether or not the speaker knew that *water* designated H_2O, or that "the watery stuff of our acquaintance" was H_2O). Hence, if (α) and (β) were correct, as Jackson takes them to be, then (C) would be **false**, and his account of the necessary aposteriori would fail at that point. Of course, the ascription *x knows apriori that water is H_2O* is not really true of any speaker, while the ascription *x knows that water is H_2O* is true only of those who have had the relevant chemistry lesson—which just goes to show that, contrary to Jackson, the conjunction of (α) and (β) cannot be correct.

Regarding (D), let the context of utterance be one in which (i) the speaker utters *He has a beard,* referring demonstratively to Saul Kripke, (ii) Jackson is told that the speaker has uttered this sentence, referring to some man or other, but Jackson is not told to whom this reference is made, (iii) Jackson also does **not** know, independently, of Saul Kripke, that he has a beard, but (iv) Jackson does believe, and even knows, that the speaker expressed some truth or other. Contrary to (D), the ascription *Jackson knows that he has a beard*, said in the same context by the same speaker referring demonstratively to Saul Kripke, would be **false**, not true. Thus, if *water* really were an indexical like *he* (the reference of which was fixed by the description *the watery stuff of our acquaintance* in the manner Jackson supposes), the ascription *x knows that water covers most of the Earth* would also be false (of a speaker who didn't know that *water* designated H_2O or that "the watery stuff of our acquaintance" was H_2O, but did know that *Water covers most of the Earth* expresses some truth or other, and that "the watery stuff of our acquaintance" covers most of the Earth). Hence, the version of principle (D) in which S is the sentence *Water covers most of the Earth* would itself be false, thereby falsifying Jackson's story yet again. What these examples indicate is that *water* is **not** indexical in the way that Jackson imagines.

Jackson's Allegiance to (Very) Strong Two-Dimensionalism

So far in this section, I have argued that Jackson's comments commit him to the version of the strong two-dimensionalist explanation of the necessary apriori sketched in the previous section—including the analysis of names and natural kind terms, and, in general, all sentences that are instances of the necessary aposteriori, as indexical. I now turn to further comments which make his allegiance to very strong two-dimensionalism even more explicit. After giving his solution to the "puzzle" about the necessary aposteriori in terms of two different senses of the truth conditions of a sentence—the conditions in which the sentence expresses a truth and the conditions in which what is expressed in a particular context is true—he goes on to express his solution explicitly in terms of the Lewis-Stalnaker model of propositions, and the strong two-dimensionalist distinction between primary and secondary intension.

Accordingly, we could say, following Tichy, Chalmers, Lewis, and Stalnaker among others, that there are *two* propositions connected with a sentence like 'Water covers most of the Earth'. The one we have been calling the proposition expressed is the set of worlds at which the sentence is true given which world is in fact the actual world [better: given which possible world-state in fact obtains (or is instantiated)]; the other is the set of worlds satisfying the following condition: given that w is the actual world [given that w obtains], then the sentence is true at w. [This is the set of contexts/world-states such that the meaning the sentence actually has—its character—determines that the sentence expresses at w a proposition that is true when evaluated at w.] In this second case, we are considering, for each world w, the truth value of S in w under the supposition that w is the actual world, our world [i.e., under the supposition that w obtains and S expresses a proposition with respect to w.]. We can call this set of truth conditions the A-proposition expressed by S—'A' for actual. [This is the primary intension of S.] In the case of the first proposition, however, we are considering, for each world w, the truth value of S, given whatever world is in fact the actual world [given whatever world-state in fact obtains], so we are considering, for all worlds except the actual world, the truth-value of S in a counterfactual world. [What we are considering is the set of possible world-states w such that the proposition expressed by S at the actual world-state—the one that really obtains—is a proposition that would have been true if w were to have obtained.] We can call this set of truth-conditions, the C-proposition expressed by T [i.e., S]—'C' for counterfactual. [This is the secondary intension.] Obviously, the A-proposition is an extension to sentences of the A-intension [primary intension] of terms, and the C-proposition is an extension to sentences of the C-intension [secondary intension] of terms. . . . It is, I take it, the C-proposition [secondary intension] that is normally meant by unadorned uses of the phrase 'proposition expressed by a sentence' *when* 'proposition' is meant in its set-of-truth-conditions sense. . . .

Thus, we have two superficially different but essentially identical accounts of the necessary aposteriori. One says a sentence like 'Water = H$_2$O' gets to be necessary a posteriori because the proposition it expresses is necessary, but which proposition this is need not be known in order to understand the sentence, and is an a posteriori matter depending on the nature of the actual world. Little wonder then that it takes empirical work and not just understanding, to see that the proposition expressed and, thereby, the sentence, is necessary. The other says that there are two propositions connected with a sentence like 'Water = H$_2$O', and the sentence counts as necessary if the C-proposition [secondary intension] is necessary, but, as understanding the sentence only requires knowing the A-proposition [primary intension], little wonder that understanding alone is not enough to see that the sentence is necessary.[20]

Here Jackson makes explicit the framework of very strong two-dimensionalism that was implicit in his earlier remarks.

The main feature of strong two-dimensionalism about which he is less than fully explicit involves the semantics of attitude ascriptions—most particularly assertion, belief, and knowledge ascriptions, *x v's that S*. For the strong two-dimensionalist these (standardly) report relations between agents and the primary intensions of their complement clauses. Although in his discussion of the necessary aposteriori, Jackson seems tacitly to assume this, the closest he comes to explicitly endorsing it is in the following passage.

It is, as Stalnaker, Tichy, and Chalmers emphasize, the A-proposition expressed by a sentence that is often best for capturing what someone believes when they use the sentence, and for capturing the information they seek to convey by uttering a sentence. **Thus, children who have not yet had the chemistry lesson in which they are told that water is H$_2$O, but who understand the sentence 'Water covers most of the Earth', will use the sentence**

---

[20] Pages 76–77.

to express their opinion that most of the Earth is covered by the watery stuff of our acquaintance.[21]

These comments are, admittedly, rather spare. However, there are several factors which lend support to the conclusion that Jackson implicitly subscribes to the strong two-dimensionalist analysis of attitude ascriptions.

First, notice the comment about "children who have not yet had the chemistry lesson in which **they are told that water is H_2O.**" Jackson here uses the attitude ascription

9. They are told that water is H_2O.

to pick out those children who have the property of having not yet had a chemistry lesson in which they are told p, for a certain proposition p that is specified by the complement clause of (9). Clearly, p is **not** intended to be the trivial, necessary proposition, that H_2O is H_2O, which Jackson takes to be the secondary intension of the complement clause. He is not imagining children who have not yet been informed of a trivial, apriori identity. Thus, as he himself uses (9), it does **not** specify a relation between an unidentified agent (the chemistry teacher), the children, and the **secondary** intension of its complement clause. Rather, he seems to imagine a chemistry lesson in which children are told that the watery stuff of our acquaintance is H_2O. Since the proposition that the watery stuff of our acquaintance is H_2O is what he takes to be the primary intension of the complement clause, he seems to be using (9) to report a relation between an unidentified agent, the children, and the **primary** intension of the complement clause. In short, his own use of (9) fits the strong two-dimensionalist semantic rule according to which attitude ascriptions relate agents to the primary rather than secondary intensions of their complement clauses.

Second, Jackson tells us the children use the sentence 'Water covers most of the Earth' to, in his words, *express their opinion that most of the Earth is covered by the watery stuff of their acquaintance.* Here, he seems implicitly to be denying that when these children sincerely utter the sentence they are asserting and expressing their belief in the secondary intension of that sentence. Rather, he takes them to be asserting and expressing their belief in its primary intension—the proposition that "the watery stuff of our acquaintance" covers most of the Earth. As before, this is fully in accord with strong two-dimensionalism.

[21] Page 76, my emphasis.

Third, not only do children use sentences containing the word *water* to express their beliefs, **we** use such sentences to report **their** beliefs. We say: *Johnny believes that water covers most of the Earth, Johnny believes that there is water in the pitcher*, or *Johnny hasn't yet learned that water is H$_2$O,* and so on. Although Jackson doesn't mention this explicitly, surely what we say in a great many of these cases is true (even when the children have not yet had their chemistry lesson). The only way these attitude ascriptions could be true, on Jackson's account, is if what we use them to report are the agent's beliefs in the primary, rather than the secondary, intensions expressed by their complement clauses. Although this doesn't strictly entail that Jackson presupposes the strong two-dimensionalist account of the semantics of attitude ascriptions, it lends credence to this interpretation.

Finally, any account which, like Jackson's, claims to explain why S is an instance of the necessary aposteriori by claiming (i) that the secondary intension of S is necessary, while (ii) the primary intension of S is knowable only aposteriori, must connect (i) and (ii) to the truth of (10a), (10b), and (10c).

10a. *It is a necessary truth that S.*

 b. *It is not knowable apriori that S.*

 c. *It is knowable only aposteriori that S.*

The needed connection is, of course, provided by the theses (iii) that (10a) is used to ascribe necessity to the secondary intension of S and (iv) that (10b) is used to deny that the primary intension of S is knowable apriori, while (10c) ascribes to it the property of being knowable only aposteriori. Without theses (iii–iv), Jackson has no explanation of the truth of (10a), (10b), and (10c)—and hence no account of the necessary aposteriori. Since he surely **does** have such an account, he should be interpreted as committed to (iii) and (iv). Moreover, once (iv) is in place, there is no denying that the examples in (11) have uses in which they report relations between agents and the primary intensions of their complement clauses.

11a. *John knows apriori that S.*

 b. *John knows only aposteriori that S.*

 c. *John knows that S.*

 d. *John believes that S.*

It could, of course, be maintained that in addition to having these uses, some or all of the ascriptions in (11) have other uses as well. As far as I know, Jackson leaves this possibility open. What is not left open is that he needs the strong two-dimensionalist uses. If these are not to be obtained by adopting the strong two-dimensionalist semantics of attitude ascriptions, how are they to be obtained?

Two-Dimensionalism and Physicalism

Having explained Jackson's route to strong two-dimensionalism, I will now review what he takes to be his most important application of it. As indicated earlier, he wants to show that if physicalism is true, in the sense that all truths are necessary consequences of the explicitly physical truths of an ideal physics, then all truths must be apriori consequences of those physical truths.[22] In stating his thesis, we will suppose that it is possible to give some finite formulation P of all the explicitly physical truths, and we will let S express any other truth. Physicalism, then, holds that $P \supset S$ is necessary. Jackson's thesis is that if physicalism is correct, then the claim *It is knowable apriori that $P \supset S$* must also be true. The argument he gives in *From Metaphysics to Ethics* is designed to rebut the most obvious objection to this thesis: namely, that since we know from Kripke that some sentences are necessary but not apriori, we have no reason to think that the physicalist's crucial conditionals, $P \supset S$, may not be among them. Jackson attempts to show that, in fact, they are not among them—i.e., they are not instances of the necessary aposteriori. Not surprisingly, his argument makes significant use of his strong two-dimensionalist account of what it is for a sentence to be an instance of the necessary aposteriori.

He begins with a paradigmatic Kripkean instance of what may be called *necessary aposteriori consequence*.

12a. H_2O covers most of the Earth.

13. Water covers most of the Earth.

---

[22] See pp. 7–8 of *From Ethics to Metaphysics* for Jackson's characterization of the class of explicitly physical truths. From his discussion there, it appears that, as he sees it, the truths on which, according to physicalism, all other truths depend are those that express claims concerning the sorts of micro-properties and relations that are posited by current physical science to explain observable macro-phenomena. For a very useful and illuminating discussion of Jackson's argument about physicalism, see Alex Byrne, "Cosmic Hermeneutics," *Philosophical Perspectives* 13 (1999): 347–83.

As Jackson frames the example, (12a) plays the role of an explicitly physical truth, while (13) plays the role of a nonphysical truth that is a necessary consequence of the physical truths. (So, for purposes of this example, *water* is understood as not being part of the explicitly physicalistic vocabulary.) Jackson notes that (13) is a necessary consequence of (12a) in the sense that the proposition expressed by (13) is a necessary consequence of the proposition expressed by (12a). The *C-propositions*, as he calls them (i.e., the secondary intensions), stand in this relation.[23] Thus, the conditional (14)—with (12a) as antecedent and (13) as consequent—is necessary.[24]

14. H_2O covers most of the Earth $\supset$ water covers most of the Earth.

However, this conditional is **not** apriori on Jackson's account, since one can understand it without being in a position to determine that it expresses a truth. Recall that *water* is supposed to have the content of the rigidified description—*dthat [the watery stuff of our acquaintance]*. Hence, Jackson takes (14) to be synonymous with (15).

15. H_2O covers most of the Earth $\supset$ dthat [the watery stuff of our acquaintance] covers most of the Earth.

The conditional (15) will fail to express a truth in some context/ world-state w, if in w H_2O covers the Earth, but it is not the case that the stuff which is watery covers most of the Earth. This might come about because, in w, H_2O has different observable properties from those it has in the world as it actually is, and for that reason does **not** count as watery stuff, in w. So here we have a pair of conditional sentences—(14) and (15)—which, on Jackson's account, are necessary but **not** apriori.

Jackson next claims that we can get necessary **apriori** conditionals connecting the physical with the nonphysical by conjoining (12a) with (12b), and using the conjunction as antecedent.

[23] Page 81, fn. 35.
[24] In this discussion, we follow Jackson in connecting talk of necessary and apriori consequence of sentences with talk of the necessity and apriority of conditional sentences as follows: S_2 is a necessary consequence of S_1 iff $S_1 \supset S_2$ is necessary (which holds iff the secondary intension S_2 is true at all world-states w at which the secondary intension of S_1 is); S_2 is an apriori consequence of S_1 iff $S_1 \supset S_2$ is apriori (which, according to Jackson, holds iff the primary intension of this conditional is knowable apriori). Jackson believes that this primary intension is knowable apriori iff the primary intension of S_2 is true at all world-states w at which the primary intension of S_1 is true.

12b. H_2O is the watery stuff of our acquaintance.

The resulting conditionals are those in (16).

16a. H_2O covers most of the Earth & H_2O is the watery stuff of our acquaintance ⊃ the watery stuff of our acquaintance covers most of the Earth.

  b. H_2O covers most of the Earth & H_2O is the watery stuff of our acquaintance ⊃ dthat [the watery stuff of our acquaintance] covers most of the Earth.

  c. H_2O covers most of the Earth & H_2O is the watery stuff of our acquaintance ⊃ water covers most of the Earth.

Since, according to Jackson, these conditionals all have the same primary intension, his strong two-dimensionalism leads him to the view that one of these conditionals is apriori iff they all are. Since (16a) is, without a doubt, apriori (its primary intension is, according to Jackson, identical with the trivial necessary truth which is its secondary intension), he concludes that (16c) is too, and hence that it is both necessary and apriori.

Jackson takes this to be a vindication of his thesis about physicalism. Since he regards the needed supplementary conjunct (12b) to be one that is itself determined by the explicitly physical truths, he concludes that the finite formulation P of all the explicitly physical truths either already contains it explicitly, or has it as an apriori consequence—in which case *P ⊃ water covers most of the Earth* will also be apriori. He further assumes that the same argument could be repeated for all pairs of sentences S_{1a}, S_2 for which $S_{1a} ⊃ S_2$ is a Kripkean example of the necessary aposteriori, where S_{1a} is a physical truth and S_2 is nonphysical. In all such cases, he believes, the conjunction of S_{1a} with some further truth S_{1b} will be an apriori consequence of the physical truths that has S_2 as one of its apriori consequences. If this is right, then Kripkean instances of the necessary aposteriori pose no threat to his thesis about physicalism.

With this in mind, let us review the argument involving *water* and *H_2O*, as Jackson sees it.

(i) (14) is an example of the necessary aposteriori since, although the proposition p it expresses (its secondary intension) is necessary, understanding (14) is not sufficient for one to know that it expresses a truth. The reason this isn't sufficient is that understanding (14) does not guarantee that one knows that it expresses p. In order to know this, one must know that its consequent, (13), expresses q (where q is the proposition that H_2O covers most of the Earth). Since understanding (14) does not, by itself, guarantee that one knows this, additional empirical information is needed.

(ii)   *Water* functions on the model of the demonstrative *he*; its analysis is *dthat [the watery stuff of our acquaintance]*. Hence, if S is a sentence containing the word *water*, and S expresses a proposition p, then in order for one who understands S to know that it expresses p, one must know of the referent of *water*—namely the chemical kind H_2O—that it is the watery stuff of our acquaintance. Thus, the empirical information needed to know that (13) expresses the proposition that H_2O covers most of the Earth—and that (14) expresses the trivial necessary proposition that if H_2O covers most of the Earth, then H_2O covers most of the Earth—is the information that H_2O is the watery stuff of our acquaintance.

(iii) Next consider the conjunction of (12a) and (12b), which is the antecedent of (16c). One who understands (16c) must also understand this conjunction, in which case one will know that if this conjunction is true, then (i) the consequent, (13), of (16c) expresses the proposition that H_2O covers most of the Earth, and (ii) (16c) itself expresses a trivial necessary truth. Of course, one who understands (16c) also knows that if its antecedent is false, then (16c) will, again, express a truth. Hence, understanding (16c) is sufficient to know that it must be true—which means that it is apriori, in addition to being necessary.

(iv) Since, according to physicalism, (12b) is determined by the physical truths, it is an apriori consequence of the physical truths, as is the antecedent of (16c), which is the conjunction of (12a) and (12b).

(v)   Since the antecedent of (16c) is an apriori consequence of the physical truths P, and (16c) is itself apriori, the consequent, (13), of (16c) is an apriori consequence of P, and the physicalist's conditional *P ⊃ water covers most of the Earth* is apriori—in which cases the Kripkean example (14) of the necessary aposteriori poses no problem for Jackson's thesis about physicalism.

(vi) The same style argument can be given for all Kripkean examples of the necessary aposteriori.

This argument is, of course, dependent on Jackson's strong two-dimensionalist treatment of the necessary aposteriori—which, as we have seen, is more than a little questionable. Before worrying about that, however, there is an immediate difficulty that must be faced. Step (iv) in the argument equates the determination of (12b) by the physical truths with (12b)'s being an apriori consequence of those truths. But what is it for S to be determined by the physical truths? If it is for S to be a necessary consequence of the physical truths, then of course physicalism maintains that (12b) is so determined, but it doesn't follow without further argument that (12b) is also an apriori consequence of the physical truths. Nor can we simply interpret the claim that (12b) is determined by the physical truths to be the claim that (12b) is an apriori consequence of those truths, since we have yet been given no argument that it is. Thus, even if everything else in the argument were correct, (iv) would be unsupported.

In the following passage I quote Jackson's own presentation of the argument—beginning with his discussion of (14), and then moving to the conditional (16c) that results from adding to the antecedent of (14) an extra conjunct supplying the information needed to know that the consequent of these conditionals expresses the proposition that H_2O covers most of the Earth. I have emphasized the remarks at the end of the passage expressing step (iv) in the argument. The point to notice is that Jackson merely assumes the crucial point, without giving any argument for it.

What understanding [of (14)] alone does give, though, is the way the proposition expressed depends on context, on the relevant facts outside the head, on the relevant facts about how things actually are. Thus, if the two-dimensional explanation of the necessary a posteriori is correct, the appropriate supplementation of the premises [e.g., of (12a)] by contextual information [(12b)] will give a set of premises that do lead a priori to the conclusion [(13)]. We will be able to move a priori from, for example, sentences about the distribution of H_2O *combined* with the right context-giving statements, to the distribution of water. And exactly this is true for the inference just given. . . . Although the passage from [12a] to [13] is a posteriori, the passage from [12a] together with [12b] to [13] is a priori in view of the a priori status of 'Water is the watery stuff of our acquaintance'. Although our understanding of the sentence 'Water covers most of the Earth' does not in itself give the proposition it expresses, it does give the proposition it expresses when we know the context and [12b] gives the context, for it gives the relevant fact about us and our world. . . . The crucial point here is the way that the contextual information, the relevant information about how things actually are, by virtue of telling us in principle the propositions expressed by the various sentences (or, equivalently, the C-propositions associated with them) enables us to move a priori from the H_2O way things are to the water way they are. **But if physicalism is true, all the information needed to yield the propositions being expressed about what the actual world is like in various physical sentences can be given in physical terms, for the actual context is givable in physical terms according to physicalism. Therefore, physicalism is committed to the in principle a priori deducibility of the psychological from the physical.**[25]

Here, it appears, Jackson simply begs the question. What he needs is the premise that if physicalism is true, then every truth about context that is relevant to determining the proposition expressed by a sentence will be an **apriori** consequence of the physical truths. But that isn't what physicalism states. What physicalism says is that all such truths are **necessary** consequences of the physical truths. The claim that they are also **apriori** consequences of the physical truths is not a **premise** that Jackson can rely on: rather it is an instance of the general thesis his argument is designed to defend.[26]

Nevertheless, there is something interesting to be learned from the difficulty he encounters at this point. We have already seen that he is committed to the strong two-dimensionalist view that all names and natural kind terms are semantically equivalent to rigidified descriptions that don't themselves contain any names or natural kind terms. Suppose one also thought that these descriptions were made up entirely of vocabulary the primary intensions of which were identical with their

[25] Pages 82–83.
[26] Byrne makes this point on p. 371 of "Cosmic Hermeneutics."

secondary intensions. If one thought that this were the case, then one might think that his argument could be reinstated.

Consider, in this connection, Jackson's made-up description *the watery stuff of our acquaintance*, which he asks us to suppose fixes the reference of the term *water*. If the primary intension of this description were identical with its secondary intension, then, the primary intension of (12b) would be identical with its secondary intension, in which case strong two-dimensionalism would dictate that it could not be a necessary consequence of the physical truths without also being an apriori consequence of them (assuming that the physical truths themselves display no distinction between primary and secondary intension). This, of course, is the result Jackson needs.

However, it is far from clear that it is really achievable. For one thing, it is hard to see how the primary intension of his description *the watery stuff of our acquaintance* could turn out to be identical with its secondary intension, containing as it does the ordinary indexical *our*. For another, it would have to be explained how it could be that ordinary terms like proper names and natural kind terms require complex semantic analyses that impose a distinction between primary intension and secondary intension, whereas the highly sophisticated language of the most advanced physical science does not. Nor is this all. Since understanding names and natural kind terms does not require knowing any physics, there would have to be further, nonphysical vocabulary—used to give the descriptive meanings of names and natural kind terms—the expressions of which are themselves innocent of the distinction between primary and secondary intension. What does this other vocabulary consist in, and how could it possibly be shown to be sufficient for the descriptive semantic analysis of all names and natural kind terms, while also being such that the truths formulated in it are apriori consequences of the truths of physics? Since Jackson does not address these challenges, the crucial steps (iv) and (vi) in his argument concerning physicalism remain unsupported. However, this is not the end of the matter.

Confusions about Reference-Fixing Descriptions

There is more at stake here than the argument about physicalism. In addition, there are deeper worries about the strong two-dimensionalist doctrine that all names and natural kind terms must be synonymous with rigidified versions of descriptions that semantically fix their referents. That there must be such reference-fixing descriptions is something Jackson seems to regard as obvious, and beyond serious doubt—as is indicated by the following footnote in which he acknowledges that his treatment of (12) and (13) depends on his analysis of *water* as involving the rigidification of *the watery stuff of our acquaintance*.

> I assume the particular reference-fixing story told earlier for 'water' about, that is, the A-intension of 'water'. Other views about how the reference-fixing story should go would require appropriately different versions of [12b]. **Although any view about how 'water' gets to pick out what it does will be controversial, it is incredible that there is *no* story to tell—it is not magic that 'water' picks out what it does pick out—so we can be confident that there is a reference-fixing story to tell.**[27]

I will return in a moment to "the particular reference-fixing story told earlier for 'water'" mentioned in the first sentence. Before doing that, however, I want to bring out an important confusion underlying the remarks I have highlighted.

Recall that Jackson is here defending a view about the meaning of the word *water*, in the sense of what a competent speaker who understands the term knows. The view being defended in the footnote is that *water* is synonymous with *dthat [the watery stuff of our acquaintance]*. If this view is correct, then anyone who understands (13)—*Water covers most of the Earth*—knows that it is true iff the watery stuff of our acquaintance covers the Earth. (Pretend that it has been specified what the content of this dummy description is.) Hence, if such a person also understands the conditional (16c), with (13) as consequent and the conjunction of (12a) and (12b) as antecedent, then that person will have all the information needed to conclude that it is true—which, according to Jackson, shows that the conditional is apriori. In the footnote, he is defending the claim about the meaning of *water* that allows him to draw this conclusion. His point is that even though the precise content of his imaginary reference-fixing description *the watery stuff of our acquaintance* must be regarded as controversial, there can be no controversy that there is such a description. After all, *water* doesn't get its reference by magic!

Jackson's defense confuses two things: (i) the facts that originally brought it about that *water* stands for what it does, and that have sustained the reference of the word since it was initially established, and (ii) the facts about the meaning of *water* that speakers must master in order to understand the word. Since the position Jackson is defending is one about meaning and understanding, what he needs to establish as uncontroversial is that the facts in (ii) include facts that specify descriptive characteristics which are necessary and sufficient for a kind to be designated by *water*. However, this is **not** uncontroversial. What is uncontroversial is that since *water* didn't get its reference by magic, some facts of type (i) must exist, or have existed. If we knew these facts, they could, of course, be described. But it does not follow from this that such descriptions are parts of the meaning of the term, or that speakers who understand *water* must associate them with the word.

Suppose, for the sake of argument, that *water* originally got its meaning and reference by some Kripke-style baptism involving particular samples presumed to share some common, but then unknown, underlying material constitution which the word was stipulated to stand for. On the basis of this stipulation, the word came to stand for the physically constitutive kind shared by certain samples. Suppose further that later speakers used the word with the intention that it should stand for whatever kind had already been associated with it in the common language. To complete the story, let us assume that there was no period of wholesale confusion of that kind with some different kind. So *water* didn't change its reference over time.[28]

This story provides a sketch of the facts of type (i) that explain why *water* refers to what it does. But there is no requirement that competent speakers who understand the word know these facts. In order to understand *water*, one doesn't have to know which samples were originally involved, where they were located, or where they can be found today. One doesn't even have to know that the word was originally introduced by an ostensive baptism involving samples with which the original stipulators were acquainted. One also doesn't have to know whether or not there has been reference change over time. One certainly doesn't have to be able to reliably identify samples when confronted with them; nor is it required that one be personally acquainted with any samples of water. Rather, an otherwise competent English speaker is counted as a competent user of the word, if he or she knows that *water* is a term that stands for some natural kind

---

[28] We here rule out cases like that described in Evans's 'Madagascar' example.

that determines its extension at different world-states—even if one doesn't have any reliable way of describing that kind, other than the kind the word stands for in English. Perhaps one also has to have some idea of what type of kind it is—i. e., that it has something to do with physically constitutive characteristics—and that the stuff in question sometimes comes in liquid form. But this knowledge is quite meager and falls far short of any noncircular, uniquely identifying description of the sort that could possibly qualify as giving the meaning of the term.

If this Kripkean picture is correct, then there may be no description of the type required by Jackson's argument—even though it is not magic that *water* refers to what it does. Since Jackson has done nothing to undermine this picture, he has not given credence to one of the central planks of his strong two-dimensionalism. He hasn't provided any reason to believe the doctrine that all names and natural kind terms are synonymous with indexical, rigidified descriptions that do not themselves contain any names or natural kind terms.

With this in mind, I return to the particular reference-fixing story, alluded to in his footnote, that Jackson tells about *water*. This is what he says:

> 'Water' is a rigid designator for the kind common to the watery exemplars we are, or the appropriate baptizers in our language community were, acquainted with. This is what we grasp when we come to understand the word. This is what we all knew about water before 1750, before we discovered the chemical composition of water. What then does the word 'water' denote in a world where the kind common to the relevant watery exemplars in that world is kind K under the supposition that that world is the actual world? [That is, what would the content assigned to a world-state w by the character of *water* pick out when evaluated relative to w, where w is as much like the actual world-state as possible except for having kind K everywhere water is standardly found in the actual world-state?] Kind K, of course, be that kind H_2O, XYZ, or whatever. In short, we take Kripke's story about reference fixing, and apply it to each world under the supposition that it is the actual world [i.e., under the supposition that it is functioning as a context of utterance], to get the A-extension of 'water' in that world.[29]

[29] Page 49.

This passage illustrates a serious error growing out of certain misleading aspects of Kripke's discussion of reference fixing that I warned about in chapter 4. As I there pointed out, except for some relatively rare special cases, the vast majority of ordinary proper names do **not**, according to Kripke, have their referents semantically fixed by description. The same may be said for natural kind terms—at least after a brief period following their original introduction.[30] So how is their reference determined? In answer to this question, Kripke offers his conception of reference transmission by historical chains, which often begin with episodes of baptism, or ostensive definition. What is not always noticed—and what Kripke himself did not emphasize sufficiently strongly—is that "reference fixing by description" and "reference fixing by historical chain" are not on a par.

Reference fixing by description is, as Kripke standardly understands it, a matter of linguistic rules that competent speakers must master if they are to understand the relevant terms. By contrast, when one speaks of reference fixing by historical chain, one is alluding to certain foundational facts of the sort (i) above that bring it about that a name or natural kind term comes to refer to what it does, and that play important roles in determining that the original reference is preserved over time. These foundational facts are not parts of the meanings of names or kind terms of which competent speakers must be aware. Speakers have to know what the words of their language mean and refer to, and they must know how to use them. They don't have to know how those words got to mean and refer to what they do; nor do they have to know how the conditions for their proper use arose and are sustained.

Much of this is, I think, more or less implicit in Kripke himself. The main problem with his discussion is that the crucial distinction between facts of types (i) and (ii) is not made explicit or developed. In

---

[30] One of the misleading aspects of Kripke's discussion, noted in chapter 4, was his tendency to speak as if when natural kind terms are introduced ostensively we may, at least for a short time, think of descriptions incorporating the contents of such introductions as semantically fixing the reference of the terms, and as thereby giving rise to apriori knowledge. For my critique, see the section "Natural Kind Terms, Reference Fixing, and the Apriori." Evidence of the fact that this unfortunate aspect of Kripke's discussion influenced Jackson is given by Jackson's fn. 34 of chapter 2 of *From Ethics to Metaphysics*: "Although Kripke does not use the terminology of two-dimensional modal logic, the crucial point is implicit in his writings, or so it seems to me. For he insists that sentences of the form 'K is . . .' where 'K' is a natural-kind term, and the dots are filled with an account of how reference to Ks is fixed are a priori, and the way reference to Ks is fixed gives the A-extension of K in every possible world, that is, gives the A-intension" (pp. 51–52).

addition, his way of putting matters may sometimes be misleading. In particular, his way of framing the general discussion—*What fixes reference?*—has, I think, suggested to some that the two answers he gives to this question—*Descriptions in certain unusual cases* and *Historical chains of reference transmission for the great mass of proper names and natural kind terms*—are on a par. Since the claim about descriptions is understood to be semantic, and hence about the linguistic rules that speakers must master in learning various names, philosophers like Jackson have been encouraged to think of the claim about historical chains in the same way. This, as I have argued, is a mistake.

The point at issue strikes at the heart of all forms of ambitious two-dimensionalism. Without the analysis of proper names and natural kind terms as rigidified descriptions, there is no case for taking them to be indexical at all. But if they are not indexical, then their primary intensions are identical with their secondary intensions, in which case the distinction between the two cannot be used to explain, or explain away, the necessary aposteriori. Perhaps because of this, Jackson is tenacious in defending the idea that whenever a speaker s understands a name or natural kind term, and is competent to use it, s will possess a reference-fixing description that uniquely determines its reference. In many cases, Jackson thinks, this description may define s's reference in terms of the reference of others more expert than s, with whom s is connected by a historical chain or reference transmission. But no matter, whenever s is competent, there will always be such a description. Jackson expresses this idea in the following passage.

> [I]t is observed that it may be unclear who the experts are in the sense that it is unknown to the ignorant users, and yet reference still occurs. Many folk refer to quarks when they use the word 'quark', despite the fact that they do not know whether it is a term from physics or from biology, and so do not know which department contains the experts. . . . However, these folk do know that there are some experts somewhere or other, and that **these experts lie at one end of a reference borrowing chain that has whoever they themselves borrowed the term from at the other**. . . . But now we can specify the property these folk associate with the word 'quark'. **It is having the property the group**

of users of the word 'quark' that they are borrowing from associate with the word 'quark'.[31]

The suggestion here seems to be that for many speakers the reference-fixing description they associate with *quark* is something like *the kind of thing referred to by those from whom my use of the term borrows its reference*. If a speaker s has borrowed from others who are themselves borrowing, then their use of a similar parasitic description will push back the determination of s's reference one step further, and so on until the genuine experts are reached. At that stage, it is assumed that reference of *quark* in the mouths of the experts is determined by their detailed descriptive knowledge of quarks.

Although there are several serious problems with this picture, we will pause over only one.[32] The description imagined cannot possibly be the mechanism by which reference is determined. Rather, it assumes that there is some other process of reference transmission by which the referent of s's use of *quark* has already been inherited from previous uses of the term. That is what it is for reference to have been **borrowed**. Without such an independent process that really determines how reference is fixed, the description designates nothing. With such an independent process, the description accurately picks out the referent, but only because reference has already been determined independently of any consideration of the description itself.

---

[31] "Reference and Description Revisited," *Philosophical Perspectives* 12,: *Language, Mind, and Ontology* (1998), p. 210, my emphasis.

[32] Additional problems include the following: (i) if *quark* in s's language were synonymous with *dthat [the kind of thing referred to by those from whom my use of the term 'quark' borrows its reference]*, then the primary intension of a sentence S containing the term would be a proposition about reference borrowing, in which case a speaker who said *so and so believes, knows, etc. that S* would—according to the strong two-dimensionalist construal of attitude ascriptions—standardly (or at any rate often) be interpreted as attributing to so and so beliefs in, and knowledge about, how s's use of the term *quark* got its referent (which is absurd); (ii) if the reference-fixing descriptions in terms of which *quark* were semantically analyzed depended on the knowledge of particular speakers, then the word would have different meanings for different speakers, and no account of the meaning of the word in the common language would be given; (iii) if the reference of terms of physics, like *quark*, were semantically determined by descriptions mentioning semantic and psychological facts about people and their use of words, then Jackson's project of showing that all truths—including the truths of semantics and psychology—must, if physicalism is correct, be apriori consequences of the physical truths (i.e., the project of showing that the primary intensions of the relevant conditionals must be apriori) would be threatened, or at least complicated, since on this account the primary intensions of some physical truths (for at least some speakers) would themselves be semantic and psychological.

Moreover, it is not clear that other descriptions that specify the referent of one's use of a term would do much better. Consider, in this respect, the description *the thing/kind, etc., to which the person or persons from whom I first acquired the term referred when they used it.* Although this description doesn't beg the question by specifying reference borrowing that must have occurred independently, there is no guarantee that it picks out what one's use of the term really refers to. After all, it is conceivable that the person from whom one picked up the term initially was using it nonstandardly, in a way that doesn't determine the reference of one's current use. It is also conceivable that the term has changed reference since one originally encountered it, in which case the description may again be inaccurate. It would be nice for the description theorist if there were available a complete, explicit, accurate, and non-question-begging theory of the process by which the reference of speakers' use of names and natural kind terms is always inherited that could be put to use to formulate the reference-fixing descriptions the descriptivist needs. But there isn't.[33]

However, this is not Jackson's last line of defense. As I indicated in chapter 3, he believes that it is demonstrable that speakers must have at their disposal some implicit theory that does the work of semantically determining the reference of their terms, whether or not they are able to explicitly state the relevant reference-fixing descriptions. Thus, in "Reference and Description Revisited" he says:

> [I]f speakers can say what refers to what when various possible worlds are described to them, description theorists can identify the property associated in their minds with, for example, the word 'water': it is the disjunction of the properties that guide the speakers in each particular possible world when they say which stuff, if any, in each world counts as water. This disjunction is in their minds in the sense that they can deliver the answer for each possible world when it is described in sufficient detail, but it is implicit in the sense that the pattern that brings the various disjuncts together as part of the, possibly highly complex, disjunction may be one they cannot state.[34]

Jackson believes that ordinary speakers' dispositions to respond to elaborate Kripke-style thought experiments about the reference of *water* in different possible contexts of use must be the product of their

[33] For discussion, see chapter 14 of *The Age of Meaning.*
[34] Page 212.

implicit understanding of what the term means. He takes this understanding to consist, at least in part, in their associating *water* with a property which defines necessary and sufficient conditions for something to count as designated by it in any possible context. In his two-dimensionalist terminology, this property amounts to the primary intension, or as he calls it, the *A-intension*, of the term—which is why he takes the intuitive judgments of speakers about what a word would refer to if used in contexts of different sorts to provide information that is definitive of its meaning.

From this perspective, the fact that there are easily imagined contexts of utterance in which uses of *water* just like ours refer to XYZ, rather than H_2O, is taken to conclusively demonstrate that *water* is indexical, and that its reference **must** vary from context to context. For Jackson, the only remaining question is the content of the descriptive conditions which must be satisfied in order for *water* to refer to a kind K in a possible context/world-state—not whether there are such conditions. To answer this question, familiar Kripke/Putnam-style thought experiments are the guides. The same view is advanced for proper names. For example, the fact that there are easily imagined contexts in which uses of *Hesperus* and *Phosphorus* refer to different planets, while being in other respects just like our own actual context, is taken to demonstrate that these names have different indexical meanings (A-intensions), and that their reference must vary from one context to the next.

Jackson's thinking may be illustrated with the help of the following scenarios.

SCENARIO 1

World-state w is as much like our actual world-state as possible, except that in w the clear, drinkable stuff that falls from the sky and fills lakes, rivers, and oceans is not H_2O, but XYZ. In w, there are speakers like us, who use the word *water* in ways that are indiscernible from the ways that we actually use the word *water*.

Question: What does *water*, as used in w, refer to? Answer: To XYZ.

SCENARIO 2

Word-state w is as much like our actual world-state as possible, except that in w (i) the clear, drinkable stuff that falls from the sky and fills lakes, rivers, and oceans throughout the entire inhabited part of the world is XYZ, and (ii) there are undiscovered samples of H_2O elsewhere which are observationally indistinguishable from XYZ. In w, there are speakers like us, who use the word *water* in ways that are indiscernible from the ways that we actually use the word *water*. However, all of their uses of the term have been in conjunction with XYZ; they have never encountered H_2O.

Question: What does *water*, as used in w, refer to? Answer: To XYZ.

SCENARIO 3

World-state w is as much like our actual world-state as possible, except that in w about half of the clear, drinkable stuff that falls from the sky and fills lakes, rivers, and oceans is XYZ, and the other half is H_2O. The inhabitants of w, who are in all significant respects just like us, causally interact with both, in more or less equal proportions. Since the two kinds are observationally indistinguishable in all everyday situations, the inhabitants don't realize that they are interacting with two kinds, rather than one. Since they use the word *water* in ways that are indiscernible from the ways that we actually use it, they are equally disposed to apply it to samples of both kinds.

Question: What does *water*, as used in w, refer to? Natural Answer: To both kinds (or to instances of both kinds).

Scenario 1 is an abbreviated version of Putnam's Twin Earth fable, while the other two scenarios are just variations on the same theme.[35] If one assumes at the outset (i) that the contexts/world-states in these scenarios are genuinely possible, and (ii) that the word *water* used in these scenarios has the same character (A-intension) as *water* has in our actual, everyday context, then the judgments made about the reference of *water* in these scenarios provide information about the character (A-intension) that *water* actually has for us. On these assumptions, one concludes from these examples that the semantic rule governing the word has something to do with applying to whatever kind or kinds (with which we are acquainted) instances of which are clear, drinkable, fall from the sky, and fill the rivers, lakes, and oceans. Doubtless this is only a first approximation that could, in principle, be refined by considering additional, more complicated scenarios. As a first approximation, though, one might say that the semantic rule governing *water* dictates

[35] Hilary Putnam, "The Meaning of 'Meaning'."

that it is to apply to instances of whatever kind or kinds of stuff (with which we are acquainted) have the familiar "watery" properties. You know, it means *the watery stuff of our acquaintance!*

There are two problems with this line of reasoning. First, it is not obvious that the possibilities outlined in Putnam's Twin Earth fable, and related scenarios, are genuinely possible in the sense required by Jackson. They are, of course, epistemologically possible—we can't know apriori that a world-state doesn't obtain in which something other than H_2O—call it *XYZ*—has all the normal observational properties that water actually has, including falling from the sky, filling the rivers, lakes, and oceans, being drinkable by us, and playing the role in our lives that H_2O actually does. But this is not enough for Jackson. Since he refuses to countenance epistemological possibilities that are not metaphysically possible, he is obliged to tell us why we should think that such world-states really are metaphysically possible. Like virtually everyone else discussing Putnam-style scenarios, he doesn't do this. How, then, can we be confident that they are possible in this sense? I don't know enough chemistry to be able to tell you whether any of the metaphysically possible molecular structures we are aware of—significantly different from H_2O but constructed out of basic elements we know about—could reproduce all the normal observational and functional properties of water. Surely, it can't be ruled out apriori that there are none, and philosophical discussions of this issue never specify empirical reasons for ruling this out. Thus, it is not obvious—to me at least—that Putnam's familiar scenarios represent genuine metaphysical possibilities. This wouldn't matter if everyone recognized that they were to be accepted as epistemologically possible, without prejudging whether or not they are metaphysically possible. But this is not Jackson's position. Given his restriction of the epistemologically possible to the metaphysically possible, for him to treat them as epistemologically possible—which they surely are—is for him to presuppose that they are also metaphysically possible—which they may or may not be. In light of this, it would seem that he ought to be more cautious about placing the weight on these scenarios that he does. That he isn't cautious suggests to me that—like all too many of us at one time or another—he is unwittingly engaging in the age-old philosophical practice of helping himself to a commonplace notion—epistemological possibility (distinct from metaphysical possibility)—the legitimacy of which is rendered questionable by his central philosophical doctrines.

The second problem with his use of scenarios like 1–3 to draw con-

clusions about the meanings of words like *water* is that the central assumption on which his reasoning is based is completely unsupported.
There is **nothing** in the scenarios that indicates that *water*, as used in
the contexts/world-states there described, has the same character as it
actually has for us. Suppose—as I, and others, do—that natural kind
terms like *water* (as well as proper names) have nonindexical meanings—i.e., constant characters, which assign the same content to every
context.[36] Then the contexts/world-states described in scenarios 1–3
are ones in which speakers use the word *water* with meanings which
differ from the meaning it actually has for us. This is perfectly compatible with their use of the word *water* being indiscernible from ours.
Since we actually apply the word to instances of the clear, drinkable
stuff that falls from the sky and fills the rivers, lakes, and oceans of our
acquaintance, we naturally assume that speakers in our illustrative scenarios do too. These are simply contingent, aposteriori facts about our
actual use of the term that are preserved in the imagined scenarios.
What our intuitions about the scenarios provide us with information
about is the role played by these contingent facts in determining what
character (meaning) *water* has when used by speakers in various situations—not what the actual character of *water* assigns to the contexts in
these situations.[37]

There are both strong and weak theses here. The strong thesis is
that names and natural kind terms are not indexical, rigidified descriptions, but rather are nonindexical, nondescriptive terms with constant
characters. The weak thesis is that Jackson has done nothing to show
that the strong thesis isn't correct. Although I have already touched
on important considerations favoring the strong thesis—e.g., the
seeming unavailability of substantive, necessary and sufficient, descriptive, reference-determining conditions that all competent speakers
who understand a given name or natural kind term are required to
know—the full argument for the strong thesis will have to wait until
chapter 10. For now, it is only the weak thesis that I take to have established. If I am right, then Jackson has failed to establish, or provide

[36] See, for example, section XXII of David Kaplan's "Demonstratives."

[37] Although these scenarios don't tell us about the meaning that *water* actually has, it
might be thought (i) that they shed light on the meaning of notions like *reference, name,* and
natural kind term, and (ii) that these scenarios provide information about what we can know
apriori about the reference of various names and natural kind terms in different possible situations. Although I am skeptical about even this, I note only that the position differs sharply
from Jackson's, and provides no support for the idea that claims like *Water is the watery stuff*
are knowable apriori.

any significant evidence for one of the essential tenets of all forms of ambitious two-dimensionalism—the claim that all names and natural kind terms are equivalent to indexical, rigidified versions of descriptions that do not themselves contain any uneliminable names or natural kind terms.

Conclusions

In this chapter, I have argued that Jackson is a very strong two-dimensionalist, I have explicated his particular version of this position, and I have examined how he uses it in dealing with an important philosophical problem—the relationship between physical and nonphysical facts (or statements). Although I have pointed out numerous problems with his two-dimensionalist views, and their application to physicalism, I have not yet attempted to provide a conclusive refutation of strong two-dimensionalism itself—something that will come in chapter 10. In my opinion, the most striking result to emerge from the discussion thus far is the paucity of Jackson's positive arguments for strong two-dimensionalism, and the almost complete lack of support they provide for its central tenets.

Although this judgment may sound harsh, I believe it is quite understandable when put in proper perspective. Jackson starts from a position that simply takes it for granted (i) that meanings of expressions must ultimately be descriptive,[38] (ii) that metaphysical possibility is the only possibility, (iii) that propositions are sets of truth conditions, which in turn can be identified with (metaphysically) possible world-states, and (iv) that Kripke's examples of the necessary aposteriori and the contingent apriori are, in some sense, legitimate (even though the sentences in question cannot express propositions which are necessary but knowable only aposteriori, or contingent but knowable apriori). Given this starting point, he had very little choice but to tell a story quite like the one he did. Seen in this way, his views are nuanced, sophisticated, and thoroughly understandable. The problems and implausibilities we have found seem to be testaments not so much to faults in the execution of his chosen philosophical program, but to the fundamental philosophical assumptions of the program itself. In the next chapter, we will examine the work of another leading ambitious two-dimensionalist, David Chalmers, to see if the same point holds true.

---

[38] See the first few pages of "Reference and Description Revisited."

CHAPTER 9

CHALMERS'S TWO-DIMENSIONALIST
DEFENSE OF ZOMBIES

The topic of this chapter is the two-dimensionalist system of David Chalmers. As in the case of Jackson, the discussion will focus on, though not be limited to, his most systematic, widely known, and influential work, *The Conscious Mind*, in which he is concerned with physicalism, understood as the doctrine that all truths are necessary consequences of the explicitly physical truths. Like Jackson, Chalmers argues that if physicalism is true, then all truths must be apriori consequences of the physical truths. Unlike Jackson, he thinks that it is clear that certain truths are **not** apriori consequences of the physical truths, and so physicalism is false. Among these crucial nonphysical truths are descriptions of the contents of conscious experiences—e.g., of visual sensations, of other perceptual and imaginative seemings, and of aches, pains, pangs of hunger, and other bodily sensations. Chalmers claims, not implausibly, that truths of this sort are not apriori deducible from the explicitly physical truths. Given his thesis that any truth is a necessary consequence of the physical truths only if it is an apriori consequence of the physical truths, he concludes that statements about conscious experiences and their contents are not necessary consequences of the physical truths. This leads him to the view that zombies are genuinely possible—where zombies are beings that are molecule for molecule, and in all other physical respects, completely identical with us, but who have absolutely no conscious experiences, and for whom, as Chalmers puts it, "all is dark inside."[1] His thesis is that the universe could have been exactly as it actually is, with beings physically identical to us, whose every brain event matched ours down to the smallest detail, and who behaved at every moment exactly as we actually behave—who say the same words, make the same sounds, and who respond to the same stimuli exactly as we actually do—without these beings having any conscious experiences whatsoever. This provocative, if outlandish, fantasy is then used to illustrate

[1] *The Conscious Mind*, p. 96.

the need for a way of understanding and thinking about consciousness that is, in some important measure, independent of the physical.

Two-dimensionalism enters this picture in Chalmers's defense of the view that a truth is a necessary consequence of the physical truths only if it is an apriori consequence of those truths—just as it did for Jackson. As illustrated in the last chapter, anyone defending this thesis must deal with the obvious Kripkean objection. Since some truths are necessary but knowable only aposteriori, some necessary consequences of a given statement are **not** apriori consequences of it. How, then, does Chalmers know that his statements about conscious experiences aren't necessary consequences of the totality of physical truths, without being apriori consequences of them? His response to this challenge is, in broad outline, the same as Jackson's. Kripkean examples of the necessary aposteriori are explained using the apparatus of ambitious two-dimensionalism. It is then argued that this explanation doesn't apply when we consider the conditional, $P \supset S$, where P encompasses the totality of explicitly physical truths, and S is any other truth. In all cases of this sort, the conditional is necessary only if it is also apriori—which is just to say that S is a necessary consequence of P only if S is an apriori consequence of P.

This chapter will investigate Chalmers's version of ambitious two-dimensionalism, and the use to which he puts it in his argument against physicalism. As with Jackson, I will argue that, with certain qualifications, Chalmers is most naturally understood as espousing strong two-dimensionalism. In addition to explicating his version of this view, noting the problems with it, and scrutinizing the argument against physicalism in which it plays so prominent a part, I will carefully examine the central ideas that motivate and lead him to his philosophical position.

The two most important of these central ideas are expressed by (i) and (ii).

(i) Epistemic and metaphysical possibility are one and the same in the following sense: for all world-states w, w is a state that the world could genuinely have been in, and hence is metaphysically possible, iff w is not knowable apriori not to obtain, and hence is epistemically possible. Kripkean examples of the necessary aposteriori are not cases in which a single proposition is evaluated differently with respect to two different spaces of possible world-states. Rather, they are cases in which the primary and secondary intensions (propositions) associated with a sentence receive different evaluations with respect to the same space of possible world-states.

(ii) Meaning, in the sense of that which a speaker knows in virtue of understanding an expression (or a sentence), is primary intension—thought of as a function from world-states to extensions (or truth values). In the case of names and natural kind terms, speakers' intuitions about the proper use of these terms in different scenarios can be used to demonstrate that they have primary intensions which are distinct from their secondary intensions, as well as to elucidate what these primary intensions are.

These principles lie at the heart of the views of Chalmers and Jackson. Although both are familiar from Jackson, Chalmers has something distinctive to add to each—which is where I begin.

Epistemic and Metaphysical Possibility

According to Chalmers, the important lesson to draw from Kripkean examples of the necessary aposteriori is that they don't require different kinds of possible world-states; in particular, they don't require epistemically possible but metaphysically impossible world-states. Rather, when we call a statement (Chalmers uses this word to refer to sentences) *aposteriori*, or merely *epistemically possible*, we are saying that its **primary** intension is true in some, but not all, possible world-states, and when we call a statement *necessary* we are saying that its **secondary** intension is true in all possible world-states—in the same sense of *possible world-states*. For Chalmers, a possible world-state is a way the world either is or could have been, which, in turn, is a way one could consistently and coherently conceive the world as being, and which one cannot know apriori that it isn't. He calls such world-states *logically possible worlds*.

Here are some illustrative comments:

As for the notion of a logically possible world, this is something of a primitive: as before, we can intuitively think of a logically possible world as a world that God might have made. . . . As for the *ex-*

tent of the class, the most important feature is that every conceivable world is logically possible.[2]

It follows from all this that the oft-cited distinction between "logical" [epistemic] and "metaphysical" possibility stemming from the Kripkean cases—on which it is held to be logically possible but not metaphysically possible that water is XYZ—is not a distinction at the level of *worlds*, but at most a distinction at the level of *statements*. A statement is "logically possible" [epistemically possible] in this sense if it is true in some world when evaluated according to primary intensions; a statement is "metaphysically possible" if it is true in some world when evaluated according to secondary intensions. The relevant space of worlds is the same in both cases. Most importantly, none of the cases we have seen give reason to believe that any conceivable *worlds* are impossible. . . . So there seems to be no reason to deny that conceivability of a world implies possibility. . . . An implication in the other direction, from logical possibility to conceivability, is trickier in that limits on our cognitive capacity imply that there are some possible situations that we cannot conceive, perhaps due to their great complexity. However, if we understand conceivability as conceivability-in-principle—perhaps conceivability by a super being—then it is plausible that logical possibility of a world implies conceivability of the world, and therefore that logical possibility of a statement implies conceivability of the statement.[3]

If a statement is logically possible or necessary according to its primary intension, the possibility or necessity is knowable *a priori*, at least in principle. Modality is not epistemically inaccessible: the possibility of a statement is a function of the intensions involved and the space of possible worlds, both of which are epistemically accessible in principle, and neither of which is dependent on *a posteriori* facts in this case. . . . The class of 1-necessary truths [sentences the primary intensions of which are true in all possible world-states] corresponds directly to the class of *a priori* truths. If a statement is true *a priori*, then it is true no matter how the actual world turns out; that is, it is true in all worlds considered

---

[2] Page 66.
[3] Pages 67–68.

as actual, so it is 1-necessary. And conversely, if a statement is 1-necessary, then it will be true no matter how the actual world turns out, so it will be true *a priori*. In most such cases, the statement's truth will be knowable by us *a priori*; the exceptions may be certain mathematical statements whose truth we cannot determine, and certain statements that are so complex that we cannot comprehend them. Even in these cases, it seems reasonable to say that they are knowable *a priori* at least *in principle*, although they are beyond our limited cognitive capacity.[4]

Though familiar by now, this view is really quite startling. Without getting into fancy arguments about the semantics of modal and epistemic operators, I ask you to recall a homely example that underscores how implausible this basic picture is. I show you this paperweight. You can see it, you can pick it up and feel it, but you may not be able to make out what it is made of. You imagine that it might be made of plastic, or metal, or wood. In imagining this, you are imagining the very object itself having the property of being made of plastic, being made of metal, or being made of wood. Hence, you are imagining the universe containing a certain object—this one—having been constructed of plastic, having been constructed of metal, or having been constructed of wood. This is just another way of saying that there are properties that you can imagine the universe having—the property of containing this very object, made of plastic, the property of containing this very object, made of metal, and so on—which you are not sure whether the universe really does have. Moreover, you can't tell by apriori reasoning alone which of these properties is instantiated. They are conceivable ways the world might be that are epistemically possible. When you finally learn that the paperweight is, in fact, made out of wood, you realize that it **couldn't** have existed without being made out of wood, and so you realize that certain epistemically possible ways the world might be are **not** ways that the world could genuinely be, and so are metaphysically impossible. Since these ways are just what Chalmers calls *worlds*, this elementary Kripke-style example of the necessary aposteriori leads to precisely the conclusion that Chalmers denies—namely that these examples of the necessary aposteriori show that certain epistemically possible world-states are metaphysically impossible.

This, I believe, is the correct description of the case involving my

[4] Pages 68–69.

paperweight. Notice, by contrast, how unnatural the alternative, two-dimensionalist description would have to be: According to it, there is **no** possible world-state whatsoever in which this very object—this paperweight—is made out of plastic. So you can't coherently imagine the universe having the property of containing this very object being made out of plastic. What you are really imagining is the universe containing **another** very similar paperweight that is made out of plastic. By the same token, you can't really imagine this very object—this paperweight—having the property of being made of plastic, which is to say you can't really imagine this very object being plastic. This is highly counterintuitive.

There are other counterintuitive consequences of Chalmers's two-dimensionalist picture, as well. For one thing, intuitively it seems obvious that you know that you are holding this paperweight, and no other. It is not just that you know that you are holding **some** paperweight or other (and that you are not holding more than one). Yet, before you examine the paperweight carefully, you may not know that it is made out of wood. If so, then there will be no way you could draw the conclusion that it is made of wood, simply by relying on apriori reasoning, without further empirical evidence. How would Chalmers describe this? He has to admit that you can't, on the basis of what you now know, rule out the possibility that the one and only one paperweight you are holding is made of plastic. That means there are genuinely possible world-states compatible with what you know in which you are holding **some** paperweight which is made of plastic. But since, in point of actual fact, the object you are holding is essentially made out of wood, there are no possible world-states in which it—this very object—is made out of plastic. Once this is admitted, Chalmers will have to maintain that you **don't** know, of this very paperweight, that it is the one and only one paperweight that you are holding.

That, it seems to me, is an absurdity that comes from refusing to admit epistemically possible world-states over and above metaphysically possible world-states. In my view, the natural, default position is that, of course, there are metaphysically impossible but epistemically possible world-states—ways the world could not genuinely be which we cannot know apriori that it isn't. Hence, the way to proceed in philosophy is to presume that there are such world-states, unless some very powerful objections to the contrary are produced. In a moment, I will examine Chalmers's objections on this score. Before I do, however, it is worthwhile stepping back briefly to gain some perspective on what we mean when we talk about possible and impossible world-states.

Why do many philosophers resist the idea of impossible world-states? One reason, I think, is that many are already uneasy about metaphysically possible world-states, and so adding impossible world-states to the mix seems incredible to them. But why are they uneasy about metaphysically possible world-states in the first place? Often, I think, it is because they are in the grip of an utterly fantastic picture of what possible world-states are. The problem begins with the disastrously misleading terminology *possible worlds* as opposed to the more intuitive *possible states of the world*—understood as *ways the world could be*. What do we mean—outside of philosophy—when we use the expression *the world*? Often we use *the world* to mean the Earth—a large concrete object that is part of the universe. People say *the world is round*, or *I want someday to travel all around the world*, meaning that the Earth is round, and that they want to travel all around it. But *the world* can also be used in a more expansive sense to designate the Earth and the heavens together—the whole universe, thought of as the maximally inclusive concrete object. It is this that many people (including a good many philosophers) think that philosophers are taking about when they speak of *the actual world*. But if the existing concrete universe is the actual world, what are possible worlds? The natural answer is that they must be large concrete objects too—alternate universes. Thus, when philosophers insist that there are other possible worlds, they are often taken to be saying that in addition to the actual universe we live in, there are other universes disconnected from ours with other inhabitants in them who, though they may be similar to us in various ways, are, of course, not really us, but our counterparts. According to this picture, reality is not the universe; it is the pluriverse.[5]

Since the picture that emerges contains huge metaphysical assumptions, it is natural that when metaphysically possible worlds are understood in this way, many people feel uneasy admitting that they exist. Still, some philosophers have been bullied into submission. The method most often used to bring this about goes something like this. First, it is pointed out that modal talk is ubiquitous and indispensable; there is no way we could get along without it—in philosophy, science, or everyday life. Next, it is said that the meanings of ordinary modal language sentences are given by the standard possible world semantics

---

[5] See David Lewis, On The Plurality of Worlds (Oxford: Blackwell, 1986).

for modal discourse, which analyzes talk involving *could, would,* and the like as involving claims about possible worlds. According to the semantics, the truth of many indispensable modal sentences requires the existence of metaphysically possible worlds. Having accepted these points, some philosophers find that since they can't bring themselves to deny the ordinary modal truths, they must grudgingly admit the existence of metaphysically possible worlds—despite continuing to feel uneasy about them.[6] Feeling this way, they are not inclined to be very receptive to the idea that in addition to metaphysically possible worlds, there are also epistemically possible but metaphysically **impossible** worlds; and they regard it as truly incredible when this view is accompanied by the claim that the view that there are such worlds (really world-states) is the obvious, intuitive one.

From my perspective, all of this is wrong-headed. In my opinion, the idea that by analyzing the meanings of ordinary truths involving locutions like *could, would, possibly,* and *necessarily,* we come to learn of the existence of alternate concrete universes is one of the most bizarre ideas in the history of a discipline known for such ideas. It is obvious that we don't mean anything of the kind by our ordinary modal talk, and if we did, we would have no justification for accepting what we regard as ordinary modal truths. The main errors in the view are (i) identifying ways the world could possibly be—i.e., properties the world could have—with alternate concrete universes, (ii) taking possible world semantics to give meanings of ordinary sentences containing modal notions—as opposed to providing a useful model theory for modal logics, and (iii) thinking that modal notions can be analyzed away by the semantics, as opposed to taken as primitive. Although these ideas are connected, the main point I have concentrated on up to now is (i). We don't have to take ways the world could be to be alternate concrete universes; we can take them to be properties. If we do, then the idea that there are properties the universe couldn't have

---

[6] A different response by some philosophers is to take world talk to be about concrete universes, but to treat modal talk as being about a certain fiction concerning such universes. On this view, *It is a necessary truth that S* means something like *According to the fiction about concrete worlds written by David Lewis, augmented by an encyclopedia listing all actual facts about the world we inhabit, 'S' is true in all concrete universes.* Although one might well be able to make a distinction between epistemic and metaphysical possibility within this framework, in my view the position gets off on the wrong foot by granting Lewis's so-called "metaphysical realism" too much priority in the first place. No one should think that the choice is between construing modal talk as fictional and taking it to be literal but utterly incredible.

had (*could* here is a primitive), but which we can't know apriori it doesn't have, won't involve bizarre or obviously counterintuitive consequences.[7]

Still, one might wonder whether there are good philosophical arguments against recognizing epistemically possible, but metaphysically impossible, world-states. Chalmers does argue against this in the section "Strong Metaphysical Necessity" of chapter 4 of *The Conscious Mind*. He begins with the following statement of the issue.

> It could be held that there is a modality of metaphysical possibility that is distinct from and more constrained than logical possibility [conceivability], and that arises for reasons independent of the Kripkean considerations. On this view, there are fewer metaphysically possible worlds than there are logically possible worlds, and the *a posteriori* necessity of certain statements can stem from factors quite independent of the semantics of the terms involved. We can call this hypothesized modality *strong metaphysical necessity*, as opposed to the *weak metaphysical necessity* introduced by the Kripkean framework. On this view, there are worlds that are entirely conceivable, even according to the strongest strictures on conceivability, but which are not possible at all.[8]

Here, a clarification is in order. At this point in his discussion, Chalmers believes that he has explained away all standard Kripkean examples of the necessary aposteriori—in essentially the same manner as Jackson—and shown them to be instances of an entirely linguistic phenomenon involving the distinction between primary and secondary intensions, with no larger metaphysical implications. For Chalmers, this means that "the Kripkean framework" does not require any notion of a possible world-state that is more restrictive (stronger) than that of an epistemically possible world-state, and that the sense of *necessity* relevant to Kripkean examples of the necessary aposteriori requires truth in all world-states in a space of such states that is only weakly restricted (to include all and only those that are epistemically possible) rather

---

[7] Although I favor taking world-states to be potential properties of the universe, and although this account makes for a plausible distinction between epistemic and metaphysical possibility that gives rise to a compelling explanation of the necessary aposteriori, I leave it open whether there may be other reasonable ways of distinguishing between epistemic and metaphysical possibility that do not rest on this potentially controversial conception of world-states, while giving rise to similarly plausible (non-two-dimensional) accounts of the necessary aposteriori. The crucial point is not to think of world-states as concrete universes.

[8] *The Conscious Mind*, p. 137.

than strongly restricted (to some proper subset of the epistemically possible states).

This was not, of course, Kripke's picture. In contrast to Chalmers, Kripke did **not** identify metaphysically possible world-states with epistemically possible world-states, and he did **not** view language as the source of the necessary and aposteriori status of his examples. Instead, he looked to metaphysics. For Kripke, the source of many necessary aposteriori truths—e.g., those involving necessity of origin, as well as membership in certain natural kinds—involved nontrivial essential properties of things that can be known to be possessed by those things only aposteriori. In such cases, the only role played by language is in allowing one to state that the things in question have the relevant properties essentially—and for this the main requirement is the availability of rigid designators, the reference of which doesn't vary from one world-state to the next.[9] If one has linguistic worries about proper names or natural kind terms in this regard, one can usually make do without them by employing other rigid designators—e.g., ordinary demonstratives like *this (individual), that (object), I, you, he, she,* and *it,* or even quantificational variables x, y, and z (which clearly don't show any distinction between primary and secondary intension). Thus, for Kripke, the import of many of his examples of the necessary aposteriori was precisely to establish the modality of *strong metaphysical necessity* that Chalmers contrasts with the *weak metaphysical necessity* that characterizes his reinterpretation of Kripke's examples.

In this section of his book, Chalmers offers a general argument designed to show not just that Kripke's examples are insufficient to establish what Chalmers calls *strong metaphysical necessity,* but that no examples, or philosophical argument, could ever do the job. His target is any philosophical position which claims that there are fully conceivable, epistemically possible, world-states that are metaphysically impossible, as well as sentences the necessary aposteriority of which stems from metaphysical rather than purely semantical considerations. Thus, if his argument is successful, it should provide both a general, apriori reason—independent of positive proposals about the semantics of particular words or constructions—for rejecting what I take to be the correct construal of Kripke's examples, and an objection to any attempt to establish the basic Kripkean picture of modality in another way.

Here is Chalmers's argument.

---

[9] See chapter 14 of Soames; *The Age of Meaning.*

There is a sense in which the truth of *statements* such as "Water is XYZ" is conceivable but not possible, but these examples never rule out the possibility of any conceivable *world*. They are merely instances in which such a world is misdescribed. Strong metaphysical necessity goes beyond this. . . . there is no reason to believe that such a modality exists. Such "metaphysical necessities" will put constraints on the space of possible worlds that are brute and inexplicable. It may be reasonable to countenance brute, inexplicable facts about *our* world, but the existence of such facts about the space of possible worlds would be quite bizarre. . . . **Indeed, if some worlds are logically possible [i.e., coherently conceivable] but metaphysically impossible, it seems that we could never know it. By assumption the information is not available *a priori*, and *a posteriori* information only tells us about *our* world. This can serve to locate our world in the space of possible worlds, but it is hard to see how it could give information about the extent of that space.** Any claims about the added constraints of metaphysical possibility would seem to be a matter of arbitrary stipulation.[10]

Chalmers argues that if we distinguish epistemically possible world-states from metaphysically possible world-states, and hold that some of the former are metaphysically impossible, then we will have to admit that one can never know which world-states these are.

The argument is essentially this:

P1. Suppose there are epistemically possible (conceivable) world-states that are metaphysically impossible (but not knowable apriori not to be instantiated).

P2. We can't know apriori which epistemically possible world-states are metaphysically impossible.

P3. Knowledge that can be acquired only aposteriori can't tell us which epistemically possible world-states are metaphysically impossible; the only thing such knowledge can tell us is which possible world-states are, or are not, instantiated.

C. Since all knowledge is either apriori or aposteriori, if there are epistemically possible world-states that are metaphysically impossible, we can never know which states they are.

[10] *The Conscious Mind*, p. 137, my emphasis.

The problem with the argument is that P3 is false, as is the conclusion. Think again about my paperweight. Prior to investigating it, I know that it is perfectly conceivable that it is made out of plastic or metal. Surely, I can't know apriori that it isn't. Thus, I know that there are fully conceivable—epistemically possible—world-states in which it is made of metal or plastic. Suppose I come to learn **aposteriori** that the actual state of the world is one in which my paperweight is made of wood. Next I combine this aposteriori knowledge with my **apriori** knowledge that **if** the actual state of the world is one in which a paperweight is made of wood, then the paperweight couldn't have existed without being made out of wood, and so there are no metaphysically possible states of the world in which it is made of metal or plastic. From these two premises I conclude that there are no metaphysically possible world-states in which my paperweight is made of metal or plastic. This means that the fully conceivable, epistemically possible, world-states in which it is made out of metal or plastic are metaphysically impossible. Since I derived this result from a pair of premises, one of which is aposteriori, it qualifies as aposteriori. Since this is aposteriori knowledge of which epistemically possible world-states are metaphysically impossible, both P3 and the conclusion, C, of Chalmers's argument are false.

This refutation is, of course, just an elaboration of the old Kripkean idea that we can know apriori of certain properties that they are essential properties of things that have them, even though finding out which objects have them is an aposteriori matter. Cases like this give rise to genuine instances of the necessary aposteriori. In these cases, finding out that something is true in the actual world-state gives us information about what is true in all, or in no, metaphysically possible world-states.[11] Chalmers misses this. One reason he does may be that he has his own nonstandard account of many necessary aposteriori sentences containing names or natural kind terms—which may lead him to think that all Kripkean examples must be amenable to such a treatment, and that the source of the necessary aposteriori must always be linguistic, rather than metaphysical. This, as I have emphasized, is a mistake.

Whether or not one agrees with me about this, two conclusions about Chalmers's general argument against metaphysically impossible,

---

[11] For a particularly clear discussion of this in Kripke, see pp. 152–53 of "Identity and Necessity," in Milton Munitz (ed.), *Identity and Individuation* (New York: New York University Press, 1971).

yet conceivable, and epistemically possible, world-states should be un-controversial. First, since his argument fails to comes to grips with a highly plausible Kripkean account of how knowledge of the actual is sometimes required to determine the scope of the possible, it does **not** establish its conclusion. Second, since it simply ignores the obvious Kripkean account of the matter, it cannot provide any **independent** objection to the orthodox Kripkean account of the necessary aposteri-ori. Thus, the entire force of Chalmers's critique will have to rest on the positive case he can make for his ambitious two-dimensionalist reinterpretation of Kripke. This is significant, since—as in the case of Jackson—Chalmers's two-dimensionalist semantic theory is both highly programmatic and problematic in itself. It is motivated not by the success of any careful and detailed semantic analyses, but by the conviction that it provides the only possible explanation of the neces-sary aposteriori (and the contingent apriori) that is compatible with what we know antecedently about modality and the nature of possible world-states.

The roots of this conviction can, I think, be traced to the plausible idea that there must be some connection between conceivability and possibility. Although this idea is correct, in my opinion, Chalmers is too quick to generalize from it. As a result, he comes to view conceivability and possibility as coextensive, with the former being perhaps defini-tional of the latter. What he fails to see is that a significant and illumi-nating link between the two can be preserved, even if one recognizes the existence of world-states that are fully conceivable, and yet meta-physically impossible. It is, I think, because he fails to see this interme-diate position that the only alternative he recognizes to the view that conceivability and possibility (of world-states) come to essentially the same thing is a view which distinguishes genuine metaphysical possibil-ity from mere conceivability by imposing some entirely arbitrary con-straints on the former over and above of those required by the latter. As he puts it, "any claims about the added constraints of metaphysical pos-sibility would seem to be a matter of arbitrary stipulation."[12]

The central reason this is incorrect is, as I see it, that the objects of conceivability—the things we conceive when trying to determine what is metaphysically possible—are not simply world-states, but entire sys-tems of metaphysical possibility, each with a designated "actual" world-state and a space of related states, some of which are possible

---

[12] *The Conscious Mind*, p. 137.

relative to it, others of which are possible relative to those, and so on. Think again about the paperweight. I can conceive of a world-state in which it is made of wood, a world-state in which it is made of metal, and a world-state in which it is made of plastic. That is, I can conceive of each of these states as obtaining, or being instantiated. Accompanying each state, I can conceive of a set of related states that I recognize as having the following property: they will be genuine metaphysical possibilities if the initial, designated state is instantiated. So accompanying the designated state in which the paperweight is made of wood and is of just this color (gold on one side and brown on the others), I can conceive of related world-states in which it is made of wood and is of another color. But given the supposition that the original state is instantiated, I can conceive of no state that is possible relative to it in which the paperweight is made of material other than wood. A similar point holds for the other epistemically possible world-states in which the paperweight is made of metal, or of plastic. When they play the role of the designated "actual" world-state—i.e., when I consider them as instantiated and ask which states are possible relative to them—I regard world-states in which the paperweight is made of wood as impossible **in those systems**.

So we have a set of epistemically possible world-states, each of which can be conceived as being instantiated. Along with each such state w_1, we have a set of (epistemically possible) world-states w_2 which we recognize to be metaphysically possible, if the initial, designated "actual" state w_1 is instantiated—i.e., we recognize that if w_1 were instantiated, then w_2 would be a property that the universe could have had. Moreover, for each such state w_2 there is a set of (epistemically possible) world-states w_3 which we recognize to be metaphysically possible, if w_2 is instantiated. This reflects the fact that we recognize that if w_1 were instantiated, then w_3 would be (metaphysically) possibly possible.[13] Repeating this process indefinitely, we end up with a conceivable—epistemically possible—system of metaphysical possibility. Collecting all such systems together, we have a set of epistemically possible systems of metaphysical possibility. Roughly speaking, for a world-state to be genuinely metaphysically possible is for it to be a metaphys-

---

[13] As Nathan Salmon has argued (especially in the case of ship of Theseus type examples), it should not be assumed that if w_3 is possibly possible, then it must be possible. For an explanation and defense of the philosophical underpinnings of the basic conception of world-states presented here, see Salmon, "The Logic of What Might Have Been," *Philosophical Review* 98, 1 (1989): 3–34.

ically possible member of some epistemically possible system of meta-physical possibility, **the designated world-state of which is the state that the world really is in**. For a world-state to be genuinely meta-physically possibly possible is for it to be a possibly possible member of such a system, and so on. Obviously, this is not a definition of meta-physical possibility in nonmodal terms. Rather, it is a way of thinking about the relationship between metaphysical possibility, epistemic pos-sibility, and conceivability involving the primitive notion of a property that the world could have instantiated.

On this picture, conceivability is a fallible but useful guide to what is metaphysically possible. It is fallible because before we know very much about what is actual, there are many epistemically possible world-states that seem to us to be genuinely possible, and so remain candidates for being metaphysically possible. The more we learn about the actual world, the more we whittle down this field of candidates, and the better able we are to identify the scope of genuine metaphysi-cal possibility. To put it in a nutshell, **our guide to metaphysical pos-sibility is conceivability plus our knowledge of actuality.**

There is, however, a potentially significant question that remains open. If, somehow, we could discover all actual, nonmodal facts, would we be in a position to know precisely which world-states were metaphysically possible (and possibly possible, etc.) and which not? Otherwise put, once ignorance of actuality is factored out, are facts about which world-states are genuinely metaphysically possible relative to other world-states, always knowable, in principle, by us, apriori? The most optimistic view is, of course, that they are; and perhaps this is right. But, since nothing I have said guarantees, or requires, this, I leave it as an open question. For present purposes, the chief lesson to be learned is that distinguishing epistemically possible from metaphys-ically possible world-states does **not** require divorcing genuine, meta-physical possibility from conceivability, or making the connection between the two "arbitrary," "inexplicable," or "bizarre." On the con-trary, the connection is natural, illuminating, and robust. It is simply more complex than it is on any account that identifies the metaphysi-cally possible world-states with those that are coherently conceivable (and not knowable apriori not to obtain).

All of this is foreign to Chalmers. Having started out with the pre-conceived idea that all and only the ways that the world could gen-uinely be are ways that it can coherently be conceived to be, he cannot recognize the metaphysical source of any instances of the necessary aposteriori, nor can he explain the function of evidence in justifying knowledge of such truths as that of ruling out epistemically possible world-states that are metaphysically impossible. If empirical evidence is to play a role in eliminating possibilities with respect to which what is to be known is false, then what is to be known cannot be necessary. This suggests that each sentence S that is an instance of the necessary aposteriori **must** be associated with two propositions—one necessary and relevant to modal claims in which S figures, and the other contingent and relevant to knowledge ascriptions in which S is involved. Chalmers's way of getting this result is to motivate the distinction between primary and secondary intension, which is the second fundamental idea upon which his system is based. For this, he appeals to an idealized Fregean conception of linguistic competence in which a speaker's understanding of an expression, plus a complete description of an epistemically/metaphysically possible world-state, is, in principle, always sufficient to allow the speaker to identify, by apriori reasoning alone, the extension of the expression (provided that the expression has a determinate extension relative to the world-state, and provided that the speaker reasons correctly). It is to this idea that I turn next.

Linguistic Competence and the Distinction between Primary and Secondary Intensions

Chalmers introduces this idea in *The Conscious Mind*. After describing his "two-dimensional picture of meaning and necessity" as a synthesis of views suggested by Kripke, Putnam, Kaplan, Stalnaker, Lewis, Evans, Davies, and Humberstone, he articulates the basic distinction as follows:

> On the traditional view of reference, derived from Frege although cloaked here in modern terminology, a concept determines a function *f*: W → R from possible worlds to referents. Such a function is often called an *intension*; together with a specification of a world w, it determines an *extension* *f*(w). In Frege's own view, every concept [Chalmers often uses *concept* to mean *word* or *expression*] had a *sense,* which was supposed to determine the reference of the concept depending on the state of the world; so these senses correspond closely to intensions. The sense was often thought of as the *meaning* of the concept in question.

More recent work has recognized that no single intension can do all the work that a meaning needs to do. The picture developed by Kripke complicates things by noting that reference in the actual world and in counterfactual possible worlds is determined by quite different mechanisms. In a way, the Kripkean picture can be seen to split the Fregean picture into two separate levels.

Kripke's insight can be expressed by saying that there are in fact *two* intensions associated with a given concept. That is, there are two quite distinct patterns of dependence of the referent of a concept on the state of the world. First, there is the dependence by which reference is fixed in the *actual* world, depending on how the world turns out: if it turns out one way, a concept will pick out one thing, but if it turns out another way, the concept will pick out something else. Second, there is the dependence by which reference in *counterfactual* worlds is determined, given that reference in the actual world is already fixed. Corresponding to each of these dependencies is an intension, which I will call the *primary* and *secondary* intensions, respectively.[14]

For Chalmers, the primary intension of an expression E (or a sentence S) is a function from possible—i.e., conceivable—world-states, thought of in their role of contexts, to extensions of E (or truth values of S) when evaluated at those world-states. As he puts it, primary intension "picks out what the referent of the concept would be if that world turned out to be actual."[15] As usual with ambitious two-dimensionalists, care must be taken in interpreting what they mean when using *actual*, not in its normal use as a rigidifier (*the actual F*), but as a predicate of world-states. When used in this way, it seems to mean something like *to obtain* or *to be instantiated*; a world-state is actual iff it obtains, or is instantiated, and to imagine it as actual is to imagine that being so. However, this can't be the whole story, as is clear when one attempts to distinguish primary from secondary intension.

Chalmers draws the distinction as follows:

> We might say that the primary intension picks out the referent of a concept in a world when it is *considered as actual*—that is, when it is considered as a candidate for the actual world of the thinker—whereas the secondary intension picks out the referent

---

[14] *The Conscious Mind*, pp. 56–57.
[15] Page 57.

of a concept in a world when it is *considered as counterfactual,* given that the actual world of the thinker is already fixed.[16]

Chalmers's parenthetical remark in this passage—*that is, when it is considered as a candidate for the actual world of the thinker*—isn't very helpful. Typically thinkers exist, and think, with respect to many possible world-states. So there is no such thing as **the** world-state of the thinker; nor will adding *actual* help, since that is what is supposed to be explained. Still, the idea is not hard to see. To consider a world-state as actual is to consider it as a potential context of utterance.[17] Primary intensions are functions which are determined by two more basic functions—(i) character: the mapping from contexts to contents and (ii) content (or secondary intension): the mapping from world-states to extensions. The primary intension of an expression E maps a context C onto the result of applying the content (secondary intension) of E in C to the world-state of C. If one identifies contexts with world-states, then the primary intension of E maps a world-state w (considered as a context) onto the result of applying the content (secondary intension) of E in w to w itself.

This distinction between primary and secondary intension applies to expressions of all types, including sentences. Combining Kaplan's terminology with Chalmers's, one might say that the secondary intension of a sentence S (at a world-state w considered as a context) is a function from arbitrary world-states w* to truth values of S at w*, *considered as counterfactual.* To say that, relative to a context w, S is true at w*, *considered as counterfactual,* is to say that the proposition p expressed by S relative to w (i.e., the proposition p assigned by the character of S to w) would be true if w* were instantiated. To say that S is true at w, *considered as actual,* is to say that the meaning of S as we actually use it—its Kaplan-style character—assigns to w, as context, a proposition q that would be true if w were instantiated. The idea is similar, though a bit more convoluted, when a singular term t is involved. To say that (relative to a world-state w considered as a context)

[16] Page 60.

[17] Intuitively, to consider a world-state w as a potential context of utterance is to consider the contribution w would make to what would be said or expressed by utterances of sentences, carrying the meanings they have for us here and now, were they uttered in w. The notion of context needed for the above account of what it is to "consider a world-state as actual" is a theoretical refinement of this intuitive notion. In the theoretical sense, developed by Kaplan, a context is an abstract perspective containing information needed by the meanings of a certain class of sentences to determine semantic contents of those sentences, relative to the context.

t refers to o at w*, *considered as counterfactual,* is to say that the content of t relative to w (i.e., the content determined by applying the character of t to w) either is the object o itself, or would determine the object o if w* were instantiated. To say that t refers to o at w, *considered as actual,* is to say that the meaning of t as we actually use it—its Kaplan-style character—assigns to w as context a content that either is o itself, or that would determine o if w were instantiated.

This is, of course, the same distinction we saw in Jackson. Although Chalmers doesn't give the long-winded, but accurate, Kaplan-style explanation of it given here, he seems to realize that an explanation along these lines is perfectly correct.

> The distinction between these ways of looking at worlds [i.e., considering them *as actual* and *as counterfactual*] corresponds closely to Kaplan's (1989) distinction between the *context of utterance* of an expression and the *circumstance of evaluation.* When we consider a world w as counterfactual, we keep the actual world as the context of utterance, but use w as a circumstance of evaluation. For example, if I utter, "There is water in the ocean" in this world and *evaluate* it in the XYZ world, "water" refers to H_2O and the statement is false. But when we consider w as actual we think of it as a potential context of utterance, and wonder how things would be if the context of the expression turned out to be w. If the context of my sentence "There is water in the ocean" turned out to be the XYZ world, then the statement would be true when evaluated at that world. The primary intension is therefore closely related to what Kaplan calls the *character* of a term, although there are a few differences, and the secondary intension corresponds to what he calls a term's *content.*[18]

Given this, I will gloss what Chalmers would express using (1a,b,c, or d)

1a. t refers to o relative to w, considered as actual.

b. t would refer to o, if w turned out to be actual.

c. t will refer to o, if w turns out to be actual.

d. t refers to o, on the hypothesis that w is actual.

as being what is expressed by (2).

[18] Page 60.

2. If w were to be instantiated, and t were available for use with the meaning it actually has—i.e., with the Kaplan-style character $C_{t@}$ that t has in the actual world-state @—then it would refer to o (by virtue of the fact that the content obtained by applying $C_{t@}$ to w either would be o itself, or would determine o).

Similarly, I will gloss what Chalmers would express using (3a,b,c, or d)

3a. S is true relative to w, considered as actual.

 b. S would be true, if w turned out to be actual.

 c. S will be true, if w turns out to be actual.

 d. S is true, on the hypothesis that w is actual.

as being essentially the same as that expressed by (4).

4. If w were instantiated, and S were available for use with the meaning it actually has—i.e., with the Kaplan-style character $C_{S@}$ that S has in the actual world-state @—then the proposition S would express (i.e., the proposition obtained by applying $C_{S@}$ to w) would be true.

There are, to be sure, some tricky technical issues that arise involving special cases such as world-states in which no one understands English, or no one ever speaks, or there are no sentences. However, these don't tell against the basic correctness of these glosses. Like Kaplan, Chalmers wants sentences such as *No one understands English*, *No one ever uses a sentence*, and *There are no sentences* to come out true when set in such world-states, as contexts. To get this result, we may follow Kaplan in thinking of sentences, carrying the meanings they actually have, as being capable of expressing true propositions, even when set in world-states with respect to which they don't exist, or in which no one uses or understands them. For our purposes, tricky cases like *There are no sentences* can, for the most part, be set aside. However, the lesson they teach remains important when considering Chalmers's more prosaic examples. In order to evaluate these examples correctly, one must always have a firm grip on the distinction between (5a), on the one hand, and (5b), on the other.

5a. the referent assigned to a potential context of utterance w by **the actual meaning of a term t** (via the application to w of the actual character $C_{t@}$ of t, plus the further application of the content thereby determined to w), and the proposition assigned to w by **the actual meaning $C_{S@}$ of S**

b. the referent assigned to w by **the meaning of t as used by speakers in w** (via the application to w of the character C_{tw} that t has when used by speakers in w, plus the further application of the content thereby determined to w), and the proposition assigned to w by **the meaning C_{Sw} that S has as used by speakers in w**

With this in mind, I turn to Chalmers's crucial doctrine about the relationship between primary intension and the linguistic competence of speakers. He addresses this issue in an article, "On Sense and Intension," published six years after *The Conscious Mind*.[19] In section 3, "What Are Senses?," he advocates the Fregean idea that they are conditions on extension. As he sees it, their crucial property is that they give a competent speaker "a way of identifying an expression's extension [where the expression is one that the speaker understands], given full knowledge of how the world turns out."[20] Given that he takes possible world-states to be maximally complete ways that, for all we know apriori, the world could be, Chalmers identifies the sense (primary intension) of an expression with something that a speaker who understands it tacitly grasps which, in principle, is sufficient to allow the speaker to be able to identify the extension of the expression in an arbitrary world-state w, when provided with a complete specification of w.

Here is how he begins his discussion of the matter.

The extensions of our expressions depend on how our world turns out. That is, they depend on which scenario is actual [obtains, or is instantiated]. Once we know enough about the nature of our world, we are usually in a position to know what our expressions refer to. Once we do enough astronomical work investigating the nature of the objects in the evening sky, we know that 'Hesperus' refers to Venus, not Jupiter. . . . Once we know about the chemical makeup of the various substances in our environment, we know that 'water' refers to H_2O, not to a basic element.[21]

At this point we pause for clarification. Prior to doing any astronomical work, speakers were able to identify the referent of 'Hesperus'.

[19] Chalmers, "On Sense and Intension," *Philosophical Perspectives* 16 (2002): 135–82.
[20] Ibid., p. 143.
[21] Ibid., p. 144.

They looked at the sky at night, pointed to Venus, and said *That is Hesperus*, or *That is what 'Hesperus' refers to*. If Venus had been listening, she could have truly reported such speakers by saying *They know that I am Hesperus*, or *They know that 'Hesperus' refers to me*. Thus, Venus is such that speakers who understood 'Hesperus' knew that it was the referent of 'Hesperus', even before doing the astronomical work that Chalmers has in mind. Of course, such speakers may not have known at the time that Hesperus was not Jupiter, or that 'Hesperus' did not refer to Jupiter, and reflecting on their linguistic competence with the terms would not have been sufficient to learn those things. For that, astronomical discovery was needed.

The same is true for 'water'. Prior to the chemical discovery, speakers were able to identify the kind designated by *water*. As explained in chapter 4, familiarity with instances of a kind typically brings with it acquaintance with the kind. Thus, with a little idealization, we may imagine speakers who understood the term 'water' pointing to certain samples and saying *Water designates the physically constitutive kind of which these are instances*. Hence, the kind water is such that speakers who understood the term knew that 'water' designated it. Of course, such speakers didn't know the molecular structure of its instances, and for that reflection on their linguistic competence would not have helped; chemistry was needed. Here, it is important to emphasize that I treat H_2O not as a Millian name of the kind water, but as a description of that kind. One can understand the word 'water' and thereby know, of the kind water, that 'water' designates it, without knowing that the description H_2O also designates it, that water is H_2O, or that 'water' designates H_2O.

These niceties about what is, and what is not, known on the basis of linguistic competence alone will come in handy later. For now, I return to Chalmers's discussion of the relationship between understanding the primary intension of an expression and knowing the extension of that expression. I pick up with Chalmers illustrating the point that knowing more about a world-state puts us "in a position to know what our expressions refer to." He continues:

> **We can think of this as being part of what using a language involves. If a subject uses an expression** [that the subject understands], **then given sufficient information about the world, the subject will be in a position to know the extension of the expression. Furthermore, something like this will be the case**

however **the world turns out: for any scenario** [possible world-state], **given sufficient information about that scenario** [possible world-state], **the subject will be in a position to determine what the extension of the expression will be** *if* **that scenario** [possible world-state] **is actual** [is instantiated, or obtains]. [That is, the subject will be in a position to determine the object o to which the term would refer if the world-state in question were to be instantiated, and t were to be available for use with the meaning it actually has—its actual Kaplan-style character]. **Of course in some cases the extension may be indeterminate, as it sometimes is in the actual world; but in such a case, the subject will be in a position to determine that too.**[22]

Here, Chalmers expresses the view that a speaker who understands an expression has the tacit ability to identify the extension of the expression (in some informative way) relative to any possible world-state w, considered as a potential context of utterance, given sufficient information about w. His idea is that the primary intension of any expression—that which a competent speaker grasps when understanding the sentence—can be read off the responses that such a speaker would, in principle, give, if he reasoned carefully and correctly, to questions about what the expression would designate, relative to different possible world-states, *considered as actual.*

One of the serious difficulties raised by this view, which I will simply note before going further, involves the vocabulary in which the possible world-states are to be described to the subject. As Chalmers recognizes, if the subject is going to answer questions about what his terms refer to relative to different possible world-states, these world-states will have to be described. This raises the question of what vocabulary is to be used in giving these descriptions. If the descriptive vocabulary itself involves expressions the primary intensions of which are distinct from their secondary intensions, then more than one possible world-state may correspond to a single world-state description, depending on whether one considers the world-state corresponding to the description's primary intension or its secondary intension. To avoid this difficulty, Chalmers requires that the world-state descriptions be free of any names or natural kind terms, the primary intensions of which diverge from their secondary intensions. He also disallows most ordinary indexical phrases. Since for Chalmers all, or nearly all, names, nat-

---

[22] Ibid., p. 144, my emphasis and, of course, parenthetical additions.

ural kind terms, and ordinary indexical phrases fall into the excluded category, this restriction is very severe. What remains? His official view seems to be that what remains is the language of fundamental physics, plus mentalistic vocabulary describing the phenomenal contents of conscious experiences—e.g., descriptions of visual sensations, of other perceptual and imaginative seemings, and of aches, pains, pangs of hunger, and other bodily sensations. The view is, then, that for every expression E and speaker s who understands E, s has the tacit ability to identify (using apriori reasoning alone) the extension of E relative to any possible world-state w, *considered as actual*, when given a description of w in the vocabulary of theoretical physics, augmented by descriptions of the phenomenal contents of conscious experiences (provided that s reasons carefully and correctly).

Here, for example, is Chalmers's account of what is involved when a speaker identifies the extension of an expression relative to a possible world-state w, considered as actual.

> To consider a scenario W as actual is to consider the hypothesis that D is the case, where D is a *canonical description* of W. When scenarios are understood as centered worlds, a canonical description will conjoin an *objective* description of the character of W (including its physical and mental character, for example), with an indexical description of the center's location within W. The objective description will be restricted to *semantically neutral* terms: roughly, terms that are not themselves vulnerable to Twin Earth thought experiments (thus excluding most names, natural kind terms, indexicals, and terms used with semantic deference).[23]

The reference here to "centered worlds" is to world-states, considered in their role as contexts of utterance, augmented by, or centered on, a designated agent and time to provide interpretations for *I* and *now*. Since I will discuss these in more detail a little later, I will put them aside for now. The key point to notice is how severe are the restrictions on the canonical description of possible world-states used in determin-

---

[23] Page 611 of David Chalmers, "The Components of Content," in David Chalmers (ed.), *The Philosophy of Mind: Classical and Contemporary Readings* (New York and Oxford: Oxford University Press, 2002), 608–33. For other statements of the restriction of the vocabulary of canonical descriptions, see fn. 5, p. 180 of "On Sense and Intension," and p. 319 of Chalmers and Jackson, "Conceptual Analysis and Reductive Explanation," *Philosophical Review* 110 (2001): 315–60. In the latter, the vocabulary is specified to be one that includes that of fundamental physics plus vocabulary describing "the phenomenal states and properties instantiated by every subject bearing such states and properties, at every time."

ing the primary intensions of expressions and in testing the abilities of competent speakers. These descriptions are required to be stated exclusively in *semantically neutral* terms—terms that show no distinction between primary and secondary intension.[24] As Chalmers recognizes, this excludes most names, natural kind terms, ordinary indexicals (presumably except for *I* and *now*), and all words that the speaker is able to use competently only by virtue of relying on experts who, supposedly, have the tacit ability to give "non-deferential" necessary and sufficient conditions for being in the extension of the term. The claim that speakers have the ability to identify the extension of every term they understand, relative to every possible world-state (considered as a potential context of utterance), when that world-state is described in the highly restricted vocabulary allowed by Chalmers, is an extraordinarily strong and implausible claim, which—though required by his central doctrines—is not supported by detailed semantic analyses of any individual words. Although, I can't, myself, see how the claim could possibly be correct, I will not pause over this point now, but will instead leave open the possibility that some modification or weakening of it might be found. With this in mind, I will move on to other features of Chalmers's view of the relationship between linguistic competence and primary intension that merit further consideration.

The view under investigation is that speakers have the ability to correctly identify the extension of every term they understand, relative to every possible world-state, when *considered as actual.* Chalmers and Jackson express this view as follows.

> [P]ossession of a concept such as 'knowledge' or 'water' [i.e., understanding a term such as 'knowledge' or 'water'] bestows a *conditional ability* to identify the concept's [term's] extension under a hypothetical epistemic possibility, given sufficient information about that epistemic possibility and sufficient reasoning. That is, possession of these concepts [understanding of these terms] in a sufficiently rational subject bestows an ability to evaluate certain conditionals of the form $E \rightarrow C$, where E contains sufficient information about an epistemic possibility [a possible world-state] and where C is a statement using the concept [term] and charac-

---

[24] The further requirement that the world-state descriptions be couched entirely in the vocabulary of physics plus vocabulary for describing subjective conscious experiences is more important for Chalmers's views about physicalism than it is for his basic semantic framework. Since that requirement makes his position even more implausible, I will put it aside in assessing his semantic theses.

terizing its extension, for arbitrary epistemic possibilities [world-states, "considered as actual"].[25]

In "On Sense and Intension," Chalmers gives two examples of what he takes this ability to amount to involving the words 'Hesperus' and 'water'.

Let scenario W_2 be one on which the brightest object visible in the evening is Jupiter, and where the brightest object visible in the morning is Neptune. For all we know a priori, W_2 is actual [i.e., we don't know apriori that world-state W_2 isn't instantiated, though we do of course know this aposteriori]. If it turns out that W_2 is actual, then it will turn out that Hesperus is Jupiter [and that 'Hesperus' refers to Jupiter]. If one hypothetically accepts that W_2 is actual, one should rationally conclude that Hesperus is Jupiter [and that 'Hesperus' refers to Jupiter]. So when evaluated at W_2, the intension of 'Hesperus' returns Jupiter. If it turns out that A is actual [i.e., if it turns out that the world-state @ that really does obtain, but which we don't know apriori to obtain, does obtain], then it will turn out that Hesperus is Venus [and that 'Hesperus' refers to Venus]. So when evaluated at A [i.e., @] the intension of 'Hesperus' returns Venus. The same applies to a term such as 'water'. Let W_3 be a 'Twin Earth' scenario, where the clear, drinkable liquid in the oceans and lakes is XYZ. For all we know a priori, W_3 is actual [i.e., although we know that W_3 is not instantiated, this knowledge is aposteriori]. If it turns out that W_3 is actual, then intuitively, it will turn out that water is XYZ [and that 'water' designates the kind XYZ]. If one hypothetically accepts that W_3 is actual, one should rationally conclude that water is XYZ [and that 'water' designates the kind XYZ]. So when evaluated at W_3, the intension of 'water' returns XYZ. If it turns out that A is actual [if the world-state @ that really obtains does obtain], then it will turn out that water is H_2O. So when evaluated at A [i.e., @], the intension of 'water' returns H_2O.[26]

Chalmers takes these examples to be indicative of results that could be achieved for virtually any name or natural kind term. The important point about these alleged results is that, if he is right, they show that the extensions of names and natural kind terms vary from context to

[25] "Conceptual Analysis and Reductive Explanation," p. 324.
[26] "On Sense and Intension," pp. 145–46.

context, which, in conjunction with the view that these expressions are rigid designators, is sufficient to establish the thesis—essential to all forms of ambitious two-dimensionalism—that their secondary intensions are distinct from their primary intensions.

A Crucial Equivocation in Chalmers's Argument

However, Chalmers is not right. The statements of the forms (1) and (3) (and closely related locutions) that he uses to establish his results can be understood in two quite different ways.

la. t refers to o relative to w, considered as actual.

  b. t would refer to o, if w turned out to be actual.

  c. t will refer to o, if w turns out to be actual.

  d. t refers to o, on the hypothesis that w is actual.

3a. S is true relative to w, considered as actual.

  b. S would be true, if w turned out to be actual.

  c. S will be true, if w turns out to be actual.

  d. S is true, on the hypothesis that w is actual.

On one natural understanding of these statements, they are clearly correct, but on this understanding they do **not** establish the results about primary intensions that Chalmers draws from them. On a different understanding, these statements would, if true, establish those results, but on this understanding the intuitive considerations offered in their favor do **not** support them. In short, the plausibility of Chalmers's argument for this essential tenet of ambitious two-dimensionalism—that names and natural kind terms have primary intensions that are distinct from their secondary intensions—is the result of equivocating on what one means when one uses locutions such as *the extension (truth value) of an expression E (or a sentence S), under the hypothesis that scenario w is actual.*

In order to bring this equivocation into the open, one must remember what these locutions have to mean, if they are to bear directly on the conclusions about the primary intensions of terms and sentences that he draws from them. This was expressed by the glosses (2) and (4) of (1) and (3), respectively.

2. If w were to be instantiated, and t were available for use with the meaning it actually has—i.e., with the Kaplan-style character $C_{t@}$ that t has in the actual world-state @—then it would refer to o (by virtue of the fact that the content obtained by applying $C_{t@}$ to w either would be o itself, or would determine o).

4. If w were instantiated, and S were available for use with the meaning it actually has—i.e., with the Kaplan-style character $C_{S@}$ that S has in the actual world-state @—then the proposition S would express (i.e., the proposition obtained by applying $C_{S@}$ to w) would be true.

When considering a nonactual world-state w—like the one in which Jupiter rather than Venus is visible in the evening, or the one in which the liquid in the oceans is XYZ rather than H_2O—for the purpose of determining the extension of a term t, or the truth value of a sentence S, relative to the hypothesis that w is actual, one must, at all costs, avoid a certain mistake that is all but inevitable when matters are not made explicit. One must **not** conflate the "real" actual world-state @ with the state w that one is *considering as actual* by confusing (a) the referent of t, or the truth value of S, when used in context w with **their actual meanings $C_{t,@}$ and $C_{S,@}$** with (b) the referent of t, or the truth value of S, when used in context w with **the meanings $C_{t,w}$ and $C_{S,w}$ they carry when used by speakers in w**. This distinction is particularly important to keep in mind in cases in which we are asked to determine *the referent of t, or the truth value of S (where S contains t), on the hypothesis that w is actual*, when w is just like the actual world-state @, except that something that we (correctly) take to be a fact that is crucial to bringing it about that t refers to o, when used by us in @, is different in w—with the result that speakers in w (namely, us) use t to refer to a different object o*. These are the kinds of cases that Chalmers invokes. Unfortunately, the language he uses when asking us to consider these cases is virtually guaranteed to confuse the issue.

Let us see how this works in his scenario involving *water*. The background presupposed by the scenario, which it shares with the actual world-state @, may be taken to be something like the following: We know that, in fact, *water* was introduced, and has long been used to stand for the physically constitutive kind instances of which fall from the sky in rain, fill the oceans, lakes, and rivers, and are clear and drinkable. We also know that at some point chemists discovered the chemical composition of these instances. As a result, we found out that water was H_2O. Against this background, Chalmers asks us to consider a different possible scenario w—one which is as much like our actual world-state as possible, except for the fact that in w we learn that the supposed chemical discovery identifying the molecular structure of the clear, drinkable liquid that falls from the sky in rain, and fills the oceans, rivers, and lakes, etc. was in error. That stuff, it turns out, is not H_2O, but XYZ. Since chemistry has become a dim memory for many of us anyway, we find that we can imagine w turning out to be instantiated, or, as Chalmers puts it, "to be actual."

With this in mind, he asks:

6a. What does 'water' refer to relative to a scenario (w), considered as actual, in which it is discovered that, contrary to what had previously been thought, the clear drinkable liquid that falls from the sky in rain and fills the oceans, lakes, and rivers is XYZ, not H_2O?

  b. What would 'water' refer to, if the scenario w turned out to be actual? That is, what would 'water' refer to if it turned out that, contrary to what had previously been thought, the clear drinkable liquid that falls from the sky in rain and fills the oceans, lakes, and rivers is XYZ, not H_2O?

  c. What will 'water' refer to, if the scenario w turns out to be actual? That is, what will 'water' refer to, if it turns out that, contrary to what has previously been thought, the clear drinkable liquid that falls from the sky in rain and fills the oceans, lakes, and rivers is XYZ, not H_2O?

  d. What does 'water' refer to, on the hypothesis that the scenario in w is actual? That is, what does 'water' refer to on the hypothesis that, contrary to what has previously been thought, the clear drinkable liquid that falls from the sky in rain and fills the oceans, lakes, and rivers is XYZ, not H_2O?

The natural way of understanding these questions is to take them to be asking us to determine what we now are, and have always been, using 'water' to refer to—on the hypothesis that the world turns out to be in the state w expressed by the scenario. **In answering this question, we consider what, if w were instantiated, we would have been using 'water' to mean and refer to all along. In other words, we place ourselves in the world-state w and ask about our meaning and**

reference there. But now, the "real" actual world-state @ has gotten lost, as has the meaning $C_{water,@}$ that t actually has. Without anyone noticing, their places have been taken by the merely possible world-state w, and the meaning $C_{water,w}$ that 'water' has when used by us there. Moreover, the reference determined by $C_{water,w}$ at w is clear enough. Since w has been characterized as being as much like @ as possible, except for the changes explicitly noted in describing the scenario, it is clear that in w we use 'water' to designate the clear drinkable liquid that falls in rain, and fills the oceans, lakes, and rivers—just as we do in @—but in w this liquid is XYZ. **Although these facts about the use of 'water' by speakers of w allow us to answer Chalmers's questions, the answers we give are about the reference of 'water', as used by us in w with the meaning $C_{water,w}$—not about its reference at w, when used with the meaning $C_{water,@}$ that it has in @.**

This is very easy to miss. Because we are the speakers in both @ and w, because w is designed to preserve as much as possible of our linguistic behavior in @, and because we are asked to *consider w as actual*, any thought of the "real" actual world-state tends to get lost, or be suppressed as illegitimate. As a result, one may be lulled into ignoring a question that is vital to Chalmers's project. Does *water* change **only** its reference, as we move from one scenario to the other, or does it **also** change its meaning (character), and hence its primary intension, as well? Nothing in Chalmers's hypothetical scenarios, or in our responses to the questions in (6), provides an answer to this question. Because of this, our initial, confident answers provide **no** information about the primary intension of *water*, and **no** support for the ambitious two-dimensionalist analysis of names and natural kind terms.

Can the case be made another way? Suppose we reformulate the questions in (6) to make it clear that what is being asked about is the reference, at w, that is determined by the character that *water* has at @. Let (7) be such a reformulation.

7. Consider a possible scenario w which is as much like the actual world-state @ as possible except that in w it is discovered that, contrary to what had previously been thought, the clear drinkable liquid that falls from the sky in rain and fills the oceans, lakes, and rivers is XYZ, not H_2O. If w were to be instantiated, and if 'water' were to be available for use with the meaning it actually has—i.e., if it were associated with the same rule for

assigning contents to contexts that it has in @—what would 'water' refer to when used in w?

Although this question is perfectly coherent, it is not one that speakers' ordinary linguistic competence provides them with any special insight, or authority, for answering. In order to answer it, one has to be able to tell when a word is used with the same meaning in two possible contexts. In particular, one has to be able to tell whether (i) 'water' has a context-sensitive meaning which remains the same from its use by us in @ to its use by us in w, or (ii) the meaning of 'water' is not context-sensitive, but which context-insensitive meaning it has varies from its use in @ (to stand for one physically constitutive kind) to its use in w (to stand for a different kind). This is not something about which one is an expert just by virtue of speaking a language. It is a theoretical question that can be answered only by theoretical argument.

There are two main positions to be considered. On Chalmers's view, names and natural kind terms are indexical, rigidified descriptions, the descriptive content of which gives necessary and sufficient conditions for determining reference in the world-state of the context.[27] For example, according to Chalmers,

> "water" is conceptually equivalent to "*dthat* (watery stuff)," where *dthat* is a version of Kaplan's rigidifying operator, converting an intension into a rigid designator by evaluation at the actual world [the world-state of the context].[28]

If this theoretical analysis of names and natural kind terms is the right one, then the correct answer to the question posed in (7) is that when set in the possible context w, but used with the meaning it has in @, 'water' designates the physically constitutive kind instances of which have the molecular structure XYZ, not H_2O.

In contrast to this position, the view which I favor holds that names and natural kind terms are not indexical, but stand directly for individuals and kinds, which are included in their semantic contents. In some cases, these terms may also carry modest descriptive content as well— e.g., the meaning of the name *Princeton University* seems to carry the

---

[27] As mentioned in chapter 7, analyzing names and natural kind terms of a language L as rigidified descriptions does not require the descriptions to be nonindexically expressible in L. On the contrary, the descriptions may contain indexicals, or descriptive vocabulary that is new to L, or both.

[28] *The Conscious Mind*, p. 59. On p. 61, he adds a bit more detail, saying that 'water' "can be roughly analyzed as '*dthat* (the dominant clear, drinkable liquid *in our environment*).'"

information that its referent is a university, and the meaning of *New Jersey* may carry the information that its referent is a state—but such descriptive content virtually never constitutes necessary and sufficient conditions for determining the extension of the term at a world-state.[29] Moreover, when t is a name or natural kind term, and o is the individual or kind designated by t, speakers who understand t know of o that t designates it. However, this doesn't mean that they are capable of giving a noncircular description of o that distinguishes it from all other things, or of being able to reliably pick it out of a lineup when it is presented in the company of imposters. Nevertheless, they do know, or at any rate can be brought to see, that t is rigid in the sense that when used (by us in the actual world-state) to describe how things would be if a given possible world-state were instantiated, t picks out the same thing that it does when describing how things actually are.

For example, let k_{water} be the kind that 'water' rigidly designates, and let w^* be a possible world-state at which instances of k_{water} exist, but don't fall in rain, don't fill the oceans, lakes, or rivers, and are not clear or drinkable.[30] Instead, instances of a different kind—the molecular structure of which is XYZ—have those properties. It is, of course, common ground between Chalmers and me that 'water' designates k_{water} and not k_{XYZ} when we use it in @ to talk counterfactually about w^*. Since I don't see 'water' as indexical, I take the meaning it actually has—the character—$C_{water,@}$—to be a constant function from arbitrary contexts to contents that include its referent k_{water} in those contexts. If this is right, then it doesn't matter what the context is—the referent of 'water' will always remain the same. Thus, it makes no difference whether we ask for the reference of 'water' with respect to the pair consisting of our actual context @ and w^* as circumstance of evaluation, or whether we ask for its reference relative to the pair consisting of w^* as both context and circumstance of evaluation. In both cases the reference is k_{water}, and not k_{XYZ}. Moreover, this answer is natural, as is seen if we imagine that there are no speakers at all in w^*. Without such speakers there simply is no clear difference between the cases.

This result translates directly into an answer to the question posed in (7); the answer is that in the context w there imagined, 'water' designates k_{water} and not k_{XYZ}, just as it does in the potential context w^*. In evaluating this answer, it is crucial to remember that the fact that

---

[29] See chapters 3 and 5 of *Beyond Rigidity*.

[30] For purposes of the argument we assume that w^* is genuinely possible, rather than simply epistemically conceivable.

there are speakers in w (us) who themselves use 'water' is simply a source of confusion that must be ignored. To avoid this confusion, one should eliminate all language users from w, in which case w may be identified with w*. When this is done, the nonindexical view of 'water' emerges as completely natural.

It is worth noting that, given Chalmers's way of setting up the problem, one can scarcely even state this position. He wants to know what 'water', used with the meaning it has in @, designates in context w* ("considered as actual"). My answer is k_{water}, or, as we might put it, *the kind water*, or *the kind designated by 'water' in the actual world-state @*. However, Chalmers won't accept these as even possible answers, since in giving the first I have used (rather than simply mentioned) the term 'water', and in giving the second I have referred to @. In Chalmers's thought experiments, these linguistic moves are forbidden. As he frames the issue, it is about the answers a subject s would be able to give, using only apriori reasoning from the meanings of words s understands, to questions about the reference of those words, given certain **descriptions** of epistemically conceivable world-states. Since Chalmers thinks it would be trivial or question-begging for s to give the answer *'water' refers to water*, or in general *'n' refers to n*, he excludes the terms asked about from the admissible descriptions of the world-states, and, by extension, from the answers based on those descriptions.[31] He also precludes any reference to the actual world-state @.

Since s is dealing with descriptions of world-states, there is no place for pointing to things either. But even if s somehow had nonlinguistic access to the possible world-state as well, it is not clear how s would know what to point at, short of being able to describe it. Imagine s— with our actual understanding of the word 'water' but none of our aposteriori knowledge about water—contemplating the speakerless world-state w* in which k_{water} exists, but instances of k_{XYZ} fill the rivers, lakes, and oceans. The question before s is: If you were to use

8. The stuff in that puddle is water.

in the imagined context to express a proposition, what stuff would have to be in the puddle in order for the proposition expressed to be true? In attempting to answer this question, s might manage, by luck, to point at an instance of k_{water} in w*, but since s's apriori knowledge of the meaning of *water* doesn't, on my view, provide necessary and

[31] "On Sense and Intension," p. 144.

sufficient conditions for identifying instances of the kind it designates, s wouldn't know what to point at, and so would not be in a position to give any confident answer to the question that Chalmers poses. In short, the subjects of Chalmers's thought experiments are denied the resources to knowingly and justifiably express what I take to be the correct answer to the question.[32] But this only shows that his framework for discussing the issue was too narrow from the beginning. If a framework for discussing the issue presupposes from the outset that understanding any expression gives one the ability to identify its extension at arbitrary world-states from descriptions of those states, then it is hardly surprising that it will eliminate all accounts of meaning except those in which meanings are descriptive. However, for the descriptivist to proceed in this way is for him to stack the deck in his favor.

So far, I have only stated the indexical and nonindexical positions; I have not given theoretical reasons that conclusively decide the issue between them. Although I find the nonindexical position compelling, I recognize that it is theoretical in nature, and that it stands in need of further argument that goes beyond appeal to untutored linguistic intuition. Such arguments can, and will, be given. But whether or not one comes, in the end, to share my views about this, one should recognize that speakers do **not** have strong and definite intuitions supporting Chalmers's alternative view—since to have such intuitions, speakers would have to find it obvious that names and natural kind terms are indexical, which they certainly do not.

Conclusion

I have now reached precisely the same conclusion about Chalmers that I did about Jackson in the penultimate section of chapter 8 on refer-

[32] Although Chalmers does allow them the resources to give the answer 'Water' designates the kind instances of which have the molecular structure H_2O, and although that would, on my view, be the correct answer, it is not an answer that, on my view, subjects are in a position to give solely on the basis of apriori reasoning from the meaning of 'water'. Note that the answer Chalmers prefers—namely, 'Water' designates the kind instances of which fall from the sky in rain, and fill the oceans, lakes, and rivers—is really no better in this regard. It too relies on aposteriori information (not contained in the meaning of the term) about what 'water' refers to in @. The defect in Chalmers's argumentative strategy is that it simply presupposes that certain favored answers to questions about the designation of terms in different scenarios are derived solely from subjects' understanding of the meaning of the term, whereas other disfavored answers do not. But Chalmers has no non-question-begging way of making this distinction.

ence-fixing descriptions. Both philosophers hold that names and natural kind terms are to be analyzed as indexical, rigidified descriptions. Both argue for this by citing the results of thought experiments in which subjects who understand the terms are asked to identify what they would refer to if different possible world-states, described to them in certain ways, were to *turn out to be actual.* However, in both cases, when one examines these thought experiments, one sees that their presuppositions stack the deck in favor of descriptivism, and that the imagined scenarios do nothing to rule out the possibility that names and natural kind terms are nonindexical and nondescriptive. Because of this, the considerations cited by Chalmers and Jackson do **not** provide persuasive support for the crucial two-dimensionalist doctrine that the primary and secondary intensions of names and natural kind terms are distinct.

There is, of course, a stronger thesis that remains to be established—the thesis that the Chalmers-Jackson analysis is not just unsupported, but false. There are two related types of consideration that lead to this result, and support the alternative nonindexical, nondescriptive (or at least partially nondescriptive) view of names and natural kind terms. The first involves Kripkean difficulties—which Chalmers and Jackson are far too sanguine about avoiding—that one encounters when trying to come up with accurate, noncircular descriptions that speakers supposedly associate with these terms simply by virtue of understanding them. The second involves problematic consequences of rigidifying those descriptions in certain ways. Establishing these points will be among the central tasks of chapter 10, where I will attempt to refute several leading theses of different versions of ambitious two-dimensionalism. But first, we must finish the sketch of Chalmers's brand of the view.

Chalmers's Treatment of the Necessary Aposteriori and the Contingent Apriori

To this point, I have examined the case Chalmers makes for two essential tenets of ambitious two-dimensionalism. I began with his reasons for identifying metaphysically possible world-states with epistemically possible world-states—ways the world genuinely could be (or could have been) with ways that we can coherently conceive it to be, and cannot know apriori that it is not. Given this identification, one cannot explain the function of evidence required for knowledge of necessary aposteriori truths as that of ruling out epistemically possible world-states that are metaphysically impossible. If empirical evidence is to play a role in eliminating possibilities with respect to which what is known is false, then what is known cannot be necessary. This invites the idea that each sentence that is an instance of the necessary aposteriori must be associated with two propositions—one necessary, and relevant to modal claims, and the other contingent, and relevant to knowledge ascriptions. This is where the second essential tenet of ambitious two-dimensionalism kicks in. The distinction between the primary and secondary intensions of terms, which Chalmers grounds in his idealized, Fregean conception of linguistic competence, naturally extends to sentences. Whereas the primary intension of a sentence is a function from world-states (in their role as potential contexts of utterance) to truth values, its secondary intension at a context is a function from world-states (in their role as circumstances of evaluation) to truth values. The primary intension of a sentence S either is itself, or closely corresponds to, the proposition associated with S that determines the status of S as apriori or aposteriori. The secondary intension of S in a context either is itself, or closely corresponds to, the proposition associated with S in the context that determines the status of S as necessary or contingent. What remains is to see how Chalmers develops this idea.

Here is how he introduces it in *The Conscious Mind*.

> Both the primary and the secondary intensions can be thought of as candidates for the "meaning" of a concept [expression]. . . . We might as well think of the primary and secondary intensions as the *a priori* and *a posteriori* aspects of meaning, respectively. If we make this equation, both of these intensions will back a certain kind of conceptual truth, or truth in virtue of meaning. The primary intension backs *a priori* truths, such as "Water is watery stuff." Such a statement [sentence] will be true no matter how the actual world turns out, although it need not hold in all non-actual possible worlds. The secondary intension does not back *a priori* truths, but backs truths that hold in all counterfactual possible worlds, such as "Water is H_2O." Both varieties qualify as truths in virtue of meaning; they are simply true in virtue of different aspects of meaning.[33]

[33] Page 62.

In the passage, Chalmers indicates that if S is apriori, then S will be true *no matter how the actual world turns out*—i.e., it will express a truth with respect to any world-state taken as a context (*considered as actual*). Later, he strengthens this by maintaining that S is apriori **iff** S expresses a truth with respect to all contexts, i.e., iff the primary intension of S maps every context onto the value truth.[34] This makes sense, from Chalmers's point of view, because if the primary intension of S assigns truth to every context, then—given that a competent speaker doesn't need any further empirical information to know what this primary intension is—Chalmers reasons that such a speaker also won't need any empirical information about the context to know that S expresses a truth in the context. In the other direction, if one can know apriori, just by understanding S, that it expresses a truth, then, Chalmers thinks, empirical information about the context can't be relevant to determining whether S expresses a truth, and so the primary intension of S must assign truth to every context. By contrast, a sentence that is not true in all contexts, but the secondary intension of which (with respect to our actual context) assigns truth to all other possible world-states (*considered as counterfactual*), is standardly known as a (metaphysically) *necessary truth*. We may express this by saying that for a sentence to count as apriori is for its primary intension to be necessary (i.e., true with respect to all contexts/world-states), whereas for it to be necessary in the more familiar (metaphysical) sense is for its secondary intension to be necessary (i.e., true with respect to all counterfactual circumstances of evaluation).

Chalmers makes this explicit in the following passage.

> It is also possible to see both [types of conceptual truths or "truths in virtue of meaning"] as varieties of *necessary* truth. The latter [necessity of secondary intension] corresponds to the more standard construal of necessary truth. The former [necessity of primary intension], however, can also be construed as truth across possible worlds, as long as those possible worlds are construed as contexts of utterance, or ways the actual world might turn out. On this subtly different construal, a statement [sentence] S is necessarily true if no matter how the actual world turns out, it would turn out that S was true. . . . This kind of necessity is what Evans (1979) calls "deep necessity," as opposed to "superficial" necessi-

---

[34] Page 66.

ties like "Water is H_2O." It is analyzed in detail by Davies and Humberstone (1980) by means of a modal operator they call "fixedly actually." Deep necessity, unlike superficial necessity, is unaffected by *a posteriori* considerations. These two varieties of possibility and necessity apply always to *statements* [sentences]. There is only one relevant kind of possibility of *worlds*, the two approaches differ on how the truth of a statement [sentence] is evaluated in a world.[35]

This is the standard formula of ambitious two-dimensionalism. Apriori truth is equated with what Evans called *deep necessity*, and which Davies and Humberstone analyzed in terms of an operator that produces a truth when attached to S iff S is true with respect to all contexts, or, as they would put it, to all world-states, *considered as actual*. This was one of their two "notions of necessity." The other was expressed by the familiar '□' operator of standard systems of modal logic. That operator produces a truth when attached to S iff for some fixed world-state *considered as actual* (i.e., for some fixed context) S comes out true with respect to all world-states (*considered as counterfactual*). Sentences which are true in this sense—those traditionally regarded as *metaphysically necessary*—have necessary secondary intensions. Chalmers endorses the view that S is apriori iff its primary intension is, as one may say, necessary, and that S is necessary in the traditional metaphysical sense iff its secondary intension is necessary.

Since *is necessary* and *is apriori* are often thought of as predicates of the propositions expressed by sentences, in adopting this terminology and applying it to primary and secondary intensions, Chalmers is implicitly treating them as propositions. He makes this explicit by explaining how to express his position in the language of *propositions*.

If we see a proposition as a function from possible worlds to truth-values, then these two sets of truth conditions [those that arise from evaluating a sentence according to its primary intension and those that arise from evaluating it according to its secondary intension] yield two *propositions* associated with any statement [sentence]. Composing the primary intensions of the terms involved yields a *primary proposition*, which holds in precisely those contexts of utterance in which the statement would turn

---

[35] *The Conscious Mind*, p. 63.

out to express a truth. (This is the "diagonal proposition" of Stalnaker 1978. Strictly speaking, it is a centered proposition, or a function from centered worlds to truth values.) The secondary intensions yield a *secondary* proposition, which holds in those counterfactual circumstances in which the statement [sentence], as uttered in the actual world, is true. The secondary proposition is Kaplan's "content" of an utterance and is more commonly seen as the proposition expressed by a statement [sentence], but the primary proposition is also central.

The two kinds of necessary truth of a statement [sentence] correspond precisely to the necessity of the two kinds of associated proposition. A statement [sentence] is necessarily true in the first (*a priori*) sense if [iff] the associated primary proposition holds in all centered possible worlds (that is, if the statement would turn out to express a truth in any context of utterance). A statement [sentence] is necessarily true in the *a posteriori* sense if [iff] the associated secondary proposition holds in all possible worlds (that is, if the statement as uttered in the *actual* world is true in all counterfactual worlds).[36]

Clearly, the view Chalmers is working up to is one in which S is an instance of the necessary aposteriori iff the primary proposition associated with S is contingent and knowable only aposteriori, while the secondary proposition associated with S is necessary (and knowable apriori).

An Excursion into "Centered Worlds" and "Centered Propositions"

At this point, a word should be said about the "centered world-states" and "centered propositions" mentioned in the above passage. A centered world-state is a world-state with the addition of a designated agent and time to provide interpretations for *I, we, now*, and grammatically related expressions, when world-states function as contexts of utterance. For example, the character of *I* is a function that maps a context—i.e., a centered world-state—onto the designated agent of that state, and the character of a sentence containing *I*—e.g., the character of *I am so and so*—is a function that maps a centered world-state onto the proposition which attributes the property of being so and so to the designated agent of that world-state. Since the designated agent may change from context to context, *I* refers to different individuals,

---

[36] Pages 63–64.

and the sentence expresses different propositions, in different contexts of utterance—which is just to say that their primary intensions are not constant functions. By contrast, since I is a rigid designator, the secondary intension of I relative to a context C is a constant function, which always picks out, with respect to any possible world-state w, the individual that is the referent of I in C. Similar remarks apply to *we*, *now*, and certain closely grammatically related expressions.[37]

This has an immediate formal consequence. Up to now I have been cleaving to my Kaplanesque understanding of the simple, Davies-Humberstone two-dimensionalist semantic picture. According to this picture, (i) the character of S is a function from world-states w to the secondary intension, fs_{2w}, of S relative to w, (ii) the secondary intension fs_{2w} is a function from world-states w* to truth values, and (iii) the primary intension fs_1 of S is a function that assigns a world-state w the value that fs_{2w} assigns to w. Adopting the familiar two-dimensionalist identification of propositions with functions from world-states to truth values, and trading each such function for the set of world-states that it assigns truth, one gets the result that the primary proposition associated with S is the set of world-states w which are members of the set of world-states assigned to w by the character of S.[38] Here, the primary intension of S and the secondary intension of S (relative to a context) are both propositions (sets of world-states), and the roles of being a context in which sentences express propositions, and of being a counterfactual circumstance in which propositions are evaluated, are two different dimensions of the same thing—a world-state.

This pleasing symmetry is lost when contexts (but not circumstances of evaluation) are expanded to include designated agents and times. Although the secondary intension of S relative to C remains a set of ordinary world-states, which we may continue to call a *proposition*, the primary intension of S is now identified with the set of contexts—i.e., centered world-states—to which the meaning of S assigns ordinary propositions that are true in (i.e., contain) the ordinary world-states on which the contexts are centered. Such a primary intension is what Chalmers calls a *centered proposition*. Notice, there is no longer a single kind of thing which plays the roles of both context and circumstance of

---

[37] See pp. 60–61 of *The Conscious Mind* for Chalmers's discussion.

[38] On the simplifying assumption that all propositions are either true or false, the two characterizations of propositions—functions from world-states to truth values, and sets of world-states—are equivalent. Differences can result if propositions can have a third truth value, or if they can be undefined for truth value. For present purposes these can be ignored.

evaluation; nor is there one kind of thing that can be identified with primary and secondary intensions of sentences. Instead, there are centered world-states and ordinary world-states in the first case, and centered propositions and ordinary propositions in the second.

Formally this is all straightforward, and the terminology may make it sound philosophically innocent. In fact, however, it is philosophically puzzling. There is a tradition of treating sets of (ordinary) world-states as propositions, and it is not immediately obvious that it makes sense to treat sets of contexts, or centered world-states, as propositions along more or less the same lines. To get a grip on the issues at stake, it is helpful to focus on two central roles played by propositions in semantical and philosophical theories. One role is being the bearer of truth value; the other is being the object of propositional attitudes. Propositions are supposed to be things that can be true or false when evaluated at different world-states, and they are also supposed to be things that can be asserted, believed, known, and the like. When propositions are identified with sets of (ordinary) world-states, it is easy to see what it means to evaluate a proposition p as true with respect to a way w that the world could be. On this picture, p is true at w iff w is a member of p. What do we say about a "centered proposition," thought of as a set of centered world-states? What is it for such a "proposition" to be true at a world-state?

I don't know of any very good answer to this question. One answer, which is, I think, as good as any, grows out of the observation that the addition of a "center" to what is already a complete way that the world could be adds no further fact about what the world would be like if it were that way. On this answer to the question, a set p of centered world-states is true when evaluated at an uncentered world-state w iff some centering of w is a member of p. By that criterion, the "centered proposition" which is the primary intension of *I am Saul Kripke* is true at @, since there is some centering of the actual world-state—namely one with Saul Kripke as designated agent—which it contains. However, this truth value is not very interesting for evaluating what I (Scott Soames) say when I assertively utter the sentence, or what I believe when I sincerely accept it.[39]

---

[39] One might think that "centered propositions" should be evaluated at "centered world-states," so that the "centered proposition" expressed by *I am Saul Kripke* is true when evaluated at a world-state centered on Saul Kripke, but not at a world-state centered on me. Still, one wants to know whether potential truth bearers—species of propositions that may be asserted and believed—are true or false *simpliciter*. To answer this question, it would seem that one must determine whether the "centered proposition" is true with respect to some centering of the actual world-state—which is just the proposal we already have.

This raises the question of what it would mean for sets of centered worlds to be among the things we assert, believe, and know. Suppose, for the sake of argument, that we take the "centered proposition" that Chalmers identifies with the primary intension of an indexical sentence S to be what is reported, believed, or known in attitude ascriptions such as *I believe that S* and *I know that S*. If we adopted this analysis, we would fail to get the obviously correct result that if Saul and I both say *I know/believe that I am Saul Kripke*, what he claims to know or believe is true, while what I claim to know or believe isn't. On the supposition just made, this can't be so, since on that supposition, we both reported knowing or believing the same "centered proposition" (primary intension). Presumably one and the same proposition—whether "centered" or not—cannot be both true and not true.

The moral here is that adding centering to world-states, and then taking sets of such states to play the roles standardly played by propositions, is no mere technicality or minor formal complication. Even the most elementary philosophical and semantic implications of this move are quite unclear. Chalmers himself doesn't raise the question of what it would mean for what he calls a *centered proposition* (primary intension) to be true, and he has very little explicitly to say about the semantics of propositional attitude ascriptions in *The Conscious Mind*.[40] It is, of course, true that world-states by themselves are too impoverished to serve as contexts for any but the most impoverished indexical languages. Although centering (around a designated agent and time) certainly helps, I believe that additional contextual parameters will also be needed, in which case the contrast between "centered" and "uncentered" world-states will not fully do justice to the differences between contexts and circumstances of evaluation.[41] Putting that aside, however, the most serious problem for the ambitious two-dimensionalist arises from the suggestion that the primary intensions and secondary intensions of sentences (Chalmers's "centered" and "uncentered" propositions) are capable of playing very similar roles (as bearers of truth values and objects of attitudes) despite the fact that they are thought of as constructed out of quite different things— contexts of utterances and circumstances of evaluation, respectively.

[40] Though, as we will see shortly, he does address the issue in "Components of Content," published six years later.
[41] See the excellent discussion of demonstrations as needed additions to contexts in Nathan Salmon, "Demonstrating and Necessity," *Philosophical Review* 111, 4 (2003): 497–537.

All of this is scanted in *The Conscious Mind*. There, the feeling one gets from Chalmers's brief remarks on the topic is that one needs to center worlds so they can play the role of contexts, but other than that, the centering doesn't have substantial philosophical consequences worth mentioning. This seems to me quite wrong. However, since this aspect of his view is left undeveloped, I will put it aside until chapter 10, when the problems posed by sentences containing ordinary indexicals will be considered in more detail.

The Connection between Apriori Sentences and "knowing apriori that"

Before breaking off to discuss "centered world-states" and "centered propositions," I had traced Chalmers's route to the conclusion that S is an instance of the necessary aposteriori iff the primary proposition associated with S is contingent, while the secondary proposition associated with S is necessary. Having arrived at this point, he illustrates and extends it with a telling example.

> To illustrate, take the statement "Water is H_2O." The primary intensions of "water" and "H_2O" differ, **so that we cannot know *a priori* that water is H_2O; the associated *primary* proposition is not necessary (it holds in those centered worlds in which the watery stuff has a certain molecular structure).** Nevertheless, the secondary intensions coincide, so that "Water is H_2O" is true in all possible worlds when evaluated according to the secondary intensions—that is, the associated *secondary* proposition is necessary. Kripkean *a posteriori* necessity arises just when the secondary intensions in a statement back a necessary proposition, but the primary intensions do not.[42]

We are told that the sentence *Water is H_2O* is **not** apriori, and hence that we can't know apriori **that water is H_2O**. The reason for this is that its primary intension—the primary proposition pp associated with it—is contingent. The idea here is that since pp is contingent, it cannot be known apriori to be true; moreover, since what one can know apriori about *Water is H_2O* is just that it expresses a truth iff pp is true, this means that one can't know apriori that *Water is H_2O* expresses a truth. So this sentence is not correctly classified as apriori, and the claims *We can know apriori that water is H_2O* and *It is knowable apri-*

---

[42] *The Conscious Mind*, p. 64, my emphasis.

ori that water is H_2O are false. Of course, what holds for this sentence is supposed to hold for all sentences the primary intensions of which are contingent.

There are several important points to notice here.

(i) Chalmers' argument presumes that if the primary proposition associated with S is contingent, then one cannot know that S is true just by understanding it; hence S is not apriori.

(ii) This presumption is based on the prior assumption that if a proposition is contingent, then it cannot be known apriori to be true. For if the primary proposition pp could be so known, then one could know apriori that S expressed a truth. And why can't pp be known apriori? Because, Chalmers tells us, it is contingent.

(iii) All of this presupposes that primary propositions—despite being "centered"—can be believed, known, and the like. Whatever problems there may be with making sense of this are ignored, or at any rate put aside, by Chalmers at this point.

(iv) In the passage, Chalmers shows that he is perfectly content to move from characterizing S as not being apriori, due to the contingency of the primary proposition associated with S, to using the indirect discourse report *We cannot know apriori that S* or *It is not knowable apriori that S*, and hence to implicitly characterizing them as true. This strongly suggests that whenever S is not apriori, the indirect discourse reports *We cannot know apriori that S* and *It is not knowable apriori that S* are taken by Chalmers to be true, and the reports *We can know apriori that S* and *It is knowable apriori that S* are taken to be false.

(v) This in turn suggests that the operator *it is knowable apriori that* does **not** operate on the secondary proposition associated with its sentential argument. If, as one naturally imagines, *It is knowable apriori that S* is to be taken to be **true** whenever S **is** apriori (because its primary proposition is necessary), then we have reason to conclude that, for Chalmers, *it is knowable apriori that* **does** operate on the primary proposition associated with its sentential argument, or—if it operates on a complex containing the primary proposition plus something else—only the primary proposition matters. Presumably, similar remarks apply to *A knows apriori that S, A knows that S, A believes that S,* and *A asserted that S.*

This general picture is born out in Chalmers's discussion of a closely related example.

> Consider by contrast the statement "Water is watery stuff." Here the associated primary intensions of "water" and "watery stuff" are the same, **so that we can know this statement to be true *a priori*, as long as we possess the concepts** [understand the words]. **The associated primary proposition is necessary, so that the statement is necessarily true in Evans's "deep" sense.** However, the secondary intensions differ, as "water" is rigidified but "watery stuff" is not. . . . The associated *secondary* proposition is therefore not necessary, and the statement is not a necessary truth in the more familiar sense; it is an example of Kripke's "contingent *a priori*."[43]

We are told, not surprisingly, that the sentence *Water is watery stuff* is apriori. The reason for this is that its primary intension—the primary proposition pp associated with it—is necessary. The idea here is that since pp is necessary, it can be known apriori to be true; moreover, since one can know apriori that *Water is watery stuff* expresses a truth iff pp is true, this means that one can know apriori that *Water is watery stuff* expresses a truth. So this sentence is classified as apriori. Presumably, though Chalmers doesn't explicitly say so here, this means *It is knowable apriori that water is watery stuff* is true. Of course, what holds for this sentence is supposed to hold for all sentences the primary intensions of which are necessary.

Points to notice about this argument are parallel to those pertaining to the previous argument:

(i)   Chalmers's argument presumes that if the primary proposition associated with S is necessary, then one can know that S is true just by understanding it; hence S is apriori.

(ii) This presumption is based on the prior assumption that if a proposition is necessary, it can be known apriori to be true.

---

[43] Ibid., p. 64.

For if the necessary primary proposition pp could **not** be so known, then one could **not** know apriori that S expresses a truth. And why is it that the primary proposition pp **can** be known apriori? Because, Chalmers tells us, it is necessary.

(iii) All of this presupposes that primary propositions—despite being "centered"—can be believed, known, and the like. Whatever problems there may be with making sense of this are ignored, or at any rate put aside, by Chalmers at this point.

(iv) Although in the most recently quoted passage, Chalmers does not move from characterizing 'Water is watery stuff' as being apriori to using the indirect discourse report *It is knowable apriori that water is watery stuff*, and thereby to implicitly characterizing it as true, it is hard to imagine that he would object to this move. For one thing, we have the parallel with the previously quoted passage. For another, when he describes the use of hypothetical scenarios to determine the primary intensions of sentences, he repeatedly indicates that although (a) speakers should "**accept that** water is H_2O" (indirect discourse) on the hypothesis that certain scenarios (possible world-states) are actual, and reject it on the hypothesis that others are actual, (b) they should always "**accept that** water is watery stuff" on any hypothesis about what is actual. This strongly suggests that he thinks that accepting that water is watery stuff doesn't require any empirical justification, which in turn implies that the belief that water is watery stuff is apriori, and—since it is true that water is watery stuff—that it is knowable apriori that water is watery stuff. This indicates that he takes *It is knowable apriori that water is watery stuff* to be true, and, more generally, that whenever S is apriori, he takes the indirect discourse report *It is knowable apriori that S* to be true.

(v) This in turn conforms to the idea that the operator *it is knowable apriori that* operates on the primary proposition associated with its sentential argument, or—if it operates on a complex containing the primary proposition plus something else—only the primary proposition matters. Presumably, similar remarks apply to *A knows apriori that S, A knows that S, A believes that S,* and *A asserts that S.*[44]

In addition, one further point emerges from the two examples taken together.

(vi)   Chalmers assumes that p is knowable apriori iff p is necessary. Although this assumption doesn't strictly **require** that propositions be sets of world-states (centered or not), it does exert pressure in that direction, since it is hard to see how other conceptions of propositions—e.g., structured neo-Russellian or neo-Fregean propositions—could validate the assumption.

Consider, for example, the test case (9).

9.   Meyer Kripke is Saul Kripke's father.

Assuming the necessity of origins, we may classify (9) as an example of the necessary aposteriori.[45] Thus, for Chalmers, the primary proposition associated with it is contingent, whereas the secondary proposition is necessary. Since he assumes that every necessary proposition is knowable apriori, he must take this one to be. If propositions are just sets of world-states, then the explanation of how the secondary proposition associated with (9) can be known apriori is straightforward. On this view, there is only one necessary proposition, and knowledge of it is trivial. Suppose, however, that propositions are structured complexes of the sorts identified with either Russell or Frege. If the secondary proposition associated with (9) is Russellian, then it is a structured complex the components of which are two distinct individuals plus the fatherhood relation. Since there is nothing in this structure the contemplation of which could possibly reveal that

[44] Further support for this final remark comes from Chalmers's comment: "The primary proposition, more than the secondary proposition, captures how things seem from the point of view of the subject: it delivers the set of centered worlds which the subject, in having the belief, is endorsing as potential environments in which he or she might be living (in **believing that Hesperus is Phosphorus**, I endorse all those centered worlds in which the evening star and the morning star around the center are identical). It is also fairly easy to argue that the primary proposition, rather than the secondary proposition, governs the cognitive and rational relations between thoughts. For this reason it is natural to think of the primary proposition as the *cognitive* content of a thought." *The Conscious Mind*, p. 65, my emphasis.

[45] Don't worry about world-states in which Saul Kripke doesn't exist. I am simplifying to streamline the discussion.

the predication indicated in the proposition was true, it would be very difficult to justify the conclusion that the proposition is knowable apriori. The same is true regarding the neo-Fregean conception of the proposition, once it is remembered that the senses of the two names that would replace their referents in the structured proposition would not, on any reasonable construal, include information about who is the father of whom.[46] Thus, if one is, like Chalmers, committed to the view that all necessary propositions are knowable apriori, then one has good reason to reject neo-Russellian and neo-Fregean conceptions of propositions in favor of the possible world-state conception— as indicated in (vi).

Additional confirmation of this point is found in "On Sense and Intension," where Chalmers endorses the idea that two sentences S and T will have the same primary intensions iff the material biconditional *S iff T* is apriori.[47] Since, on his view, S is apriori iff its primary intension is necessary, this means that the primary intensions of two sentences are identical iff they are necessarily equivalent. Identifying these with propositions, and taking what holds of primary propositions to hold of propositions generally, one gets the result that propositions ("centered" or "uncentered") can be identified with sets of (centered or uncentered) world-states.

This completes my interpretation of the fundamental tenets of Chalmers's two-dimensional semantic system. As I have shown, there are strong and persuasive reasons for taking the position advocated in *The Conscious Mind* (and amplified elsewhere) to be a version of strong—even very strong—two-dimensionalism, in the sense defined in chapter 7. Even though Chalmers did not explicitly formulate all the crucial theses, his discussion strongly suggests and may even require them or their near equivalents, in order to make fully coherent sense. At the end of this chapter, I will return to the issue of interpretation to discuss a significant complication involving propositional attitude ascriptions introduced by a more recent discussion, published several years after *The Conscious Mind*. Before addressing this issue, however, I will say a word about how he uses his two-dimensional semantic apparatus to argue against physicalism, and for the possibility of zombies.

---

[46] These general points about neo-Russellian and neo-Fregean propositions are made, very persuasively, by Alex Byrne in section 7 of "Chalmers' Two-Dimensional Argument against Physicalism," *MIT Working Papers in Linguistics and Philosophy* 1 (2000).

[47] "On Sense and Intension," p. 151.

For Zombies and against Physicalism

Chalmers wants to show that there are aspects of reality, indeed aspects of us, that go beyond the purely physical, in the sense that some truths about the world, and about us, are not necessary consequences of the physical truths.[48] He begins by observing that there is a perfectly conceivable world-state just like ours in all physical respects—in which our bodies exist and function just as they actually do, and in which all our brain activity is the same as it is in the actual world—but in which there are no conscious experiences. In that world-state your body exists, it is reading right now, your brain is in exactly the same state that it is now actually in, but your body is a zombie—and all other human bodies are too. Although they can interact intelligently with the world, they feel no pleasures or pains, they never experience pangs of hunger or other bodily sensations, and they have no sense experiences in virtue of which the world appears to them in one way rather than another—e.g., nothing ever appears black or white, red or green, loud or quiet, sour or sweet to them. They are, in effect, complicated organic machines with no conscious lives whatsoever.

Physicalists contend that the imagined world-state is not really possible. According to them, truths about conscious experiences are necessary consequences of the totality of underlying physical truths. Why then is Chalmers's zombie fantasy coherent, conceivable, and not knowable apriori not to be so? If the fantasy is coherently conceivable in this sense, it is because the relationship between the physical and the mental is not apriori. If one can't derive the mental from the physical by apriori reasoning alone, then there is no apriori incoherence in the conjunction of the physical with the negation of the mental. But the fact that there is no apriori incoherence doesn't show that the fantasy is genuinely possible. It is not possible; the world couldn't have been that way. So says the physicalist.

Chalmers considers this physicalist response to his zombie scenario in chapter 4 of *The Conscious Mind*.[49] He imagines the physicalist invoking Kripke's example of the necessary aposteriori, *Water is H_2O*, to illustrate the point. If there can be statements (sentences) that are necessary without being apriori, then there is no reason why the relation-

---

[48] For an illuminating discussion of the architecture of Chalmers's argument against physicalism, see Byrne, "Chalmers' Two-Dimensional Argument against Physicalism."

[49] Page 131.

ship between the mental and the physical can't be one of necessary consequence without being one of apriori consequence. Chalmers responds to this by invoking his strong two-dimensionalist framework for understanding the necessary aposteriori, which he summarizes as follows:

> Recall that in this framework there are two intensions (functions from possible worlds to referents) associated with any concept [expression]. . . . The primary intension associated with "water" is something like "watery stuff." The secondary intension is "H_2O," which is derived from the primary intension by applying Kaplan's *dthat* operator: "*dthat* (watery stuff)" picks out H_2O in all possible worlds, as watery stuff is H_2O in the actual world. "Logical possibility" comes down to the possible truth of a statement when evaluated according to the primary intensions involved. . . . The primary intension of "water" and "H_2O" differ, **so it is logically possible in this sense that water is not H_2O.**[50]

Here we have the familiar explanation. The sentence *Water is not H_2O* is logically possible (i.e., conceivable, or epistemically possible) because its primary intension (proposition) assigns truth to some (centered) world-states. Since the primary intensions of 'water' and 'H_2O' differ, there are world-states in which they pick out different things. This guarantees that the primary intension (proposition) pp of the sentence is possible in the ordinary sense—i.e., pp is true with respect to some ways that the world genuinely could be. Hence, Chalmers concludes, "**it is logically possible that water is not H_2O.**" Again one finds the seamless transition from talk about words and their intensions, to talk of the possible truth of the primary intension (proposition) of the sentence *Water is not H_2O*, to the use of the sentence in **indirect discourse**, where it is said that it is logically possible **that water is not H_2O**.

The same sort of transition is made when the passage continues with Chalmers's remarks about metaphysical necessity.

> "Metaphysical possibility" comes down to the possible truth of a statement when evaluated according to the secondary intensions involved. The secondary intensions of "water" and "H_2O" are the same, **so it is metaphysically necessary that water is H_2O.**[51]

[50] Page 132.
[51] Page 132.

In the language of strong two-dimensionalism, the sentence *Water is H_2O* is metaphysically necessary because its secondary intension (proposition) assigns truth to all world-states. Since the secondary intensions of 'water' and 'H_2O' are the same, they pick out the same extensions in all world-states, and the secondary intension (proposition) sp of the sentence is necessary in the ordinary sense—i.e., sp is true with respect to every way that the world genuinely could be. Hence, Chalmers concludes, "it is metaphysically necessary **that water is H_2O.**"

In general, Chalmers accepts the following claims as true

It is metaphysically necessary that S.

It is logically possible that ~S.

It is not logically necessary that S.

whenever one has a pair of sentences, *S* and *~S*, the first of which is "metaphysically necessary"—because its secondary intension (proposition) is necessary—and the second of which is "logically possible"—because its primary intension (proposition) is contingent. Moreover, he takes it to be obvious that there are such sentences. In light of this, one can ask whether the operator *it is metaphysically necessary that* operates on the same semantic value of its sentential arguments as do *it is logically necessary that* and *it is logically possible that*. In principle these operators could do so—if one recognized that there were two kinds of possible world-states, and that a single proposition could be true in all metaphysically possible world-states, while being false in some logically possible— i.e., epistemologically conceivable—world-states. But Chalmers adamantly rejects this picture. For him, (i–iii) are articles of faith.

(i)   There is just one kind of possible world-state.

(ii)   Necessity, whether of the logical (epistemic) or the metaphysical kind, is always a matter of truth with respect to all possible world-states.

(iii)   The reason that both *It is metaphysically necessary that S* and *It is not logically necessary that S* can jointly be true is that S is associated with two intensions (propositions)—primary and secondary—the former being determinative of logical necessity and the latter being determinative of metaphysical necessity.

This picture strongly suggests that the two operators operate on different semantic values of their arguments—that *it is metaphysically necessary that* operates on the secondary intension (proposition) of S, while *it is logically necessary that* operates on the primary intension (proposition) of S. Of course, both operators could operate on the pair of primary and secondary intensions (propositions) of S, with one operator looking only at one member of the pair and the other operator looking only at the other—but that is just a notational variant of the idea that they operate on different semantic values. This result comports well with the conclusion of the previous section. There I indicated that for Chalmers *It is knowable apriori that* S is true iff the primary intension of S is necessary. Hence, I argued that he is properly interpreted as holding that *it is knowable apriori that* operates on the primary proposition associated with S, or—if it operates on a complex containing the primary proposition plus something else—only the primary proposition matters. To this I now add that, in his system, *It is knowable apriori that* S and *It is logically necessary that* S come to the same thing.

With his strong two-dimensionalist treatment of the necessary aposteriori in place, Chalmers is in position to make short work of the physicalist. First, he restates the physicalist's objection from a perspective that presupposes the truth of his two-dimensionalist account of the necessary aposteriori. Then, he quickly disposes of it.

> The objection therefore comes down to the point that in using arguments from conceivability and the like, we have demonstrated the possibility of a zombie world using the *primary* intensions of the notions [expressions] involved, but not using the more appropriate *secondary* intensions. While the primary intension of phenomenal notions [mentalistic vocabulary] may not correspond to that of any physical notion [expression], the secondary intensions may be the same. If so, the phenomenal [mental] and physical/functional concepts [words and phrases] may pick out the same properties *a posteriori* [i.e., they may have the same secondary intensions] despite the *a priori* distinction [i.e., despite the distinction in their primary intensions]. . . . The easiest way to see that none of this affects the arguments for dualism is to note that the argument I have given goes through if we concentrate on the primary intension throughout and ignore the secondary intension. . . . For note that whether or not the primary and sec-

ondary intensions coincide, the primary intension determines a perfectly good property of objects in possible worlds. The property of being watery stuff is a perfectly reasonable property, even though it is not the same property as the property of being H_2O. If we can show that there are possible worlds that are physically identical to ours but in which the property introduced by the primary intension is lacking, then dualism will follow. This is just what has been done with consciousness.[52]

Given Chalmers's assumptions, one cannot fault this argument. Here is how it can be reconstructed. Let P be some finite formulation that entails all the explicitly physical truths. Let S be some mentalistic truth that talks about conscious experiences. Then according to Chalmers's physicalist opponent, $P \supset S$ is necessary but not knowable apriori. Treating this in accord with his strong two-dimensionalism, Chalmers takes the physicalist's contention to mean that the secondary intension of the sentence is necessary, while the primary intension is contingent. What is the primary intension of $P \supset S$? It is the proposition expressed by a corresponding conditional in which P and S are replaced by sentences P_P and S_P, the secondary intensions of which are the primary intensions of P and S, respectively. However, it is part of Chalmers's story that when we reach the vocabulary of fundamental physics—the terms used to formulate P—the primary and secondary intensions of these expressions always coincide. Hence, no replacement is really needed in the case of P.[53] However, since the whole conditional is an example of the necessary aposteriori, Chalmers's two-dimensionalism dictates that the primary and secondary intensions of S must be different. The result is $P \supset S_P$.

On the strong two-dimensionalist view, this sentence has got to be contingent (on the assumption that the original conditional was a genuine case of the necessary aposteriori). But if it is contingent, then there is a possible world-state in which all the actual truths of physics are true and S_P is false. Hence S_P is **not** a necessary consequence of the physical truths. Since S_P is, like S, true in the actual world-state, this means that some actual truth is not a necessary consequence of the physical truths. Consequently, physicalism is false. In effect, if you

[52] Page 132.

[53] If we had to replace P with a distinct physicalist sentence P_P, then the argument wouldn't go through, since the demonstration that a truth S_P is not a necessary consequence of P_P would not show that some truth is not a necessary consequence of the totality of the physical truths.

think of mentalistic terms as being rigidified descriptions that designate psychological kinds, and you accept the whole of Chalmers's two-dimensionalist picture—while admitting that claims about conscious experiences are not apriori consequences of the underlying physical truths—then you must also admit that there are possible world-states in which our bodies and brains exist and have all the physical properties they have in the actual world, while failing to have a certain nonphysical property NP that we actually have—where the possession of NP provides the basis for correctly attributing conscious experiences to us.

Of course, this argument is only as strong as its premises, about which I have evinced strong reasons to be skeptical. Although I agree with Chalmers that claims about conscious experiences are not apriori consequences of the underlying physical truths, I have questioned the account of the necessary aposteriori that emerges from his basic two-dimensionalist semantic theory, as well as the use of the vocabulary of theoretical physics to provide a supposedly two-dimension–free foundation for that theory. In the discussions of Jackson and Chalmers, I have argued that none of the central tenets of strong two-dimensionalist semantics, and the resulting treatment of the necessary aposteriori, are well motivated. I have also argued that there are plausible alternatives to each such tenet, and that the resulting two-dimensionalist systems lead to serious difficulties. In the next chapter I will extend this critique by providing arguments that the main tenets of ambitious two-dimensionalism are false. As for the idea that the vocabulary of theoretical physics can be used to provide a two-dimension–free foundation for two-dimensionalist semantic analysis, all I can say is that the idea is extremely implausible on its face, and that it has not been worked out in enough detail to determine whether it is even coherent. For these reasons, serious doubts remain about Chalmers's attempted refutation of physicalism.

In addition to these, there is one further question worth asking. Suppose, for the sake of argument, that Chalmers's refutation of physicalism is correct. Would it follow that there is a way that the world genuinely could be which is such that if the world were that way, then zombies would exist—i.e., our bodies and brains would have no consciousness, even though they would have all the physical properties they do in the actual world-state? I don't see that this would follow, any more than it would follow that if in some world-state there were no watery stuff—i.e., stuff with the familiar observable properties of water in the actual world-state—then there would be no H_2O (i.e., water) in that world-state. Suppose you thought, as Chalmers does, that *water* is equivalent to the rigidified description *dthat[the watery stuff]*, where the unrigidified description designates something other than H_2O in some world-states. Given this, you might still recognize the existence of H_2O (water) in a world-state in which there was no watery stuff. By analogy, even if Chalmers's argument against physicalism were accepted, this would not by itself show that there is a possible world-state w with respect to which zombies exist, even though all the physical facts in w are the same as they are in the actual world-state. To establish that, further argument (perhaps involving the analysis of mentalistic vocabulary) is needed.

Although I think that Chalmers recognizes this, certain of his formulations can give one the wrong impression. For example, immediately after making his argument against physicalism—based on the primary intension of the conditional $P \supset S$ that the physicalist labels *necessary aposteriori*—Chalmers says the following.

> **We have seen that there are worlds physically just like ours that lack consciousness, according to the primary intension thereof.** This difference in worlds is sufficient to show that there are properties of our world over and above the physical properties. **By analogy, if we could show that there were worlds physically identical to ours in which there was no watery stuff, we would have established dualism about water just as well as if we had established that there were worlds physically identical to ours in which there was no H_2O.**[54]

I am not sure precisely what the two highlighted sentences are supposed to mean, especially the latter, *if we could show that there were worlds physically identical to ours in which there was no watery stuff, we would have established **dualism about water** just as well as if we had established that there were worlds physically identical to ours in which there was no H_2O.* Certainly what we would establish—by showing that there are world-states physically identical with ours in which there was no watery stuff—is **not** that there are genuine possible world-states physically identical with ours in which there is no water. By analogy, if one thought that words for conscious experiences were, like water, equivalent to dthat-rigidified descriptions, one would have to recog-

---

[54] *The Conscious Mind*, pp. 132–33, my emphasis.

nize that Chalmers's argument against the physicalist does **not** show there are genuine possible world-states physically identical to ours in which there are no conscious experiences.

However, in the end Chalmers does not accept this semantic analysis of conscious-experience terms.

> The irrelevance of *a posteriori* necessity can be further supported by the observation that with consciousness, the primary and secondary intensions coincide. What it takes for a state to be a conscious experience in the actual world is for it to have a phenomenal feel, and what it takes for something to be a conscious experience in a counterfactual world is for it to have a phenomenal feel. The difference between the primary and secondary intensions for the concept water reflects the fact that there could be something that looks and feels like water in some counterfactual world that in fact is not water, but merely watery stuff. But if something feels like a conscious experience, even in some counterfactual world, it *is* a conscious experience. All it means to be a conscious experience, in any possible world, is to have a certain feel. (Kripke makes a similar point, although he puts the point in terms of essential properties rather than in terms of meaning.)[55]

This passage announces a number of controversial assumptions about the metaphysical nature of conscious phenomena, their epistemological availability to us, and the supposed lack of any distinction between the primary and secondary intensions of terms designating them. In order for Chalmers's argument for mind/body dualism to work, these assumptions must be added to those we have already listed. I will not attempt to evaluate these new assumptions here. It is enough to point out their role in his response to the physicalist. The crucial point is that Chalmers thinks that, unlike proper names and natural kind terms, terms for conscious experiences are special in not being equivalent to rigidified descriptions. In his two-dimensionalist framework, this means they don't have distinct primary and secondary intensions, and that the crucial physicalist conditionals $P \supset S$ can't be instances of the necessary aposteriori. Since they do seem, clearly, to be aposteriori, it follows that they can't be necessary. Hence, the mental is not a necessary consequence of the physical. Q.E.D.

[55] Page 133. The reference to Kripke is to his (in my opinion seriously misleading) discussion at the end of lecture 3 of *Naming and Necessity*, of pain, c-fiber stimulation, and the mind/body identity theory.

An Added Complication Involving Propositional Attitude Ascriptions

As previously shown, theses T1–T3 are central to Chalmers's two-dimensionalist account of the necessary aposteriori and the contingent apriori.

T1. A proposition is knowable apriori iff it is necessary.

T2. A sentence S is an instance of the apriori iff its primary intension is necessary—i.e., iff the "centered" proposition it expresses is true in all contexts.

T3. S is an instance of the apriori iff *It is knowable apriori that S* is true.

This led me to conclude that, for Chalmers, *it is knowable apriori that* operates on the primary proposition associated with its sentential argument, or—if it operates on a complex containing the primary proposition plus something else—only the primary proposition matters. Given the evident semantic connections between *It is knowable apriori that S*, on the one hand, and *A knows apriori that S, A knows that S, A believes that S,* and *A asserted that S,* on the other, I concluded that "similar remarks apply" to the latter sentences as well. The reasons I contented myself with this rather vague formulation were (a) that Chalmers does not make explicit proposals about the semantics of ordinary propositional attitude ascriptions in *The Conscious Mind*, and (b) that when he does discuss this topic, in "Components of Content," published six years later, what he has to say is not easy to square with the account of *it is knowable apriori that* which emerges from *The Conscious Mind*. It is now time to address this topic.

In section 8 of "Components of Content," Chalmers discusses ascriptions of the form *x believes that S*. Although he doesn't offer an explicit semantic theory of these sentences, he does make it clear that their truth conditions depend on the relationship the agent bears not just to the primary intension of S, but also to its secondary intension.

> It is easy to see that ordinary belief ascriptions ascribe both epistemic and subjunctive content [i.e., primary and secondary intension]. If I say 'Ralph believes that Clark Kent is muscular', then in order for my utterance to be true, Ralph must have a belief that satisfies two sorts of constraints. First, the belief must have the

subjunctive content of the proposition that Clark Kent is muscular [i.e., the secondary intension, or secondary proposition, associated with the belief must be the proposition that Clark Kent is muscular, which is the secondary intension of the sentence *Clark Kent is muscular*]. . . . But that alone is not enough: a belief that Superman is muscular would have the same subjunctive content, but would not make my ascription true. As is often noted . . . for the ascription to be true, the belief must involve a concept that refers to its object (Clark Kent) under an appropriate mode of presentation. In the current framework, modes of presentation are naturally seen as epistemic [i.e., primary] intensions. If Ralph refers to Clark Kent under an epistemic [primary] intension that picks out whoever is called 'Clark Kent', or one that picks out whoever is the reporter with glasses at the *Daily Planet*, or some more complex intension in the vicinity, my belief ascription will be true. If Ralph refers to Clark Kent under any epistemic [primary] intension that picks out the guy in the cape, or one that picks out the strongest man in the world, my belief ascription will be false. One might say that for the ascription to be true, Ralph must refer to Clark Kent under a 'Clark Kent'-appropriate epistemic [primary] intension. Here, the conditions on a 'Clark Kent'-appropriate epistemic [primary] intension are somewhat vague and unclear, and they may well be context-dependent, but it is clear from an examination of cases that they are substantive.[56]

Several conclusions about Chalmers's view of belief ascriptions are suggested by this passage.

C1. Although both the primary and secondary propositions (intensions) associated with S are responsible for necessary conditions on the truth of *x believes that S*, neither provides sufficient conditions.

C2. In order for *x believes that S*, as used in a context C, to be true of an agent a in a circumstance of evaluation w, the secondary proposition (intension) associated with a's belief in w must be the same as that associated with S in C.

C3. The necessary condition on the truth of *x believes that S* supplied by the primary proposition (intension) associated with

[56] Page 622.

S is much weaker and vaguer. Nevertheless there are cases in which the ascription is false of an agent a even though the secondary intension of a's belief in w matches that of S (in the context of ascription), just as there are cases in which the ascription is false, even though the primary intension of the agent's belief matches that of S.

These conclusions are borne out by Chalmers's most explicit statement of his treatment of belief ascriptions.

> The general principle here is something like the following. A belief ascription 'x believes that S' is true when the ascribee has a belief with the subjunctive [secondary] intension of S (in the mouth of the ascriber), and with an S-appropriate epistemic [primary] intension. Here the epistemic [primary] intension is usually much less strongly constrained than the subjunctive [secondary] intension. The conditions on S-appropriateness may well be complex and context-dependent. . . . Still, one can make a few generalizations. Much of the time, an epistemic [primary] intension that is not too different from the ascriber's will be S-appropriate, and much of the time, an epistemic intension that involves the terms in S itself will be S-appropriate.[57]

One question left open by Chalmers's remarks concerns the entities he calls 'beliefs', which are presumed to have primary and secondary intensions that must bear appropriate relations to the primary and secondary intensions of the complement sentences of attitude ascriptions, in order for the ascriptions to be true of an agent. There are different possibilities for what these entities might be. However, since he is not specific about what he means, I will make do with sentences or mental representations that the agent would accept. Using this idea, one may state the truth-conditional principle that Chalmers seems to have in mind.

C4. The ascription *x believes that S* is true with respect to an assignment A of values to variables, a context C, and a world-state w iff in w, the individual a assigned to 'x' by A accepts some sentence or mental representation M which is such that (i) the secondary intension of M in a's context in w is identical with the secondary intension of S with respect to C and

A, and (ii) the primary intension of M is "appropriately related" to the primary intension of S with respect to A.[58]

This principle is, of course, vague and provisional. In addition to
containing the clause requiring primary intensions to be "appropriately related," there is another way in which C4 is incomplete. It
doesn't explicitly characterize the belief predicate as relational, nor
does it identify the objects of belief. Sentences in which *believes* takes
as grammatical objects either ordinary noun phrases—e.g., *the proposition that all truths are determined by the physical truths, the physicalist's
thesis, what David denied*—or variables of objectual quantification indicate that *believe* stands for a relation between believers (agents) and
things believed (objects of belief). The close semantic relationship (indicated by a variety of semantically valid arguments) between belief ascriptions of the form *x believes that S* and those of the form *x believes
NP*, or *x believes p*—where NP is a noun phrase and p is an objectual
variable—suggests that even belief ascriptions of the first sort are relational. Hence, a fully developed semantic theory would state the truth
conditions of belief ascriptions in this way. However, I will make do
with C4.

In chapter 10, I will give arguments against C3 (and its incorpora-
tion into C1 and C4), as well as against systems of ambitious two-
dimensionalism that embrace them, and related principles for other
propositional attitude ascriptions. For now, I will focus on how these
principles lead to conflicts with some of the central ideas of Chalmers's own version of two-dimensionalism. To do this, one first needs
to connect belief ascriptions to ascriptions of knowledge and apriori
knowledge.

10a. John believes that S.

  b. John knows that S.

  c. John knows apriori that S.

For any assignment A, context C, and possible world-state w, if (10c)
is true with respect to A, C and w, then (10b) is too; and for any A, C,

---

[58] Since primary intension is derived from character, and character is relativized to assignments of values to variables (to allow for quantifying in), primary intension must be similarly
relativized. On a separate point, talk of a's context in w refers to a context in which a is the
designated agent and w is the designated world-state. (For simplicity, I ignore times in stating C4.) Thought of in this way, a's context in w need not be one in which a uses any sentences or has any beliefs (in which case the belief ascription will, correctly, come out false).

and w, if (10b) is true with respect to A, C, and w, then (10a) is too.[59] Thus, any case in which (10a) is false with respect to A, C, and w— because in w John does not bear the right relation to either the primary or secondary intension of S with respect to A and C—is one in which (10b) and (10c) are false with respect to A, C, and w, for the same reason. As a result, the necessary conditions involving primary and secondary intensions of S that Chalmers imposes on the truth conditions of belief ascriptions (10a) must also be imposed on the truth conditions of knowledge ascriptions (10b) and (10c).

The constraints on the truth conditions of sentences like (10c), containing *knows apriori that*, carry over to ascriptions of the form (10d).

10d. Someone knows apriori that S.

However, the relationship between these ascriptions and those of the form (10e) is a little tricky.

10e. It is knowable apriori that S.

Presumably, the truth of the latter does not strictly require the truth of the former—since the only existing agents might not have done the required apriori reasoning. This suggests that (10e) is equivalent to something along the lines of one of the claims in (11).

11a. There is some agent x such that in some possible world-state w, x knows apriori that S.

b. In some possible world-state w there are agents who know apriori that S.

c. If there were agents who were perfect apriori reasoners, then they would know apriori that S.

I suspect that (11a) is still too restrictive (suppose that existing agents are essentially subject to certain significant cognitive limitations), and that something along the lines of (11b) or (11c) most closely approximates (10e). For the sake of simplicity—not having to raise the issues of what being a perfect reasoner would amount to, of whether such perfection is even possible, or of what the minimal change in the actual world-state would have to be to make the antecedent of (11c) true—I will opt for (11b). Although this will affect the way in which certain points that follow are expressed, it won't, I think, affect the central un-

---

[59] I include assignments to allow for the possibility of quantifying in.

derlying issues. The main thing to notice is that the Chalmers-inspired constraints on sentences containing the predicate *knows apriori* will now carry over to constraints on the operator, *it is knowable apriori that*.

With this in mind, I will consider how his new treatment of attitude ascriptions and operators affects his previously enunciated two-dimensionalist account of the apriori. I have already shown that the doctrines Apriori 1 and Apriori 2 are central to his account.

APRIORI I

A sentence S is an instance of the apriori iff the primary intension of S is necessary iff the character of S assigns every context a proposition that is true in that context.

APRIORI 2

It is knowable apriori that S is true iff S is an instance of the apriori.

Next, I will show how Chalmers's new analysis of attitude ascriptions threatens the conjunction of these two principles.

Taking the first principle as fixed (and assuming the two-dimensionalist analysis of names), I begin with an argument that puts pressure on the left-to-right direction of the second principle.

Step 1. If the new semantic analysis of attitude ascriptions is correct, then there will be cases in which an utterance, by a_1 in context C_1, of A_2 *knows that n is F* is true, where (i) the referent a_2 of A_2 justifiably accepts a true sentence *m is F* the secondary intension of which in a_2's context C_2 is the same as the secondary intension of *n is F* in C_1, and (ii) the primary intensions of these two sentences are at least somewhat different because the primary intension of m (as used in C_2) differs somewhat from that of n (as used in C_1). (Here, n is a name, and m is either a name or an indexical. The term m may even be the same name as n, provided that we recognize that different speakers may use it with somewhat different primary intensions in their respective contexts.)

Step 2. If there are cases of the sort indicated in step 1, then it is extremely natural to suppose that some of these cases will be symmetrical in that while a_1 uses A_2 *knows that n is F* to truly report about a_2, the latter can use A_1 *knows that m is F* to truly report about a_1. These reports can be jointly true because (i) the secondary intensions of the two complement clauses are the same in their respective contexts, and (ii) the primary intensions of these clauses, though different, are close enough to satisfy constraints imposed by the new semantic analysis of attitude ascriptions.

Step 3.   To make matters concrete, assume that the primary intensions of n and m are given by a pair of descriptions D_n and D_m which pick out the same objects in their respective contexts, but which denote different objects with respect to at least some pairs of contexts. One natural way for this to happen is for both descriptions to be conjunctive, for both to share a core of common conjuncts, and for the two to differ in that D_n contains a conjunct that predicates G of its denotation whereas the corresponding conjunct in D_m predicates the unrelated predicate F. Although nothing in two-dimensionalism explicitly mandates the existence of cases like this, nothing excludes them, and the implicitly assumed speaker-relativity of the primary intensions of many proper names strongly suggests them.

Step 4.   Now consider a_1's utterance in C_1 of the ascription A_2 *knows that if n exists, then n is F*. For the reasons given in step 2, this ascription should be true, since a_2 justifiably accepts the true sentence *If m exists, then m is F*, the secondary intension of which in C_2 is the same as the secondary intension of *If n exists, then n is F* in C_1. As before, although the primary intensions of the two sentences (as used in their respective contexts) are different, they should be close enough to satisfy the constraints imposed by the new semantic analysis of attitude ascriptions.

Step 5.   Since F is included in the reference-fixing conditions for m, the primary intension of *If m exists, then m is F* (as used in C_2) should be necessary, and so the knowledge correctly attributed to a_2 by a_1's utterance of A_2 *knows that if n exists, then n is F* should (according to the two-dimensionalist) be counted as apriori.

Step 6. So A_2 *knows apriori that if n exists, then n is F* should be true, as used in context C_1.

Step 7. But then *It is knowable apriori that if n exists, then n is F* must also be true as used in C_1.

Step 8. This is so even though the primary intension of *If n exists, then n is F* (as used in C_1) is not necessary.

Clearly, this argument threatens the conjunction of Apriori 1 with the left-to-right direction of Apriori 2. Since this conjunction was central to the version of two-dimensionalism espoused in *The Conscious Mind*, Chalmers's new semantic treatment of attitude ascriptions puts his previous two-dimensionalism at risk. Although it is conceivable that restrictions could be imposed blocking certain moves in the above argument, it is unlikely that such argument-blocking restrictions could be given principled, non–ad hoc justifications. At the very least, Chalmers's new analysis of attitude ascriptions creates a serious prima facie problem for his two-dimensionalism.

There are also potential problems involving truths which, though classified as apriori, resist being known by certain agents—even though their powers of reflection are unimpaired and their apriori reasoning is flawless. The relevant examples are instances of the contingent apriori—which, on Chalmers's account, are ubiquitous. Since every name and natural kind term n can, in principle, be analyzed as a *dthat*-rigidified description *dthat D*, for each such term there will be a sentence *n is D*, or *ns are Ds*, that is classified as an instance of the contingent apriori.[60] For purposes of illustration I start with the favorite example of ambitious two-dimensionalists, (12).

12. Water is (the) watery stuff.

We have seen that Chalmers takes this to be apriori, and hence regards

13. It is knowable apriori that water is (the) watery stuff.

to be true. Nevertheless, C4 (together with related principles for ascriptions of other attitudes, including knowledge) has the consequence that, in the possible (counterfactual) scenario of Twin Earth, agents whose apriori reasoning is just as good as ours actually is do not

---

[60] I here ignore worries about world-states in which the referent of n doesn't exist. As usual, such questions could be sidestepped by considering examples *If n exists (or if there is such a thing as n), then n is D*, and related variants.

know apriori that water is (the) watery stuff—despite the fact that they recognize full well that the primary proposition associated with (12) is necessary. We may suppose that these agents do accept (12) (without needing empirical justification), but since the secondary intension of (12) in their context is different from its secondary intension in the actual world, any actual report by us ascribing to them apriori knowledge that water is (the) watery stuff will **not** (given the new semantic analysis of attitude ascriptions) be verified by their attitude toward (12). In addition, we may suppose that there our Twin Earth brothers and sisters accept no other sentence S the secondary intension of which (in their context) matches the secondary intension of (12) in ours. Hence, although it is (according to Chalmers) knowable apriori that water is (the) watery stuff, and although we (supposedly) know it apriori, the Twin Eartheans don't know that water is (the) watery stuff, and they couldn't come to know it by matching our reasoning about it, or by any amount of apriori reasoning, no matter how good.

This is not a result that one would get from an orthodox strong two-dimensionalist system, since in such systems the Twin Eartheans **are** correctly describable by us as *knowing apriori that water is (the) watery stuff,* due to the fact that they know the primary intension of the complement clause to be true. So in adopting C4 (and presumably other principles for attitude ascriptions), Chalmers has taken a substantial step away from his previous implicit strong two-dimensionalism. This, of course, may not be bad. Though surprising when judged from the perspective of standard strong two-dimensionalism, the new characterization of the Twin Eartheans has elements in common with familiar non–two-dimensionalist accounts. On any such account of the contingent apriori, there will be some sentences S such that the proposition expressed by S is knowable apriori, even though that very proposition is false, and hence unknowable, at some world-states. On the version of this view that I favor (in which propositions are seen as structured, rather than as sets of world-states), these examples are rare, they never hinge on *dthat*-rigidified descriptions, ordinary proper names, or natural kind terms, but they may make crucial use of the actuality operator.[61] For example, when S expresses any contingent truth p, *It is knowable apriori that if actually S, then S* is true, *it is knowable apriori that* operates solely on the proposition expressed by its complement clause (what two-dimensionalists call its secondary inten-

[61] See chapters 4 and 6.

sion), and this proposition is knowable in the actual world-state @ without appeal to evidence. The reason this is true is, roughly, that knowing that the proposition that if p is true in @ then p is true, is something that agents in @ are in a position to know simply by virtue of knowing that the proposition that if p is true, then p is true (even though the same cannot be said for agents in other world-states).[62]

Chalmers certainly would not go this far. There is no indication that he would accept my explanation of this particular example, and it is clear that he would not restrict the contingent apriori to examples that are explainable in this way. Rather, it seems evident that he remains intent on retaining as much of strong two-dimensionalism as possible. Unfortunately, what the resulting system amounts to is quite unclear. However, since he doesn't indicate any slacking in his commitment to the other doctrines of strong two-dimensionalism, the best course is to take them to remain in place, so far as possible, and to assess his view under that assumption. When this is done, a number of problems come to the fore.

The first of these involves a slight variation on the familiar Twin Earth scenario. In the new (counterfactual) scenario, although XYZ is the watery stuff, H_2O also exists in certain isolated locations, with some, but not all, of the properties of watery stuff. Let us (here in @) use *sort of watery stuff* to stand for those properties (a proper subset of the properties that *watery stuff* is supposed to stand for). At some point, agents on Twin Earth come across the H_2O—i.e., water—that exists there, and discover, by empirical investigation, that it is sort of watery stuff, which they express by saying (14).[63]

14. That stuff [pointing at one of the pools] is sort of watery stuff.

Intuitively, it would seem that, on the basis of this, these agents are truly describable as knowing (aposteriori) that water is sort of watery stuff. Thus (15), as said by us in @, is true when evaluated with respect to their world-state w_{TE}.

15. They know that water is sort of watery stuff.

If the new semantic analysis of attitude ascriptions is correct, this means that the secondary intension of (14) in their context is the same

---

[62] See chapter 6.

[63] Don't think of (14) as a strict identity statement. Rather think of *is sort of watery stuff* as a predicate that is applied to instances of the kind demonstrated by the speaker in using the demonstrative subject.

as the secondary intension of (16) in ours, and that the primary intension of (14) for them must be "appropriately related" to that of (16) for us.

16. Water is sort of watery stuff.

So far so good. But now there is a puzzle. According to Chalmers's two-dimensionalism, the primary intension of (16) is necessary, which means (by the principle Apriori 1) that (16) is an instance of the apriori, and (by the right-to-left direction of Apriori 2) that (17) is true (with respect to our actual context C, and both @ and w_{TE} as circumstances of evaluation).[64]

17. It is knowable apriori that water is sort of watery stuff.

Moreover, since Chalmers's constraints involving the primary and secondary intensions of the sentential complements of *knows* and *knows apriori* are, apparently, satisfied, it would seem that a two-dimensionalist system of the sort envisioned in *The Conscious Mind* should count (18), or at least (19), as said by us in @, as true when evaluated at w_{TE}. After all, if it is knowable apriori that water is watery stuff, if, like us, the Twin Eartheans are able to entertain the proposition that water is watery stuff by virtue of being acquainted with water, if, furthermore, they know this proposition to be true, while being expert apriori reasoners, then it would seem that they should be in a position to know **apriori** that water is sort of watery stuff.

18. They know apriori that water is sort of watery stuff.

19. They are in a position to know apriori—by proper reasoning and reflection—that water is sort of watery stuff.

However, it is intuitively clear from the scenario that (18) and (19) are **not** true. It is not obvious what, if any, reasonable combination of standard two-dimensionalist theses plus Chalmers's new views about attitude ascriptions might provide an adequate explanation of this fact. However, since this issue pushes strongly in the direction of weak two-dimensionalism, which will be extensively critiqued in chapter 10, I will put off further consideration of this issue until then, when I will

---

[64] Assuming that *It is knowable apriori that water is sort of watery stuff* is to be understood along the lines of (11b), one may characterize it as true not only with respect to our actual context C and world-state @, but also with respect to C and the Twin Earth world-state w_{TE}, since, presumably, @ is possible relative to w_{TE}, and, according to Chalmers, agents in @ know apriori that water is sort of watery stuff.

revisit the question of what sort of hybrid two-dimensionalist view may be available to Chalmers.

The next class of problematic examples also involve sentences that Chalmers takes to be instances of the contingent apriori. This time I focus on another favorite of ambitious two-dimensionalists.

20. Hesperus is visible in the evening sky, if there is a unique thing which is D.

For the sake of argument, assume with Chalmers that *Hesperus* is equivalent to *dthat D*, where D involves, perhaps among other things, predication of the property of being visible in the evening sky. Then, (20) will be classified as an instance of the contingent apriori, and (21) will be counted as true. (Again we use Apriori 1 and the right-to-left version of Apriori 2.)

21. It is knowable apriori that (Hesperus is visible in the evening sky, if there is a unique thing which is D).

I now invoke the intuitively compelling exportation principle E.

E. For any name n and predicate F, if α *knows/believes that n is F* is true (with respect to A, C, and w), and o is the referent of n (with respect to C and w), then α *knows/believes that x is F* is true (with respect to A', C, and w, where A' differs from A at most in assigning o to 'x', and 'x' is new to the sentence). So is α *knows/believes that I am F* (relative to A, C', and w, where C' differs from C at most in that o is the agent of C'). Ditto when *n is F* is replaced by the slightly more complicated *n is F, if there is a unique thing which is D*.

Sentences (22a) and (22b), in which 'it' functions as a bound variable, are examples of this principle—which I take to be correct.[65]

22a. If John knows that Hesperus is visible in the evening sky, then there is something, namely Hesperus, which is such that John knows that it is visible in the evening sky.

22b. If John knows that (Hesperus is visible in the evening sky, if there is a unique thing which is D), then there is something, namely Hesperus, which is such that John knows that (it is

---

[65] See chapter 3 of *Beyond Rigidity* for a defense and explanation of E, which is restricted to cases in which n has a referent.

visible in the evening sky, if there is a unique thing which
is D).

But now, if the knowledge reported by the antecedent of (22b) is apriori, as it is on Chalmers's account, then the knowledge reported by its
consequent must also be apriori—since in order to have this knowledge, it is only necessary to have the knowledge reported by the antecedent of (22b). Thus, we get the result that (23a,b) are true, as are
(24a,b), relative to an assignment of Hesperus to the variable 'x'.[66]

23a. There is something, namely Hesperus, which is such that
John knows apriori that (it is visible in the evening sky, if
there is a unique thing which is D).

   b. There is something, namely Hesperus, which is such that it
is knowable apriori that (it is visible in the evening sky, if
there is a unique thing which D).

24a. John knows apriori that x is seen in the evening sky, if there
is a unique thing that is D.

   b. It is knowable apriori that x is seen in the evening sky, if
there is a unique thing that is D.

This result holds even though the primary intension of *x is visible in
the evening sky*, relative to an assignment of Hesperus to 'x', is contingent (and identical with its secondary intension). Clearly, this violates
a central tenet—the conjunction of Apriori 1 with the left-to-right direction of Apriori 2—of Chalmers' two-dimensionalism.[67]

With a little poetic license, the same sort of counterexample can
be produced by imagining a context C′, just like the actual present

[66] Here, I implicitly appeal to the principle that if *a knows that S* entails that *a knows that
R*, then *a knows apriori that S* entails *a knows apriori that R*. The justification of this principle is as follows: (i) if *a knows apriori that S* is true, then *a knows that S* is true and a's justification for this knowledge does not rely on empirical evidence; (ii) since *a knows that S* entails *a knows that R*, and since (presumably) any justification for the knowledge reported by
the former is sufficient justification for the knowledge reported by the latter, *a knows that
R* is true and a's justification for this knowledge does not rely on empirical evidence; (iii) so
a knows apriori that R is true. The only potentially questionable step here is (ii)—which
could, in principle, fail only if the truth of *a knows that S* required a to possess empirical evidence justifying R that was not needed to justify S. Whether or not any cases of this sort can
be found, (23) and (24) do not fall into this category.
[67] Here, and in what follows, I assume formulations of Apriori 1 and 2 in which S may
contain a free occurrence of a variable, and the truth, primary intension, and character of S
are relativized to assignments of values to variables.

context, except that in C′ Hesperus is the agent. Reasoning parallel to that which just given leads to the result that in C′ Hesperus expresses truths by uttering (25a) and (25b)—to her neighbor Mercury.

25a. John knows apriori that (I am visible in the evening sky, if there is a unique thing that is D).

b. It is knowable apriori that (I am visible in the evening sky, if there is a unique thing that is D).

This result holds even though the primary intension of *I am visible in the evening sky* is contingent. Again, this is a violation of the central tenets of Chalmers's two-dimensionalism.

One could, of course, block (23), (24), and (25) by rejecting E. But that, in my opinion, is untenable. Hence, the problems we have found are not easily avoidable. It is worth noting here that they are **not** created by Chalmers's new view of the semantics of attitude ascriptions. On the contrary, it might be counted as a virtue of the view that it makes room for the results we have derived from his initial two-dimensionalist characterizations of (20) and (21). What we have seen is **not** that C1–C4 (and related principles for other attitudes) are false (though I will argue in chapter 10 that C1 and C3 are), but that combining them with Chalmers's other commitments to ambitious two-dimensionalism creates certain conflicts and problems, while leaving other antecedent problems intact. The earlier, eight-step argument against the left-to-right direction of Apriori 2 illustrated how the new analysis of attitude ascriptions leads to conflicts with central principles of Chalmers's ambitious two-dimensionalism. The present problem with the standard ambitious two-dimensionalist analysis of examples like (20) and (21) is an example of an inherent problem in the analysis that remains, even after the new analysis of attitude ascriptions is adopted.

One final class of problematic examples draws from instances of the necessary aposteriori to reach a result similar to that involving (20). Here I let *Pappy* be the name of my wooden paperweight, and *is not made out of metal* express a property in virtue of which *x is not made out of metal* is true, relative to an assignment of Pappy as value of the variable 'x', in all possible world-states. Then (26) is a Kripkean example of the necessary aposteriori.

26. If Pappy exists, then Pappy is not made out of metal.

As previously seen, in Chalmers's two-dimensionalist system, *Pappy* will be analyzed as equivalent to ***dthat D***, for some D, and the primary intension of (26) will be seen as contingent, while its secondary intension is recognized to be necessary.

With this in mind, consider the open sentence (27), relative to an assignment of the referent of *Pappy* to the variable 'x'.

27. If Pappy exists, then x is not made out of metal & Pappy = Pappy.

Since the primary intension of (27), relative to an assignment of Pappy to 'x', is true in all contexts, it will be characterized as apriori by Chalmers's two-dimensionalist principle Apriori 1. The right-to-left direction of Apriori 2 will then classify (28a) as true, relative to an assignment of Pappy to 'x', which means that (28b) will be judged to be true *simpliciter*.

28a. It is knowable apriori that (if Pappy exists, then x is not made out of metal & Pappy = Pappy).

b. There is an x, namely Pappy, which is such that it is knowable apriori that (if Pappy exists, then x is not made out of metal & Pappy = Pappy).

But now, applying the principle E to these examples, we get the results that (29a) is true, relative to an assignment of Pappy as values of both 'x' and 'y', and that (29b) is true *simpliciter*.

29a. It is knowable apriori that (if Pappy exists, then x is not made out of metal & y = Pappy).

b. There is an x and there is a y, both of which are identical with Pappy, such that it is knowable apriori that (if Pappy exists, then x is not made out of metal & y = Pappy).

Appealing to Leibniz's Law (the standard quantified version), one may conclude that (30a) is true, relative to an assignment of Pappy to 'x', and that (30b) is true *simpliciter*.

30a. It is knowable apriori that (if Pappy exists, then x is not made out of metal & x = Pappy).

b. There is an x, namely Pappy, which is such that it is knowable apriori that (if Pappy exists, then x is not made out of metal & x = Pappy).

Notice, however, that the primary intension of

31. If Pappy exists, then x is not made out of metal & x = Pappy.

relative to an assignment of Pappy to 'x' is **not** necessary—with the re-sult that the conclusions just drawn about (30) again conflict with the conjunction of Apriori 1 and the left-to-right direction of Apriori 2. Moreover, it is exceedingly strange, and counterintuitive, that (30b) could be **true**, while (30c), and hence, (30d), were **false**—which they must be, if (26) is to be an example of the necessary aposteriori.

30c. It is knowable apriori that (if Pappy exists, then Pappy is not made out of metal & Pappy = Pappy).

   d. It is knowable apriori that (if Pappy exists, then Pappy is not made out of metal).

As before, some of these problems could be avoided by rejecting E. However, since E is quite compelling, I believe the proper lesson to draw is that Chalmers's two-dimensionalist account of the necessary aposteriori is at fault.

Conclusions

In this chapter I have examined Chalmers's version of ambitious two-dimensionalism, and the use to which he puts it in arguing against physicalism and for mind/body dualism. I paid close attention to his arguments for two essential prerequisites of strong two-dimensional-ism—the identification of epistemically possible (conceivable) world-states with metaphysically possible world-states, and the analysis of names and natural kind terms as indexical, rigidified descriptions with distinct primary and secondary intensions. In each case, I found the ar-guments wanting. I then turned to his treatment, in *The Conscious Mind*, of the necessary aposteriori and the contingent apriori—which closely followed the classical strong (even very strong) two-dimension-alist model. After examining the argumentative use to which his two-dimensionalist doctrines were put in his inconclusive argument for du-alism, I turned to his more recent suggestions for the semantic analysis of propositional attitude ascriptions. At this point I noted that al-though they diverge from classical strong two-dimensionalism in cer-tain respects, enough of that system remains to create serious problems for a variety of examples involving the contingent apriori and the necessary aposteriori.

Having discussed the main systems of ambitious two-dimensionalism in the existing literature, I will, in the next chapter, draw some general conclusions about different possible versions of this doctrine. To that end, I will offer what I take to be a conclusive refutation of classical strong two-dimensionalism, plus strong, and I believe telling, objections to weak two-dimensionalism—in the sense in which those doctrines were defined in chapter 7. I will then consider other, hybrid views of the general sort that Chalmers may have been gesturing toward with his recent discussion of propositional attitude ascriptions. I will try to determine whether these views are plausible, or whether an entirely different approach to the semantic analysis of names and natural kind terms, and to the explanation of the contingent apriori and the necessary aposteriori, is needed. I will argue that it is.

CHAPTER 10

CRITIQUE OF AMBITIOUS
TWO-DIMENSIONALISM

In chapter 7, I outlined two distinctive versions of ambitious two-dimensionalism—strong and weak. In chapters 8 and 9, I examined the views of two leading proponents of ambitious two-dimensionalism. Although Jackson and Chalmers lean heavily toward the strong version of the view, they are not fully explicit and unequivocal in their support of it, and Chalmers's recent discussion of propositional attitude ascriptions can be seen as a step toward weak two-dimensionalism. Hence, it will be important to critique both versions of the view. After these critiques are in place, I will consider certain hybrid versions, including Chalmers's own, which don't fit completely into either category. My thesis will be that no form of ambitious two-dimensionalism is capable of reviving descriptivism, and that the attempt to explain away the necessary aposteriori and the contingent apriori by associating sentences in these categories with pairs of propositions which receive different modal evaluations with respect to a single space of epistemically conceivable, metaphysically possible world-states cannot succeed.

Critique of Strong Two-Dimensionalism

I begin with the purest form of ambitious two-dimensionalism, the central tenets of which are T1–T6.

T1. Each sentence is semantically associated with a pair of semantic values—its primary intension, and its secondary intension. Its primary intension is a proposition which is true with respect to all and only those contexts C to which the Kaplan-style character of S assigns a proposition that is true at C. When contexts are identified with world-states, and propositions are taken to be sets of such states, the primary proposition associated with S is the set of world-states w which is such that the character of S assigns to w (considered as a context of utterance) a set of world-states (i.e., a proposition) that contains (i.e., is true at) w. The secondary intension of (or proposition expressed by) S at a context C is the proposition assigned by the character of S to C.

T2. Understanding S consists in knowing its character and primary intension. Although this knowledge, plus complete knowledge of a given context C, would always give one knowledge of the secondary intension of—i.e., the proposition expressed by—S in C, sometimes one does not have such knowledge. Since we never know all there is to know about the context/world-state C, sometimes we don't know precisely which proposition is expressed by S in C. However, this does not prevent us from using S correctly in C.

T3a. Examples of the necessary aposteriori are sentences the secondary intensions of which are necessary, and the characters of which assign false propositions to some contexts. Since the character of such a sentence sometimes assigns propositions to contexts that are false in those contexts, the primary intension of such a sentence is contingent.

T3b. Examples of the contingent apriori are sentences the secondary intensions of which are contingent, and the characters of which assign true propositions to every context. Since the character of such a sentence always assigns propositions to contexts that are true in those contexts, the primary intension of such a sentence is necessary.

T4a. All proper names and natural kind terms have their reference semantically fixed by descriptions not containing any (uneliminable) proper names or natural kind terms.

T4b. These names and natural kind terms are synonymous with context-sensitive, rigidified descriptions (involving *dthat* or *actually*).

T5a. **It is a necessary truth that S** is true with respect to a context C and world-state w iff the secondary intension of S in C is true with respect to all (metaphysically possible) world-states w* that are possible relative to w. Similarly for other modal operators.

T5b. ***It is knowable apriori that*** S is true with respect to C and w iff the primary intension of S in C is knowable apriori in w; ***x knows/believes that*** S is true of an individual i with respect to C and w iff in w, i knows/believes the primary intension of S with respect to C. Similarly for other epistemic operators.

T6a. S is an example of the necessary aposteriori iff the secondary intension of S (with respect to C) is a necessary truth, but the primary intension of S is contingent and, though knowable, not knowable apriori. To say that the primary intension of S is contingent is, in effect, to say that there are contexts C* to which the character of S assigns a proposition that is false in C*. Thus, examples of the necessary aposteriori express necessary truths in our actual context, while expressing falsehoods in other contexts. Primary intensions of these sentences are not knowable apriori because we require empirical information to determine that our context is not one to which the character assigns a falsehood.

T6b. S is an example of a contingent apriori truth iff the secondary intension of S (with respect to C) is true, but not necessarily true, while the primary intension of S is necessary and knowable apriori. To say that the primary intension of S is necessary is, in effect, to say that for every context C*, the proposition assigned to C* by the character of S is true at C*. Thus, sentences that are examples of the contingent apriori express propositions which, while true in our actual context/world-state, are false when evaluated at some world-states, even though these sentences express truths in every context/world-state. Primary intensions of these sentences are knowable apriori because no empirical information is needed to determine that our context is one to which the character assigns a truth.

These points are illustrated by the sentences in (1).

1a. The actual husband of Stephanie Lewis was the actual author of *Counterfactuals.*

 b. The husband of Stephanie Lewis was the author of *Counter-factuals.*

The two rigidified descriptions in (1a) rigidly designate David Lewis. Hence, the secondary intension of (1a) is a necessary truth.[1] By contrast, the proposition expressed by (1b) is contingent, and obviously knowable only aposteriori. Since (1b) expresses the same proposition in every context of utterance, this proposition—the secondary intension of (1b)—is taken to be its primary intension as well. Of course, (1a) expresses a truth in all and only those contexts in which (1b) expresses a truth. This means that the primary intension of (1a) is necessarily equivalent to the contingent, aposteriori proposition that is both the primary and secondary intension of (1b). They may even be identified, since, for the prototypical strong two-dimensionalist, propositions are sets of possible world-states. However, even if one were to resist the identification, in this case one would have to acknowledge the trivial equivalence of these propositions. Anyone who understands both sentences knows that they have the same truth value in any context in which they are used, and one who apprehends both the primary intension of (1a) and the primary/secondary intension of (1b) can see immediately that they are equivalent. It follows that since the latter is knowable only aposteriori, so is the former. As a result, the strong two-dimensionalist maintains that sentence (1a) is an example of the necessary aposteriori, even though it is not associated with any one proposition that is both necessary and knowable only aposteriori.

This example illustrates one of the central contentions of strong two-dimensionalism: no single proposition can be both necessary and knowable only aposteriori. The thought that there are such propositions is due to an equivocation. When S embeds under a modal operator, its secondary intension is relevant; when S embeds under an epistemic operator, its primary intension is relevant. Since names and natural kind terms are analyzed as rigidified descriptions, the two intensions will be different whenever S contains any of these expressions. Hence, the strong two-dimensionalist believes he can explain away all Kripkean examples of the necessary aposteriori on the model of (1a).

The lesson of this example is incorporated in two further theses, T7a

---

[1] To keep things simple I will ignore world-states in which David doesn't exist. I will also, in discussing this example, make the simplifying assumption that the names occurring in it are non-indexical expressions with constant characters. Although this assumption runs contrary to two-dimensionalist doctrine, taking it for granted here will allow us to focus on the difference between rigidified and unrigidified descriptions in the two-dimensionalist explanation of the necessary aposteriori. Later, in criticizing strong two-dimensionalism, I will remove the simplifying assumption.

and T7b, which, as I explained in chapter 7, are all but inevitable corollaries of T1–T6.

T7a. There is no proposition that is both necessary and knowable only aposteriori; nor is there any proposition that is contingent yet knowable apriori.

T7b. The necessary aposteriori and the contingent apriori are, in effect, linguistic illusions born of a failure to notice the different roles played by primary and secondary intensions in modal and epistemic sentences.

A further thesis that suggests itself is T8, the strong two-dimensionalist rationale for which was also given in chapter 7.

T8. A proposition is necessary iff it is knowable apriori.

The previous theses already incorporate both the right-to-left direction of T8 and the claim that any necessary truth that is knowable at all is knowable apriori. What T8 adds is the claim that all necessary truths are knowable. This is attractive to the strong two-dimensionalist, who wants to explain all instances of the contingent apriori by citing the necessity of the primary intension of the sentence—an explanation that will go through with complete generality only if it is somehow guaranteed that every necessary truth is knowable. Since, as previously explained, theorists inclined toward strong two-dimensionalism have wanted to take it for granted that necessity of primary intension is always enough for apriori truth, they have reason to embrace T8. If they do, this provides an additional rationale for identifying propositions with sets of possible world-states (or functions from such to truth values)—something toward which they are also inclined.

As before, I will use the term *strong two-dimensionalism* to refer to systems incorporating T1–T7, whether or not they also incorporate T8, and I will use *very strong two-dimensionalism* for systems that include T8. I will presuppose that all these systems, and only these, identify propositions with sets of possible world-states (or functions from such states to truth values). Since some criticisms of strong two-dimensionalism apply equally to weak two-dimensionalism, I will defer those until later, when weak two-dimensionalism is on the table. In this section I will consider two classes of arguments directed specifically against the strong version of the view. The first class involves the interaction of modal and epistemic constructions concerning sentences containing names, rigidified descriptions, natural kind terms, and variables of quantification. The second class focuses on examples containing ordinary indexicals like *I*, *you*, *he/she*, and *now*.

Arguments Involving the Interaction of Modal and Epistemic Operators

I begin with two arguments that attack the central strong two-dimensionalist idea that modal and epistemic operators (and predicates) operate on different propositions associated with S in sentences like ***It is a necessary truth that S*** and ***x v's that S***. In stating these arguments, I will take for granted the prototypical, very strong two-dimensionalist identification of propositions with sets of possible world-states. In principle, this assumption can be relaxed without affecting the final conclusions reached. All one needs to do is (i) restrict oneself to agents who understand both S and ***Actually S***, and (ii) assume that any such agent who believes that one of these expresses a truth (and so believes its primary intension) also believes that the other expresses a truth (and so believes its primary intension). Using this, one can reach the conclusions of arguments 1 and 2 without appealing to the otherwise convenient premise that necessarily equivalent propositions are identical.

ARGUMENT 1

Step 1. According to strong two-dimensionalism, epistemic attitude ascriptions ***A believes that S*** report that the agent bears the belief relation to the primary intension of S— i.e., a proposition that, in effect, says of the character of S that it expresses a truth.

Step 2. Since for every context C, the character of sentence (1a) expresses a truth with respect to C iff the character of sentence (1b) does too, the two primary intensions are identical, and the ascriptions
A believes that the actual husband of Stephanie Lewis was the actual author of Counterfactuals.

and

A believes that the husband of Stephanie Lewis was the author of Counterfactuals.
are necessarily equivalent. (In fact their secondary intensions, as well as their primary intensions, are identical.)

Step 3. Hence, the truth value of

> a. It is a necessary truth that [if the actual husband of Stephanie Lewis was the actual author of *Counterfactuals* and Mary believes that the actual husband of Stephanie Lewis was the actual author of *Counterfactuals*, then Mary believes something true].

is the same as the truth value of

> b. It is a necessary truth that [if the actual husband of Stephanie Lewis was the actual author of *Counterfactuals* and Mary believes that the husband of Stephanie Lewis was the author of *Counterfactuals*, then Mary believes something true].

Since (b) is false, so is (a).

Step 4. Similarly, the truth value of

> a. It is a necessary truth that [if Mary believes that the actual husband of Stephanie Lewis was the actual author of *Counterfactuals*, and if that belief is true, then the actual husband of Stephanie Lewis was the actual author of *Counterfactuals*].

is the same as the truth value of

> b. It is a necessary truth that [if Mary believes that the husband of Stephanie Lewis was the author of *Counterfactuals*, and if that belief is true, then the actual husband of Stephanie Lewis was the actual author of *Counterfactuals*].

Since (b) is false, so is (a).

Step 5. Since, in fact, the a-sentences in steps 3 and 4 are true, the strong two-dimensionalist theses T5a and T5b are not jointly true.

The second argument of this kind turns on the strong two-dimensionalist treatment of names as synonymous with rigidified descriptions.

ARGUMENT 2

Step 1. According to strong two-dimensionalism, epistemic attitude ascriptions *A believes that S* report that the agent

bears the belief relation to the primary intension of S—
i.e., to a proposition that, in effect, says of the character
of S that it expresses a truth.

Step 2. According to strong two-dimensionalism, names are synonymous with rigidified descriptions. Let o be an object
uniquely denoted by the nonrigid description *the D*, let n
be a name of o, and let the strong two-dimensionalist
analysis of n be *the actual D*. Suppose further that *John
believes that n is D* is true.

Step 3. Let w be a world-state in which some object other than o
is uniquely denoted by *the D*, and in which John does not
believe of o that it "is D," though he does believe the
proposition expressed by *The D is D*.

Step 4. According to strong two-dimensionalism, the truth values of (a) and (b) must be the same.

   a. *Although John truly believes that n is D, had the
world been in state w, n would not have been D and
John would not have believed that n was D.*

   b. *Although John truly believes that the actual D is D,
had the world been in state w, the actual D would not
have been D and John would not have believed that
the actual D was D.*

Step 5. Since, according to strong two-dimensionalism, *John believes that the actual D is D* and *John believes that the D
is D* are necessarily equivalent, occurrences of the latter
can be substituted for occurrences of the former in (b)
without changing truth value. Hence, if (a) and (b) are
true, then (c) must also be true.

   c. *Although John truly believes that the D is D, had the
world been in state w, the actual D would not have been
D and John would not have believed that the D was D.*

Step 6. In fact, however, (a) is true and (c) is false. Hence the
conjunction of the strong two-dimensionalist theses T4
and T5 is false. (Analyzing names as rigidified descriptions compounds the problem revealed in argument 1.)

There are four points to notice about these arguments before we go
further. First, since strong two-dimensionalists treat natural kind terms

as rigidified descriptions—essentially on a par with proper names—corresponding arguments involving natural kind terms can be constructed that are parallel to argument 2. Second, whereas argument 1 involves the interaction of the belief predicate with the modal operator *it is a necessary truth that*, argument 2 involves the interaction of the belief predicate with a counterfactual conditional that mentions a certain possible world-state. In general, arguments corresponding to 1 and 2 can be constructed using any of a broad variety of modal locutions—modal operators, quantification over possible world-states, counterfactual conditionals, and the like. This is significant when considering a certain possible objection on the part of the strong two-dimensionalist—who might maintain that the operator *necessarily*, or *it is a necessary truth that*, is ambiguous, sometimes standing for what is true in all world-states *considered as counterfactual*, and sometimes standing for what is true in all world-states *considered as actual*. The response to this objection is that it seems unlikely that all modal notions should be subject to the same ambiguity, and that for any modal locution one chooses—even those that seem clearly to involve counterfactual evaluation—sentences that obviously differ in truth value will be wrongly characterized as agreeing in truth value by the hypothesis that the central semantic tenets of strong two-dimensionalism accurately describe English. Third, appeals to alleged instances of ambiguity in one or another of the expressions that occur in our arguments against strong two-dimensionalism will be of limited utility, in any case. No matter what the alleged source of ambiguity, the most that could be claimed by a strong two-dimensionalist proponent of the ambiguity strategy is that his theory allows some readings of the relevant English sentences in which they are properly characterized as having the right truth values. But even if this turns out to be so in some particular case, the strong two-dimensionalist will still be saddled with the prediction that the sentences in question also have the problematic readings—which, in fact, they don't.

The fourth point to notice is that what the arguments show about one propositional attitude verb—*believe*—can be generalized to other propositional attitude verbs and operators—such as *know, know apriori*, and *is knowable apriori*. What arguments 1 and 2 show is that, contrary to strong two-dimensionalism, the belief predicate in an ascription **x believes that S** takes the same semantic value of S as argument as do the modal and counterfactual operators in sentences like **It is a necessary truth that S** and **If it had been the case that R, then it would have been the case that S**. Given that the modal and counterfactual operators take the secondary intensions of their complement sentences as arguments, one must conclude that *believe* does too. But if this is true of *believe*, then surely it must also be true of *know* and *know apriori*. Thus, it is not surprising that an argument parallel to argument 1 can be given in which *know* is substituted for *believe*.

ARGUMENT 3

Step 1. According to strong two-dimensionalism, knowledge ascriptions *A knows that S* report that the agent bears the knowledge relation to the primary intension of S—i.e., to a proposition that, in effect, says of the character of S that it expresses a truth.

Step 2. Since for every context C, the character of sentence (1a) expresses a truth with respect to C iff the character of sentence (1b) does too, the two primary intensions are identical, and the ascriptions

A knows that the actual husband of Stephanie Lewis was the actual author of Counterfactuals.

and

A knows that the husband of Stephanie Lewis was the author of Counterfactuals.

are necessarily equivalent. (In fact, their secondary intensions, as well as their primary intensions, are identical.)

Step 3. Hence, the truth value of

a. *It is a necessary truth that [if Mary knows that the actual husband of Stephanie Lewis was the actual author of Counterfactuals, then the actual husband of Stephanie Lewis was the actual author of Counterfactuals].*

is the same as the truth value of

b. *It is a necessary truth that [if Mary knows that the husband of Stephanie Lewis was the author of Counterfactuals, then the actual husband of Stephanie Lewis was the actual author of Counterfactuals].*

Since the b-sentence is false, so is the a-sentence.

Step 4. However, in point of fact, the a-sentence in step 3 is true. Hence, the strong two-dimensionalist theses T5a and T5b are not jointly true.

Arguments to the same effect can be constructed using *knows apriori* and *it is knowable apriori that*.

Step 1. According to strong two-dimensionalism, ascriptions of apriori knowledge, *A knows apriori that S*, report that the agent bears the relation of knowing apriori to the primary intension of S—i.e., to a proposition that, in effect, says of the character of S that it expresses a truth.

Step 2. Since for every context C, the character of *If there is a unique thing which is D, then the actual D is D* expresses a truth with respect to C iff the character of *If there is a unique thing which is D, then the D is D* does too, the two primary intensions are identical, and the ascriptions *A knows apriori that if there is a unique thing which is D, then the actual D is D.*

and

A knows apriori that if there is a unique thing which is D, then the D is D.

are necessarily equivalent. (In fact, their secondary intensions, as well as their primary intensions, are identical.)

Step 3. Hence, the truth value of

a. *It is a necessary truth that [if Mary knows apriori that if there is a unique thing which is D, then the D is D, then Mary knows apriori that if there is a unique thing which is D, then the D is D].*

is the same as the truth value of

b. *It is a necessary truth that [if Mary knows apriori that if there is a unique thing which is D, then the D is D, then Mary knows apriori that if there is a unique thing which is D, then the actual D is D].*

Step 4. Sentence (b) of Step 3 is false—as is shown by any world-state w which is such that (i) *Mary knows apriori that if there is a unique thing which is D, then the D is D* is true with respect to w, but (ii) *If there is a unique thing which is D, then the actual D is D* is false with respect to w—and hence not known by Mary—because the thing which "is actually D" (i.e., the thing which is denoted by *the D* in the world-state @) is not the thing denoted by *the D* with respect to w. Since the b-sentence in step 3 is false, so is the a-sentence.

Step 5. In point of fact, however, the a-sentence in step 3 is true. Hence, the strong two-dimensionalist theses T5a and T5b are not jointly true.

ARGUMENT 5

Step 1. According to strong two-dimensionalism, apriori-knowledge ascriptions *It is knowable apriori that S* report that the primary intension of S can be known apriori.

Step 2. Since for every context C, the character of *If there is a unique thing which is D, then the actual D is D* expresses a truth with respect to C iff the character of *If there is a unique thing which is D, then the D is D* does too, the two primary intensions are identical, and the ascriptions

It is knowable apriori that if there is a unique thing which is D, then the actual D is D.

and

It is knowable apriori that if there is a unique thing which is D, then the D is D.

are necessarily equivalent. (In fact, their secondary intensions, as well as their primary intensions, are identical.)

Step 3. Hence, the truth value of

a. *It is a necessary truth that [if it is knowable apriori that if there is a unique thing which is D, then the D is D, then it is knowable apriori that if there is a unique thing which is D, then the D is D].*

is the same as the truth value of

b. *It is a necessary truth that [if it is knowable apriori that if there is a unique thing which is D, then the D is D, then it is knowable apriori that if there is a unique thing which is D, then the actual D is D].*

Step 4. One cannot know something apriori, if it is false. More precisely, ***It is knowable apriori that S*** is true with respect to a context C and world-state w, only if S is true with respect to C and w.

Step 5. Hence, sentence (b) of step 3 is false—as is shown by any world-state w which is such that (i) ***It is knowable apriori that if there is a unique thing which is D, then the D is D*** is true with respect to w, but (ii) ***If there is a unique thing which is D, then the actual D is D*** is false with respect to w—and hence is not knowable apriori in w—because the thing which "is actually D" (i.e., the thing which is denoted by ***the D*** in the world-state @) is not the thing denoted by ***the D*** with respect to w. Since the b-sentence in step 3 is false, so is the a-sentence.

Step 6. In point of fact, however, the a-sentence in step 3 is true. Hence, the strong two dimensionalist theses T5a and T5b are not jointly true.

Arguments 3–5 extend the objections to strong two-dimensionalism illustrated by arguments 1 and 2 from examples involving belief ascriptions to those involving knowledge and apriori-knowledge ascriptions. The next argument brings in a new element—namely the semantic relationship between proper names and variables of quantification. It exploits the relationship between the a-sentences and the b-sentences in the following examples, where n is a name, F is a predicate, and the truth of ***n is F*** guarantees the truth of ***There is such a thing as n***.

2a. John truly believes that n is F, but had the world been in state w, n would not have been F.

b. There is an x such that John truly believes that x is F, but had the world been in state w, x would not have been F.

3a. John truly believes that n is F, but had the world been in state w, John would not have believed that n was F.

b. There is an x such that John truly believes that x is F, but had the world been in state w, John would not have believed that x was F.

Ill-founded doubts about the legitimacy of quantifying-in aside, it is an obvious fact of English that the a-sentences entail the b-sentences, in the sense that for any context C and world-state w, if the a-sentences are true with respect to C and w, then the b-sentences are too. Similarly obvious facts—parallel to those illustrated by (2) and (3) but involving knowledge and apriori-knowledge ascriptions—can easily be found. These facts constrain the semantic analyses of names, variables, attitude ascriptions, and modal operators in ways that are inconsistent with strong two-dimensionalism, as is indicated by the following argument.

ARGUMENT 6

Step 1. The following a-sentence entails the b-sentence—when the truth of *n is D* is such that it guarantees the truth of *There is such a thing as n.*

 a. *John truly believes that n is D, but had the world been in state w, n would not have been D and John would not have believed that n was D.*

 b. *There is an x such that John truly believes that x is D, but had the world been in state w, x would not have been D and John would not have believed that x was D.*

Step 2. If the semantics of strong two-dimensionalism were correct, there would be no such entailment, since (b) could be false with respect to a context C and world-state w, when (a) was true with respect to C and w. This result is due to the fact that (i) there is no distinction between primary and secondary intensions for variables even though (ii) strong two-dimensionalists are committed to sharply distinguishing the primary and secondary intensions of names, and to analyzing attitude ascriptions as reporting relations between agents and the primary intensions of their complements.

Step 3. Hence, the semantics of strong two-dimensionalism is incorrect; it misses the elementary fact that if *John believes (knows/knows apriori) that n is F* is true at world-state w at which n designates o, then at w John believes of o that it "is F," and *John believes (knows/knows apriori) that x is F* is true at w with respect to an assignment of o to 'x'.

The lesson of this argument is obvious. Since n is rigid, there is an object o (its referent) which is such that at any world w, *n is F* is true at w iff at w it is a fact that o has the property expressed by F. For this reason, it ought to be the case that for any world w, *John's belief that n is F* stands for a belief about o—i.e., one that is true at w only if at w o has the property expressed by F. But according to strong two-dimensionalism this is not so; instead, "the fact that n is F" and "the belief that n is F" are (wrongly) allowed to come apart.

The final argument in this class of arguments against strong two-dimensionalism extends the point of the previous argument to a case involving what is arguably—but perhaps controversially—an instance of objectual quantification over propositions.

ARGUMENT 7

Step 1. Let S be an example of the necessary aposteriori that the strong two-dimensionalist characterizes as such. Let it further be the case that *John doesn't know that S* is true because John lacks the empirical information required for such knowledge.

Step 2. Then, according to the strong two-dimensionalist, (a) is true.

   a. *It is a necessary truth that S, but it is not knowable apriori that S, and although it is knowable that S, John doesn't know that S.*

Step 3. In point of fact, (a) entails (b).

   b. There is some necessary truth p, which is not knowable apriori, and although p is knowable, John doesn't know p.

Step 4. (b) contradicts the strong two-dimensionalist's central thesis that no single proposition is both necessary and knowable only aposteriori. In addition, it conflicts with the very strong two-dimensionalist's identification of propositions with sets of possible world-states, since if p is the unique necessary truth, then John surely knows it.

Step 5. So strong two-dimensionalism is incorrect.

Although I believe this argument to be sound, I recognize that a staunch defender of strong two-dimensionalism might doubt that (b) really does follow from (a), on the intended objectual interpretation of the propositional quantifier. Such quantification is an immediate threat to the strong two-dimensionalist, since objectual variables are not associated with distinct primary and secondary intensions, and so cannot be given a two-dimensionalist treatment. However, to say this is not to justify the strong two-dimensionalist's rejection of the move from (a) to (b). We could easily devise languages with strong two-dimensionalist semantics, which also allowed objectual propositional quantification. In such languages, both (a) and (b) could be formulated, but it would be obvious that (b) didn't follow from (a). What argument 7 seems to show is that English is not such a language. To get the further result that English does not have a strong two-dimensionalist semantics, the argument relies on the implicit assumption, which I believe to be correct, that the quantification in (b) is, indeed, objectual quantification over propositions. Since the case against strong two-dimensionalism already seems overdetermined, I will not pause here to debate this assumption.[2] For those who remain in doubt about it, think of argument 7 as raising a prima facie objection to strong two-dimensionalism that is an immediate consequence of its very formulation. At the very least, the strong two-dimensionalist owes the rest of us a response.

Arguments Involving Nondescriptive Indexicals

In chapter 2 I showed that at least some indexicals must have their reference fixed, not by any reference-fixing descriptions, but directly by parameters of the context. In what follows, I will assume that *I* and *now* are two such indexicals. Up to now—in chapter 7 and in the early part of this chapter—I have stated strong two-dimensionalism in its simplest form, without the complications introduced by these nondescriptive indexicals (though I briefly mentioned these complications when discussing Chalmers's "centered worlds" in chapter 9). I now turn to the issues raised for strong two-dimensionalism by sentences containing indexicals of this sort. The most obvious change that is required is the expansion of contexts to include a designated agent and time, in addition to the designated actual world-state of the original Davies-Humberstone models. This changes the nature of primary intensions as compared with secondary intensions. In the original ambitious two-dimensional framework, the meaning (character) of S was a function from world-states, considered as contexts, to propositions expressed by S relative to those world-states, and the primary intension of S was a proposition that is true when evaluated at a world-state w iff

---

[2] See pp. 40–46 of my *Understanding Truth* (New York: Oxford University Press, 1999) for considerations favoring the objectual interpretation of propositional quantifiers in examples like (b).

the meaning of S assigns w a proposition that is true at w. Cleaving to the familiar, very strong two-dimensionalist identification of propositions with sets of world-states, one may identify the primary intension of S with the set of world-states w, such that the meaning of S assigns to w a set of world-states that contains w. Thus, in the original framework, the primary intension of S and the secondary intension of S (relative to a context) are both propositions (sets of world-states), and the roles of being a context in which a sentence expresses a proposition, and of being a counterfactual circumstance in which a proposition is evaluated, are two different dimensions, or uses, of the same thing—a world-state.

This changes when contexts (but not circumstances of evaluation) are expanded to include designated agents and times. Although the secondary intension of S relative to C remains a set of world-states, which may be called an *ordinary proposition*, the primary intension of S is now identified with the set of contexts to which the meaning of S assigns ordinary propositions that are true in (i.e., contain) the world-states of the contexts. Call these *pseudo-propositions*. There is no longer one thing which plays both the role of context and the role of circumstance of evaluation, and there is no longer one kind of thing that occurs as arguments of both modal operators, like *it is a necessary truth that*, and epistemic operators, like *John knows that* and *it is knowable apriori that*. Instead, there are contexts and world-states in the first case, and ordinary propositions and pseudo-propositions in the second. Since, according to strong two-dimensionalism, primary intensions are the objects of the attitudes, and hence the things that are knowable apriori or only aposteriori, some account of attitude ascriptions is now needed that makes sense of this. It is not clear that there is any acceptable account to be had.

What is it to know, apriori or aposteriori, something which is not an ordinary proposition? Perhaps a pair of examples will help.

4a. I am here now.

  b. I am not Saul Kripke.

We may suppose that if I were to assertively utter (4a) now, I would express the (ordinary) proposition that Scott Soames is in Princeton at 10 A.M., September 24, 2003. Although this proposition is contingent, the meaning of (4a) generates a truth in every context. As a result, strong two-dimensionalism would, presumably, classify it as an example of the contingent apriori. The situation is just the reverse with (4b), which, one supposes, would be classified as an instance of the necessary aposteriori.

Fair enough; those characterizations are at least defensible. But what do I know in these cases, and what do I report myself as knowing when, in the same context, I assertively utter (5a) or (5b)?

5a. I know that I am here now.

  b. I know that I am not Saul Kripke.

The natural answer is that what I know, and report myself as knowing, is the same as what I (truly) report Gideon as knowing when I assertively utter (6a,b), and what I (truly) report our new graduate student, Harold, as not knowing when I assertively utter (7a,b).

6a. Gideon knows that I am here now.

  b. Gideon knows that I am not Saul Kripke.

7a. Harold doesn't know that I am here now.

  b. Harold doesn't know that I am not Saul Kripke.

And what is that? Clearly the primary intensions of (4a,b) are not what is known, and reported to be known (or unknown), in these cases. Each of us accepts (in his own context) the meanings of (4a,b), which in turn generate these primary intensions. Each of us would sincerely say "I am here now" and "I am not Saul Kripke." However, although each of us bears the same relation to the primary intensions of these sentences, Harold doesn't know what Gideon and I know, and Gideon's knowledge, unlike mine (in the case of (5a)), is obviously not apriori.

Is there any reasonable way in which primary intensions might be brought into play here? I don't see that there is. Consider the following suggestion.

SUGGESTED STRONG TWO-DIMENSIONALIST TREATMENT
OF PROBLEMS POSED BY (5–7)

When the complement clause of an attitude ascription contains the indexical 'I', all occurrences of the indexical will be replaced by occurrences of a new variable v, and the original ascription will be regarded as true w.r.t. a context C, world-state w, and assignment A of values to variables iff its translation (in which occurrences of v replace occurrences of 'I') is true w.r.t. to C, w, and an assignment A* that differs from A at most in assigning to v the agent of C. (The proposal could be expanded to treat other non-descriptive indexicals.)

On this picture, (6b) would be true with respect to a context C with me as agent and world-state w iff its translation

6c. Gideon knows that x is not Saul Kripke.

is true, with respect to C, w, and an assignment of me to 'x'. The point of this maneuver is to preserve the orthodox strong two-dimensionalist analysis of the semantics of knowledge ascriptions, which takes the objects of *know* to be the **primary intensions** of their complement clauses—something clearly threatened by (5–7) in their unanalyzed form. Ignoring, for the moment, any context sensitivity that might be introduced by the analysis of the name *Saul Kripke*, one may take the character of the formula *x is not Saul Kripke* relative to an assignment of me to 'x' to be a constant function from different contexts to the same proposition. In cases like this, the distinction between primary intension and secondary intension all but disappears, and the knowledge ascriptions can be treated as reporting that the putative knower **knows of** me that I am not Saul Kripke, or, what amounts to the same thing, that the putative knower knows the singular proposition expressed by *x is not Saul Kripke*, relative to an assignment of me to 'x'.

This is a good result in the sense that it correctly describes the truth conditions of the original attitude ascriptions. However, there are two problems with this maneuver for the strong two-dimensionalist. First, the attempt to save the strong two-dimensionalist semantic rule that knowledge ascriptions report a relation between the knower and the **primary intension** of their complement clauses is nothing more than a subterfuge. After translation and reanalysis, attitude ascriptions like those in (5–7) end up being true iff the putative knower bears the relevant relation to the **secondary intension** of their original (untranslated) complement clauses. The only way in which the proposal differs from a straightforward recognition that in these cases attitude ascriptions semantically report relations between putative knowers and the secondary intensions of their complement clauses is by covering up this recognition with a misleading and pointless detour. Second, the maneuver falsifies central two-dimensionalist claims anyway. For surely, even after the translation required by the analysis, (6b) remains an example of the necessary aposteriori, in the sense that the knowledge it correctly reports Gideon as having is aposteriori, despite the fact that the truth he is reported as knowing—i.e., the proposition expressed by *x is not Saul Kripke* relative to an assignment of me to 'x'—is necessary. If this is right, then there is a proposition p which is both necessary and knowable only aposteriori, contrary to thesis T7 of strong two-dimensionalism. Moreover, the result is inconsistent with the very strong two-dimensionalist identification of propositions with sets of world-states, since, on that identification, there is only one necessary truth, and it is knowable apriori by everyone. Hence, the suggested treatment of attitude ascriptions containing nondescriptive indexicals doesn't do the strong two-dimensionalist much good.

Next, consider a different attempt to save two-dimensionalism.

ANOTHER ATTEMPT TO SAVE STRONG TWO-DIMENSIONALIST DESCRIPTIVISM FROM THE PROBLEMS POSED BY (5–7)

Occurrences of 'I' (and other indexicals) in the complement clauses of knowledge ascriptions are to be replaced by contextually rigidified descriptions that refer to the agent of the context. (Replacement with a name wouldn't do any good, since names themselves are all to be analyzed in terms of rigidified descriptions.)

So, on this proposal, (6b) is translated into something of the form (6d).

6d. Gideon knows that dthat [the x: SSx] is not Saul Kripke.

When the name *Saul Kripke* is replaced by the reference-fixing description supposedly associated with it, one ends up with something of the form (6e).

6e. Gideon knows that dthat [the x: SSx] is not dthat [the y: SKy].

The idea is that although the **secondary intension** of the complement clause is necessary, it is not the thing that (6e) reports Gideon as knowing. Instead, the object of knowledge is taken to be the **primary intension** of the complement clause, which, may be identified with the contingent aposteriori proposition expressed by (8).

8. [the x: SSx] is not [the y: SKy]

In this way, the proposal attempts to explain why the knowledge reported in (6b) is aposteriori, even though the complement sentence of (6b) expresses a necessary truth.

In the end, however, this won't work. All one needs to ask is *What are these descriptions?* If one consults the writings of ambitious two-dimensionalists like Lewis, Jackson, and Chalmers, the most consistent and promising suggestion one finds for associating descriptions with proper names of more or less ordinary, unfamous people and things attempts to piggyback on what they imagine to be a tolerably well-understood *causal-historical chain theory.*[3] Since this strategy will be scrutinized in the next section of this chapter, I will here simply assume that the reference-fixing description associated with many names n will be something along the lines of the indexical description, *the individual whom I have heard of under the name 'n'*, suggested by David Lewis. But now the problem is transparent. When one encounters a name (like *Saul Kripke*) in the complement clause of an attitude ascription, one is told to analyze it in terms of an indexical description. But when one encounters an indexical in such a clause, the proposal under consideration directs that it too is to be replaced. The problem is that any replacement one comes up with will either lead in a circle, or be utterly implausible.

The problem is illustrated by the example at hand. Adopting the Lewisian suggestion, (6e) becomes (6f).

6f. Gideon knows that dthat [the x: SSx] is not dthat [the individual I have heard of under the name 'Saul Kripke'].

There is already a difficulty here—namely, that whether or not Gideon knows that I am not Saul Kripke is conceptually independent of whatever knowledge he may or may not have about whether I have ever heard the name 'Saul Kripke'. (Remember that, according to strong two-dimensionalism, the proposition that (6f) reports Gideon as knowing is, roughly, the one that we get by stripping off the occurrences of *dthat.*) Nor would it help to fiddle with this result so that it spoke of the person Gideon has heard of under the name 'Saul Kripke'. After all, this is supposed to be an analysis of **my** utterance; the truth conditions of what I said do not depend on whether or not Gideon has heard the name 'Saul Kripke'. So the analysis is empirically wrong.

But put that aside. A further difficulty is that the first person singular pronoun has been reintroduced in to the complement clause of the analysis of my attitude ascription. Since the proposal directs that this

[3] See David Lewis, "Naming the Colors," fn. 22, and "Putnam's Paradox"; Fred Kroon, "Causal Descriptivism"; Frank Jackson, "Reference and Description Revisited," pp. 209–12; and David Chalmers, "On Sense and Intension"; all cited in chapter 3, fns. 6 and 7.

term must be eliminated in favor of its own reference-fixing description, one must now transform (6f) into (6g).

6g. Gideon knows that dthat [the x: SSx] is not dthat [the individual that dthat [the x: SSx] has heard of under the name 'Saul Kripke'].

What is this remaining description, *the x: SSx*? Any attempt to identify it with one containing a name, or natural kind term, such as the descriptions in (9), will be fruitless.

9. the oldest son of **Bill** and **Ruth Soames**
   the **Seattle** native who teaches philosophy at **Princeton**
   the **man** standing next to **Mark Johnston**
   the professor whose office is room 113 **1879 Hall**

According to strong two-dimensionalism, each name and kind term in (9) must itself be replaced by a description, and, again, the favored descriptions tend to be of the form *the individual I have heard of under the name (or kind term) 'n'*. Thus, replacing the description *the x: SSx* in (6g) with any of the descriptions in (9) would reintroduce the original problem.

What about indexical descriptions such as those in (10)?

10. the individual who is **now here** working on **this manuscript**
    the person who produced **this inscription**
    the individual in the foreground of **that picture**

As before, there are obvious empirical problems with each of these alternatives, since the truth or falsity of my report that Gideon knows that I am not Saul Kripke does not depend on whether or not he knows where I am, what inscriptions I am producing, or which pictures I am in. So the truth conditions assigned by the strong two-dimensionalist analysis to the resulting attitude ascriptions (relative to my context) are badly off target. But put that, too, aside. Again, there is a further problem to be faced. The difficulties posed by indexicals in attitude ascriptions for strong two-dimensionalism are not limited to cases in which the first person singular pronoun explicitly occurs in the complement clause of the attitude report. The same difficulties will be raised by the presence of any expression which is analyzed in terms of the first person singular pronoun, as well as by any other indexical primitive that is not itself to be replaced by a description.

Suppose the strong two-dimensionalist maintains that although some indexicals are primitive, others are definable in terms of the primitives. Suppose further that these primitives include 'I' and 'now'. Using these primitives, one might propose definitions along the lines of those in (11).

11a. *Here* (used in the absence of any demonstration) is defined as *dthat [my location now]*.

b. *this N* (accompanied by a demonstration and a guiding intention) is defined as **dthat [the N that I am demonstrating (and intend to refer to) now]**.

However, if one does take this route, then the descriptions in (10) will reintroduce the first person singular pronoun, and so be of no help to the strong two-dimensionalist in identifying the description **the x: SSx** needed in his proposed analysis (6g) of my remark (6b). What if indexicals like those in (10) are not defined, but are themselves primitive? In that case, the problems posed by (6b) are multiplied by focusing on examples like (12).

12. Gideon knows that this man [pointing to me] is not that man [pointing to Saul Kripke].

It is, I think, time to call a halt to all this. The problems we have encountered in this section give every indication of being intractable—stemming as they do from the confrontation of central tenets of strong two-dimensionalism with obvious linguistic facts. First, in order to explain away all examples of the necessary aposteriori and the contingent apriori involving names and natural kind terms, it must be possible, in principle, to find a reference-fixing description for each name and natural kind term that doesn't itself contain any other such term. Second, as Twin Earth–style examples involving qualitatively identical agents in qualitatively identical situations indicate, such descriptions typically must contain indexicals like 'I', 'now', 'here', or 'this'. Third, since there are examples of the necessary aposteriori and the contingent apriori involving these indexicals, the strong two-dimensionalist must somehow explain them away too. However, this is impossible, since the theorist has no resources left to do the job. Although the strong two-dimensionalist might try to analyze some indexicals in terms of others, certain indexicals must be taken as primitive, without any descriptive analysis. When one reaches these, one will be left with instances of the necessary aposteriori and the contingent apriori for which no strong two-dimensionalist explanation is possible. Putting this result together with the battery of objections—arguments 1–7—developed in the previous section, one has little choice but to conclude that strong two-dimensionalism is untenable. If ambitious two-dimensionalism is to have a future, some other version of the view must be found to be defensible.

Critique of Weak Two-Dimensionalism

As indicated in chapter 7, the essential difference between strong and weak two-dimensionalism that drives all other differences is that whereas the strong two-dimensionalist seeks to explain away the necessary aposteriori and the contingent apriori as an illusion—in the manner of T7—the weak two-dimensionalist accepts the existence of propositions that are both necessary and knowable only aposteriori, as well as those that are both contingent and knowable apriori, while attempting to give deflationary explanations of how there can be such propositions. In doing this, the weak two-dimensionalist rejects T7, T8, and the identification of propositions with sets of possible world-states (or functions from such states to truth values), while sharply modifying the semantic analysis of propositional attitude ascriptions given in T5b, and the explanations of the necessary aposteriori and the contingent apriori given in T6. The resulting version of ambitious two-dimensionalism is characterized by the following theses.

WT1.   Each sentence is semantically associated with a pair of semantic values—a primary intension, and a secondary intension. The primary intension of S is its Kaplan-style character. The secondary intension of (or proposition expressed by) S at a context C is the proposition assigned by its primary intension to C.

WT2.   Understanding S consists in knowing its primary intension—i.e., its meaning, or character. Although this knowledge, plus complete knowledge of the context C, would always give one knowledge of the proposition expressed by S in C, sometimes one does not have such knowledge. Since we never know all there is to know about the designated world-state of C, sometimes we don't know precisely which proposition is expressed by S in C. However, this does not stop us from using S correctly in C.

WT3a.   Examples of the necessary aposteriori are sentences the secondary intensions of which are necessary, and the primary intensions of which assign false propositions to some contexts.

WT3b.   Examples of the contingent apriori are sentences the secondary intensions of which are contingent, and the primary intensions of which assign true propositions to every context.[4]

WT4a.   All proper names and natural kind terms have their reference semantically fixed by descriptions not containing any (uneliminable) proper names or natural kind terms.

WT4b.   These names and natural kind terms are synonymous with descriptions rigidified using *actually* or *dthat*.[5]

WT5a.   *It is a necessary truth that S* is true w.r.t. a context C and world-state w iff the secondary intension of S in C is true w.r.t. all (metaphysically possible) world-states w* that are possible relative to w.

WT5b.   Standardly, an attitude ascription *x v's that S*, when taken in a context C, is true of an individual a with respect to a possible world-state w iff there is some meaning (character) M such that (i) in w, a bears R to M (which relation depends on which verb v is involved), and (ii) M assigns the **secondary intension** of S relative to C to a related context with a as agent and w as world-state. So propositions are objects of the attitudes, and attitude verbs are two-place predicates of agents and their objects. However, this two-place relation holds between an agent a and a proposition p in virtue of a three-place relation

---

[4] As explained in chapter 7, WT3a and WT3b are to be taken as universally quantified conditionals, rather than universally quantified biconditionals. For example, WT3a tells us that for every sentence S, if S is an example of the necessary aposteriori, then the secondary intension of S is necessary and the primary intension of S assigns false propositions to some contexts. It does **not** assert the converse of this claim.

[5] As indicated in chapter 7, WT4a and WT4b do not require the relevant descriptions to be non-indexical or to contain vocabulary drawn exclusively from the language of which the names and natural kind terms are parts. However, they do require the properties expressed to be purely descriptive.

holding between a, a character, and p. To believe p is to **accept** a character M that expresses p, and to believe that M expresses a truth. To know a true proposition p is to **justifiably accept** a character M that expresses p, and to know that M expresses a truth.

WT5c.   In addition, some attitude ascriptions *x v's that S* have a secondary reading in which they are true of an individual a with respect to a context C and world-state w iff in w, a bears a certain relation R to the character M of S (or, in certain cases, to the character of a specified transformation of S). For example, when v = 'believe', R is the attitude of accepting M and believing it to express a truth; when v = 'know', R is the attitude of justifiably accepting M and knowing it to express a truth.[6]

WT6a.   For all propositions p, p is both necessary and knowable only aposteriori iff (i) p is necessary; (ii) p is knowable **in virtue of** one's justifiably accepting some meaning M and knowing that it expresses a truth, where M is such that (a) it assigns p to one's context, (b) it assigns a false proposition to some other context, and (c) one's justification for accepting M, and believing it to express a truth, requires one to possess empirical evidence; and (iii) p is knowable **only** in this way.

WT6b.   For all propositions p, p is both contingently true and knowable apriori iff in addition to being contingently true, p is knowable **in virtue of** one's justifiably accepting some meaning M and knowing that it expresses a truth, where M is such that (a) it assigns p to one's context, (b) it assigns a true proposition to every context, and (c) one's justification for accepting M, and believing it to express a truth, does not require one to possess empirical evidence.

The difference between weak and strong two-dimensionalism can be illustrated by contrasting the weak two-dimensionalist explanation

---

[6] For the weak two-dimensionalist, WT5b is the central semantic principle applying to propositional attitude ascriptions. WT5c specifies an additional reading of some attitude ascriptions posited by some theorists to handle a limited range of special so-called *de se* cases. See chapter 7 for explanation.

of the necessary-aposteriori classification of (1a) with the strong two-dimensionalist explanation given earlier.

    1a. The actual husband of Stephanie Lewis was the actual author of *Counterfactuals*.

    b. The husband of Stephanie Lewis was the author of *Counterfactuals*.

Since the two rigidified descriptions in (1a) are codesignative, the secondary intension of (1a)—the proposition it expresses—is a necessary truth.[7] According to the weak two-dimensionalist, this proposition counts as knowable only aposteriori because (a) it is knowable in virtue of one's justifiably accepting the character of (1a) and knowing that it expresses a truth, (b) this character assigns false propositions to contexts the designated world-states of which are precisely those in which the contingent, aposteriori proposition expressed by (1b) is false, (c) one's justification for accepting this character in the actual context, and believing it to express a truth, requires one to possess empirical evidence that the proposition expressed by (1b) is true, and (d) the secondary intension of (1a) isn't knowable in any fundamentally different way. In the case of this particular example, the chief difference between strong and weak two-dimensionalism is that although both count the **sentence** (1a) as an example of the necessary aposteriori, only weak two-dimensionalism classifies the **proposition** it expresses—its secondary intension—in this way. In other cases, the difference between these two versions of ambitious two-dimensionalism goes well beyond this.

One big difference is that whereas strong two-dimensionalism incorporates the thesis T5b—analyzing propositional attitude ascriptions *x v's that S* as reporting relations between agents and the primary intensions of S—weak two-dimensionalism rejects T5b in favor of WT5b—which analyzes the ascriptions as relating agents to the secondary intensions of S. Because of this, none of the previous arguments falsifying strong two-dimensionalism tell against weak two-dimensionalism. However, there are other differences that don't reflect so favorably on it. One of the most notable of these bears directly on the weak two-dimensionalist account of the necessary aposteriori and the contingent apriori.

---

[7] As before, in order to simplify the discussion, I ignore world-states with respect to which David Lewis doesn't exist.

The explanations of these categories of truth summarized in WT6 seem to presuppose that there is some connection between a character expressing a falsehood in some, or no, contexts and one's needing, or not needing, empirical evidence in order to justifiably accept it. This is reflected by the fact that if, as I will assume, everything that can be known is either knowable apriori or knowable only aposteriori, then WT6 rules out the following possibilities:

(i)   There is a necessary proposition p expressed by a sentence S satisfying the following conditions: (a) the character M of S expresses a truth in every context, (b) one can know p by virtue of understanding S, justifiably accepting it (i.e., accepting M), and knowing it to express a truth, (c) justifiably accepting M and knowing it to express a truth requires empirical evidence, and (d) there is no other, apriori, route to p.

(ii) There is a contingent proposition p expressed (in some context C) by a sentence S satisfying the following conditions: (a) the character M of S expresses a truth in C, but in other contexts it expresses something false, (b) in C, one can know p by virtue of understanding S, justifiably accepting it (i.e., accepting M) and knowing it to express a truth (in C), and (c) justifiably accepting M and knowing it to express a truth (in C) does not require empirical evidence.

In the case of (i), the combination of (a), (b), and WT6a rule out the possibility that p is an instance of the necessary aposteriori, while the combination of (c), (d), and the account of apriority embedded in WT6b rule out the possibility that p is an instance of the necessary apriori. Assuming that if there is such a p (and sentence that expresses it), then p must be one or the other, the weak two-dimensionalist must conclude that there is no such p (and sentence that expresses it). A similar argument holds for (ii).

What reason is there to believe these conclusions? Here, it should be remembered that the central tenets of weak two-dimensionalism, and the conclusions just drawn from them, do not result from exhaustive and painstaking analyses of the constructions actually found in English and other natural languages. Rather, they reflect views about what sorts of linguistic phenomena are possible. The analyses offered of the necessary aposteriori and the contingent apriori are not simply claims about which linguistic categories actually existing examples happen to fall into—as if in the next language one looks at one might find examples of the necessary aposteriori conforming to (i). On the contrary, the weak two-dimensionalist believes that there simply could not be instances of the necessary aposteriori and the contingent apriori of any kind other than those postulated in WT6. Why not?

Faced with this question, the weak two-dimensionalist is at a distinct disadvantage, when compared with the very strong two-dimensionalist. When asked why there can be no propositions that are necessary yet knowable only aposteriori, the very strong two-dimensionalist answers that this follows from the nature of propositions—which are nothing more than sets of metaphysically possible world-states (or functions from such to truth values). As a result, any sentences that are classified as instances of the necessary aposteriori **must** be associated with two propositions—one of which is necessary and relevant to the modal evaluation of the sentence, and the other of which is contingent, aposteriori, and relevant to the epistemological evaluation of the sentence. There simply are no other possible analyses. Moreover, once the mechanism of assigning pairs of propositions to sentences is in place, the explanation of the contingent apriori follows in train. Sentences that are classified in this way are such that the epistemically relevant propositions associated with them are necessary. And why does that make them apriori? Because, on the possible world-state analysis of propositions, there is only one necessary proposition, and it is automatically known apriori by everyone.

The beauty of very strong two-dimensionalism is its ability to give principled answers to these questions. In the end, of course, this is small comfort, since the system is demonstrably incorrect. However, the point to notice is that in retreating to weak two-dimensionalism, we are not just avoiding undesirable consequences of the original view, we are also giving up some of its initial attractiveness and motivation. When asked why there **couldn't possibly be** an instance of the necessary aposteriori conforming to (i), the weak two-dimensionalist has, as far as I can see, no principled answer. Why, for example, couldn't there be a sentence S in any **possible** language which was such that (a) S consists of a proper name for an object o together with a predicate expressing a necessary property of o, (b) the character S is a **constant** function from contexts to a necessary proposition p, yet (c) justifiably accepting that character, and knowing it to express a truth, requires empirical evidence, and (d) there is no apriori route to p. Although the doctrines of weak two-dimensionalism rule this out, they don't provide any clear rationale for doing so. A related lacuna comes up in the discussion of the contingent apriori, where it is tacitly assumed that if M is a character that can justifiably be accepted and known to be true without evidence, then M must assign a true proposition to every context.

This provides a place to begin my critique. If it is not clear why things **have to be** as they are stipulated to be by weak two-dimensionalism, then it may not be so clear that they really **are** that way in the first place. In particular, it may not be that names and natural kind terms are indexical, rigidified descriptions with primary intensions that are distinct from their secondary intensions. If they are not, then not only are the theses WT4a,b about names and natural kind terms incorrect, the theses WT3a,b and WT6a,b about the necessary aposteriori and the contingent apriori are also in doubt. I will start out by focusing on WT4a, which maintains that the reference of names and natural kind terms is semantically fixed to be whatever is denoted by certain descriptions associated with them by speakers. I will then move on to WT4b, which analyzes names as rigidified versions of these descriptions. I will argue that these theses are false: names and natural kind terms do **not** have descriptive meanings which determine their reference, and even if they did, rigidification would cause further problems. If this is right, then there is no avoiding the view that the characters of names and natural kind terms are constant functions, in which case the weak two-dimensionalist accounts of the necessary apriori and the contingent apriori collapse.

Critique of WT4a: Against the View That Reference Must Be Fixed by Description

In the discussions of Jackson and Chalmers in chapters 8 and 9 I indicated that the analysis of names and natural kind terms as having their reference semantically fixed by descriptions does not arise from examination of particular cases, but rather from apriori arguments that there are no other possible ways in which these terms could secure their reference. As Jackson puts it in *From Metaphysics to Ethics*, "it is not **magic** that 'water' picks out what it does pick out."[8] The idea is that terms must get their reference in some way, and whatever way that turns out to be can be described. However, this hardly settles the issue.

---

[8] Page 82, my emphasis.

As I explained in the penultimate section of chapter 8, Jackson's idea confuses the foundational facts which bring it about that words have the meaning and reference they do with the semantic facts about meaning and reference that competent speakers must know in order to understand them. Once this confusion is cleared up, it is obvious that more is needed to establish that names and natural kind terms have descriptive semantics than the commitment to eschew magic.

A different route to descriptive analyses about names and natural kind terms, employed by both Jackson and Chalmers, came from commonsense answers to questions about what our terms would refer to if certain scenarios "turned out to be actual." In chapter 9, I argued that this line of argument fails because (i) the constraints under which the scenarios are described illicitly presuppose descriptivism to begin with, and (ii) the questions themselves confuse (a) what we would have meant by our words if the described scenarios had been instantiated with (b) what the actual meanings of our words tell us about their referents when set in those scenarios. Once this confusion is resolved, the case for descriptivism based on these thought experiments falls apart.

One particularly bold variant of this last, flawed, defense of descriptivism is expressed by Jackson in the following passage, cited in chapters 3 and 8.

Our ability to answer questions about what various words refer to in various possible worlds, it should be emphasized, is common ground with critics of the description theory. The critics' writings are full of descriptions (*descriptions*) of possible worlds and claims about what refers, or fails to refer, to what in these possible worlds. Indeed, their impact has derived precisely from the intuitive plausibility of many of their claims about what refers, or fails to refer, to what in various possible worlds. But if speakers can say what refers to what when various possible worlds are described to them, description theorists can identify the property associated in their minds with, for example, the word 'water': it is the disjunction of the properties that guide the speakers in each particular possible world when they say which stuff, if any, in each world counts as water. This disjunction is in their minds in the sense that they can deliver the answer for each possible world when it is described in sufficient detail, but it is implicit in the sense that the pattern that brings the various disjuncts together as part of the, possibly highly complex, disjunction may be one they cannot state.[9]

What is new, and quite remarkable, about this passage is the suggestion that the claim that the referents of expressions are semantically fixed by descriptions is, for all intents and purposes, irrefutable—since any refutation requires clear intuitions about what refers to what in different situations, and these can only be explained as arising from reference-fixing descriptions semantically associated with expressions by speakers.[10] There are several crippling problems with this suggestion. First, there are clear cases in which we have no trouble identifying the referent of a term t (in a given scenario), even though it is clear that there is no reference-fixing description associated with t by speakers. Kaplan's example of the qualitative duplicates, the identical twins Castor and Pollux discussed in chapter 2, is a case in point. We have no trouble identifying Castor as the referent of his use of *I*, and Pollux as the referent of his, just as we have no trouble recognizing ourselves as referents of our own uses. This is so despite the fact that the referent of *I* is **not** semantically fixed, for any of us, by descriptions we semantically associate with it. If this is true of *I*, it is surely also true of *now*, and may be true of other expressions as well. Second, neither Kripke's overall methodology, nor his refutations of the claim that most names and natural kind terms n have their reference semantically fixed by associated descriptions, presuppose that ordinary speakers can correctly determine the reference of n in all contexts in which n has a determinate reference (where the contexts are given appropriately neutral descriptions and n is used by speakers in the context with the same meaning it has when actually used by us). The most that is presupposed is that for each candidate description D, there is **at least one** such context in which we can recognize that n does **not** refer to the individual or kind denoted by D (or that D does not denote the individual or kind to which n refers). This is far weaker than what Jackson's suggestion of irrefutability requires. Third, even in cases in which there may be descriptions picking out the referent of a term that are, in some sense, associated with it by speakers, it remains to be shown that these descriptions are included in the meaning of the term, in the sense of being included in the necessary conditions for understanding the word

---

[9] "Reference and Descriptions Revisited," p. 212.

[10] This suggestion can also be found in Chalmers, "The Components of Content," p. 630, fn. 11, and Chalmers and Jackson, "Conceptual Analysis and Reductive Explanation," pp. 326–27.

and being a competent user of it. One can describe possible scenarios in which our intuitions tell us that speakers use the word *and* to mean disjunction, the material conditional, the property of being a necessary truth, or the property of being a philosopher. Even if one were to grant the contentious assumption that these intuitions arise from some internalized theory T that unconsciously guides us, it would not follow that the **meaning** of *and*—its character in Kaplan's sense—is one that yields as content in a context whatever satisfies the relevant description extractable from T. **Surely not every word is a descriptive indexical in Kaplan's sense.** To miss this point is to miss the distinction between (i) semantic facts about what an expression means, or what its referent and content are in a context, and (ii) presemantic, foundational facts in virtue of which the expression has the meaning, and hence the referents and contents in different contexts, that it does. Whereas the descriptivist needs reference-fixing descriptions to be involved in (i), Jackson's argument can't exclude the possibility that where descriptions are available at all, their only role is in (ii). Finally, the claim that our ability to categorize cases in certain ways presupposes the sort of underlying descriptive knowledge supposed by Jackson is tendentious in something like the way that Plato's attribution of apriori knowledge of mathematics to the slave boy in the *Meno* is tendentious. There are other ways to explain the recognition of new facts. Since we are thoroughly familiar with language and its use, it would not be surprising to learn that we have a generally reliable ability to recognize new linguistic facts, and to generate reasonable linguistic hypotheses, given elaborate descriptions of previously unconsidered cases, without having antecedently possessed, either consciously or unconsciously, any developed theory of the matter.

For these reasons, it is an error to assume that descriptions semantically fixing the referents of names and natural kind terms **must** be available. Instead of looking for some apriori guarantee, one must consider candidate descriptions, case by case. When one does this, the results are not promising. An often noted fact about proper names is the enormous variability in the descriptive information associated with the same name by different competent speakers.[11] Although most speakers who have enough familiarity with a name to be able to use it possess some descriptive information about its referent, little, if any, of this information is common to all of them—certainly not enough to

---

[11] See Gareth Evans, *Varieties of Reference* (New York and Oxford: Clarendon Press, 1982), chapter 11, and my *Beyond Rigidity*, chapter 3.

uniquely identify the referent. What is more, many speakers would not be able to articulate any uniquely identifying description.

The same point applies to natural kind terms like *water*, for which, Jackson suggests (in the above passage) the reference-fixing description—"*something like: belonging to the kind which most of the clear, potable samples, acquaintance with which lead* [led?] *to the introduction of the word 'water' in our language* [belong to]."[12] This clearly won't do. First, in order to understand *water*, an ordinary speaker doesn't have to have a view about what led to its introduction into our language. Second, one doesn't have to know that samples of water are standardly clear and potable. Imagine an unusually unfortunate English speaker, brought up in dismal and restricted circumstances, who never drank water, never imagined that anyone else did, and whose only acquaintance with it was with a cloudy stream of water spilling out of a drainpipe from a laundry. This person might correctly use *water* to refer to water, and might say and know, just as we do, that water is used for washing, but not know that water is often clear and potable. Since such a speaker may well understand the word, and use it to designate instances of the same kind that we do, without associating it with Jackson's proposed description, that description is not part of its meaning in the language, and does not qualify as semantically fixing its referent.

As indicated in chapters 3 and 8, considerations like these have led several descriptivists to embrace causal descriptivism—according to which the reference-fixing description for a name (or natural kind term) n is something like **the thing I have heard of under the name 'n'** or, perhaps, **the causal source of this token of 'n'**, where, David Lewis reminds us, to find "*an account of the relation being invoked here, just consult the writings of causal theorists of reference.*"[13] There are three main problems with this view. First, the descriptions cited are not always accurate. For example, I might use *Zaza* to refer to a certain dog in the neighborhood, having forgotten that I introduced the name myself, and wrongly thinking that I picked it up from someone else. Since in such a case I use the name to refer to the dog, though I may never have heard it used by anyone else, there is some difficulty with Lewis's first description.[14] The second problem is common to both descriptions, and to certain versions of the so-called causal-historical theory of reference from which they are extracted. As Jonathan McKeown-

[12] "Reference and Description Revisited," p. 212.
[13] "Naming the Colors," fn. 22.
[14] For more problems of this sort see the penultimate section of chapter 8.

Green has pointed out, not all cases in which a speaker successfully uses a name n to refer are cases in which he has either introduced n himself, or acquired n from someone else with the intention of preserving the reference of his source. Suppose, for example, that you know of a certain region in Ireland in which the residents of different towns see to it that there is always exactly one person bearing the name *Patrick O'Grady*. Learning of this curious fact, you set out to visit the region to interview the different men bearing that name. On entering a pub in a new town, you announce "*I am looking for Patrick O'Grady, whom I am willing to pay for an interview for my new book.*" In so doing you successfully use the name to refer to the man, and say something about him—not because you have acquired the name through a causal-historical chain of reference transmission, but because you are able to speak the language of the community in which the referent of the name has already been established.

This brings us to the third, and most fundamental, problem with the attempt to appropriate causal-historical theories of reference transmission for the purposes of descriptivism. Egocentric, metalinguistic descriptions associated with names are no more parts of their meanings than similar egocentric, metalinguistic descriptions are parts of the meanings of other words in the language. As indicated in chapter 4, standardly, when a speaker uses any word—*magenta, abode, osteopath, alphabetize, necessarily*, etc.—the speaker intends to use it in accord with the linguistic conventions of the community. The speaker intends to use it to refer to, or express, whatever other competent members of the community do. In the case of proper names, it is recognized both that a given name may be used by only a subpart of the community, and that different members of the relevant subcommunity (who use the name to refer to the same individual) may associate it with very different descriptive information without the name meaning something different for each of them. Thus, the general intention that one's use of words conform with the linguistic conventions of one's community translates, in the case of most names, into the intention to use them to refer to whomever or whatever other relevant members of the community use them to refer to. Some such intention is a standard condition on normal language use, not a part of meaning.

There is a larger lesson here involving historical chains of reference transmission. On the picture one often gets, a name isn't part of my language at all until I either introduce it myself, or encounter someone else using it, and form the reference-fixing intention that in my idiolect it will refer to whatever it refers to in the idiolect of those from whom I acquire it. This picture is misleading. The language I speak is a common language, of which the name is normally a part before I ever encounter it. As a speaker, I need not know all the linguistic properties of the words in my language; my knowledge is partial, just as my knowledge of other social institutions of which I am a part is partial. Nevertheless, since I am a competent member of the linguistic community, I can appropriate a word that may be new to me, and use it with the meaning and reference it has already acquired. In the case of a name, the word probably entered the language via the stipulation of some authorities—say, the parents of a newborn child. It is retained in the language by a practice of various speakers using it to refer to that individual; and speakers normally encounter it for the first time by hearing others use it—everyone intending to use it with the meaning or reference it has already attained. If this picture is right, then historical chains, though they exist, are not themselves reference-determining mechanisms.[15] Thus, as I pointed out in chapter 4 in the discussion of Kripke, no metalinguistic descriptions invoking them play the role of semantically fixing the reference of names (or natural kind terms).

All of this adds up to an argument against the ambitious two-dimensionalist thesis WT4a. As I see it, the dialectical situation is this:

(i) In *Naming and Necessity*, Kripke refuted specific proposals for descriptive analyses according to which ordinary proper names have their referents semantically fixed by descriptions commonly associated with them.

(ii) Descriptivists, including ambitious two-dimensionalists like Jackson and Chalmers, have tried to answer Kripke's challenge, not by formulating specific and detailed descriptive analyses of particular terms that can be shown to be immune to his objections, but rather by offering general apriori arguments that such analyses must be possible, since there is no other way in which reference could be fixed.

(iii) All of these general arguments have now been found wanting.

(iv) In particular, the claim that Kripke's own negative arguments against descriptivism, as well as his positive historical-chain

---

[15] This conception of the proper way to view historical chains of reference transmission is developed in chapter 9 of Jonathan McKeown Green's dissertation, *The Primacy of Public Language* (Princeton University, 2002).

theories of reference transmission, presuppose that, in the end, names and natural kind terms have their reference semantically fixed by description, has been shown to be incorrect.

(v)   Although we saw, in chapter 4, that Kripke can be criticized for sometimes writing in a way that might seem to suggest that chains of reference transmission may have a semantic role to play, this suggestion is misleading; there is a natural conception of language as a social institution in which they play a role in preserving and communicating the meanings and reference of words, once those have been established, rather than being themselves parts of meaning that semantically determine reference.

In short, we have a plausible and natural conception of language according to which names and natural kind terms do not have their reference semantically fixed by descriptions, we have telling Kripke-style objections against every descriptive analysis—metalinguistic or non-metalinguistic—ever proposed for particular expressions, and we have refutations of general, apriori arguments that these expressions must have their referents fixed descriptively. As I see it, this adds up to a strong case against WT4a.

Critique of WT4b: Against Taking Names to Be Rigidified Descriptions

In this section I put aside problems about finding reference-fixing descriptions in order to focus on the problems that would confront the weak two-dimensionalist even if such descriptions could be found. In order to avoid Kripke's modal argument against descriptivism (see chapter 2), such descriptions must be rigidified. Hence, the need for WT4b. There are two ways in which this might be done—with the actuality operator or the *dthat*-operator. If one assumed—with the very strong two-dimensionalist—that propositions were sets of possible world-states (or functions from such to truth values), then it wouldn't make much difference which operator was used. But now that the weak two-dimensionalist has set that assumption aside, the different means of rigidification turn out to have very different consequences.

First, consider *actually*-rigidified descriptions. Suppose (i) that *Saul Kripke ≠ David Kaplan* is an example of the necessary aposteriori, (ii) that *the x: SKx* and *the x: DKx* are descriptions that semantically fix the referents of the two names, (iii) that *the x: SKx ≠ the x: DKx* is contingent because there are world-states in which the two descriptions denote the same person, and (iv) that the two names are synonymous with *the x :actually SKx* and *the x: actually DKx*, respectively. On these assumptions, *Saul Kripke ≠ David Kaplan* conforms to WT4a and WT4b. However, the analysis is incorrect, because (iv) is false—since it doesn't do full justice to the fact that actual believers share many beliefs with merely possible believers. For example, I, along with others, believe that Saul Kripke ≠ David Kaplan; and it is not unreasonable to suppose that we also believe, of the actual world-state @, that it is a world-state with respect to which it is true that Saul Kripke ≠ David Kaplan. A similar point holds for merely possible believers. In some possible world-states w, various agents believe that Saul Kripke ≠ David Kaplan; in addition, they believe, of w, that it is a world-state with respect to which it is true that Saul Kripke ≠ David Kaplan. However, they need not have any beliefs about @. Supposing they don't, I would say something false if I were now to say *In w, they believe that the x: actually SKx ≠ the x: actually DKx*—since in saying this I would be saying that in w they believe, **of** @, that the unique individual who "is SK" in it is not the unique individual who "is DK" in it. Thus, if (iv) were correct, I would say something false if I were now to say *In w, they believe that Saul Kripke ≠ David Kaplan*. But I wouldn't be saying something false. Hence, (iv) is incorrect.

When spelled out in detail, this argument makes use of the weak two-dimensionalist thesis, WT5b, which specifies that, on a standard reading of *x believes that S*, the ascription is true with respect to a context C and world-state w iff in w, the agent believes the proposition expressed by S in C—an assumption traditional descriptivists typically rely on when using Frege's puzzle and Russell's problem of negative existentials to argue against nondescriptive analyses. What the argument shows is that if the content of a name n is given by an *actually*-rigidified description, then, on this reading, a belief ascription containing n in the complement clause is true of an agent x with respect to a merely possible world-state w only if, in w, x believes certain things about, not w, but the world C_W of the context in which the ascription is used to report x's belief. Since there is no such reading of these English belief ascriptions, the descriptivist proponent of weak two-dimensionalism cannot take the contents of names to be given by *actually*-rigidified descriptions.[16]

---

[16] This argument is presented and defended in detail on pp. 39–49 of *Beyond Rigidity*. A different argument for the same conclusion involves the possibility, mentioned on page 122,

Although some may wish to avoid this argument by denying that belief ascriptions report relations to the secondary intensions of their complement clauses, this analysis is more difficult to reject than is often realized. In order to save the thesis that names are *actually*-rigidified descriptions, one would have to reject not only this analysis, but also analyses in which the secondary intension of the complement is merely included as part of what the agent is reported to believe. There is, I think, no future in this.[17] In any case, it is not an option for the weak two-dimensionalist, who is committed to analyzing attitude ascriptions in a way that conforms to the argument.

The problem gets worse when one realizes (i) that in virtually all cases, the only plausible reference-fixing descriptions to which the actuality operator might be attached contain indexicals referring to the speaker and/or his utterance and time of utterance,[18] and (ii) that the only remotely plausible candidates for such descriptions are variants of those put forward by Lewis and other causal descriptivists. For example, consider Lewis's *thing I have heard of under the name 'Venus'* or *causal source of this token of 'Venus'*. Under the reading of belief ascriptions just indicated, my utterance of

that one can know apriori, of @, that a proposition p is true with respect to it, without thereby knowing p. If this is possible, then it is possible to satisfy *x knows apriori that actually S* without satisfying *x knows that S*, thereby undermining all putative examples of the necessary aposteriori hinging on *actually*. On this view, names and natural kind terms, which do give rise to instances of the necessary aposteriori, cannot be *actually*-rigidified descriptions.

[17] Michael Nelson takes this line in "Descriptivism Defended," *Noûs* 36 (2002): 408–36. His aim is to defend the view that names are *actually*-rigidified descriptions by offering an account in which *x believes that S* doesn't report a relation between the agent and any semantic value of S. One problem with the view is the lack of any explicit semantics for overtly relational ascriptions in which the belief predicate is followed by a propositional variable or a description, rather than a sentential clause. As a consequence, the analysis misses the obvious semantic relationship between clausal and nonclausal belief ascriptions. Moreover, on the most natural way of extending it to these ascriptions, implicitly endorsed by Nelson on p. 426, one gets the result that *John believes that S* can be false when *John believes the proposition that Sally just denied & the proposition that Sally just denied = the proposition that S* is true (see his note 22), as well as when *There is a proposition p such that John believes p & p = the proposition that S* is true. The same extension gives the result that *Bill believes everything Mary believes & Mary believes that S, but Bill doesn't believe that S* can be true with respect to certain contexts and world-states. Since these results are clearly unacceptable, Nelson has not shown that the descriptivist has any viable strategy for avoiding the argument in *Beyond Rigidity*.

[18] Both I and my Twin Earth duplicate (on another planet in the same possible world-state) associate the same purely qualitative descriptions with n, while using it to refer to different things. If this is to be accounted for by reference-fixing descriptions, they will have to contain indexicals referring to particular contextual parameters.

13. The ancient Babylonians believed that Venus was a star.

will then be true only if the ancients had views about me and which things I have heard of under which names, or about the causal sources of specific utterances of mine. Obviously, this is absurd; these ascriptions have no such readings.[19]

Nor do they have the other reading that the two-dimensionalist sometimes alleges them to have—namely one, specified in WT5c, in which (13) is true only if the ancient Babylonians accepted the character of the complement of (13), which, on the Lewis causal-descriptivist analysis, they would do only if they took themselves to have heard of some object under the name 'Venus'. In fact, my utterance of (13) is true, even though they were not familiar with the name 'Venus', and so would not have accepted this character. Finally, the absurdity of combining this analysis of names with the reading of belief ascriptions specified by WT5c is brought out by (14).

14a. Rudolf Lingens believes that his companion in the library, Jorge, is my brother.

b. Rudolf Lingens believes that his companion, the x: actually I have heard of x under the name 'Jorge', is my brother.

On this analysis, (14a) is analyzed as (14b), and hence is predicted to be true iff Rudolf accepts the character of the relevant transform—*my companion, the x: actually I have heard of x under the name 'Jorge', is my brother*—of the complement sentence, and so believes that his companion, whom **he** has heard of under the name 'Jorge', is **his** brother. Clearly, these are not the truth conditions of (14a), on any reading it has in English.[20]

[19] These considerations also rule out another popular (though non–two-dimensionalist) descriptivist strategy for dealing with the modal argument—namely, analyzing names as (nonrigid) descriptions that are required to take wide-scope over modal operators, while retaining narrow scope when they occur embedded under verbs of propositional attitude. This strategy can scarcely get off the ground because the only feasible candidates for reference-fixing descriptions contain indexicals referring to the speaker and/or the speaker's utterance and utterance time. Since the content of such a description is never what a name n contributes to the proposition expressed by *x believes that n is F*, this approach cannot plausibly account for elementary examples like (13). In addition, the strategy of assigning different scopes to the alleged descriptive contents of names embedded in modal and epistemic constructions leads to absurdities similar to those revealed by the arguments given above against strong two-dimensionalism, as is shown on pp. 25–39 of *Beyond Rigidity*.

[20] This example really reveals two problem: (i) coming up with the relevant transform of the complement sentence when that sentence already contains indexicals, and (ii) dealing with the indexicals introduced by analyses of names as indexical, *actually*-rigidified descriptions.

The lesson to be drawn is that even if the causal descriptivist could provide reference-fixing descriptions for names and natural kind terms, the semantic contents of these terms could **not** be given by rigidifying these descriptions using the actuality operator. What about using *dthat*? Although this avoids some of the absurdities involving *actually*, others remain, and two new problems are added. The main difficulty that remains concerns the alleged reading of attitude ascriptions specified by WT5c. If the purportedly reference-fixing descriptions to which *dthat* is attached are—as they must be— egocentric, metalinguistic descriptions of the sort provided by the causal descriptivist, then the absurdities just discussed involving ascriptions like (13) and (14) carry over to analyses employing *dthat* rather than *actually*. The main difficulty that is avoided involves the standard reading of attitude ascriptions specified by WT5b. If names are taken to be *dthat*-rigidified descriptions, we get the desired result that it is possible to believe that Saul Kripke ≠ David Kaplan without believing anything about the actual world-state, or other contextual parameters. This is all to the good. However, we also get the result that the semantic content of a name, relative to a context C, is just its referent in C. This leads to two new difficulties for weak two-dimensionalism.

First, it renders weak two-dimensionalism equivalent to familiar versions of Millianism regarding precisely those consequences of Millianism that descriptivists have traditionally found most objectionable— namely, (i) that coreferential names are substitutable without change in content or truth value in attitude ascriptions, and (ii) that negative existentials involving so-called empty names are characterized as expressing either no propositions at all, or propositions with gaps in them. In short, this version of weak two-dimensionalism faces Frege's puzzle and Russell's problem in essentially the same way that the most anti-descriptivist theories do. Since the desire to avoid these perceived problems with descriptivism's main competitor was one of the central factors motivating two-dimensionalism in the first place, this cannot be a happy result for the weak two-dimensionalist.

The second new difficulty is that wholesale appeal to *dthat*-rigidified descriptions wreaks havoc with the weak two-dimensionalist's account of the necessary aposteriori and the contingent apriori. Think again about the two-dimensionalist assumptions made about

15. Saul Kripke ≠ David Kaplan

when considering what sorts of rigidified descriptions could be taken as analyses of the two names. These assumptions were (i) that (15) is an example of the necessary aposteriori, (ii) that *the x: SKx* and *the x: DKx* are descriptions that semantically fix the referents of the two names, and (iii) that *the x: SKx ≠ the x: DKx* is contingent because there are world-states in which the two descriptions denote the same person. I have already shown that the names cannot be analyzed as synonymous with rigidified versions of these descriptions containing the actuality operator. However, if one substitutes the new principle (iv$_{dthat}$) for the original principle (iv), one puts assumption (i) at risk, thereby threatening weak two-dimensionalism in a new way.

> (iv$_{dthat}$) The two names *Saul Kripke* and *David Kaplan* are synonymous with *dthat [the x: SKx]* and *dthat [the x: DKx]*, respectively.

The problem, which is illustrated by (16), arises from (iv$_{dthat}$), WT5, WT6, and the nature of *dthat*.

16. *dthat [the x: SKx] ≠ dthat [the x: DKx & x ≠ the z: SKz]*

Since the two *dthat*-rigidified descriptions denote Saul Kripke and David Kaplan, respectively, the proposition expressed by (16)—its secondary intension—is, according to this version of weak two-dimensionalism, the same as the proposition expressed by (15). Moreover, given the nature of the unrigidified versions of the descriptions in (16)—i.e., *[the x: SKx]* and *[the x: DKx & x ≠ the z: SKz]*—one can easily see that there is no context C in which they designate the same thing. To simplify matters, I here stipulate that ≠ is to be understood in such a way that a sentence in which it is flanked by terms that designate the same thing is false, but a sentence in which it is flanked by terms that designate different things, or by terms that fail to designate at all, is true. Then the primary intension of (16) will express a truth in every context.

Now suppose that I understand (16), but don't know of the man, Saul Kripke, that he is designated by the rigidified description *dthat [the x: SKx]*, nor do I know of David Kaplan that he is designated by the rigidified description *dthat [the x: DKx]*.[21] Despite the fact that I don't know which individuals are designated in (16), I can see that it

---

[21] If the descriptions *the x: SKx* and *the x: DKx* happen to make this impossible, substitute any other pair of descriptions the first of which denotes Saul Kripke and the second of which denotes David Kaplan. The argument will not be affected.

must express a truth in every context. Hence I accept it, and believe it to express a truth in my context. From this, plus WT5b, it follows that I believe the proposition expressed by (16). In fact, for the weak two-dimensionalist, it should follow that I count as knowing this proposition to be true, and indeed knowing it apriori, since my acceptance of (16) is justified solely by my understanding the sentence, independent of additional empirical evidence. Since, by hypothesis, this proposition is the proposition that Saul Kripke ≠ David Kaplan, it should also follow that this proposition **isn't** an example of the necessary aposteriori after all. Checking WT6a, we see that indeed this is so, since clause (iii) of that thesis isn't satisfied. Thus, the version of weak two-dimensionalism under consideration conflicts with the claim—widely accepted by two-dimensionalists and non–two-dimensionalists alike—that (15) **is** an instance of the necessary aposteriori.

This is no isolated example. As is illustrated by (17) and (18), a similar result can be reached for virtually every standardly accepted instance of the necessary aposteriori.[22]

17a. That is not made out of metal (said pointing at the paperweight on my desk).

   b. Dthat [the paperweight that I am pointing at which is made of wood and not metal] is not made out of metal.

18a. Molecules of water have two hydrogen atoms and one oxygen atom.

   b. Molecules of dthat [the watery stuff, which is H_2O] have two hydrogen atoms and one oxygen atom.

Although (17a) and (18a) are widely recognized examples of the necessary aposteriori, the propositions they express are the same as those expressed by (17b) and (18b), the primary intensions of which express truths in every context. If, as ambitious two-dimensionalists standardly assume, understanding sentences like these is sufficient for (justifiably) accepting them, and knowing that they express truths, then the account of propositional attitude ascriptions embedded in WT5b will yield the conclusion that it is also sufficient for knowing the propositions they express to be true, and even for knowing these propositions apriori. By this route, the version of weak two-dimensionalism under

---

[22] Let the negation in the predicate of (17a,b) have wide scope, and treat (18a,b) as universally quantified conditionals.

consideration can be seen to be inconsistent with standard characterizations of sentences as instances of the necessary aposteriori that are
now accepted by nearly everyone.

Similar reasoning could be used to establish a drastic expansion of
the contingent apriori, and of the apriori in general, under this version
of weak two-dimensionalism. For example, let o be any object whatsoever, and let {P$_1$, ... P$_n$} be any set of properties the conjunction of
which uniquely applies to o. Given the unrestricted ability to use
dthat-rigidified descriptions to form singular terms the semantic contents of which are the objects they rigidly designate, one could always
form a description *the D* denoting the object uniquely possessing the
conjunction of the P$_i$'s, and then rigidify it using *dthat* to form a term
the semantic content of which was o itself. Finally, let p be any proposition that says of o that, if it exists, then it has one or more of the P$_i$'s.
Using *dthat [the D]*, we could formulate a sentence S expressing p
which was such that the primary intension of S expressed a truth in
every context, and was known by linguistically competent speakers to
do so. Under the usual assumption that understanding a sentence like
this is sufficient for (justifiably) accepting it, and knowing it to express
a truth, the account of propositional attitude ascriptions embedded in
WT5b will lead to the conclusion that p is knowable apriori.

These, I take it, are intolerable results. However, it would not be
easy for the weak two-dimensionalist to avoid them. One step in the
right direction would be to repudiate a principle, implicit in many ambitious two-dimensionalist discussions, which I have elsewhere called
weak linguisticism about the apriori.[23]

WEAK LINGUISTICISM ABOUT THE APRIORI
If one knows a proposition p solely by virtue of understanding a sentence that expresses p, and knowing semantics facts
about it, then one knows p apriori.

The important point neglected by this principle is that a piece of evidence e needed to understand the meaning of a sentence S may also
play a role in **justifying** the proposition p expressed by S. In such
cases, one who understands S will have all the evidence needed to
know that p is true, but p won't correctly be counted as apriori because to know p one must have empirical evidence that justifies it.[24]

However, rejecting this principle is not enough to save weak two-

---
[23] Soames, *The Age of Meaning*, p. 407.
[24] This is argued on pp. 408–10 of *The Age of Meaning*.

dimensionalism from the falsifying results I have adduced. The heart of the problem lies in the combination of (i) the unrestricted availability of rigidified descriptions, *dthat [the D]*, the semantic contents of which are the denotations of *the D*, (ii) the fact that understanding *dthat [the D] is F* does not require knowing of any object o that it is designated by *the D*, or knowing of any proposition p that *dthat [the D] is F* expresses p, and (iii) the contention that understanding and accepting *dthat [the D] is F* (and believing it to express a truth) is sufficient for believing the proposition it expresses, and similarly that understanding and justifiably accepting *dthat [the D] is F* (and knowing it to express a truth) is sufficient for knowing the proposition it expresses. Given the account of the necessary aposteriori and the contingent apriori specified in WT6, the weak two-dimensionalist must reject at least one of these principles, in order to avoid my falsifying counterexamples.

Since (ii) is part of the very characterization of how *dthat* is supposed to be understood, the best candidates for rejection are (i) and (iii). My own view, based on an obvious extension of an argument given in chapter 16 of *The Age of Meaning*,[25] is that (i) should be rejected, since no expression with the semantic properties that Kaplan assigned to *dthat* is capable of being a meaningful part of any possible human language. For suppose it were. Then there would be many sentences *dthat [the D] is F* the semantic contents of which were propositions p, even though understanding these sentences would not be sufficient to know that they expressed p. If this were so, then competent speakers could not routinely use such a sentence to entertain p, and assertive utterances of the sentence could not, reasonably, be counted as assertions of p, or expressions of one's belief in p.[26] Since, in my view, the semantic content of a sentence S just is information associated with S which is reliably connected to the propositions competent speakers use S to entertain, assert, and express their beliefs in, no sentences can have the semantic properties that Kaplan assigns to *dthat [the D] is F*.[27] If I am right about this, then it is the final nail in the coffin of weak two-dimensionalism, for if *dthat* is not available to rigidify descriptions, then the last hope of saving WT4b will be gone.

There is, however, another possible position. One could retain (i)

---

[25] Pages 414–16.

[26] See *The Age of Meaning* for details.

[27] See chapter 3 of *Beyond Rigidity*, plus "Naming and Asserting," in Zoltan Szabo (ed.), *Semantics vs. Pragmatics* (New York and Oxford: Oxford University Press, 2004).

while rejecting (iii)—thereby severing the connection between the semantic content of sentences containing *dthat* and the ability of competent speakers to use those sentences in the usual way to express attitudes toward their contents. For example, on this view, understanding
and (justifiably) accepting (17b) and (18b) (and knowing them to express truths) is **not** regarded as sufficient for knowing, or even believing, the propositions they express. In order for one's attitudes toward
these sentences to result in one's knowing or believing the propositions they express, it is required, in addition, that one know of, or believe of, my paperweight (in the case of (17b)) and the kind water (in
the case of (18b)) that they are designated by the relevant *dthat*-rigid-
ified descriptions—i.e., by *dthat [the paperweight that I am pointing at*
which is made of wood and not metal] (in the case of (17b)), and by
dthat [the watery stuff, which is H₂O] (in the case of (18b)). Since this
required *de re* knowledge cannot be had apriori, one's attitudes toward
(17b) and (18b) pose no threat to the classification of (17a), (18a)—
and the propositions they express—as instances of the necessary aposteriori. Similar reasoning could be adduced for other putative counterexamples.

Although this implicit rejection of WT5b is the best the weak two-
dimensionalist can do in defense of WT4b, the position is not a happy
one. The argument just given for salvaging (17a) and (18a) as instances of the necessary aposteriori postulates (i) that understanding
and (justifiably) accepting (17b) and (18b) is **not** sufficient for knowing or believing the propositions they express, and (ii) that what is required in order to explain this *de re* knowledge and belief is some independent *de re* knowledge and belief of essentially the same kind. It is
precisely this that the weak two-dimensionalist cannot explain. The *de*
re knowledge that must be presupposed by the weak two-dimensionalist, if the system is to be saved from falsifying counterexamples, is itself
knowledge of propositions in which kinds or individuals occur as constituents.[28] How does this knowledge arise? Since it can't be explained
as the result of understanding and (justifiably) accepting indexical sentences, some further, non–two-dimensionalist explanation of it must
be given. Once we have such an explanation, however, it would seem

---

[28] The connection between *de re* knowledge of an object and knowing a proposition in
which the object is a constituent is brilliantly discussed in David Kaplan, "Opacity," in Lewis
Edwin Hahn and Paul Arthur Schilpp (eds.), *The Philosophy of W. V. Quine* (La Salle, IL:
Open Court, 1986). For a brief summary of my own, see pp. 150–53 of "Donnellan's
Referential/Attributive Distinction," *Philosophical Studies* 73 (1994): 149–68.

that we should be able to apply it directly to paradigmatic Kripkean examples in which an essential property P is predicated of an object o, even though knowledge of o that it has P can only be aposteriori. But then we have recreated an instance of the Kripkean necessary aposteriori that cannot be forced into the weak two-dimensionalist mold.

Summary

This completes my case against weak two-dimensionalism. I have argued that the weak two-dimensionalist's contention that names and natural kind terms are rigidified descriptions is incorrect. My grounds for this conclusion are (i) that names and natural kind terms are not **semantically** associated with the descriptive information required by the analysis, and (ii) that no means of rigidification is available that both fits the assumptions of weak two-dimensionalism and results in rigidified descriptions the semantic behavior of which matches that of names and natural kind terms. If this is right, then there is no basis for thinking that names and natural kind terms are indexical at all, with primary intensions that are distinct from their secondary intensions. As a result, both WT4 and WT6 should be rejected, and with them the weak two-dimensionalist account of the necessary aposteriori and the contingent apriori.

Hybrid Views

Confronted with powerful objections to both strong and weak two-dimensionalism, ambitious two-dimensionalists might naturally wonder whether there might be some third version of their program which is immune to the problems of the other two. I don't believe there is. However, the matter is not easily resolved, since it is not clear what modifications of either strong or weak two-dimensionalism are possible without abandoning essential features of the approach. Fortunately, there is a place to begin. In chapter 9 I explained how David Chalmers, after seeming to champion strong two-dimensionalism in *The Conscious Mind*, adopts a position in "The Components of Content" that rejects both the strong two-dimensionalist analysis of propositional attitude ascriptions given by T5b and the weak two-dimensionalist analysis given by WT5b. In their place, he suggests a point of view that can be reconstructed as follows:

C1. Although both the primary and secondary propositions (intensions) associated with S are responsible for necessary conditions on the truth of *x believes that S*, neither provide sufficient conditions.

C2. In order for *x believes that S*, as used in a context C, to be true of an agent a in a circumstance of evaluation w, the secondary proposition (intension) associated with a's belief in w must be the same as that associated with S in C.

C3. The necessary condition on the truth of *x believes that S* supplied by the primary proposition (intension) associated with S is much weaker and vaguer. Nevertheless, there are cases in which the ascription is false of an agent a even though the secondary intension of a's belief in w matches that of S (in the context of ascription), just as there are cases in which the ascription is false, even though the primary intension of the agent's belief matches that of S.

C4. The ascription *x believes that S* is true with respect to an assignment A of values to variables, a context C, and a worldstate w iff in w, the individual a assigned to 'x' by A accepts some sentence or mental representation M which is such that (i) the secondary intension of M in a's context in w is identical with the secondary intension of S with respect to C and A, and (ii) the primary intension of M is "appropriately related" to the primary intension of S with respect to A.

There are several respects in which the resulting system is vague or underspecified. First, the "appropriate relationship" which must exist between the primary intension of S and the primary intension of the sentence or representation M accepted by the agent in order for *x believes that S* to be true of the agent is left vague and unspecified by Chalmers. As a result, no definite predictions are made about which substitutions within S that leave its secondary intension intact, while changing its primary intension, are semantically guaranteed to preserve the truth value of *x believes that S*, and which are not. It is compatible with the new view that most such substitutions are guaranteed to preserve truth value, or that few are. In its present form, the theory simply makes no predictions, positive or negative, about this. Second, it is not clear what range of propositional attitude verbs are to be given semantic analyses along the lines of C4—though we will assume that *know, know apriori,* and *know aposteriori* are among them. Third, we need to be told what the other theses of the new two-dimensionalist system are. In particular, we need to be told what the new account of the necessary aposteriori and the contingent apriori is to be. An essential prerequisite for doing this is to identify the things that are taken to fall into these categories. As we have seen, for the strong two-dimensionalist, instances of the necessary aposteriori and the contingent apriori are **sentences** (classified modally on the basis of their secondary intensions and epistemically on the basis of their primary intensions). For the weak two-dimensionalist, **propositions** (secondary intensions) are also classified as instances of the necessary aposteriori and the contingent apriori. However, this classification—spelled out in WT6—is possible only because propositions (secondary intensions) are taken by the weak two-dimensionalist to be the objects of propositional attitudes like belief and knowledge. Although much is unclear about C1–C4, one thing that is obvious is that if they are adopted, then the objects of the attitudes cannot be characterized in this way. This brings us to the fourth, and final, way in which C1–C4 are underspecified. As noted in chapter 9, neither the new theses nor Chalmers's own comments identify the objects of knowledge and belief, or explain the relational character of knowledge and belief predicates. This is necessary, not only to account for the full range of belief and knowledge ascriptions, but also to formulate a new ambitious two-dimensionalist account of the necessary aposteriori and the contingent apriori—distinct from those found in either strong two-dimensionalism or weak two-dimensionalism. For all these reasons, the rejection of T5b and WT5b, and their replacement by C1–C4, results not in a well-defined hybrid version of two-dimensionalism, but, at best, in an underspecified class of hybrid views the contents of which are not fully clear.

Presumably, however, some things are fixed. Names and natural kind terms must continue to be analyzed as rigidified descriptions, with distinct primary and secondary intensions. As a result, sentences containing these terms, as well as those containing ordinary indexicals, will be characterized as having distinct primary and secondary intensions. Moreover, the explanation of the necessary aposteriori and the contingent apriori must essentially involve the difference between primary and secondary intensions. More specifically, in order to retain the animating spirit of ambitious two-dimensionalism, the explanation of the necessary aposteriori must not require metaphysically impossible world-states that are epistemically possible (conceivable). Finally, the same argument that was used in connection with weak two-dimensionalism to show that names and natural kind cannot be *actually-*rigidified descriptions will carry over to the hybrid views considered here. Thus, a good place to begin examining these views is with the hypothesis that names and natural kind terms are synonymous with *dthat-*rigidified descriptions.

Of course, the argument given against WT4a still applies. Since this argument maintains that there is no descriptive, reference-fixing information semantically associated with names and natural kind terms in the first place, it is unaffected by issues that depend on the specific form of rigidification chosen by the ambitious two-dimensionalist. For this reason alone, the hybrid views should, I believe, be rejected. However, in the interest of strengthening the case, it is worth looking further. Suppose, then, for the sake of argument, that the rigidified description **dthat [the D]** is a candidate for the analysis of a name or natural kind term n. Then, the proposition expressed by (i.e., the secondary intension of) (19a) relative to a context C may be taken to be the same as the proposition expressed by (the secondary intension of) (19b) relative to C—which in turn will be the same as the proposition expressed by (the secondary intension of) (19c) relative to an assignment of the referent of n to 'x', and the proposition expressed by (the secondary intension of) (19d) relative to a context in which the referent of n is the agent. (Similar identifications hold in the case of more complex sentences.)

19a. n is F.

   b. dthat [the D] is F.

   c. x is F.

   d. I am F.

Next consider the attitude ascriptions in (20)—relative, in the case of (20c), to an assignment of the referent of n to 'x', and, in the case of (20d), to a context in which the referent of n is the agent.

20a. a knows/believes that n is F.

   b. a knows/believes that dthat [the D] is F.

   c. a knows/believes that x is F (relative to an assignment of the referent of n to 'x').

d. a knows/believes that I am F (relative to a context in which the referent of n is the agent).

Since, by hypothesis, the primary intensions of (19a) and (19b) are the same, the ascriptions (20a) and (20b) must agree in truth value. Since, as a matter of obvious empirical fact, (20c) and (20d) will be true whenever (20a) is true and n has a referent, the hybrid two-dimensionalist has no choice but to hold that the primary intensions of (19c) (relative to an assignment of the referent of n to 'x') and (19d) (relative to a context in which the referent of n is the agent) are "appropriately related" to the primary intensions of (19a,b) in the sense of C4.

This is almost enough to recreate for the hybridist a version of the same set of problems that undermined the weak two-dimensionalist's use of *dthat*-rigidified descriptions. The other needed piece of the puzzle is the view, shared by all ambitious two-dimensionalists, that apriori truths based on the primary intensions of names and natural kind terms are easy to come by—e.g., (21a) and (21b).

21a. Hesperus is visible in the evening (if anything is the brightest heavenly body seen in the evening sky at times t and places p).

b. Water is watery stuff.

For any such example *n is F (if anything is the . . .)*, the hybrid two-dimensionalist's characterization of (22a,b) as true will carry with it a commitment to the truth of (22c), relative to an assignment of the referent of n to 'x', and of (22d), relative to a context in which the referent of n is the agent.[29] (The description *the D* is taken to include the predication of F.)

22a. a knows apriori that n is F (if anything is the ...).

b. a knows apriori that dthat [the D] is F (if anything is the ...).

c. a knows apriori that x is F (if anything is the ...).

d. a knows apriori that I am F (if anything is the ...).

---

[29] The reason for this may be expressed abstractly as follows. If *a knows apriori that S* is true, then *a knows that S* is true and a's justification for this knowledge does not rely on empirical evidence. But since in these cases *a knows that R* follows from *a knows that S,* and since any justification for the knowledge reported by the latter is sufficient justification for the knowledge reported by the former, *a knows that R* is true and a's justification for this knowledge does not rely on empirical evidence. Thus, *a knows apriori that R* is true. See note 66 of chapter 9 for elaboration.

There are two problems with this result. First, whatever it is that is supposed to be known apriori in the case of (22c,d)—whether it be the complement clause, the secondary intension of the clause, or a "two-dimensional proposition" consisting of the primary and secondary intensions of the clause—need not either itself be necessary, or have a necessary primary intension. Thus, the connection between apriority and necessity of primary intension—so central to ambitious two-dimensionalism—seems to have been lost. Second, *de re* knowledge of the sort reported by (22c) and (22d) is **never** apriori. For example, one simply can't know apriori, of any object, that it is visible in the evening (if anything is the brightest heavenly body visible in the evening sky at times t and places p), or, of any kind, that instances of it are clear, potable, etc. As argued in chapter 4, such knowledge is always grounded in empirical knowledge derived, ultimately, from someone's acquaintance with the object or kind.[30] Hence—contra the ambitious two-dimensionalist—ascriptions along the lines of (22a,b) are (in the relevant cases) always false.

Failure to recognize this also infects the hybridist's account of the necessary aposteriori. If, as the hybridist supposes, Venus can be given a name n that grounds apriori knowledge that it **is** visible in the evening (if anything is the brightest heavenly body visible in the evening sky at times t and places p), then surely Mercury can be given a name m that grounds apriori knowledge that it is **not** visible in the evening (if anything is the heavenly body that is not visible in the evening but rather is . . .). But then, the primary intension of $n \neq m$ will be necessary, $n \neq m$ will be characterized as apriori, and (23a,b) will be counted as true. As before, this leads to classifying (23c) as true, relative to an assignment of Venus to 'x' and Mercury to 'y'.

23a. a knows apriori that n ≠ m.

   b. a knows apriori that dthat [the x: . . . x is visible in the evening . . .] ≠ dthat [the x: . . . x is not visible in the evening . . .]

   c. a knows apriori that x ≠ y.

---

[30] See the section "Reference-Fixing Descriptions and the Contingent Apriori." For further discussion, see chapter 16 of *The Age of Meaning*, as well as my "Knowledge of Manifest Natural Kinds."

However, this is incorrect, since it conflicts with the widely recognized fact that the nonidentity of the two objects is something which, though necessary, is knowable only **aposteriori**.

What we have here is a version of the same problem that was posed by (15) for weak two-dimensionalism. As before, the problem generalizes to many other instances of the necessary aposteriori. For example, corresponding to the problems posed by (17) and (18) for weak two-dimensionalism, we have the problems posed by (23) and (24) for the hybrid view.[31]

23a. Agent a knows apriori that Pappy is not made out of metal.

  b. Agent a knows apriori that dthat [the paperweight that I am pointing at which is made of wood and not metal] is not made out of metal.

  c. Agent a knows apriori that x is not made out of metal.

24a. Agent a knows apriori that molecules of water* have two hydrogen atoms and one oxygen atom.

  b. Agent a knows apriori that molecules of dthat [the watery stuff, which is H_2O] have two hydrogen atoms and one oxygen atom.

  c. Agent a knows apriori that molecules of k have two hydrogen atoms and one oxygen atom.

In considering these examples, suppose that the names *Pappy* and *water*—of my paperweight and the kind water—have been introduced with the meanings of the *dthat*-rigidified descriptions in the (b) sentences. Surely, if *Hesperus* and *water* can carry the descriptive meanings that ambitious two-dimensionalists imagine, then these new names can carry the meanings indicated. Similarly, if, as the two-dimensionalist contends, the fact that *Hesperus* and *water* have these meanings is enough to guarantee the apriority of (21a) and (21b), then, by parity of reasoning, (23a) and (24a) must be characterized as capable of being true. But if they are true, then there will be no blocking the characterization of (23c) and (24c) as true, relative to an assignment of my paperweight to the variable 'x', and the kind water to the variable 'k'. As before, these results are intolerable, since what we have here are examples of the necessary aposteriori—not the necessary apriori.

---

[31] As before, we interpret negation as taking wide scope.

The moral of the story is that ambitious two-dimensionalists of all stripes are wrong in claiming that examples like (21a) and (21b)—based on alleged descriptive meanings of natural kind terms—are instances of apriori truth. There are no such apriori truths. Rather, names and natural kind terms are used in sentences like these to express *de re* knowledge of individuals and kinds that is aposteriori, and ultimately grounded in acquaintance with these items. This fact leaves the ambitious two-dimensionalist with an unpalatable choice. The theorist must either give up the view that names and natural kind terms are *dthat*-rigidified descriptions—and with it the view that they have descriptive meanings at all—or admit that

25. If there is a unique thing which is D, then n is the D.

is **not** apriori, even when n is analyzed as **dthat [the D]**, and (25) expresses a truth in every context. To opt for the former course would be, in effect, to abandon ambitious two-dimensionalism altogether—since without descriptive meanings there is no distinction between the primary and secondary intensions of names and natural kind terms, and without this the entire ambitious two-dimensional treatment of Kripkean examples of the necessary aposteriori and the contingent apriori will evaporate. To avoid this, the theorist must, at the very least, break the connection between apriority and the necessity of primary intension by granting that the two come apart in cases like (25). Although this involves giving up a fundamental tenet of ambitious two-dimensionalism (the conjunction of the principle Apriori 1 and the right-to-left direction of Apriori 2 discussed in the penultimate section of chapter 9), I don't see how the theorist who wishes to salvage something from the view can avoid this.

However, the hybrid two-dimensionalist is still not out of the woods. In order to maintain the view that names and natural kind terms are synonymous with *dthat*-rigidified descriptions, the theorist must identify the kinds of descriptions that can play this role. Here it is important to recognize a certain fact about names that leads to an acquaintance constraint on descriptions **the D** which are such that **dthat [the D]** might qualify as candidates for giving the analysis of names.[32]

DE RE KNOWLEDGE OF REFERENCE

If there is an object o such that n designates o, and a speaker s understands n, then *x knows that 'n' designates n (if 'n'*

---

[32] A similar constraint holds for natural kind terms. I leave it open that a stronger version of these constraints, in which the parenthetical clauses are deleted, might also be justified.

designates anything at all) is true of s, as is ***There is an object o such that x knows that 'n' designates o (if 'n' designates anything at all).***

THE ACQUAINTANCE CONSTRAINT ON DESCRIPTIVE ANALYSES OF NAMES

If *dthat [the D]* is the analysis of n (which designates o), and s understands *dthat [the D]*, then ***x knows that 'dthat [the D]' designates dthat [the D] (if 'dthat [the D]' designates anything at all)*** is true of s, as is ***There is an object o such that x knows that 'dthat [the D]' designates o (if 'dthat [the D]' designates anything at all)***. Since to understand *dthat [the D]* is just to understand both the description *the D* and the operator *dthat*, and since understanding the operator doesn't play any role in being able to identify the object designated by the description, understanding *dthat [the D]* will be sufficient to know that it designates o (if it designates anything at all), only if understanding *the D* is sufficient to know that it designates o (if it designates anything at all). Thus, if *dthat [the D]* is the analysis of n (which designates o), and s understands *the D*, then ***There is an object o such that x knows that 'the D' designates o (if 'the D' designates anything at all)*** is true of s.

Descriptions satisfying this constraint are **not** common. As a result, the constraint severely restricts the range of possible descriptive analyses of names. Examples of descriptions that, arguably, do pass the test include those in (26).

26. the individual whom I believe to be my brother
    the object which I believe to be a paperweight on my desk
    the thing which is now looking to me to be a computer screen
    the pebble on the floor which I can feel with my left foot

In general, the descriptions satisfying the constraint are those that characterize the speaker as having some *de re* belief or other cognitive attitude toward the object designated by the description. Perhaps this characterization can be extended to include objects described in terms of the speaker's acquaintance with or causal connection to them, even if the descriptions don't explicitly mention *de re* attitudes—provided it is a (necessary) consequence of the satisfaction of the description that certain *de re* attitudes are had. These are descriptions the rigidifications of which are candidates for providing descriptive analyses of names.

The striking thing to notice about this is that what guarantees the *de re* attitudes is simply that the descriptions are satisfied, and so succeed in denoting something. Whether or not the speaker understands the descriptions, or accepts sentences containing them, is immaterial. What an anti–two-dimensionalist result this is! One of the central characteristics of all forms of ambitious two-dimensionalism is the view that *de re* belief, knowledge, and the like, about individuals or kinds, is to be explained as arising from the attitudes agents bear to indexical sentences, or mental representations, that express propositions directly involving those individuals or kinds. But now we see that this, apparently, can't always be so—since the very indexical sentences that the two-dimensionalist posits to provide this explanation (when names or natural kind terms are involved) are such that understanding and accepting them signals *de re* belief only if antecedently attained *de re* beliefs and other cognitive attitudes are presupposed. Since the two-dimensionalist appears to have no ready explanation of these beliefs and attitudes—some of which may themselves be instances of the necessary aposteriori—this problem (which is common to weak two-dimensionalism and the hybrid views alike) strikes at the heart of the program, and signals its demise.

Finally, a word needs to be said about attempts to appeal to primary intensions of names to resolve instances of Frege's puzzle. The attempt to resolve some instances of the puzzle by using descriptive information attributed to the referent of a name by uses of attitude ascriptions containing it is not unreasonable. However, in the vast majority of cases, the enormous variability of the information associated with names from one speaker to the next, and one conversational context to the next, militates against attempts to locate the puzzle-resolving information in the meanings of the names. There are, of course, a few rare examples—like the name *Superman* (used by Chalmers to motivate his appeal to primary intensions)—in which a case can be made for the inclusion of descriptive information in the meaning of the name. However, when this is so, I believe that the model of partially descriptive names presented in *Beyond Rigidity* works better than the model which takes names to be *dthat*-rigidified descriptions.[33] If descriptive information about superpowers really is included in the meaning of the name *Superman*, then, according to the *Beyond Rigidity* model, the name may be analyzed as semantically equivalent to the description *the x: x has superpowers & x = y*, relative to an assignment of the man Superman–Clark Kent to the variable 'y'. One virtue of the

---

[33] See chapter 5 of *Beyond Rigidity*.

model is that it explains the intuitive judgment that (27) has a reading in which it is true, in a way in which the rigidified description model does not.[34]

27. Since the individual who is actually Superman could have existed without having superpowers, he could have existed without being Superman.

Opinions may vary about whether intuitions like this are clear and strong enough to justify taking *Superman* to be partially descriptive. However, whatever conclusion one ultimately adopts about this example, the general point remains clear. Names like this—for which any reasonable case can be made that their names might include substantial descriptive information—are few and far between. Although it is not unreasonable to hold that (28) is true, a similar claim cannot be made for the overwhelming majority of linguistically simple proper names.

28. Necessarily anyone who believes that Superman exists believes that someone with superpowers exists.

For example, (29) is not true.

29. Necessarily anyone who believes that Aristotle existed believes that a philosopher existed.

We all know that Aristotle himself could have existed without being a philosopher; and surely if that had been so, people who knew Aristotle might well have believed that Aristotle existed without believing that any philosopher existed. From this it follows that being a philosopher is not part of the meaning of the name *Aristotle* in any way in which the attribution of that property constitutes a necessary condition on the truth of belief ascriptions *x believes that ... Aristotle ....* The same argument can be repeated for nearly all linguistically simple proper names n and contingent properties p of their referents.[35] In each such case, what the argument shows is that n is not partially descriptive in a way that involves the attribution of p, nor does n have a primary intension involving the attribution of p which affects the truth condi-

---

[34] See p. 121 of *Beyond Rigidity*. Note, on this analysis *Superman could have existed without having superpowers* has a wide-scope reading in which it is true, even though the proposition expressed by *Superman exists but does not have superpowers* is untrue in all possible circumstances.

[35] A linguistically simple name is one which contrasts with names like *Princeton University* and *New York City*, which, due to their syntactic complexity, are naturally analyzed as *the x: x is a university and x = y* and *the x: x is a city and x = y*, relative to appropriate assignments to 'y'.

tions of attitude ascriptions in the way envisioned by Chalmers's theses C1, C3, and C4.

I would say that this result straightforwardly falsified the conjunction of those theses with the analysis of linguistically simple names as *dthat*-rigidified descriptions, but for the fact that Chalmers adds, at one point, that the relation of "appropriateness" mentioned in C4— which is supposed to hold between the primary intension of S in *x believes that S* and the primary intension of the sentence or representation accepted by the agent—may vary from context to context. This wild card allows one the flexibility to include the property of being a philosopher in the primary intension of *Aristotle*, if one wishes, while ignoring it in a case like our example (29), where paying attention to that aspect of the primary intension would give the wrong result. However, I doubt that this is a strength of the theory.

It is not that I disagree with the idea that different descriptive enrichments are relevant in different contexts to the truth conditions of that which is asserted and conveyed by assertive utterances of an ascription *a believes that S*. On the contrary.[36] However, when one thinks about the wide variability that exists, the natural conclusion to reach is that it results from free, pragmatic enrichment of the semantic content of the attitude ascription uttered, rather than from the selection of stronger or weaker standards of appropriateness to a single, fixed, descriptive content (given by the primary intension). This point becomes all the more compelling when one realizes that for the defender of the hybrid version of ambitious two-dimensionalism, the primary intensions of names must be given by descriptions like those in (26). The salient feature of these descriptions is that they describe idiosyncratic relationships between the referent of a name and a speaker. Since there is no reason to think that agents to which such a speaker may wish to ascribe beliefs have any knowledge of this relationship, these descriptions are particularly poor candidates for constraining the truth conditions of the assertions made by utterances of belief ascriptions.

Conclusions

This completes my critique of ambitious two-dimensionalism. In the case of strong two-dimensionalism—which is, I think, the purest and

---

[36] See chapter 8 of *Beyond Rigidity*.

most coherent form of the view—I take the critique to be a refutation. The same is true of the critique of Stalnaker's pragmatic version of strong two-dimensionalism, discussed in chapter 5. In the case of weak two-dimensionalism, as well as the family of hybrid views, I take the objections to be very strong. The key issues involve the descriptive analyses of names and natural kind terms as rigidified descriptions, the semantics of knowledge and other attitude ascriptions, and the account of the necessary aposteriori and the contingent apriori. Regarding these, I believe I have established (i) that names and natural kind terms cannot be *actually*-rigidified descriptions, (ii) that there are very serious obstacles to taking them to be *dthat*-rigidified descriptions, or to having their reference semantically fixed by descriptions at all, (iii) that the claim that apriority is coextensive with having a primary intension that is true in all contexts cannot be maintained, (iv) that ambitious two-dimensionalist accounts of *de re* attitudes do not cover all instances of *de re* knowledge and belief, (v) that among the instances not covered may be genuine cases of the necessary aposteriori, and (vi) that the hybridist's appeal to primary intensions is not a promising way of dealing with Frege's puzzle. Along the way I have made some positive suggestions about how to deal with the problems that ambitious two-dimensionalism has tried, unsuccessfully, to solve. In the next and final chapter, I will bring these suggestions together to form an alternative positive picture, to assess where things stand, and to indicate the work that remains to be done.

PART FOUR

THE WAY FORWARD

CHAPTER 11

POSITIVE NONDESCRIPTIVISM

The subject under investigation, ambitious two-dimensionalism, has, in my view, been one of the most important philosophical developments in the past twenty-five years. It is the most concerted and systematic attempt among many to reinstate descriptivism in the philosophy of language, internalism in the philosophy of mind, and some version of conceptualism in our understanding of modality in the face of the challenges that rocked these positions more than thirty years ago. Having argued that ambitious two-dimensionalism has failed, I see its failure as a testament to the power of the original challenges— of Kripke, Putnam, Kaplan, and others—and to the lasting significance of their most central insights. Broadly speaking, the lessons of their works, and of the line of philosophical investigation that arose from them, were (i) that for many expressions, neither their semantic contents, nor the mechanisms that determine their reference, are wholly, or even predominantly, descriptive, (ii) that understanding these expressions cannot, in general, be equated with associating them with the right conceptual contents, in any sense in which qualitatively identical agents share such contents, (iii) that linguistic competence and language use have important social components that are neglected by traditional descriptive analyses, which have often been individualistic in their starting points, (iv) that linguistic meaning is not wholly transparent, as is shown by the fact that expressions with the same meaning can be understood by speakers who do not recognize this sameness of meaning, (v) that the contents of the assertions made, and the beliefs expressed, by assertive utterances of sentences are often partially determined by factors external to the agent, (vi) that *de re* propositional attitudes are ubiquitous, and cannot be exhaustively explained in terms of *de dicto* attitudes to descriptive (or metalinguistic) contents, (vii) that metaphysical possibility is distinct from, and significantly narrower than, epistemic possibility, and (viii) that the relationship between linguistic and conceptual analysis, on the one hand, and conclusions about what is metaphysically necessary or possible, on the other, is more indirect than most philosophers have heretofore realized.

The importance of these lessons and their ramifications for philosophy as a whole can hardly be overestimated. By contrast, the appeal of the two-dimensionalist attempt to revive descriptivism, and the initial plausibility of some of its leading doctrines, are indications of the persistence of traditional patterns of thinking, and of the difficulty of seeing our way clear to a new point of view. Even those of us who are critics of that attempted revival are still in the process of consolidating and articulating the new, nondescriptivist perspective. This should not be surprising. In previous chapters, I have argued that when we look back at the seminal anti-descriptivist discussions of Kripke and Kaplan we find, in addition to their startling breakthroughs, certain erroneous or misleading passages that suggest an incomplete, and at times faltering, grasp of the direction in which their most powerful insights were heading. We, who are following in their footsteps, have the job of sorting through all this, of identifying their occasional missteps, and of marking the path more clearly, so that the trail they blazed can be extended. The critique of ambitious two-dimensionalism is part of this process. In chapter 3, I noted that this attempt to revive descriptivism arose as a response to certain genuine puzzles and problems. If, as I have argued, ambitious two-dimensionalism is not the correct response to these difficulties, we need to figure out what is. With this in mind, I return to the central factors that motivated the view.

One source of motivation involved concerns about the necessary aposteriori arising from certain views about the nature of propositions and "possible worlds" (or possible world-states). Thinking of necessary truths as those that are true in all possible worlds (or world-states), those philosophers who identified propositions with sets of such worlds (or with functions from them to truth values) could recognize only one necessary proposition, which, of course, had to be regarded as knowable apriori. Confronted with Kripkean examples of the necessary aposteriori, they had little choice but to attempt to explain the examples by associating these sentences with pairs of propositions—one necessary and knowable apriori, the other contingent and knowable only aposteriori. As we have seen, this idea received different formulations, including Stalnaker's pragmatic version, as well as the more familiar semantic version that I have called *(very) strong two-dimensionalism*. Having chronicled the failure of these views in chapters 5 and 10, I take this result to reinforce the already plausible conclusion that the possible-worlds analysis of propositions on which it was based is incorrect. Propositions are not sets of "possible worlds" (or world-states), nor are they functions from such to truth values. Rather, they are structured complexes constructed out of the semantic contents of the constituents of sentences that express them. Far from being an unwelcome result that has been forced on us, this is a position for which there is abundant, independent evidence.[1]

Views about the nature of propositions were, of course, not the only, or perhaps even the chief, source of ambitious two-dimensionalist worries about the necessary aposteriori. In addition, there was the puzzle about how a proposition p that would be true no matter what possible state the world was in could be such that knowledge of p required empirical evidence about the way the world actually is. If p is true with respect to every possible world-state, then it would seem that the function of evidence cannot be to rule out world-states in which p is false. Given that the function of evidence is to rule out the falsity of something, the ambitious two-dimensionalist naturally concluded that evidence is needed to rule out the possibility that a certain proposition q, distinct from but related to p, is false. Ambitious two-dimensionalism emerged as a view according to which each sentence S that is an instance of the necessary aposteriori is associated with two propositions—one, its so-called secondary intension, which is necessary and relevant to modal claims in which S figures, and the other, its so-called primary intension, which is contingent, knowable only aposteriori, and relevant to knowledge ascriptions in which S is involved. As I have emphasized, the fundamental presupposition of this line of reasoning is that epistemic and metaphysical possibility are one and the same; there is only one kind of possible world-state, and what Kripkean examples of the necessary aposteriori show is that each of his sentences is associated with two propositions, which are evaluated differently with respect to the same space of such states.

The failure of ambitious two-dimensionalism points to the failure of this underlying presupposition. Epistemic and metaphysical possibility

---

[1] See Scott Soames, "Direct Reference, Propositional Attitudes, and Semantic Content," originally published in *Philosophical Topics* 15 (1987): 47–87; reprinted in N. Salmon and S. Soames (eds.), *Propositions and Attitudes* (Oxford: Oxford University Press, 1988); also "Semantics and Semantic Competence," *Philosophical Perspectives* 3: *Philosophy of Mind and Action Theory* (1989), pp. 575–96. For other criticism of the possible-worlds analysis of propositions and/or defenses of structured propositions, see Nathan Salmon, *Frege's Puzzle* (Cambridge MA: MIT Press, 1986), especially appendix C; Mark Richard, *Propositional Attitudes* (Cambridge: Cambridge University Press, 1990), especially chapter 1; and Jeff King, "Structured Propositions and Sentence Structure," *Journal of Philosophical Logic* 25 (1996): 495–521.

are **not** one and the same. Rather, there are states of the world that are metaphysically impossible while being epistemically possible—in the sense that we cannot know apriori that they do not obtain, or are not instantiated. The propositions expressed by instances of the necessary aposteriori are true in all metaphysically possible world-states, but false in certain epistemically possible states. The function of the empirical evidence needed for knowledge of these propositions is to rule out such states.

The attractiveness of this view is based on many factors, not least of which is an intuitively satisfying conception of what philosophers are fond of calling "possible worlds." On this view, "possible worlds," or, more properly, possible world-states, are not large concrete objects— alternate universes that exist in regions of reality temporally and spatially disconnected from our actual universe. Instead, they are properties that we can conceive the universe as having. Just as there are properties that ordinary objects could possibly have had, and other properties they couldn't possibly have had, so there are maximally complete properties that the universe could have had—**possible states of the world**—and other maximally complete properties that the universe could not have had—**impossible states of the world**. Just as some of the properties that objects couldn't have had are properties that one can conceive them as having, and which one cannot know apriori that they don't have, so some maximally complete properties that the universe could not have had (some impossible states of the world) are properties one can conceive it as having, and which one cannot know apriori that it doesn't have. The informativeness of aposteriori necessary truths results, in part, from the fact that learning them allows one to rule out certain impossible, but nevertheless conceivable, states of the world. These are the sorts of world-states that are ruled out by the empirical evidence required to know such truths.[2]

Although the conception of world-states as properties contributes substantially to this explanation of the necessary aposteriori, it does not, of course, dictate the explanation all by itself. As a result, it is possible to accept the conception, while rejecting the explanation— perhaps because the explanation brings with it what some philoso-

---

[2] By a conceivable state of the world I mean one which we cannot know apriori not to be instantiated. Ruling these out is only part of the story behind the informativeness of different necessary truths—as is shown by the fact that some necessary apriori truths, like Fermat's last theorem, may be informative, in the natural sense of providing us with new information we may not already know, even though such truths are true in all epistemically possible world-states.

phers may regard as excessive philosophical costs.[3] The best example of such a philosopher that I know of is Robert Stalnaker—who is as clear as anyone about the status of "possible worlds" as properties, but who nevertheless continues to recognize only metaphysically possible world-states, and even to identify propositions with sets of such states.[4] His most important reason for refusing to recognize epistemically possible world-states (in the sense defined here), over and above the metaphysically possible, stems from his desire to ground all intentionality—including all forms of belief and knowledge—in nonintentional, modal facts involving metaphysical possibility. Since he recognizes that admitting epistemically possible world-states—characterized in terms of what can, and what cannot, be known apriori—would threaten this project, he declines to do so.[5] As I see it, however, this reason is undermined by the facts (i) that Stalnaker's project requires the notoriously problematic identification of propositions with sets of metaphysically possible world-states, (ii) that, in addition to this, his attempted explication of the intentional in terms of the metaphysically possible fails for independent reasons,[6] (iii) that, as seen in chapter 5, his pragmatic two-dimensionalist model of discourse cannot account for straightforward uses of sentences that are instances of the necessary aposteriori, and (iv) that, as seen in chapter 10, the restriction of epistemic possibility to metaphysical possibility cannot be saved by resorting to semantic versions of ambitious two-dimensionalism. The proper response, in light of all this, is to view world-states as properties that can coherently (i.e., without apriori-detectible inconsistency) be attributed to the universe, and to recognize the distinction between epistemically possible and metaphysically possible states.

A related source of motivation for ambitious two-dimensionalism arose from concern over Kripke's proposed examples of the contingent apriori, including his famous case (1) of the standard meter.

1. One meter is the length of stick s, if s exists at t (and hence has a length).

---

[3] It may also be possible to reject the conception while embracing some variant of the explanation. See fns. 6 and 7 of chapter 9.

[4] See his "Possible Worlds," *Noûs* 10 (1976); 65–75 for his account of possible worlds as properties.

[5] See *Inquiry* (Cambridge, MA: MIT Press, 1984), chapter 1, pp. 24–25.

[6] See Jeff Speaks, *Three Views of Language and the Mind* (unpublished Princeton dissertation, 2003).

How can a sentence such as this—containing a name (or natural kind term) n—express something knowable apriori about the referent r of n, when the sentence is contingent, and predicates of r a property (like being the length of a certain stick) which we normally regard as something one can know an entity to possess only by appeal to empirical evidence? The answer is that it can't. Contrary to Kripke, no such sentences are instances of the contingent apriori—as I have argued, briefly in chapters 4, 6, and 10 above, and at greater length in chapter 16 of *The Age of Meaning*. Sentences containing names or natural kind terms express (Russellian) propositions about individuals or kinds. As a result, knowing these propositions involves having *de re* knowledge of these individuals or kinds, the justification of which is inevitably empirical and aposteriori.[7]

In reaching this conclusion, one must be careful to distinguish genuine apriori knowledge of p—which does not require any empirical justification—from (i) knowledge of p the justification for which one is guaranteed to possess by virtue of understanding some sentence S that expresses p, and (ii) knowledge that S expresses a truth (no matter what the context), in cases in which understanding S is sufficient to justify this metalinguistic knowledge. If there are sentences S that one can understand without knowing of any proposition p that S expresses p, then (ii) may be possible without (i). The important point, however, is that both (i) and (ii) are possible without apriori knowledge of p in cases in which S expresses p, and understanding S requires one to possess empirical information which is necessary and sufficient for justifying p.

Here, it is important to distinguish the role played by experience in allowing us to grasp, or entertain, certain propositions, and the role played by experience in providing empirical evidence that justifies us in believing those propositions to be true. Although propositions which are knowable apriori do not require us to possess empirical evidence to justify believing them, they may require certain experiences in order for us to be able to grasp them. For a certain interesting class of propositions p, the very experiences that allow us to grasp p also provide em-

---

[7] As Mark Kalderon has reminded me, there may be an exception to this generalization. Although a meter is an abstract unit of length, our *de re* knowledge of it that it is the length of a certain stick is clearly aposteriori. Thus (1) is aposteriori. In certain other cases, however, our *de re* knowledge of abstract objects—e.g., natural numbers—may not be based on empirical evidence, and so may count as apriori. If so, then some sentences containing names for these numbers may express Russellian propositions that can be known apriori.

pirical evidence that justifies believing p. Since these propositions cannot be known without such justifying evidence, they are not properly classified as apriori—even though the empirical evidence required is provided by the experience that enables us to entertain them.[8]

This point is illustrated by an example from chapter 4. Suppose I introduce the name *Φ-Saul* with the stipulation that its reference is to be semantically fixed by the description *the x: x is a philosopher and x = Saul Kripke*. Here, we may assume that to understand this description, and hence the new name it is used to introduce, one must understand its constituents, including the name *Saul Kripke*. Since understanding *Saul Kripke* requires knowing that it refers to an individual iff that individual is Saul Kripke, understanding *Φ-Saul* requires knowing that it refers to an individual iff that individual is both Saul Kripke and a philosopher. Hence, it is part of the meaning of the new name that it refers to a philosopher, if it refers to anything at all. However, the proposition semantically expressed by

2. Φ-Saul is a philosopher, if *Φ-Saul* has a referent.

is just a contingent singular proposition that says of the man, Saul Kripke, that if a certain name refers, then he is a philosopher. This proposition is **not** knowable apriori, even though the knowledge needed to understand (2), and thereby entertain the proposition it expresses, is sufficient for knowledge of that proposition.

The point can be strengthened if we adopt the plausible assumption that in order to understand any name n that refers to an individual o, one must know that which is expressed by *'n' refers to n*—which in turn requires one to have *de re* knowledge of o that n refers to it. On this assumption, understanding (3) requires knowing of Saul Kripke that he is a philosopher, and hence knowing of the proposition expressed by (3) that it is true.

3. Φ-Saul is a philosopher.

Clearly, this knowledge is not apriori, even if it is required in order to understand (3). Analogous points apply to sentences containing ordinary, nonartificial examples of names and natural kind terms. The salient lesson is that in order for a proposition p to be knowable apriori, it is not enough that there be some sentence S which both expresses p and is such that understanding S provides one with all the

---

[8] Thanks to Jim Pryor and Jeff Speaks, whose lead I follow here.

justification one needs to know p. Although such sentences and propositions do have an interesting epistemological status, and might properly be termed *analytic*, they are **not** instances of the apriori.

It is ironic that ambitious two-dimensionalists—whose treatment of the necessary aposteriori stands in sharp opposition to Kripke's deepest and most important insights about the necessary aposteriori—were so ready to accept his flawed characterization of examples like that of the standard meter as the starting point for their discussion of the contingent apriori. It was this, as much as anything else, that started them down the wrong path. Evidence of this contention can be found in one of the most important founding documents of ambitious two-dimensionalism, Gareth Evans's "Reference and Contingency."[9] The focus of this article is on alleged instances of the contingent apriori involving so-called *descriptive names*, like Kripke's *one meter*, and Evans's own *Julius*—which Evans introduces with the reference-fixing stipulation that it is to refer to whoever invented the zipper (in the absence of any knowledge of who that might be). Following reasoning analogous to Kripke's in the standard meter case, Evans concludes that (4) is an example of the contingent apriori.

4. Julius invented the zipper, if anyone did.

It is, of course, puzzling how this could be. As Evans recognizes, if knowing that which is expressed by (4) involves knowing of the referent of *Julius* that he invented the zipper, if anyone did, then this knowledge **cannot** be apriori. Moreover, knowing that which is expressed by (4) will involve knowing this, if what (4) expresses is **simply** the Russellian proposition p expressed by *x invented the zipper, if anyone did* relative to an assignment of the referent of *Julius* to *x* (or any descriptive enrichment of p which incorporates p). However, although Evans thinks that p is one of the propositions associated with (4), he believes that (4) **also** expresses the general proposition (not his word) that the inventor of the zipper invented the zipper, if anyone did. Whereas the Russellian proposition is supposed to be the argument contributed by (4) when embedded under a modal operator like *it is a necessary truth that*, the general descriptive proposition is supposed to be the argument supplied by (4) when it is the complement of an attitude verb like *assert, know,* and *believe*. Here we have an early route to strong two dimensionalism, via the contingent apriori.

---

[9] Gareth Evans, "Reference and Contingency," *The Monist* 62 (1979): 161–89.

In the very next year after the publication of "Reference and Contingency," Davies and Humberstone, using Evans as their starting point, extended that route in their highly influential article, "Two Notions of Necessity."[10] As with Evans, the central application of their ambitious two-dimensionalist ideas was to alleged instances of the contingent apriori involving either the actuality operator, or "descriptive names" (which they analyzed in terms of the actuality operator). As explained in chapter 6, they cautiously extended the ambitious two-dimensionalist explanation to instances of the necessary aposteriori involving natural kind terms. However, they also expressed well-founded doubts about this extension; and where ordinary (nondescriptive) proper names were concerned, they were creditably agnostic. Nevertheless, the die was cast, and ambitious two-dimensionalism was off and running.

Having seen the failure of this program, we are now in a position to look back on its history and pinpoint where things went wrong. As I see it, an important initial misstep was the failure to recognize that for any genuine name or natural kind term n whatsoever, knowledge of that which is expressed by sentences containing n (and reported by ascriptions *A knows that ... n ...*) is *de re* knowledge of the referent of n. Once this is recognized, there is a clear route to the conclusion that Kripkean instances of the contingent apriori involving names or natural kind terms do not exist.[11] Things are different when the actuality operator is involved. Here, Evans, Davies, and Humberstone were on the right track. However, they seem not to have realized that no ambitious two-dimensionalist explanation is needed for these genuine instances of the contingent apriori. When S is contingent, the proposition expressed by *If S, then actually S* (relative to a context in which @ is the designated world-state) is both contingent and knowable by agents (in @) by virtue of reasoning starting from the related necessary apriori proposition expressed by *If S, then S*.[12]

With this worries about the necessary aposteriori and the contingent apriori may be put aside. What about the other major factors motivating ambitious two-dimensionalism? One such factor was the conviction, shared by many descriptivists, that although Kripke's anti-

---

[10] Martin Davies and Lloyd Humberstone, "Two Notions of Necessity," *Philosophical Studies* 38 (1980): 1–30. It is interesting to note that Evans refers to Davies and Humberstone in the final footnote of "Reference and Contingency," where he credits them with drawing out further consequences of his strong two-dimensionalist idea—including, apparently, its application to the necessary aposteriori.

[11] See chapters 4, 6, and 10 above, plus *The Age of Meaning*, chapter 16.

[12] This is explained in chapter 6 above.

descriptivist arguments were powerful objections to traditional versions of descriptivism that associated names and natural kind terms with descriptions of their referents' famous deeds and most salient characteristics, new versions of descriptivism focusing on different descriptions could be found that avoided those arguments. As noted, rigidified descriptions were used to avoid the modal argument, and "causal-historical," metalinguistic descriptions were invoked to avoid Kripke's semantic arguments—while the association of different descriptions with different coreferential names was sometimes thought to be enough to solve Frege's puzzle. However, the conviction that Kripke's arguments can be so easily avoided proved to be mistaken. Not only are the individual arguments stronger and more naturally extendable than descriptivists sometimes realized, but they form a unit—each eliminates some descriptive analyses, and the effort to avoid one argument often drives the descriptivist to analyses that run afoul of the others.

For example, chapter 10 showed that although rigidified descriptions can be used to avoid Kripke's original modal argument, analyses involving the rigidifier *actually* result in insurmountable problems regarding the contribution of names and natural kind terms to the truth conditions of propositional attitude ascriptions. To make matters worse, analyses involving the rigidifier *dthat* were shown to lead to problems of their own. One such problem stemmed from the contrast between (i) the fact that understanding a name n that refers to o involves *de re* knowledge of o that n refers to it and (ii) the fact that understanding a rigidified description *dthat [the D]* that designates o involves *de re* knowledge of o that the rigidified description designates it, **only if** understanding the unrigidified description **the D** requires this. Since very few unrigidified descriptions satisfy this condition, very few *dthat*-rigidified descriptions are available as candidates for analyzing names. Moreover, those that are tend to be highly speaker- and utterance-relative, and to take for granted the kind of *de re* knowledge that acceptance of sentences containing *dthat*-rigidified descriptions is often invoked to explain. For this reason, such descriptions are not plausible candidates for giving the meanings of names (or natural kind terms) in the common language shared by speakers.

Regarding the descriptions to be rigidified, it should have been obvious from the beginning that the idea that a word like *marmot* **means the same** as some rigidified version of the description *the kind of thing that I use 'marmot' to refer to, the kind of thing that others in my community use 'marmot' to refer to,* or *the causal source of my utterance of 'mar-*

mot' in this conversation was not going to work. (The first two descriptions threaten either to be circular, or to presuppose some antecedent reference-fixing mechanism, while the third is both fallible and idiosyncratic.) This appeal to metalinguistic descriptions was, of course, intended to piggyback on Kripke's discussion of causal-historical chains of reference transmission. As such, it reflected the descriptivists' conviction that—since meaning **must** in the end be descriptive—Kripke's own methodology must itself be covertly descriptive, and, hence, capable of being turned against him. In chapters 8, 9, and 10, I argued that this is a mistake. Kripke's use of scenarios in which we can judge that a name, or kind term, refers to something other than that which is predicted by some specific descriptive analysis **does not** presuppose that we have the ability to correctly determine the reference of our terms in all possible contexts (by virtue of tacitly associating them with descriptions that really do determine their reference). From a nondescriptivist perspective, there is no reason to suppose that competent speakers have any such all-purpose, noncircular, reference-fixing beliefs and intentions.

In addition, it is crucial not to confuse (i) descriptions of the facts which explain how our terms originally acquired, and continue to retain, their meanings and referents with (ii) descriptive theories of the linguistic meanings, and reference-fixing conditions, mastered by competent speakers. If I am right, much recent discussion of chains of reference transmission, "causal descriptivism," and "deferred reference" (i.e., resolving to let one's own reference depend on that of relevant others) displays this sort of confusion. The study of language is **not** the study of the fortuitous coordination of private idiolects (each governed by the descriptive, constitutive intentions of a single speaker), with its own semantics and reference-fixing mechanisms. Rather, it is the study of a commonly shared social institution that is used in slightly different ways by different speakers. Although this social perspective is, in my opinion, part and parcel of the anti-descriptivist revolution initiated by Kripke, Putnam, and others, it may also be the part that is least developed, and least well understood. As such, it is one of the most important areas in which further work is needed to extend and deepen our understanding of the nondescriptivist perspective.[13]

---

[13] In this connection, see chapter 3 of *Beyond Rigidity*, as well as my "Naming and Asserting," in Zoltan Szabo (ed.), *Semantics vs. Pragmatics* (New York and Oxford: Oxford University Press, 2004). In addition, a systematic presentation of the public language perspective, and a discussion of its advantages over more individualistic points of view, is given in Jonathan McKeown-Green, *The Primacy of Public Language*.

The last major factor motivating ambitious two-dimensionalism was the conviction, shared by descriptivists of all stripes, that Frege's puzzle and Russell's problem of negative existentials decisively refute nondescriptivist theories. Here, it must be admitted that these problems remain serious, and that no firm consensus exists among nondescriptivists regarding their proper resolution. Nevertheless, two points stand out. First, the view that problematic instances of substitution failure demonstrate the falsity of nondescriptivist theories of the meanings of names and natural kind terms is **not** supported by an examination of all relevant data. Second, a great deal of progress on these problems has been made by contemporary Millians, and other nondescriptivists.

Let us begin with Frege's puzzle about substitution. There are several things to be noted. First, some standard examples of substitution failure—e.g., those involving *Superman/Clark Kent* (as used in the story) and *Hesperus/Phosphorus* (as used by philosophers)—are quite unusual. The idea that, unlike most linguistically simple names, these special names are associated with definite and substantial descriptive content that speakers must grasp, if they are to qualify as understanding them, has some plausibility. Perhaps one who doesn't know that *Superman* is a name of someone with superpowers doesn't understand the word; and perhaps someone who believes that *Hesperus* is a name for Venus when seen in the morning, while *Phosphorus* is a name for Venus when seen in the evening, is linguistically confused. It does not seem to be beyond the realm of possibility that these names might turn out to be what I called, in *Beyond Rigidity, partially descriptive*. Since the semantic contents of names of this sort include both their referents and certain conventionally associated descriptive information, substitutions involving them may affect what is asserted and conveyed by utterances of sentences containing them—including utterances of attitude ascriptions.

Ordinary names like *Ruth Marcus* are different. Although different speakers who are familiar with the name can be expected to associate some descriptive information or other with it, little, if any, of this information is shared by all competent users of it. Hence, the name has little or no descriptive meaning in the common language of those who employ it. This does not mean that substitution of *Ruth Barcan* for *Ruth Marcus* **never** changes what is asserted or conveyed by utterances of simple sentences or attitude ascriptions. **Sometimes**, it seems to me, it does. However, the explanation of this is, arguably, different than it is in the case of partially descriptive names. Here, if descriptive information is involved, it is more naturally regarded as a pragmatic enrich-

ment of the semantically determined content, and, hence, as something which varies from speaker to speaker, and context to context. If
these factors explain apparent instances of substitution failure, then
such instances do **not** falsify semantically nondescriptive analyses of
linguistically simple names.[14]

The second point to notice about Frege's puzzle is that some substitutions in attitude ascriptions **are** guaranteed to preserve truth
value. Among the clearest examples are those involving variables of
quantification. For example, since the planet Hesperus is in fact the
planet Phosphorus, the truth of (5a) guarantees the truth of (5b).

5a. The ancients believed, when they saw Phosphorus in the
morning, that Phosphorus was visible only in the morning,
while also believing, when they saw Hesperus in the evening,
that Hesperus was visible only in the evening.

b. There is a planet which is such that the ancients believed,
when they saw it in the morning, that **it** was visible only in
the morning, while also believing, when they saw it in the
evening, that **it** was visible only in the evening.

In this instance of **substitution success**, replacing *Hesperus* and *Phosphorus* in the belief clauses in (5a) with the variable *it* (taken relative to an assignment of Venus as value) is guaranteed (by the identity of Hesperus
with Phosphorus with Venus) to preserve truth value. Nevertheless, according to the descriptivist, these belief clauses report different propositions believed, since (i) the descriptive contents of the names are taken to
be different from the nondescriptive content of the variable (relative to
the assignment of Venus as value) and (ii) the descriptive propositions expressed by the clauses of the belief ascriptions in (5a) are different from
those expressed by the corresponding clauses in which the names are replaced by the variable (which is understood relative to the assignment of
Venus as value). Given this, the descriptivist must admit that it is **not** a
sufficient condition for (6a) and (6b) to be capable of differing in truth
value that the α and β have different contents, or that the complement
clauses in these ascriptions express different propositions.[15]

[14] See chapter 3 of *Beyond Rigidity*.

[15] The argument here is meant to present a prima facie problem for descriptivism (rather
than an attempted refutation considering all the different possible descriptivist responses).
Among other things, the argument makes the natural assumption that in English quantification into attitude ascriptions is to be understood in the same way as quantification into other
constructions.

6a. A believes that Fα.

  b. A believes that Fβ.

What, then, according to the descriptivist, does determine when substitution of β for α in (6) guarantees preservation of truth value and when it doesn't? In particular, why is it that when α is a name and β is a variable (taken relative to an assignment of the referent of α as value), preservation of truth value is guaranteed, whereas often—as in (7)—when α is a description that denotes an individual i, and β is a variable (taken relative to an assignment of i as value), substitution is **not** guaranteed to preserve truth value?

7a. Ralph believes that the shortest spy is a spy.

  b. There is someone such that Ralph believes that that person is a spy.

All too often, descriptivists don't answer these questions.

By contrast, the case of substitution success in (5) is easily explained by nondescriptive analyses of names that either identify the semantic content of a name with its referent, or at least include it in the content. Moreover, once the referent of a name is included in the content, it becomes very difficult to include very much substantive descriptive information along with it.[16] For example, when P is a nonessential property of the referent o of n, o may exist without being P, and we typically think that *n is F* may be true in such a situation, when F expresses a property that o has which is unrelated to P. Let w be a world-state with respect to which this is so. When F expresses a property (unrelated to P) which o has in w (without having P), ascriptions of the form

8. In w, agents truly believe that n is F.

are typically, and intuitively, judged as capable of being true. This would be problematic if P were part of the semantic content of n, and the truth of *A believes that n is F* required the individual designated by A to attribute P to the referent of n. But if all nonessential properties of individuals are excluded from being parts of the semantic contents of ordinary names of those individuals, descriptivists are threatened with a paucity of raw materials needed for their analysis. In this way, instances of substitution success—the mirror images of the usual

---

[16] See *Beyond Rigidity*, pp. 121–24.

POSITIVE NONDESCRIPTIVISM 343

illustrations of Frege's puzzle—make problems for descriptivism, and provide prima facie arguments for nondescriptivism.[17]

The same can be said for analogous instances of substitution success involving indexicals. For example, if Venus could talk, she could truly report the beliefs of the ancients by assertively uttering (5c), the truth of which (relative to a context with Venus as agent) is guaranteed by the truth of (5a).

> 5c. The ancients believed, when they saw me in the morning, that I was visible only in the morning, while also believing, when they saw me in the evening, that I was visible only in the evening.

Just as the semantic content of a variable (relative to an assignment) is its referent (relative to the assignment), so there is good reason to believe that the semantic content of an indexical is its referent (relative to the context). The case is strengthened by the observation that utterances of the sentences in (9) seem to express the same proposition in their respective contexts, provided that the indexicals they contain refer to the same individual in those contexts.

> 9a. I am a philosopher.
>
> b. You are a philosopher.
>
> c. He is a philosopher.

Because of this, we are inclined to assign the same truth conditions to the attitude ascriptions in (10) (relative to their respective contexts).

> 10a. Martha believes that I am a philosopher (said by x).
>
> b. Martha believes that you are a philosopher (said to x).
>
> c. Martha believes that he is a philosopher (said demonstrating x).

These examples illustrate one of the primary functions of indexicals—namely, to allow one to say the same thing (express the same proposition) from different points of view. All of this falls into place if the semantic contents of indexicals are their referents, and belief ascriptions containing them in content clauses report the singular, Russellian propositions believed by the subjects of those ascriptions. (Ditto for

---

[17] For a variant of the argument, applied to a version of the proposal that names are partially descriptive, see *Beyond Rigidity*, pp. 124–29.

belief ascriptions containing variables in their content clauses that are bound from the outside.)

Although the case for a similar conclusion involving names may not be quite as compelling, many of the same points can be made about them. First, we commonly suppose that sentences containing different but coreferential names may express the same propositions. For example, if someone speaking German utters a sentence containing the name *Deutschland*, we commonly suppose that we can use the name *Germany* to report the proposition he expressed. We are confident we can do this without inquiring into whether the descriptive information he associates with *Deutschland* matches the descriptive information we associate with *Germany*. Second, it is a commonplace that two people who utter the sentence

11. Bill Clinton is a former President of the United States.

may say the same thing—express the same proposition—even if they have sharply contrasting views of Clinton, and associate very different descriptive contents with his name. These two points seem to indicate that the particular descriptive information associated with a name by a speaker is **not** invariably part of the proposition the speaker expresses when using a sentence containing the name. Third, beliefs expressed by agents using indexicals can often be reported by third parties using an ascription in which a name is substituted for the indexical. For example, if Martha expressed her belief by assertively uttering (9c) while referring to Kripke, her belief could often be reported using (10d).

10d. Martha believes that Kripke is a philosopher.

Such a report would typically be regarded as correct, even if Martha did not know the name of the man to whom she referred.

All of this lends credence to nondescriptivist analyses of names and related expressions. Though not as easy to come by, there even seem to be cases in which examples involving proper names can be constructed that parallel (5b) and (5c) (which involved variables and indexicals). Imagine a situation in which one is speaking to an audience that is familiar with the name *Venus* but has never heard of the names *Hesperus* and *Phosphorus*. In such a situation, it seems that one might intelligibly and correctly report the beliefs of the ancients using the ascription (5d).

5d. The ancients believed, when they saw Venus in the morning, that Venus was visible only in the morning, while also believing, when they saw Venus in the evening, that Venus was visible only in the evening (though, of course, they wouldn't have put it that way—since they didn't use the name 'Venus', but instead referred to the planet using different expressions or demonstrations, morning and evening).

Such examples lend some weight to the view (i) that names belong together with variables and indexicals in contributing only their referents to the propositions semantically expressed by sentences containing them and (ii) that attitude ascriptions containing them in their content clauses report the attitudes of agents to singular, Russellian propositions about their referents.

That said, these remarks need to be qualified. The point here is **not** that these considerations, by themselves, refute all descriptive analyses of names and related expressions, and establish the correctness of a thoroughgoing nondescriptivism in which the semantic contents of all, or nearly all, linguistically simple names, natural kind terms, indexicals (relative to contexts), and variables (relative to assignments of values) are identified with the things they designate. They don't. But neither do cases of apparent substitution failure establish the global correctness of descriptivism, and the global falsehood of nondescriptivism. If I am right, the supposition that they do is based on a skewed and incomplete appreciation of the relevant facts. When one looks at **all** the data involving attitude ascriptions—including both cases of apparent substitution success and cases of apparent substitution failure—one finds that there is as much intuitive support for fundamentally nondescriptive approaches as there is for descriptive treatments. One simply can't read off the correct semantic analysis of names, indexicals, natural kind terms, and attitude ascriptions from the totality of data relevant to discussions of Frege's puzzle. Instead, one needs to construct theoretical explanations which, though unobvious initially, may ultimately provide a satisfying account of the whole mass of contextually variable, difficult-to-reconcile, and sometimes conflicting, data of this sort. The critique of ambitious two-dimensionalism in the previous chapters suggests that it cannot provide the needed answers. Thus, it is reasonable to look elsewhere.

Here, it is important to remember how daunting the task that faces the philosophically motivated descriptivist really is. Often, these theorists have linked their belief in descriptivism to a variety of overarching philosophical causes—including internalist theories of belief, conceptualist accounts of modality, the identification of metaphysical and epistemic possibility, and the analysis of propositions as sets of possible world-states. Since the threat posed by nondescriptivism to these causes would remain even if only some (possible) singular terms were nondescriptive, the data associated with Frege's puzzle is clearly not up to the task of establishing what a thoroughgoing descriptivist requires.[18] When one looks at instances of Mates's puzzle, in which apparent instances of substitution failure in attitude ascriptions can be generated even when obvious synonyms are involved—e.g., *catsup* and *ketchup*, and *fortnight* and *period of fourteen days*—it is clear that despite the theoretical challenge posed by Frege's problematic substitutions, they neither refute Millian nondescriptivism nor establish descriptivism.[19]

In my opinion, the nondescriptive, Millian approach is the most promising. The two problems I have mentioned—Frege's puzzle and Russell's problem of negative existentials—have received considerable attention in recent years from Millians and other nondescriptivists. Though this is not the place to explore this work in detail, I will mention the leading approaches and indicate the developments I find most significant. First, Frege's puzzle. Approaches to the problem that include the referent of an ordinary, linguistically simple name in its semantic content, while eschewing additional reference-fixing content or character, have been advocated recently by me, Nathan Salmon, David Braun, Mark Richard, Michael Thau, Mark Crimmins, and others. Four main strategies have been pursued.

The first, best exemplified by Salmon's *Frege's Puzzle*, holds that belief is a relation between agents and propositions that is mediated in some way by sentences or mental representations.[20] To believe a propo-

[18] See my "Direct Reference, Propositional Attitudes, and Semantic Content."

[19] See Benson Mates, "Synonymity," originally published in 1950, reprinted in Leonard Linsky (ed.), *Semantics and the Philosophy of Language* (Urbana, Chicago, and London: University of Illinois Press, 1952); Alonzo Church, "Intensional Isomorphism and Identity of Belief," *Philosophical Studies* 5 (1954): 65–73; Nathan Salmon, *Frege's Puzzle*, and "A Millian Heir Rejects the Wages of *Sinn*," in C. A. Anderson and J. Owens (eds.), *Propositional Attitudes: The Role of Content in Logic, Language, and Mind* (Stanford, CA: CSLI, 1990); my "Substitutivity," in Judith J. Thomson (ed.), *On Being and Saying: Essays for Richard Cartwright* (Cambridge, MA: MIT Press, 1987); and the introduction to Nathan Salmon and Scott Soames (eds.), *Propositions and Attitudes* (Oxford: Oxford University Press, 1988).

[20] Salmon calls these mediating entities "guises" and is noncommittal about their nature. My use of sentences and mental representations in characterizing them is a simplification, intended to skirt complications.

sition is, roughly, to understand and accept a sentence or representation that expresses it. Thus, *x believes that S* expresses in a context C something true of an agent i iff there is some sentence or representation that i understands and accepts and that expresses for i the proposition expressed by S in C. Although there is no requirement that the sentence or representation accepted by i be the same, or similar to, the sentence S used in the belief ascription, speakers sometimes take assertive utterances of such ascriptions to carry this implication. For this reason, they sometimes wrongly judge assertive utterances of examples like (12a) and (12b) (which differ only in the substitution of coreferential names) to say different things, and have different truth values.[21]

12a. Ralph believes that Carl Hempel lived on Lake Lane.

  b. Ralph believes that Peter Hempel lived on Lake Lane.

The second strategy for dealing with belief ascriptions, best represented by Mark Richard's *Propositional Attitudes*,[22] takes the thing believed to be a linguistically enhanced proposition p, which is a sort of fusion of a sentence (or mental representation) and the (Russellian) proposition it expresses. On this account, a belief ascription *x believes that S*, used in a context C, is true of an agent i iff i accepts a linguistically enhanced proposition that is similar enough to the one expressed by S in C to count as a match (where standards of similarity vary from one context to another). On this account, (12a) and (12b) mean different things and may have different truth values, despite the fact that names do not have descriptive contents.[23]

This is also true of the third strategy for dealing with belief ascriptions, advocated by Mark Crimmins in *Talk about Beliefs*.[24] According

[21] See also David Braun, "Understanding Belief Reports," *Philosophical Review* 107 (1998): 555–95, and "Cognitive Significance, Attitude Ascriptions, and Ways of Believing Propositions," *Philosophical Studies* 108 (2002): 65–81.

[22] Mark Richard, *Propositional Attitudes* (Cambridge: Cambridge University Press, 1990).

[23] Richard's approach is discussed at length in chapter 7 of *Beyond Rigidity*. Another significant theory of belief ascriptions according to which the very expressions used to express beliefs are part of the things believed is given by Richard Larson and Peter Ludlow in "Interpreted Logical Forms," *Synthese* 95 (1993). Their view is also discussed in chapter 7 of *Beyond Rigidity*, and in my "Truth and Meaning: The Role of Truth in the Semantics of Propositional Attitudes," in K. Korta and J. M. Larrazabal (eds.), *Truth, Rationality, Cognition, and Music: Proceedings of the Seventh International Colloquium on Cognitive Science* (Dordrecht: Kluwer, 2003).

[24] Mark Crimmins, *Talk about Belief* (Cambridge, MA: MIT Press, 1992). See also Mark Crimmins and John Perry, "The Prince and the Phone Booth: Reporting Puzzling Beliefs," *Journal of Philosophy* 86 (1989): 685–711.

to this view, the propositions semantically expressed by belief ascriptions in a context C contain unarticulated constituents, contributed by C, which are not part of the semantic content of any expression in the ascription itself. These "unarticulated constituents" are either the ideas in the believer's mind that express the propositions believed, or properties of those ideas. The thought behind this view is that an utterance of a belief ascription reports not only the proposition the agent believes, but the ideas, or kinds of ideas, in virtue of which he believes it. As with the second strategy, although names lack descriptive contents, attitude ascriptions that differ only in the substitution of coreferential names may semantically express different propositions, with different truth values, in a context.[25]

The final strategy for dealing with Frege's puzzle is one I develop in chapters 3, 5, and 8 of *Beyond Rigidity*.[26] Its key ideas are (i) that because of contextually shared background assumptions in a context, a speaker who assertively utters a sentence often asserts more than one proposition, (ii) that the meaning of a nonindexical sentence in a language—the proposition it semantically expresses—is (roughly) that which would be asserted in virtually any normal context involving competent speakers and hearers, and (iii) that although an unambiguous nonindexical sentence S semantically expresses the same proposition in different contexts, speakers who utter S in different contexts may (because of the presence of different contextually shared presuppositions) assert different propositions. When one applies these ideas to a linguistically simple name n, one gets the result that the proposition semantically expressed by *n is F* is the bare singular proposition that simply predicates the property expressed by F of the referent o of n. However, assertive utterances of this sentence may result in the assertion not only of this proposition, but also of propositions that include additional descriptive information. In many contexts, an agent who assertively utters *n is F* asserts the descriptively enriched proposition expressed by *The x: [Dx and x = y] is F*, with respect to an assignment of the referent o of n to 'y', where D is a predicate contextually associated with n by speaker and hearers. Since speakers in a context

[25] For a criticism of this approach see Jennifer Saul, "Still an Attitude Problem," *Linguistics and Philosophy* 16, 4 (1993).

[26] This strategy is extended and modified in my "Naming and Asserting," in Zoltan Szabo (ed.), *Semantics vs. Pragmatics* (New York and Oxford: Oxford University Press, 2004). An approach which is somewhat similar in spirit, though different regarding many significant details, is developed by Michael Thau in *Consciousness and Cognition* (Oxford and New York: Oxford University Press, 2002).

may associate different descriptive predicates with different coreferential names *Carl Hempel* and *Peter Hempel*, assertive utterances of **Carl Hempel is F** and **Peter Hempel is F** in the same context may result in the assertion of different propositions, despite the fact that the two sentences mean the same thing. In addition, when p is a descriptively enriched proposition asserted by an agent A who utters **n is F**, one can often correctly report A's assertion of p by saying **A asserted that n is F**. The proposition semantically expressed by this attitude ascription relates A to the bare singular proposition that o "is F." However, assertively uttering the attitude ascription in suitable contexts may result in the assertion not only of this proposition, but also of the proposition that A asserted (the descriptively enriched) p. As a result, substitution of coreferential, ordinary, proper names sometimes changes the truth value of the assertions made by utterances of attitude ascriptions, even though it doesn't change the propositions they semantically express. A similar point holds for belief ascriptions like (12a,b).[27]

This completes my brief survey of attempts to solve Frege's puzzle in frameworks that assign nondescriptive contents and characters to proper names (and natural kind terms). Although I haven't been able to present any of these attempts in detail, there is, I think, reason for optimism that a semantically nondescriptive solution incorporating elements of these approaches will be found. If this is right, then the puzzle need not be seen as posing an insurmountable obstacle to nondescriptive analyses of names and natural kind terms.[28]

Finally, we return to Russell's problem of negative existentials. Let n be a name such as *Socrates, Sherlock Holmes,* or *Santa Claus,* for which the associated negative existential, **n doesn't exist**, could naturally be used to express a truth. Since the negative existential sentences corresponding to these names would normally be taken to be true, many

---

[27] This account is challenged by David Braun and Ted Sider, "Kripke's Revenge," in a symposium on *Beyond Rigidity* in *Philosophical Studies* forthcoming. The symposium contains my reply.

[28] It is worth noting that analyses of names that posit thoroughly descriptive contents or characters of names have their own problems with propositional attitude ascriptions in general, and Frege's puzzle in particular. For example, a theory which holds that the meaning of n for a speaker s is the description s associates with n, may be hard pressed to explain the ability of one person who says **they both said that n is F** to correctly report the assertions of two people, both of whom have uttered **n is F**. Since, according to this theory, all three speakers may associate different descriptive contents with n, it is hard to see how the theory can explain our confidence in such reports. For further problems for descriptive theories, see Nathan Salmon, *Frege's Puzzle.*

philosophers would maintain that the names lack referents. But then, on Millian accounts, which treat names as directly referential, it might seem that both the names and the sentences containing them lack semantic contents. To say that the negative existentials lack semantic contents is to say that they fail to semantically express propositions, and so are meaningless. How, then, can they be used to assert truths? This is the problem posed by "empty names" for nondescriptive theories that identify the semantic content of a name with its referent.

There are two reasons to think this problem is not insuperable. First, most "empty names" are not really empty; they turn out to have referents of certain sorts after all. Second, the propositions asserted, and the beliefs expressed, by an utterance of a sentence containing an "empty name" are not limited to those semantically expressed by the sentence uttered. The second of these points is merely an application to empty names of a general point that the propositions asserted by an utterance of a sentence often go well beyond the proposition it semantically expresses. The first point, about the real referents of "empty names", needs more explanation.[29] Consider first the name *Socrates*. As it is generally agreed, *Socrates* refers to Socrates. However, since Socrates no longer exists, the negative existential *Socrates doesn't exist* is true. If names are directly referential, this sentence semantically expresses a bare, singular proposition in which the property expressed by the predicate is predicated of the referent of the name—a proposition that can be thought of as made up of the constituents Socrates and the property of not existing. We may even grant that since Socrates once existed, but no longer does, this proposition once existed, but no longer does. This proposition—that Socrates doesn't exist—is, of course, different from the proposition that Plato doesn't exist, which is the proposition semantically expressed by *Plato doesn't exist*. The two names, *Socrates* and *Plato*, refer to different things, even though there exists nothing that is the referent of either name; and the two negative existentials *Socrates doesn't exist* and *Plato doesn't exist* have different propositions as their semantic contents, even though there exist no propositions that are their semantic contents. Because of this,

[29] Here I follow Nathan Salmon, "Existence," in J. Tomberlin (ed.), *Philosophical Perspectives, 1: Metaphysics* (Atascadero, CA: Ridgeview, 1987), pp. 49–108, and "Nonexistence," *Noûs* 32 (1998): 277–319. See also Saul Kripke, the 1973 John Locke Lectures at Oxford University (unpublished); Peter van Inwagen, "Creatures of Fiction," *American Philosophical Quarterly* 14 (1977): 299–308; and Peter van Inwagen, "Fiction and Metaphysics," *Philosophy and Literature* 7 (1983): 67–77.

these sentences are meaningful, even though there exist no propositions which are their meanings.

All of this is coherent once we admit that it is possible for objects to have certain properties at times when they don't exist. Socrates now has the property of being designated by *Socrates* (as well as the property of not existing), even though Socrates does not now exist. Similarly, the proposition that Socrates doesn't exist is such that it now has the properties of being a proposition, and of being semantically expressed by certain sentences, even though it doesn't now exist. It also now has the properties of being true, of being believed by me, and of being asserted by utterances of *Socrates doesn't exist*. In this way, the Millian proponent of direct reference can accommodate obvious facts involving sentences containing names of once existent, but no longer existing, objects. To say that *Socrates* now refers to an object that once existed, but no longer does, is to say that there once existed an object o such that *Socrates* now refers to o, even though o does not now exist. To say that *Socrates does not exist* now semantically expresses a proposition that once existed, but no longer does, is to say that there once existed a proposition p such that *Socrates does not exist* now expresses p, even though p does not now exist. This account generalizes to sentences containing names of objects that do not exist now, but will exist in the future, as well as to objects that have never existed and will never exist, but which could have existed.[30]

Another kind of "empty name" occurs in fiction or legend—names like *Sherlock Holmes* and *Santa Claus*. The most promising account of these names that I know of has recently been developed by Nathan Salmon, building on earlier insights of Saul Kripke, Peter van Inwagen, and others.[31] The idea, in a nutshell, is this: Among the things that exist are legends, novels, plays, movies, and the like. These are abstract objects created by authors. Fictional characters are constituents of these objects. Like the fictions of which they are part, fictional characters are a special kind of real, existing object; they, too, are abstract

---

[30] The position taken here about reference to objects that once existed but no longer do (or to objects that do not yet exist but will) raises complicated questions about the metaphysics of time, and the semantics of temporal discourse, that go far beyond the scope of this book. For this reason the brief sketch given here should be understood as laying out the bare outlines of an approach I find promising, rather than reporting any final, fully worked out position. A similar point holds for reference to merely possible objects.

[31] Nathan Salmon, "Nonexistence," and Saul Kripke, *Reference and Existence: The John Locke Lectures for 1973*. In addition, see Peter van Inwagen, "Creatures of Fiction," and "Fiction and Metaphysics." All cited in fn. 29.

objects. Typically, however, they are created with the special purpose of being depicted as, or playing the role of, something quite different. For example, *Sherlock Holmes* is the name of a fictional character (an abstract object) that is depicted in the Conan Doyle stories as a brilliant detective.

Like most linguistically simple names, *Sherlock Holmes* refers to an object that is its semantic content, and sentences containing it semantically express bare, singular propositions in which properties are predicated of that object. However, sentences containing fictional names also have specialized uses. When Conan Doyle used such sentences in writing the stories, he was not attempting to assert the propositions they semantically express, or any other propositions. Rather, he was engaging in a pretense; he was, in effect, pretending to assert the propositions that make up his stories. By contrast, when we say, in talking about the stories, *Sherlock Holmes was a brilliant detective*, we may well intend to assert something, though not, of course, the singular proposition p that simply predicates the property of being a brilliant detective of the abstract object designated by *Sherlock Holmes*. What we assert is the proposition that according to the stories, Sherlock Holmes was a brilliant detective—a proposition that is true iff p follows from the propositions that make up the Holmes stories, together with whatever background propositions are presupposed by them. Finally, one can use sentences containing fictional names to assert the propositions they literally express. One can say: *Whereas Scotland Yard really is the headquarters of the London Police, Sherlock Holmes is not really a man, but only a fictional character.* Someone who assertively utters this sentence intending to make a claim about the real world, independent of the fiction, truly says, of the abstract object named by *Sherlock Holmes*, that it is not a man, but rather is a fictional character.

Finally, consider *Sherlock Holmes doesn't (really) exist*. If one says this, meaning that according to the stories Sherlock Holmes doesn't exist, then, of course, what one says is false. Similarly, if one says this, intending to make a statement about the real world to the effect that the character Sherlock Holmes doesn't exist, then, again, what one says is false—since characters, like the stories of which they are part, exist. However, there are several other propositions that one might intend to assert by uttering *Sherlock Holmes doesn't (really) exist*—most notably that there is no person in real life who has the properties that the character Sherlock Holmes is portrayed to have in the stories. This proposition is true, and our ability to assert it by uttering a negative existential that doesn't semantically express it poses no serious problems for the Millian proponent of direct reference.

What holds for *Sherlock Holmes* holds for *Santa Claus* as well. It makes no difference whether the character plays a role in a novel, short story, play, myth, or legend. Salmon's general framework can be applied straightforwardly in all such cases. Whether or not it can successfully be applied to every "empty name"—including those like *Vulcan* that occur in serious theories that turn out to be false, as well as to apparently nonreferring names that arise from more innocent mistakes in ordinary discourse—is, I believe, an open question.[32] So, although the traditional problems for directly referential accounts of names posed by descriptivists like Frege and Russell have not been fully resolved in every respect, progress has been made, and the nondescriptivist has ample grounds for optimism.

[32] A good discussion of this question can be found in Ben Caplan, *Empty Names* (unpublished Ph.D. dissertation, UCLA, 2001).

INDEX

Age of Meaning, The (Soames), 311, 334
aposteriori truth, 41, 56–57, 61–63; ana-
  lyticity and 66–67. *See also* necessary
  aposteriori truth
apriori truth, 1–4, 82; bearers of 47–51;
  Chalmers and, 195–98, 204–6, 229–32,
  236–41, 243–45; Davies and Humberstone and, 112–13; descriptivism and
  15–18; hybrid view and, 250, 253–63,
  320; Jackson and, 151–52, 169–70,
  174–81; Stalnaker and, 94–95; strong
  two-dimensionalism and, 277–79, weak
  two-dimensionalism and, 308–9. *See also*
  contingent apriori truth
assertion: content of, 116–20, context
  and, 86; Frege's Puzzle and, 348–49;
  matrices for, 87–89; Stalnaker model
  and, 85–105
"Assertion" (Stalnaker), 85
attitude ascriptions, 340–49; Chalmers
  thesis and, 250–65; descriptions and,
  15, 17–18, 20–21; direct reference and,
  35; indexicals and, 26; Jackson thesis
  and, 172–75; Kaplan and, 50–51; strong
  two-dimensionalism and, 137, 272–89;
  weak two-dimensionalism and, 141–44,
  312

Beyond Rigidity (Soames), 102, 322, 348
Braun, David, 346

Caplan, Ben, 83n41
causal descriptivism, 38, 287, 300–303, 339
causal-historical chain theory, 21, 68–71,
  287, 300–303
centered worlds. *See* world-states
Chalmers, David, 4, 37, 149, 193, 278,
  287; actuality and, 211–16, 228, 231;
  aposteriori and, 204, 228–41, 249; apriori and, 197–98, 228–65; attitude
  ascriptions and, 236–41, 250–65; centered propositions and, 232–36; centered worlds and, 217–18, 282; context
  and, 209–30, 250–65; contingency and,
  228–41; counterfactual information

and, 211–12; epistemic possibility and,
  196–209; hybrid view and, 250–65,
  313–24; Jackson and, 194–96, 212,
  228; Kaplan and, 211–13; Kripke and,
  195, 202–3, 205–6, 228; linguistic
  competence and, 209–28; metaphysical
  possibility and, 196–209; physicalism
  and, 194–96, 218n24, 242–49; primary
  intension and, 195–96, 209–32, 238–
  40, 251–53; secondary intension and,
  195–96, 209–32, 236–38, 250–53;
  strong metaphysical necessity, 203;
  strong two-dimensionalism and, 195,
  241, 259; weak two-dimensionalism
  and, 260; world-states and, 196–209,
  217–18; zombies and, 194, 242–49
characters, 25, 43–44; attitude ascriptions
  and, 50–51; Davies-Humberstone
  semantics and, 112–13, 115; *dthat*-
  operator and, 45–46; epistemic/modal
  operator interaction and, 272–82; logical truth and, 48–49, 51; propositional
  concepts and, 87; schematic, 48–49, 51;
  Stalnaker model and, 92–93; strong
  two-dimensionalism and, 133–38,
  267–90; unrelativized, 48–49; weak
  two-dimensionalism and, 140–46
circumstances of evaluation, 27n17
conceptual analysis, 149
Conscious Mind, The (Chalmers), 149, 194
context: centered worlds and, 232–36;
  characters and, 43–44; Davies-Humberstone semantics and, 110–11; indexicals
  and, 24, 44–54; rigidity and, 27–30;
  Stalnaker model and, 85–105
contingent apriori truth, 31–32, 37, 106,
  121–23, 334–36; Chalmers and, 238–
  40; Davies and Humberstone and 111–
  20, 129; Evans and 111–12, 114,
  116–20, 129, 336–37; Jackson and,
  193; Kaplan and, 46, 51–54; Kripke and,
  333–34; reference-fixing and, 55–68;
  Stalnaker and, 94–96; strong two-
  dimensionalism 40–41, 135–39, 146–
  47, 295; weak two-dimensionalism and,
  41–42, 140–41, 144–47, 294–96, 310
Crimmins, Mark, 346–48

Davies-Humberstone semantics, 106–29
deep necessity, 111–12, 231
demonstratives: *dthat*-operator and, 45–46, 49–54; Jackson thesis and, 165–67; two-dimensionalism and, 44–54
"Demonstratives" (Kaplan), 44–54
de re knowledge, 98–99, 155n7, 312–13, 329; hybrid views and, 321–24; name analyses and, 321–24; natural numbers and, 334n7
descriptivism, 1, 3; criticism of, 14–32; indexicals and, 24–30; irrefutability and, 36–37; modal argument and, 15–17; motivations for, 35–38; natural kind terms and, 22–24; traditional approach to, 7–13; two-dimensionalism and, 39–42, 267–313
"Direct Reference, Propositional Attitudes, and Semantic Content" (Soames), 331n1
Donnellan, Keith, 1, 3
dthat-operator, 27–29; demonstratives and, 45–46, 49–54; hybrid views and, 316–25; Jackson and, 160–61; name analyses and, 321–24; weak two-dimensionalism and, 307–13. *See also* indexicals

epistemic possibility, 82–83, 331–33; Chalmers and, 196–209; Jackson's restriction and, 150–52
Evans, Gareth, 109n3, 111, 114, 336

Frege, Gottlob, 7, 338; Chalmers and, 241; hybrid views and, 322; proper names and, 340–41; traditional approach and, 7–13; weak two-dimensionalism and, 307
Frege's Puzzle (Salmon), 346–47
From Metaphysics to Ethics (Jackson), 149, 175, 296

Gettier problem, 57n16
Gödel/Schmidt case, 18–19

indexicals, 24, 27–30; Jackson thesis and, 159–60, 164–70; Kaplan and, 44–54;

nondescriptive, 25–26, 282–90; reference-fixing and, 55–71; Stalnaker model and, 91, 95–105; two-dimensionalism and, 133–35, 282–90

Jackson, Frank, 4, 36–37, 149; aposteriori and, 174–75; attitude ascriptions and, 172–75; Chalmers thesis and, 228; *de re* knowledge and, 155n7; epistemic possibility and, 150–52; indexicals and, 159–60, 164–70; Lewis-Stalnaker articulations and, 153–54; metaphysical possibility and, 149–52; natural kind terms and, 164–70; necessary aposteriori and, 158–63, 165–66; primary intension and, 162–63, 171–75; proper names and, 168–70; reference-fixing and, 181–93; secondary intension and, 171–75; semantics and, 153; senses of necessity and possibility and, 151; very strong two-dimensionalism and, 158, 170–75; world-states and, 151–58, 189–90

Kalderon, Mark, 155n7, 334n7
Kaplan, David, 1, 3–4, 31; character and, 43–44; Davies-Humberstone semantics and, 109–10; *dthat*-operator and, 45–46, 49–54, 311; importance of, 329; indexicals and, 24–30, 44–54; Jackson thesis and, 159–60; semantics and, 106; Stalnaker model and, 87, 95
Kazmi, Ali, 29n21, 30n22, 83n41
Kripke, Saul, 1, 3–4, 14, 31, 334–38; causal descriptivism and, 38, 339; Chalmers and, 195, 202–3, 205–6; Davies-Humberstone semantics and, 125; importance of, 329; Jackson thesis and, 165–66, 185–86; modal argument and, 15–17; natural kind terms and, 58–68, 185n30; necessary-aposteriori puzzle and, 71–83; reference-fixing and, 55–71; Stalnaker model and, 85–86; Strong Disquotation Principle and, 77, 79–80; two-dimensionalism and, 43, 54–83, 106, 165–66, 302–3, 313, 330–32; world-states and, 82–83

Lewis, David: descriptivism and, 37–39; two-dimensionalism and, 144n2, 153, 161n13, 201n6, 287, 300–301

McGlone, Mike, 81n37
Mates, Benson, 346
metaphysical possibility: 82–83, 330–33; Chalmers and, 196–209; impossible world-states and, 199–202; Jackson's restriction and, 150–52
Millian nondescriptivism, 329–53
modal argument, 15; avoidance of, 39; 303–6; general version of, 16–17; rigidity and, 16

Naming and Necessity (Kripke), 17, 150; critique of, 54–83
natural kind terms, 22–24; apriori and, 58–68; Chalmers thesis and, 216–20; Davies-Humberstone thesis and, 125–29; Jackson thesis and, 164–70; Kripke and, 58–68, 185n30; reference-fixing and, 58–68
necessary aposteriori truth, 30–31, 37–38, 42, 44, 54, 106; Chalmers and, 195, 198, 202–9, 228–41; Davies and Humberstone and, 123–29; hybrid views and, 315, 318–22; Kaplan and, 44–46, 49–54; Kripke and, 71–84, 203–6; Jackson and, 150–75; and natural kind terms, 23–24; physicalism and, 175–81, 242–49; Stalnaker and, 84–85, 90–94, 96–99; Strong Disquotation Principle and, 77–81; strong two-dimensionalism and, 135–39, 147–48, 281, 295; weak two-dimensionalism and, 140–41, 144–45, 147–48, 293–95, 304–5, 307–10, 312–13
necessity, 2–3; actuality and, 108–9; Davies-Humberstone semantics and, 107–29; deep, 111, 231; epistemic/modal operator interaction and, 272–82; physicalism and, 175–81; strong metaphysical, 203–5; strong two-dimensionalism and, 135–39, 267–90; superficial, 111; weak two-dimensionalism and, 140–41
Nelson, Michael, 305n17

"On Sense and Intension" (Chalmers), 214, 219
"On Sense and Reference" (Frege), 7

Perry, John, 24, 142
philosophy, 1–2; import of two-dimensionalism for, 3–4; lessons for, 329–30
physicalism: 149–50, 175–81, 194–95, 217, 242–49
primary intension, 40–42, 133–38, 140–41, 147–48, 270–71; Chalmers and, 209–28, 236–41, 250–53; epistemic/modal operator interaction and, 272–82; hybrid views and, 313–25; Jackson and, 171–75; linguistic competence and, 209–28; nondescriptive indexicals and, 285–86
proper names: acquaintance constraint and, 321–24; apriori and, 56, 61, 334–36; Davies-Humberstone view of, 115, 128–29; Evans's case and, 116–23, 336; Frege-Russell theses, 8–9, 14, 17, 19, 21, 340–53; hybrid views and, 313–25; Jackson thesis and, 160–61, 168; Kripke's discussion of, 14–22; reference-fixing and, 55–71; rigidity and, 15–17, 303–13; substitution and, 340–49; traditional approach to, 7–13, 136, 141, 280–81, 296–13
Propositional Attitudes (Richard), 347
propositions: bearers of apriority, 50–51; 112–13, 137, 144, 174–75, 236–40, 245; centered, 232–36; diagonal, 90, 232; necessary aposteriori, 71–83, 138–40, 144–48; neo-Fregean and neo-Russellian conceptions of, 241; "possible worlds" analysis of, 38, 84, 139, 153, 171–72; primary, 40–41, 231–32; objects of attitudes, 50–51, 112–13, 137, 141–42, 144, 146–48, 171–75, 236–40, 250–53; secondary, 40–41, 231–32; strong two-dimensionalism and, 39–42, 133–39; 146–48; weak two-dimensionalism and, 39–42, 140–42, 144–48
Pryor, Jim, 57
Putnam, Hilary, 1, 3, 64–65, 190–91, 329, 339

Quine, W. V., 2–3

reference, 1; borrowed, 187–88; Chalmers
thesis and, 209–28; direct, 24–32;
descriptive theory of, 19–21, 35–39,
55–68, 181–93, 209–28, 296–303; historical chain theory, 21, 68–71; indexicals and, 24–25; rigidity and, 16, 27–30;
semantics and, 68–71; traditional
approach to, 7–13
"Reference and Contingency" (Evans),
336–37
Richard, Mark, 346–47
rigidity: actuality operator and, 27–30;
context and, 29–30; definition of, 16;
direct reference and, 27–30; *dthat*-
operator and, 27–30, 45–46; Evans's
case and, 116; intuitive test for, 16;
philosophical implications of, 30–32;
strong two-dimensionalism and, 236,
280; weak two-dimensionalism and,
141, 303–13
Russell, Bertrand, 7–14, 21, 26, 241, 307,
340

Salmon, Nathan, 80n36, 346–47, 350n29
secondary intension, 40–42, 133–38,
140–42, 146–48; Chalmers and, 209–
12, 250–53; epistemic/modal operator
interaction and, 272–82; hybrid views
and, 313–25; Jackson and, 171–75;
nondescriptive indexicals and,
285–86
Speaks, Jeff, 68n24
Stalnaker, Robert, 4, 85, 153, 333; aposteriori and, 90–91; apriori and, 94–95;
de re knowledge and, 98–99; diagonal
proposition and, 90; Kaplan and, 87,
92–93, 95; model matrices of, 87–89,
96, 100–101; nontransparency and,
103; rules of conversation and, 86;
semantics and, 106
Strong Disquotation Principle, 77,
79–80
Strong Disquotation and Justification
Principle, 77, 79–80
strong two-dimensionalism, 40–43; aposteriori and, 137–38, 294–96; apriori
and, 135–39; attitude ascriptions and,

137, 293; Chalmers and, 195 (*see also*
Chalmers, David); contingency and,
135–39; critique of, 272–90; Davies-
Humberstone semantics and, 113–15;
examples of, 39–42, 146–48; Jackson
and, 170–75; metaphysical possibility
and, 136–37; modal/epistemic operator
interaction and, 272–82; necessity and,
138–39; nondescriptive indexicals and,
282–90; primary intension and, 133–34,
138, 285–86; rigidity and, 136, 280;
secondary intension and, 134, 138,
285–86; tenets of, 133–39; very strong,
139, 158, 170–75, 330–31

Talk about Beliefs (Crimmins), 347–48
Thau, Michael, 346
transparency, 103
Twin Earth fable, 190–91, 258, 289, 305
"Two Notions of Necessity" (Davies and
Humberstone), 106–7, 129, 337

unarticulated constituents, 348

very strong two-dimensionalism. *See*
strong two-dimensionalism

weak two-dimensionalism, 41–43; aposteriori and, 140–41, 145, 294–96; apriori
and, 144–46, 310–13; attitude ascription and, 141–44, 293; causal-historical
chain theory and, 300–303; contingency
and, 141; critique of, 290–313; Davies-
Humberstone semantics and, 114–15;
de re knowledge and, 312–13; examples
of, 39–42, 146–48; Kaplan and, 53–54,
298–99; Kripke and, 302–3, 313;
Lewis and, 300–301; necessity and, 141;
Perry example and, 142–44; primary
intension and, 140; proper names and,
141, 296–313; reference-fixing and,
296–303; rigidity and, 303–13; secondary intension and, 140–42, 291–92;
tenets of, 140–46; Twin Earth fable
and, 305
world-states, 37; actuality and, 27–28,
108–9, 120–22, 303–5; centered worlds

and, 217–18, 232–36, 282; Chalmers and, 196–209; context and, 134–36, 211–12, 217–18, 282–83; Davies-Humberstone semantics and, 108–10; impossible, 82–83, 199–209, 332; Jackson and, 150–58, 189–90; physics and, 218n24; possible, 82–83, 196–209,

332; propositions and, 38, 84, 139, 153, 171–72, 330–33; Stalnaker model and, 85–105

zombies, 194–95; physicalism and, 242–49